Bold Relief

PRINCETON STUDIES IN AMERICAN POLITICS:
HISTORICAL, INTERNATIONAL, AND
COMPARATIVE PERSPECTIVES

SERIES EDITORS

IRA KATZNELSON, MARTIN SHEFTER, THEDA SKOCPOL, EDS.

A list of titles

in this series appears

at the back of

the book

Bold Relief

INSTITUTIONAL POLITICS AND THE ORIGINS OF MODERN AMERICAN SOCIAL POLICY

EDWIN AMENTA

PRINCETON UNIVERSITY PRESS

PRINCETON, NEW JERSEY

Library of Congress Cataloging-in-Publication Data

Amenta, Edwin 1957–
Bold relief : institutional politics and the origins
of modern American social policy / Edwin Amenta.
p.   cm. — (Princeton studies in American politics)
Includes bibliographical references and index.
ISBN 0-691-01712-3 (cl : alk. paper)
1. United States—Social policy. 2. Public welfare—
United States—History. 3. United States—Politics and
government—1933–1945. I. Title. II. Series.
HN57.A584   1998
361.6′1′0973—dc21   97-24509   CIP

This book has been composed in Sabon Typeface

Princeton University Press books are printed on acid-free paper and meet the guidelines
for permanence and durability of the Committee on Production Guidelines
for Book Longevity of the Council on Library Resources

http://pup.princeton.edu

Printed in the United States of America

1   2   3   4   5   6   7   8   9   10

CONTENTS

LIST OF ILLUSTRATIONS   vii

LIST OF TABLES AND FIGURES   ix

PREFACE   xi

INTRODUCTION
Paradoxes of American Social Policy   3

CHAPTER 1
An Institutional Politics Theory of Social Policy   18

CHAPTER 2
An Indifferent Commitment to Modern Social Policy, 1880–1934   54

CHAPTER 3
America's First Welfare Reform, 1935–1936   80

CHAPTER 4
Consolidating the Work and Relief Policy, 1937–1939   122

CHAPTER 5
Some Little New Deals Are Littler than Others   162

CHAPTER 6
Redefining the New Deal, 1940–1950   191

CHAPTER 7
A Welfare State for Britain   231

CONCLUSION   250

AFTERWORD   270

NOTES   273

INITIALS OF ORGANIZATIONS AND PROGRAMS   331

SOURCES OF ILLUSTRATIONS   333

INDEX   335

ILLUSTRATIONS

2.1.	"Pay Your Poll Tax Now" (Russell Lee)	66
2.2.	Receiving a Relief Check from the FERA (Ben Shahn)	74
2.3.	Waiting for Work at a FERA Office (Ben Shahn)	77
3.1.	Lineup of WPA Workers (Russell Lee)	85
3.2.	"He Who Is a Townsendite . . ." (Russell Lee)	113
3.3.	Applications for the Bonus (Dorothea Lange)	116
3.4.	"Less Taxes = More Jobs" (Marion Post Wolcott)	119
4.1.	Local Funding for the WPA (Russell Lee)	129
4.2.	Pickets outside a Textile Mill (Jack Delano)	139
4.3.	The Workers Alliance of America Protests WPA Cuts (Dorothea Lange)	141
4.4.	The WPA Arrives in Puerto Rico (Jack Delano)	145
4.5.	Unemployment Compensation Begins (Dorothea Lange)	147
5.1.	The WPA in Chicago (Russell Lee)	178
5.2.	"Olson Spending Plan Blocked" (Dorothea Lange)	184
6.1.	NYA Students Learn Forging (Gordon Parks)	200
6.2.	"This Way to a Job" (photographer unknown)	204
6.3.	Roosevelt's Third Inauguration (Royden Dixon)	211
6.4.	A Member of the Local Townsend Club (John Vachon)	217
6.5.	"Partners in Crime" (photographer unknown)	218

TABLES AND FIGURES

TABLES

0.1. Social Spending Efforts, Selected Countries, 1938   5
1.1. Seven Periods of U.S. Social Spending and Taxation Policies, 1930–1950   46
1.2. State Political Profiles According to Institutional and Political Categories   49
3.1. U.S. National Election Results, 1928–1934   105
3.2. Pro– and Anti–Social Spending Contingents in the U.S. House of Representatives, 1931–1936   106
4.1. U.S. National Election Results, 1936, 1938   136
4.2. Pro– and Anti–Social Spending Contingents in the U.S. House of Representatives, 1935–1940   137
4.3. The Townsend Movement: Membership, Resources, and Political Activity, and Democratic Majorities in the U.S. House of Representatives, 1934–1939   140
4.4. U.K. and U.S. Social Spending Efforts, 1929–1938   143
5.1. Top Ten States in WPA Wages, OAA Pensions, and ADC Programs, 1940   167
5.2. Bottom Ten States in WPA Wages, OAA Pensions, and ADC Programs, 1940   168
5.3. Ratio of WPA Workers to General Relief Recipients, 1940: Lowest and Highest States   169
5.4. Political Profiles of Four States According to Institutional and Political Categories   173
6.1. U.S. National Taxation Sources as a Percentage of GNP, 1932–1949   206
6.2. U.S. National Election Results, 1940–1950   212
6.3. Pro– and Anti–Social Spending Contingents in the U.S. House of Representatives, 1939–1950   213
6.4. The Townsend Movement: Membership, Resources, and Political Activity, and Democratic Majorities in the U.S. House of Representatives, 1940–1949   216
8.1. States with the Highest and Lowest WPA Wage Efforts, and Selected Institutional and Political Indicators   264
8.2. States with the Highest and Lowest OAA Pension Efforts in 1940, and Selected Institutional and Political Indicators   265

FIGURES

1.1.   U.S. Polities According to Type of Political and Party
       Systems   25
1.2.   The Institutional Politics Theory: Short-Term Expectations
       for Policy Outcomes   30
1.3.   Expected Program Outcomes under a Reform-Oriented
       Regime, According to National Bureaucratic or Social
       Movement Influence and State-Level Precedents   39
4.1.   Public Policy's Influence on Markets According to Type,
       Scope, and Benefits   150
4.2.   Public Policy According to Influence on Market Forces and
       Unequal Gender Relations   152
8.1.   Expected and Actual Program Outcomes under a Reform-
       Oriented Regime, According to National Bureaucratic or
       Social Movement Influence and State-Level Precedents   257
8.2.   Institutional Politics Theory: Short-Term Expectations and
       Policy Outcomes   258

AMERICA IS embarking on a great experiment in social policy. In the summer of 1996 President Bill Clinton signed a welfare bill devised by the Republican Congress. Among other things, the bill ended the national commitment to needy children through Aid to Families with Dependent Children (AFDC), a New Deal program replaced by Temporary Aid to Needy Families, a program providing short-term aid funded by a block grant. The recent events resemble what might be called the first episode of welfare reform in American history. I am referring to the 1934–35 version, under President Franklin D. Roosevelt, that produced the Works Progress Administration (WPA) and the Social Security Act and marked the origin of modern American social policy.

The two presidents faced political situations that were strikingly similar. Each faced a large caseload of the needy. Some 5 million adults were receiving aid through the temporary Federal Emergency Relief Administration (FERA) in 1935. Roosevelt considered some 3.5 million FERA recipients to be employable. The approximately 4 million adult recipients of AFDC in 1996 were considered fit for at least part-time work. Each president declared that programs for the poor were not working. In 1935, Roosevelt railed against the "dole"—the FERA's open-ended aid to those who could work. In terms far more eloquent than what passes for political discourse today, he called the dole a narcotic and a subtle destroyer of the human spirit. In 1992, Clinton coined a campaign slogan—let's "end welfare as we know it."

Each president faced alternative proposals that were superficial. In 1933 and 1934, Congress advanced legislation to limit hours for workers and bills to encourage unemployment insurance and old-age pensions. In 1995, Congress demanded an end to the national entitlement in AFDC and cuts in other aid to the poor. Each president convened a group to study the issue and propose a solution. Roosevelt formed the Committee on Economic Security in June 1934 to develop proposals for permanent social spending reform. Prominent on it was Harry L. Hopkins, the head of the FERA, who told his aides to develop "a complete ticket to provide security for all the folks of this country." In 1993 Clinton convened a group under David T. Ellwood, a leading expert on social policy, to devise comprehensive welfare reform. In 1994, the Clinton Administration delivered to Congress the group's proposal, which included a work program, training, and child care.

As I try to show in the book, however, Roosevelt's results were greatly different from recent ones. He and his advisors built a work and relief policy that sought to unite Americans and ensure that those who wanted useful work would have it. Although Clinton proposed something like that, he feared the high cost of such a program, or potential partisan attacks on it, and balked. He ended welfare, but without replacing it. What follows is the story of the first, more successful welfare reform.

Anyone taking as long as to write a book as I did this one runs up massive debts of gratitude. Foremost among my scholarly creditors are many friends and colleagues who had the dubious pleasure of reading some version of this book in draft form and compounded their burden by writing back. They include Ellen Benoit, Edward D. Berkowitz, Kimberly Blanton, Chris Bonastia, Bruce G. Carruthers, Nancy K. Cauthen, Jeff Goodwin, Larry J. Griffin, Drew T. Halfmann, Alexander Hicks, James M. Jasper, Edward W. Lehman, Eileen L. McDonagh, David S. Meyer, Kelly Moore, Ann Shola Orloff, Sunita Parikh, Charles C. Ragin, Willemijn Roozendaal, Elizabeth Sanders, Theda Skocpol, Yvonne Zylan, and anonymous readers. I benefited much from your comments and advice. I owe the greatest amount to the most extravagant, unidentified here in the hope that they dodge future mistreatment, who commented on the whole thing. Thank you all. For advice and encouragement, I thank, too, the members of the sociology departments at Rutgers University, Princeton University, and the University of Arizona, and the Workshop on Politics, Power, and Protest in the New York University Sociology Department. Thanks also to Malcolm Litchfield, my editor at Princeton University Press, and to the copy editor, Gavin Lewis.

I owe debt of a different sort to a number of fine young scholars for their collaborations with me on related projects and research assistance on this one. I thank Ellen Benoit, Mary Bernstein, Chris Bonastia, Nancy K. Cauthen, Kathleen Dunleavy, Drew T. Halfmann, Jane D. Poulsen, Robin Tamarelli, Michael P. Young, and Yvonne Zylan. Working with you sped the time I spent writing and, mainly, not writing this book.

I am pleased to acknowledge as well the committee that supervised my dissertation, on which this book is loosely based. It included Theda Skocpol, William Julius Wilson, Gerald D. Suttles, and the late Morris Janowitz. I thank Bill Wilson for chairing the committee and emphasizing the importance of work policy and of engaging public debate. I owe a special debt of gratitude to Theda Skocpol, without whom I would never have undertaken so ambitious a project. A young scholar could not hope for a better mentor.

I also relied on the expertise and kindness of strangers. I am grateful for the professionalism and friendliness of archivists, librarians, and scholars at the following institutions: the University of Chicago Regenstein Library, the New York University Bobst and Tamiment Libraries, the Franklin D. Roosevelt Library, the Library of Congress, the National Archives, the New York Public Library, the Metropolitan Museum of Art, the Museum of Modern Art, the Chicago Historical Society, the University of California–Los Angeles Special Collections, the University of California–Berkeley Bancroft Library, the Louisiana State University Hill Memorial Library, the British Library of Political Science, the University of London Library, and the Public Record Office. My opportunity to learn from such experts and their institutions was aided in part by grants from the NYU Research Challenge Fund, the National Endowment for the Humanities, and the National Science Foundation. Any errors are my fault.

Finally, I want to thank my friends and family and Kelly Moore. It would be impossible to recount all your contributions, but I hope you know I appreciate them.

Edwin Amenta
December 20, 1996
New York City

Bold Relief

Paradoxes of American Social Policy

AMERICAN SOCIAL POLICY is usually thought to be exceptional—exceptionally sluggish and spotty, stingy and divided. Everyone knows that America waited until the Great Depression of the 1930s to enact old-age and unemployment insurance and even then failed to embrace some programs, including health insurance and family allowances, that had swept the world. And from the beginning, the conventional wisdom holds, U.S. social policy was designed to run on two tracks. On the express track was "social security," providing generous benefits as a matter of earned right and as regularly as the U.S. mail. On the local track was "welfare," dispensing paltry, haphazard, and highly personalized grants that provided disincentives to work and openings for political attack. A late start, an unfinished social insurance system, and a two-track policy—for all of those reasons America nowadays spends less of its income on public social policy than almost all similarly rich countries. It is orthodoxy, in short, that American social policy was divided and defective at its origin.

The conventional wisdom, however, is misleading. Though flawed and tardy, social policy in President Franklin D. Roosevelt's New Deal did not attempt to create a poorly funded, two-track policy that divided recipients while encouraging idleness and retrenchment. Instead, America embarked on a bold program of work and relief. Having created the Committee on Economic Security in June 1934, President Roosevelt called for the enactment of its proposals in his annual message of January 1935. He demanded three forms of economic security—the security of a "livelihood," security against the "major hazards and vicissitudes of life," and the security of "decent homes." To secure the livelihood of Americans—his foremost demand—Roosevelt called for "a definite program for putting people to work." In this he followed his economic security committee, which declared employment assurance and public employment to be the cornerstone of an American system of social spending.[1]

Soon afterward the Works Progress Administration (WPA) was created. Led by the former social worker Harry L. Hopkins, the work program's charge was to employ 3.5 million people receiving emergency relief, or "the dole," as Roosevelt sometimes called such payments and in-kind benefits. The WPA was central to the attempt to end the dole or, to use the current political vocabulary, America's first "welfare reform." For that year Congress also passed the Administration's omnibus Social Security Act. The law included the old-age insurance (OAI) program known today as "social security," but that program was overshadowed by specialized need-based programs designed to aid those considered economically immaterial, including the aged as well as the blind and children in families without breadwinners, by unemployment compensation,[2] and by measures focused on providing work to the "employable."

What is more, New Deal reformers and their contemporaries did not intend to make distinctions, such as those in evidence today, between social security and welfare programs and their respective recipients. To the contrary, the vast majority of recipients of America's social programs received need-based benefits unconnected with previous "contributions"—what today would be called "welfare."[3] That was true of public employment through the WPA and old-age pensions through Old-Age Assistance (OAA), as well as Aid to Dependent Children (ADC), the program most closely associated with the welfare label. In that era, however, people did not invoke that demeaning term. Instead they referred to the new need-based programs by the more benign "relief," a term in today's political discourse associated almost always with reductions in taxation. With its connotations of comfort, remedy, and support, the term "relief" implied that citizens might require assistance to counter misfortunes not of their own making. New Deal reformers wanted relief, especially "work relief" through public employment, to stand at the center of American public social provision.[4] Other relief programs, including OAA and ADC, were designed to aid specific groups deemed "unemployable." When the president spoke of economic security or the Social Security Act he was not referring even primarily to old-age insurance.[5]

To the reformers' way of thinking, citizens able and willing to work should have the right to a job, provided by the government in the last resort. In his frequent "fireside chats" over the radio, Roosevelt imagined himself speaking to specific Americans— "a mason at work in a new building, a girl behind a counter, a man repairing an automobile, a farmer in the field . . ." Not surprisingly, he conjured up a specific image of what his work and security program would mean. The president saw an unemployed worker first using up his short-term unemployment insurance benefits and then being issued a green ticket entitling him to a job.[6] For those citizens considered socially valuable but economically extraneous, the state was to provide a stipend. The aged had a right to assistance because of their lifelong contributions to the nation, not because of some earmarked taxes they might have paid along the way. Children in families without breadwinners were also deemed worthy of aid. In return the aged were expected to retire and mothers with dependent children to withdraw from the labor force. To be sure, there were different forms of aid. But each was to be streamlined and to run on the same fast track. As a matter of fairness, moreover, many New Deal reformers wanted these programs to be funded by an income tax system based on the ability to pay.

These initiatives, moreover, did not imply stinginess—just the opposite. On the eve of the Second World War the United States pledged more of its

TABLE 0.1
Social Spending Efforts, Selected Countries, 1938

	Percent of GDP	*Percent of Government Spending*
United States[a]	6.31	29.4
Germany[b]	5.59	18.7
United Kingdom[b]	5.01	17.5
France[b]	3.47	11.9
Sweden[b]	3.15	17.8
Netherlands[b]	1.98	10.2
Italy[b]	1.80	7.3

Sources: Peter Flora, Jens Alber, Richard Eichenberg, Jurgen Kohl, Franz Kraus, Winfried Pfenning, and Kurt Seebohm, *State, Economy, and Society in Western Europe 1815–1975: The Growth of Mass Democracies and Welfare States* (Chicago: St. James, 1983), pp. 376, 381, 387, 391, 402, 405, 408, 412, 428, 431, 442, 446. U.S. Bureau of the Census, *Historical Statistics of the United States From Colonial Times to 1970* (Washington: U.S. Government Printing Office, 1975), series F 1–5, H 32–47, Y 533–66, pp. 224, 341, 1120.

[a] For the United States the data are from *Historical Statistics.* Social spending is taken from columns 33, 34, 39, 41, 42, 47 of the "H" series and includes spending from on "social insurance," "public aid," and "other social welfare." The figures for the United States are for fiscal year 1939, which began on July 1, 1938, and are divided by the average gross national product for 1938 and 1939.

[b] For the European countries the data are from Flora et al., *State, Economy, and Society.* Social spending, which they call "social security," is defined as public money expended on social insurance and social assistance programs. The figures for Germany are for 1935. The figures for France, Sweden, and the Netherlands are based on central government expenditures for social security and public health policies. European spending is taken as a percentage of gross domestic product.

national product to security in this larger sense than any major industrial nation. As Table 0.1 shows, these programs accounted for more than 6 percent of the U.S. gross national product and almost 30 percent of government spending. The American performance outpaced the efforts of Sweden, today's world leader in social spending. America also outdistanced the United Kingdom, which began the Depression with the world's most advanced system of public social spending.

By the end of the 1930s, reformers in the National Resources Planning Board hoped to complete New Deal social policy. The president liked to think of people as a species of natural resource. From their position in the Executive Office of the President, these officials concluded that the capriciousness of politics in the forty-eight states impeded the goal of creating universal social rights through public social provision. Programs like OAA, ADC, and Unemployment Compensation were subject to state-level decision-making and thus to great variations in quality. The New Deal reformers sought to nationalize these programs or to set strict national standards in them. They also sought to protect citizens in areas—like health care and in general relief—left uncovered by the New Deal.

There were reasons to believe the reformers might succeed. For one thing, the country was jolted by two great crises—the Great Depression and World War II. Few nations were hit as hard by the Depression—one-fourth of the U.S. labor force was unemployed by 1933. By the end of the 1930s, after the 1937–38 recession, the Depression showed little sign of lifting, and the Roosevelt Administration strengthened its commitment to its social policy. Americans were soon to be mobilized to fight fascism and militarism in the Second World War. In the wake of war democratic states often render new rights to citizens to repay their sacrifices. For America's wartime ally Great Britain and elsewhere throughout the industrialized world, the end of the war heralded the age of the welfare state.

Furthermore, in America the Depression and the war constituted the Age of Roosevelt, a reformer and Democrat who dominated political life in a way that is difficult today to imagine. Roosevelt was elected president four consecutive times. He was so popular that only his death could remove him from office, and soon afterward Congress outlawed a repeat of his performance. The Democratic party, redefined by Roosevelt's New Deal, organized every Congress but one in the 1930s and 1940s, and the party promoted and allied itself with a rising labor movement. Roosevelt and his wing of the Democratic party encouraged social mobilization. Unionization, notably, grew from about one-fifteenth of the work force at the beginning of the Depression to almost a quarter by the end of the war. Labor in turn threw its weight behind the New Deal. Further on the margins of institutional politics, the crusade of the aged led by Dr. Francis E. Townsend and the Share Our Wealth societies led by Senator Huey P. Long demanded a new and more generous relationship between state and citizenry and won millions of followers. In contrast, the American Liberty League, backed by General Motors and the Du Pont family, mobilized to stop the New Deal, but had collapsed by 1940 under the pressure of mass apathy. In his last campaign Roosevelt appealed to the nation with a radical Economic Bill of Rights. Contemporaries thought that the war and the peace would give him the chance to finish what his first two Administrations had started in modern social policy.

After all, reformers inside the state had had more state to work with since Roosevelt's inauguration in 1933. Although the popular press focused on Roosevelt's so-called Brains Trust of accomplished political advisors, the national government was being remade from the bottom up. Professional and dedicated civil servants had flooded into Washington, inundating the old patronage appointees who had dubious credentials and indifferent commitments to rational government. The new national government employees sustained greater public confidence in government action, and more than two million remained in Washington to stay after the war. Notable among them were the policy experts in newly created domestic bureaucracies who were devising plans to complete the New Deal. And funds flowed into the nation's treasury, another prosaic, but essential condition for social spending policy. New taxes, like the social security payroll tax, were created, and old ones, like the income tax, were extended. As a share of the nation's income, the expenditures of the national government increased sevenfold between 1929 and 1946 — a permanent change, not a temporary wartime increase.

Roosevelt died before the war ended, but by then the dreams of many New Deal reformers had already been dashed. Much to their dismay, at the end of 1942 the WPA was given an "honorable discharge" by the president, who along with Hopkins lost interest in social policy once America went to war. Plans to complete a work and relief state were dismissed by Congress. The war period even witnessed an attack on the old-age program known today as social security, now considered the third rail of American politics, for those who touch it face instant political death. By the end of the war, in short, U.S. social policy was in disarray. America made no national commitment to a comprehensive and coherent policy to address the major income-threatening risks of capitalist democracies. New Deal social policy had failed, and American social policy for the postwar world was made up of its remnants. That failure stands out in bold relief against the breakthroughs in modern social policy during the Great Depression.

And so this historical episode suggests two paradoxes. The far-reaching policy of work and relief challenges the conventional wisdom about American social policy. The United States became a world leader in public social spending during the Depression and did so on the basis of work and relief, not social insurance. Also, the failure to complete a work and relief state confounds standard social science arguments about the impact of crises, political regimes, and state bureaucrats and revenues on social policy. To approach these puzzles it is best to start by examining how scholars have viewed social policy and how American policy differed from their understandings.

THE WORK AND RELIEF POLICY OF THE 1930s IN CURRENT AND HISTORICAL PERSPECTIVE

When as social scientists we study social policy, we typically label our subject the "welfare state," a term forged in the social policy struggles in Britain during the Second World War. By "welfare state," we do not mean programs for poor people, in accordance with modern American usage, but mean instead five specific social insurance programs — workers' compensation, old-age pensions, health insurance, unemployment insurance, and family allowances. By the 1950s, most rich capitalist democracies had adopted each of these five programs. This has led scholars to employ the singular, "the welfare state," to indicate a convergence on similar policies. Any state that has a full complement of the five programs and that devotes most of its revenues to them, moreover, it is said to be "a welfare state." For those reasons most research on the development of welfare states focuses on two issues—the adoption of the Big Five programs or the spending efforts devoted to these programs.[7]

But the distinctiveness of U.S. public social policy in the 1930s was not that it only partially developed a welfare state, understood as the Big Five. Instead U.S. reformers sought to build an entirely different form of modern public social provision—a work and relief state. This bid made considerable progress in the 1930s, and social policy experts made efforts to complete a work and relief state—not to replace it by enacting a new set of social insurance programs. Nor was the work and relief policy a political project of the Right, designed in hopes of deflecting universal social insurance proposals.[8]

The parameters of this work and relief policy are not fully captured by standard concepts in social science. One influential view is that rich capitalist democracies have created three distinctive "welfare state regimes." The "social democratic" regime, most closely approximated by modern Scandinavia, is based on the principles of universalism and "decommodification"—the latter meaning that private markets play a minimal role in workers' lives. As typified by Austria and France, the "conservative corporatist" regime is universal, but solidifies status distinctions between groups and upholds the traditional family, with one male breadwinner bringing home a family wage. The "liberal" type of welfare state, deemed least favorable to citizens, is devoted to making markets run smoothly, by making public spending low in amount and degrading in delivery. The United States and most other English-speaking countries are typically considered to approximate liberal welfare states. Recently, feminist social scientists have criticized the focus on the market as inapplicable to the issue of gender inequality. They argue that social spending programs need to be assessed according to whether they subvert unequal and unfair relationships between men and women as well as between citizens and the marketplace. They propose more general autonomy criteria to categorize social policy.[9]

Had the incipient U.S. work and relief state of the 1930s been completed it might have substantially subverted both market- and gender-based inequalities. The work and relief policy constituted a public affirmation of the profound failure of markets, which had produced low or no incomes for many people. The work and relief policy focused on providing jobs for those whom the private market had failed. Although these employment programs and other relief benefits were based on need and never received enough funding, they were designed to be provided as a right. The aged were encouraged to retire and take a pension—as their right as citizens and as valued and long-standing contributors to American society. Similarly, the policy encouraged single caretakers of dependent children to remove themselves from the labor market—by providing a stipend for subsistence until the children left home and by providing social backing for the care-taker role. The policy had at least the potential to subvert gender inequality, for if the caretaker was a woman she would need to rely neither on a job or a man. The new policy was a dramatic shift from that of previous decades, in which only few, favored widows received public support. These pro-grams were to be undergirded with a steeply progressive income tax.[10]

In other ways, though, the work and relief policy, especially as practiced, upheld gender distinctions and inequalities. The policy anticipated one family breadwinner, who was presumed to be male in most instances. American public policy not only failed to provide access for women to the private job market, but also limited their access to work available through the government. The underfunding of the WPA, when combined with these gender attitudes, made work programs a largely male preserve. The poli-cymakers' presumptions that private jobs were highly scarce and that one person alone was sufficient to earn the family's wage tended to freeze gen-der roles and inequalities as they stood. Although stipends for taking care of dependent children raised the possibility of liberating many women from relying on a man's paycheck, as it was amended and administered in most states the program did deliver on its promise and served to reinforce stereo-typed gender roles.

Distinctive though it was, the work and relief policy was far from a work and relief state. The policy never secured adequate funding, and the rights it provided varied dramatically across the country. Nor were the reformers ever able to secure an individual's right to a job. These circumstances blunted the work and relief policy's challenge to the private market. Despite attempts to extend and complete a work and relief state, this form did not survive the wartime and immediate postwar period. Even if the right to a job was established, there would be little way to secure it, as public employ-ment programs were dismantled. The divided and incomplete social security and welfare state that exists in America today grew from the ruins of the work and relief policy.

Before detailing the questions animating this book, I want to place the incipient work and relief state of the New Deal in historical perspective. As we have seen, the United States did not always lag historically in social spending. What is most distinctive about U.S. public spending policies is their erratic historical pattern. The history of U.S. public policies is best seen as a pattern of zigzags that can be divided into four periods.[11]

American public policies in the late nineteenth century were notable for their high spending and distributive character. The most expensive program was the Civil War pension. Established for injured soldiers and widows of soldiers killed in action, the program was transmuted by 1890 into a species of old-age and survivors' benefit, selecting recipients not according to need or work record, but according to documented participation on the Union side. These pensions were complemented by a primitive public employment program—federal government jobs for those with the proper political connections. An assortment of tariffs on imported goods paid for these programs. From the Civil War to the First World War, tariffs generated about half the revenues of the national government. Together these programs were seen by middle-class reformers as paradigms of corruption and obstacles to placing social policy on a modern basis. By contrast, most poor relief was still controlled at the township level and combined corruption with low benefits and degradation.

In the second phase of American public social provision, running from the turn of the century to 1930, the reformers won half the battle. A middle-class reform movement of progressives attacked party machines and sought to establish autonomous, bureaucratic executive institutions at all levels of government. This movement numbered the days of using the government bureaucracy as an employment program, and Civil War veterans and their survivors lost a kind of war of attrition. Yet the nineteenth-century policies were not replaced by European-style programs. The few innovations of this period were meager and mainly situated in states and localities. Workmen's compensation passed in most states between 1911 and 1921, requiring businesses to insure workers against industrial accidents. At the same time, mothers' pensions passed in most states, allowing localities to provide aid for widows to raise their children. Only very few pensions were granted, however, and the reform of poor laws made significant, but only marginal progress. State-level programs for infants and pregnant mothers were encouraged by the 1921 Sheppard-Towner Act, but it was repealed before the Depression. Movements for health insurance, unemployment compensation, and old-age pensions almost invariably foundered. As a result America fell behind the industrial world in modern public spending policy. America's commitment to modern social policy was, at best, indifferent.

The Depression era witnessed the heroic period of modern American social policy, as America took leadership in public spending once again. But this time social policy addressed the needs of all Americans, especially the unemployed, rather than selected groups with the proper political, regional, or military prerequisites. And this system was placed on a modern administrative basis. Once again, however, this American predominance was only temporary. By the end of the 1940s, the bid to create a work and relief state had failed. The failure foreshadowed the future. America continued to lose ground in public policy, with only a brief period of innovation in the 1960s and early 1970s.

What remained of the New Dealers' handiwork constituted American social spending policy in the postwar world. Public employment or work-relief programs, the central innovations of New Deal public social provision, were domestic casualties of the war. When the WPA was discharged, with it went employment programs for the young—the Civilian Conservation Corps and the National Youth Administration. Unemployment would be fought in the postwar period with macroeconomic fiscal and monetary manipulations.

The most numerous and expensive programs remaining were "federal" programs, meaning those in which the national government and state-level governments shared authority. The Social Security Act mainly created power-sharing programs. Of these, the most momentous of its day was Old-Age Assistance. The act provided federal matching payments for OAA, and by the end of 1938 all states had passed programs. At the end of the 1930s, this was the only program that granted aid to the aged. Because OAA had few national standards in it, however, benefits varied dramatically around the country. The program associated in recent times with the term "welfare," Aid to Dependent Children, also covered the country, though more slowly. By the end of the 1940s, however, state-level politics was being given a full airing in ADC, which suffered from great variations in generosity and coverage. Because of the demise of work programs, moreover, ADC became overburdened as the central program to fight poverty. Unemployment Compensation also remained under the control of the states, which competed to produce favorable business climates by lowering payroll taxes at the expense of this program and its recipients.

One partial and unlikely success story was old-age insurance, a national program. Inaugurated in 1935, this program initially covered only a small fraction of the labor force and was embattled from the outset. Congress saw old-age insurance as redundant and had at one point removed the program America now calls "social security" from the Social Security Act. In wartime social security ran into more trouble—scheduled payroll tax increases to finance it were denied by Congress. For these reasons Arthur Altmeyer, the long-standing chairman of the Social Security Board, referred to the end of the 1940s as the "crucial years." Although social security became better anchored after amendments in 1950, these amendments signaled the demise of Old Age-Assistance, and its loss left the state-level relief system without its standard bearers, the aged.

Other social spending policies adopted elsewhere around the industrial world never made it past the planning stage in America. Notably, attempts to bring national health and sickness insurance failed. America's unwillingness to pass such insurance ensured that it would fall behind in overall social spending efforts. Moreover, the United States did not even seek to adopt family allowances—programs enacted around the capitalist world to aid all families. Instead, Congress passed several generous, though evanescent, programs for veterans to ease their return to civilian life. Rejecting an Economic Bill of Rights for all Americans, Congress passed the GI Bill of Rights in its place.

World War II brought tremendous gains in income taxation, but by 1950 U.S. taxation policy was at a standstill. One key problem was that the politics of social spending and the politics of taxation had become separated. In

the recession of the late 1930s, the administration, following the economic
ideas of John Maynard Keynes, proposed spending increases without taxation increases. In the postwar period a taxation system established to finance the war was pressed into service to fund social spending. That arrangement provided sufficient funds so long as the economy was growing,
but constituted precarious political footing for public social provision.
What is more, the U.S. national government adopted almost all of the major
modern methods of taxation—on personal incomes, corporations, and on
payrolls for social insurance—but no national consumption taxes were introduced. The political uncoupling of taxation and social policy and the
lack of consumption taxes made it possible for the Reagan Administration
of the 1980s to darken the future of social policy by cutting and indexing
income taxes and thereby creating a fiscal crisis.

Postwar U.S. public social provision was far from the unified system of
related programs imagined by the New Deal reformers. New Deal social
policy had failed and was redefined. Instead of being a spending system centered on work, American social policy was a mixed bag of New Deal and
wartime remnants with few logical and administrative connections among
them. Partly as a result of the failure of the New Dealers, the United States
currently ranks near the bottom of capitalist democracies in public social
spending efforts.

These developments suggest the following questions. How and why did
the bold work and relief policy emerge, making the United States a social
spending leader in the 1930s? Why did the bid to complete that policy fail,
while other rich capitalist democracies—notably Britain—enacted welfare
states after World War II? Why did some programs, such as old-age insurance and public employment, become nationalized, while others, such as
Unemployment Compensation and ADC, did not? Why did work programs
fail? Why did some states follow the lead of national New Deal social policy, while others did not? Why did America gain the taxation system that it
did? All of these questions lead back to one central one: Why do Americans
have the public social spending system that we have today—a mixed-up
policy forged haphazardly in the crucible of Depression and war?

EXPLAINING U.S. PUBLIC SPENDING: THE
INSTITUTIONAL POLITICS THEORY

To answer these questions, I propose an institutional politics theory: not a
grand one, but a middle-range theory. It indicates the key reform actors and
the institutional circumstances they must negotiate to gain new social
spending commitments. The institutional aspects of the theory are derived
from arguments by Tocqueville and Max Weber. The political aspects of
the theory owe much to class struggle ideas dating from Marx.

The theory holds that political institutions influence public policy. Key institutional conditions include the following: the degree to which political life is run by democratic processes; the nature of the political party system; the centralization of the polity; and the abilities and powers of executive institutions. Each shapes public policy. To the extent that everyday people have a say in politics—through rights of association, speech, and voting—public policy is likely to aid them, for office seekers will have to take them into account. Patronage-oriented parties tend to dampen categorical reforms and are averse to modern taxation policies—especially reform with national standards, administration, and controls, for such reform is the antithesis of pork-barrel politics. A separation of functions within the national government and between the national government and the states and localities makes it difficult for reform-oriented groups to hold power. Weakness in executive bureaucracies makes difficult the planning necessary to devise modern public policies and the capabilities needed to run them.

In comparative terms, the structure of American political institutions has been generally inauspicious for the development of modern public spending programs. The American polity was born with a strong separation of powers within the national government and between the national and subnational governments, weak executive institutions, and early white manhood suffrage. The U.S. political party system—the world's first—crystallized along ethnic and sectional lines and was dominated by organizations focused on patronage. As Madison had anticipated, the U.S. constitution provides small minorities the ability to block legislation—also including social policy. Only America's widespread suffrage, gained in the early nineteenth century, was favorable to the development of social spending policies. The early adoption of democratic practices, in combination with a nineteenth-century total war, helped to make America a leader in premodern social spending.

All the same, the one comparative advantage America had enjoyed in the early nineteenth century was a disadvantage by the beginning of the twentieth: America fell behind other countries in the extension of democratic rights. Voting and civil rights were denied African Americans and many whites throughout the South. Because the groups unable to vote or discouraged from voting corresponded to those who might benefit from permanent, national spending reforms, a significant fraction of the polity had little interest in them. The patronage-based party system and the divided and weak national state served as additional obstacles to the creation of coherent, modern, and national social spending and taxation policies.

Strong as these institutional obstacles have been, various social groups have called for American public spending, including labor movements, policy expert organizations, farmers' organizations, consumer groups, protest movements, state actors, and individual politicians. Although they aspired in some cases to the policies provided elsewhere around the world, these policy advocates had real cause for hope in the U.S. setting. Only parts of the U.S. polity were undemocratic, and patronage parties had lost their grip on many parts of the country by the end of the First World War. The executive branch was weak, but it was also relatively open, encouraging pro–social spending groups to try to capture or influence it.

According to the theory, the executive and legislative representatives of political parties are key actors, who shape and influence contention over public spending policy. These actors are most likely to win public spending struggles when they form what I am calling a reform-oriented regime. A reform-oriented regime comprises a president allied with pro-spending groups and a Congress in which left and center legislators dominate. In twentieth-century America, this amounted to the control of the government by Democrats from outside the nondemocratic South and from non-patronage-oriented party systems, augmented by radical third-party legislators. It was only in the 1930s and in the North that the Democrats became a party of the Left—based not on socialist doctrine, but on the progressive and worker-oriented reforms of the New Deal.

Reform-oriented regimes have been infrequent in American history, for good reason. They require a huge Democratic majority and often the help of third parties. In the United States, such a regime was and is more difficult to construct than elsewhere. The patronage orientation of some local parties sets them against categorical public spending reform. Most of all, the presence of legislators from underdemocratized parts of the polity has typically been substantial. For these reasons, most of the rest of the country would have to swing left to put a pro-spending regime in power.

Reform-oriented regimes are difficult but not impossible to construct, and make it possible to enact new public spending and taxation programs over the opposition of other political actors. These regimes also send signals throughout the polity that categorical social spending reforms are possible—invigorating the efforts of all those struggling for them. It is during the rule of such regimes—when a president wants reform and reformers in Congress have the votes, and they and their opponents know it—that major public spending initiatives are typically enacted. Such a reform-oriented regime, I argue, accounted for the breakthrough legislation of the New Deal.

Even when they do take power, however, these regimes do not often specify the content and form of programs. I expect instead that state actors will construct the better part of the policy agenda and that these actors in turn never work from a blank slate. The content of social spending proposals depends greatly on previous programs and the powers and outlook of those who administer them. The proposals devised by state actors are expected to reflect the programs they run and the bureaus and levels of government where they are situated. Reform-oriented regimes will also move to create new bureaucracies to run programs, but when first in power must play the bureaucratic hand dealt them.

To devise coherent national policies, moreover, national policymaking

administrators must be well established in the executive branch. To pass
national policies, these proposals must coincide with a reform-oriented regime. Without these abilities, distributive or power-sharing programs are
likely to be passed into law. Reform-oriented regimes have two major tasks
facing them—to pass legislation providing new benefits to citizens, but also
to rationalize state bureaucracies.

Other actors also have important roles in the making of public spending
policy. Movements on the margins of institutional politics can influence
public spending policies, especially in placing new issues onto the public
agenda or in granting issues a higher priority. By backing more radical alternatives with collective action, these movements can increase the public
benefits in social spending legislation. However, these movements are limited in terms of how much influence they have on the content of legislation
and its passage. Challengers—mobilized groups disadvantaged in politics—
determine the content of policy only very rarely, as they typically do not
have access to the information and analytical resources state policy experts
can easily generate. Even more rarely do challengers such as the Townsend
Movement have the political leverage to force the passage of a specific program. After all, they cannot pass programs by themselves, and the process
of gaining influence over legislators is an arduous one that strains the abilities of even widely-supported challenges. Yet their impact on public policy
is amplified when political conditions are otherwise favorable—with reform-oriented regimes in power or with strong bureaucrats with missions in
accord with the aims of the challenge.

The theory suggests that with luck and hard work, U.S. social spending
advocates, inside and outside the state, can go far in effecting public social
spending programs. They did so during the 1930s. Goaded by pro-spenders
outside the state, a powerful pro-spending regime enacted a series of reforms. Moreover, most domestic state actors, focused on emergency relief
as they were, devised a system based on relief principles.

Yet U.S. political institutions dispersed the power of pro-spending actors
and placed greater obstacles in front of them than advocates of similar policies faced elsewhere. If there is a short answer to why New Deal social
policy failed it is that the United States was not a democracy. A lack of
democratic politics in the South made it difficult to construct a reform-oriented regime and for it to maintain power. So, too, in a lesser way, did
the dominance of patronage parties. Representatives from these polities had
opportunity after opportunity to stop, delay, or weaken social spending
proposals. Given the structure of the American polity, it was impossible to
banish the Right for any decent interval. Although the open and unformed
nature of the national executive branch and its infiltration by the New Dealers encouraged social spending innovations, these same characteristics
made it likely that when policy bureaucrats had their chance, they would
work at cross-purposes—devising an assortment of programs that would
stand as obstacles to coherent reform.

THE SHAPE OF THINGS TO COME

The first chapter reviews prominent explanations of public social spending in research on relatively rich capitalist democracies and introduces the institutional politics theory. The theory is premised on the claim that purely institutional and purely political theories of social policy are incomplete, but complementary. I elaborate the institutional politics theory and draw out its implications for a variety of public spending outcomes. I also address methodological issues, indicating several strategies to improve the plausibility of my arguments in this case study. Readers with little interest in expert debates, abstract argumentation, or social science methodology may want to skip or skim this chapter. Readers who are solely interested in these issues or who cannot bear the suspense may wish to jump from chapter 1 straight to the conclusion.

The second chapter discusses social policy before the permanent reforms of the New Deal. It documents America's rejection of modern social policy before the Second New Deal and explains why that happened, especially by way of the structural-political obstacles standing in the way of reform. The chapter also introduces the experimental relief programs of Roosevelt's First New Deal of 1933. The third chapter turns to social policy reform in the Second New Deal, summarizing the heroic part of the story in which policy success followed upon policy success. The chapter also explores systematically the roles of the various actors involved in the making of this work and relief policy. I argue that the main innovations took place under reform-oriented regimes and were devised by state actors. Challengers also had an impact—when they could impinge on the electoral calculations of administration and congressional actors.

The fourth chapter deals with social policy in Roosevelt's second term—what some call his "Third" New Deal. This period served to consolidate the work and relief policies of the Second New Deal for reasons that were largely similar to those behind the origins of the programs. This chapter also analyzes the work and relief policy as it stood at the end of the 1930s, and as it might have continued without the changes soon to be brought by war. The fifth chapter explores the varying reactions to the New Deal at the state level. I examine the so-called "little New Deals," as state-level programs were called, in five states, arguing that the institutional and political aspects of the theory help to explain divergences across the little New Deals. But I also show how these divergences shaped the policy agenda for the 1940s.

Reformers within the Roosevelt Administration were dismayed by states with what might be called "tiny" New Deals, and saw them as botched experiments in federalism. New Deal planners went to work—hoping to displace the failed experiments by enacting national legislation to induce standards and rational organization in the state-level spending systems. As war broke out in Europe, the New Dealers wanted to capitalize on the crisis in order to complete a work and relief state for a postwar America. They achieved some successes, especially in taxation policy. Mainly, however, their hopes were dashed, as Congress rejected their plans, save insofar as they pertained to veterans. The sixth chapter recounts that story. Chapter 7 takes us across the Atlantic to wartime Britain. What happened there could not have been more different from what happened in America—British social policy advocates achieved their goal of creating a welfare state. In the chapter I indicate why the British social policy advocates were successful while their American counterparts were not.

The conclusion summarizes the story, the institutional politics theory, and the evidence for it. It also provides a glimpse into the future of American social policy reform. The Afterword discusses the lessons of Roosevelt's welfare reforms. First, though, I turn to the arguments and methods animating this study.

CHAPTER ONE

An Institutional Politics Theory of Social Policy

Two THEORIES currently dominate thinking about modern social policy. The best explanation of recent social spending disparities among rich capitalist democracies since World War II has been the social democratic thesis. An argument based on the ideas of Marx, this thesis focuses on the political actors that propel public spending. According to it, countries with large, centralized labor movements connected to social democratic political parties that govern political life are the likeliest candidates for extensive, redistributive social spending.[1] Among richer countries, however, most major public social spending programs were adopted prior to World War II, but very few social democratic regimes were in power during these formative years. Divergences in the timing of adoption and the form of policy innovations often have been explained by institutional or state-centered arguments, based on the ideas of Weber and Tocqueville. These theses suggest that the adoption of social spending policies is encouraged by centralized political institutions and states with greater bureaucratic and financial capacities, and frustrated by fragmented political institutions and incapable states.[2]

Both political and institutional theories provide pessimistic expectations for U.S. social policy changes. Political theories like the social democratic thesis suggest that because American lacks a centralized labor movement and a social democratic party, there are no actors here powerful enough to effect far-reaching social policy changes. Institutional theories suggest that the checks and balances in U.S. government and its historically weak executive institutions limit what is possible in social policy. These arguments, however, say little about what can and did occur. Partly for this reason the study of U.S. social politics has often generated its own hypotheses.[3] Some scholars argue that it was the collective action of state-oriented challengers that brought about U.S. public social provision, and others point to the role of enlightened businessmen. The main proving ground for American theses on public spending has been the 1935 Social Security Act.[4]

In this chapter I review prominent institutional and political explanations of public social spending policies in light of overall U.S. policy developments—especially those during the Great Depression and World War II eras.[5] My purpose in doing so is to fashion a middle-range theory of social policy—what I call the institutional politics theory. An amalgam of elements of Tocquevillian, Weberian, and Marxian arguments, the theory is premised on the idea that some theses of both the institutional and the political theories are valuable and indeed complementary. Institutional theses typically specify the limits on social policy, but often ignore what drives it. Political theories specify the actors and resources that drive public social provision, but often ignore the systemic limits on political action.

I disagree, though, with some of the specifics of the standard institutional and political arguments. Although the centralization of political institutions and the degree of state capacities matter in social spending politics, two other structural conditions matter more: the democratization of the polity and the programmatic nature of the political party system. My contention is that an underdemocratized political system and a patronage-oriented party system constitute the most powerful structural obstacles to national and modern social spending policy because they set politicians against it.

Although social democratic parties and the labor movement can drive social policy, other political actors matter in struggles over social policy—including other political parties and non-class-based proponents and opponents of social policy. Notably, I expect social policy to be promoted under the auspices of what I call a reform-oriented regime, that is, one where the government is under the political control of elected officials allied with pro-spending groups and constituencies. In addition, state bureaucrats in charge of existing social programs and challengers in favor of new ones also constitute important forces behind reform. The theory specifies how institutions and politics interact in the making of social policy.

For these reasons, my expectations for American social policy are in some ways more pessimistic that those of institutional theorists and more optimistic than those of many political theorists. I see the obstacles facing the proponents of American social spending for most of the twentieth century as peculiarly daunting, since the United States suffered from an underdemocratized polity as well as from the dominance of patronage-oriented political parties. Yet the forces for reform were also greater than expected by the social democratic thesis. Even if a social democratic political party has never made a great impact in America, reform-oriented regimes can take power here—and they have.

To appraise my claims I devise comparative analytical strategies that go beyond interpreting the Social Security Act to confront other central questions about U.S. public policy. For American public spending policy was made and unmade by more than one piece of legislation during its formative years. What is more, social spending programs were constructed in different ways and had different fates. And more than that, important developments in U.S. public policy happened at the state level, and states diverged in their social policies. Other comparisons also matter. America was developing a work and relief policy in the 1930s, while Britain was not, and Britain was creating a welfare state in the 1940s, while America was not. In each instance, these differences raise important questions: Why were some periods more productive of social policy than others? Why did programs differ? Why did states differ in their social policies? Why did the United State diverge from Britain? Each question also yields opportunities for comparative analysis.

THE IMPACT OF POLITICAL INSTITUTIONS ON SOCIAL POLICY

Enduring institutional characteristics of political systems and political parties had and have a fundamental impact on the politics of public social provision. The political rights of citizens, the character of the party system, fragmentation of functions and powers in the political system, and administrative capacities in public policies—each of these, I argue, influence public spending policy. Often these influences were unintentional. Institutional conditions were mainly set prior to the era of modern public spending and for reasons having little to do with it. As it turned out, however, the twentieth century American political context placed unusually difficult institutional obstacles in the way of those promoting social spending.[6]

Underdemocratized Polities Discourage Social Policy and Disorganize its Proponents

A relatively neglected, but crucial influence of political institutions on public policy concerns the participation of everyday people in politics. This neglect is of fairly recent vintage. Around 1950, scholars made bold statements about the impact of democratic procedures in politics on public social provision. Focusing on the American South after World War II, the American political scientist V. O. Key famously argued that disorganized, one-party politics was unlikely to produce public policy serving the interests of "have-nots."[7]

I argue that a central obstacle to social spending policy is an underdemocratized polity—something more extreme than the disorganized politics identified by Key. An underdemocratized polity is one in which political leaders are chosen by way of elections, but in which there are great restrictions on political participation, political assembly and discussion, voting, and choices among leadership groups. In an underdemocratized political system there is little electoral reason for politicians to promote policies to aid the less well off, for when there are such restrictions it is usually the less well off who find themselves on the outside looking in. When poorer people cannot vote, politicians have little incentive to appeal to them by supporting social policies. Other democratic rights are important in getting politicians to champion social policy. In particular, if everyday people cannot legally or practically assemble and discuss issues, it is difficult to gain information about social policies and to press for them effectively. A democratic polity is also characterized by meaningful choices among parties or factions.[8] With that missing, the ability to assemble for political purposes, discuss issues, and vote will likely have little influence on public policy. In underdemocratized polities, politicians will accordingly do more to seek the support of those in privileged economic positions—whose preferences generally stand opposed to social spending. Where people count little in politics, money and access matter even more.

For similar reasons it is also difficult for pro-spending mass movements to organize themselves in an underdemocratized polity. Often they do not try, as there is little electoral reason for politicians to help them or to promote their cause. If pro-spending movements attempt to organize, they are more likely to be repressed. They are unlikely to have any politicians beholden to them, their friends, or relatives for support and thus will have few defenders in the state apparatus. Even if such movements manage to coalesce in undemocratic polities, they are unlikely to achieve their goals—without first effecting basic improvements in democratic practices. And so in these ways an underdemocratized political system—characterized by highly restricted voting and democratic rights and a lack of choices between parties—discourages both public spending and pro-spending social movements.

Democracy in America has had a strange career. Most white men gained the vote by the 1830s, and, as Frances Fox Piven and Richard A. Cloward put it, "Americans generally take for granted that ours is the model of a democratic polity." As they demonstrate, however, that view is mistaken. The United States was far from a full democracy for most of the twentieth century—the era of modern social policy. Democratic rights were denied most thoroughly in the South, where an organized movement for disfranchisement of African Americans seemingly defied historical inevitability, sweeping the region like a plague in the late nineteenth century. All the states of the former Confederacy realized disfranchisement schemes by 1903. Significant institutional barriers to voting, by way of stiffened registration rules and regulations, were constructed in northern cities, especially against immigrants and their offspring. In the Far West immigrants from Asia and Mexico were often discouraged or restricted from exercising the franchise.[9]

The problems of southern polities went far beyond the disorganization identified by Key. What mattered more, I am arguing, was that they were riddled with rotten boroughs. In these undemocratic districts almost all blacks—and many poor whites—were denied the franchise by means ranging from legal devices such as the poll tax and the literacy test to illegal practices such as electoral fraud and the violence of the lynch mob.[10] As a result, in the states of the former Confederacy few people voted, and the political voices of the less well off were muted—regardless of variations in the degree to which politics was otherwise organized. There were other reasons that those southerners who could participate in politics would oppose social spending. As Jill Quadagno has argued, southern Democratic parties,

backed by a dominant planter class, viewed generous social spending policies as inimical to the system of labor control. Any program with national
control was construed as a threat to the prerogative of southern elites to
answer the race question in the oppressive fashion they saw fit.[11]

The makeup of the House of Representatives indicates the degree to
which the American polity was biased by undemocratic underpinnings. In
the 1930s, for instance, of the 435 seats, 102 were allocated to the 11 states
of the former Confederacy. In the 1940s, the South claimed 105 seats.
Needless to say, the elections for most of these seats were characterized
by low voter turnout. Worse than that, most southern House members ran
unopposed in Democratic party primaries—where most southern electoral
decision-making took place. Southern senators, subject to more statewide
competition, constituted almost one-fourth of the Senate.[12] The southern
presence in the electoral college—and potentially the region's influence on
the reform-orientation of a president—was of course based on its congressional representation.

That the American polity has been relatively underdemocratized has had
a dampening effect on national and redistributive social policy, as it might
anywhere. One-fourth of the House constituted a substantial electoral barrier facing prospective builders of American social policy, as these representatives were unlikely candidates to support social policy legislation. I would
expect, too, that any program that required state-level cooperation would
have a difficult time reaching its potential in such a polity and that there
would be discrimination in the programs that did take hold—against those
without basic rights. A lack of democracy in the South also prevented the
Democrats, who began in the twentieth century to represent workers and
the poor in the North, from swinging their party further to the left.

*Patronage-Oriented Political Parties Deflect Modern Social
and Taxation Policies*

If disorganized politics poses problems for social policy, so, too, does one
highly organized form of politics. A second key impediment to modern social
policy is the dominance of patronage-oriented political parties: hierarchical
organizations that seek to win elections and maintain their organizations
through individualized benefits to party workers and other supporters. These
organizations live in and for the world of political power, to paraphrase
Weber, but do so with delimited objectives. The leaders of such patronage-
oriented parties are concerned with the survival of the organization itself.
That depends in turn on a cycle of contesting and winning elections, using
the spoils of office to reward party workers and contributors. As many
prominent American political scientists have argued, people working for
such organizations typically do so to further their material position in
society, not to pursue an ideology or program of reform.[13] Notably, David
Mayhew claims that patronage-oriented parties avoid programmatic social

policy because they find professional bureaucracies threatening. Social insurance and social assistance programs require trained and qualified workers to operate them, and so their supporters seek to legislate merit-based hiring practices. When they are successful, a letter of recommendation from a party notable no longer constitutes a ticket to a government job.[14]

Leaders of patronage-oriented parties have other important motives to oppose modern social spending programs. For one thing, programs that provide relatively automatic benefits eliminate a degree of fiscal freedom for political operatives. Money earmarked for individuals who meet abstract criteria cannot be easily diverted to those who contribute to the life of the party. For another, social spending programs rarely provide the often remunerative, if questionably legal, opportunities provided by soliciting contracts for public business. In addition, it is more difficult for a local politician to take habitual credit for a payment guaranteed by law than for delivering a holiday turkey. The first is a right and the second a gift. Automatic social spending, moreover, potentially drains resources from programs that might be deployed in an individualistic way. Furthermore, social spending programs imply higher taxes, reducing the ability of patronage politicians to lower taxes in a selective way to contributors. Finally, patronage-oriented political parties have a motive to discourage and disrupt social movements seeking to promote modern social spending policies.

Martin Shefter has argued that because democratic practices preceded state bureaucracies in America, political parties, especially in the Northeast and Midwest, oriented themselves toward patronage. In this way the U.S. political party system resembled Italy's. The American and Italian party systems contrasted with the programmatic parties of Germany, with the British party system standing somewhere in between. In Mayhew's analyses of the political party systems of every American state, he finds that thirteen stand at or near the polar type of what I am calling a patronage-oriented party system.[15]

I do not expect American patronage-oriented parties to constitute as great a drag on modern social policy as its underdemocratized polity. Always with an eye out for the main political chance, patronage-party leaders would seem likely to cut deals with a progressive administration—federal patronage in return for programmatic social spending support. Patronage-oriented politicians might also come to terms and ally with some powerful pro-spending groups, such as organized labor became in many parts of the country. Moreover, patronage politicians are invariably connected to a national party differentiating itself from the other party on the basis of national issues. Patronage politicians connected to an otherwise pro-spending political party would not be likely to stand in unreconstructed opposition to the national party's platform. They would be more likely to try to modify the program in the direction of producing greater patronage opportunities than to block it completely. In the U.S. polity in the middle of the century, this would mean that extenuating circumstances might prompt patronage-oriented Democrats to support social spending, but in the thirteen states where these party organizations flourished Democratic congressional representatives were unlikely to be enthusiastic backers of reform proposals. Similarly, social spending programs requiring state-level cooperation would have a difficult time in such polities.

Patronage-oriented parties can cause trouble in a more insidious way for social policies. The more these parties predominate, the greater is the temptation for proponents of modern social programs to forge compromises by affording patronage opportunities—or discretion in the provision of benefits—within social policy. Programs designed like that may have greater political chances in the short run, just as shoddily contrived and underbid construction projects may seem appealing on the surface. A program compromised in this way may win the support of currently powerful patronage-oriented politicians, who will view it as an opportunity to enlarge their political organizations, but is likely to be discredited in the end. One disadvantage is that a social program with patronage possibilities will provoke the opposition of political factions not so favored. More important, designing political discretion in a social program often comes at the expense of setting up professional bureaucracies that would secure the program's foundation, and exposes it to charges of unfairness or corruption.

A summary of the structure of the American polity in the early twentieth century exhibits the predicament faced by advocates of modern social policy. As Figure 1.1 shows, one-half of the forty-eight states harbored under-democratized political institutions or dominant patronage-oriented political parties. The South was democratically backward, and much of the East and Midwest was a safe haven for patronage-party systems. In contrast, most of the West and some parts of the Midwest and East had neither patronage-oriented political parties, nor great restrictions on voting rights. These polities, shaded in the figure, were the most promising sites to produce political actors in favor of adequate social spending. It follows that comparatively speaking, the U.S. polity as a whole was in a structurally unfavorable situation for modern social policy. The American polity stood somewhere in the middle of the area defined by the table, whereas most Western European polities found themselves closer to the upper left-hand corner—the most favorable institutional place for the adoption and expansion of modern social policy.[16]

Fragmented Political Institutions Discourage and Bias the
Process of Social Spending Reforms

A consensus holds among academics today that the centralization of powers in a political system—an impact on political life emphasized first by Tocqueville—constitutes a principal influence on social politics. Specifically, scholars argue that divisions in political authority provide "veto points" where small, but strongly organized groups can prevent new and far-reaching legislation.[17] According to this way of thinking, presidential

FIGURE 1.1
U.S. Polities According to Type of Political and Party Systems

Political System

		Extensive Political Rights	Restricted Political Rights
Party System	Program-Oriented	**Open Polity:** **24 western and other states**	Underdemocratized polity: 11 southern states
	Patronage-Oriented	Patronage-based polity: 13 eastern and midwestern states	Underdemocratized patronage-based polity: no states

systems are more likely than parliamentary systems to thwart small majorities in favor of spending legislation. Federalism has a similar effect, as lower levels of government must often cooperate with innovations in public policy. Political institutions that are integrated neither at the national level (vertically) nor across the national government (horizontally) are likely to aid opponents of social spending.[18]

I do not rate such fragmentation, however, as the most important structural condition inhibiting the adoption and expansion of social policy. After all, such fragmentation does not prejudice political leaders against social spending policy, as undemocratic polities and patronage-oriented parties do. All the same, a widening of the horizontal and vertical dimensions is needed to capture cross-national differences in the fragmentation of authority and to think about their effects. Nonparliamentary systems constitute one sort of horizontal fragmentation. Independence of courts constitutes another. Fragmentation within the various political branches constitutes yet another. Moreover, although a federal system constitutes the most obvious type of vertical fragmentation, greater distinctions are needed here, too. Lower levels of government can have greater or lesser powers, and there can be more than one lower level of government.

It is well known that political authority in the United States has never been horizontally or vertically integrated. It seems, though, that the powers of U.S. government are fragmented in ways that run off of the standard maps of horizontal and vertical integration. Political fragmentation here is greater and more multifaceted than that found in other democracies and has an impact on public policy that goes beyond merely inhibiting it.[19] At the national level of government, the United States has a presidential and non-parliamentary system, with the standard effects on social policy. Elected mainly by the people at large, presidents can promote programs and use various means to get Congress to consider them. The nonparliamentary nature of the U.S. political system allows intramural conflict. Members of Congress from the same party can defect from the president's legislative program without risking loss of office and can initiate competing programs. The Congress and the legislatures in the states diverge from parliamentary standards also in that legislators represent districts, not parties. Legislators ally with presidents and party leaders typically only when ideologically similar or for political expedience.

That is not all. The fragmentation of authority in the national legislature itself is also more substantial than elsewhere—with negative consequences for modern, national, and comprehensive social policies. Well-situated members of Congress can stall or diminish public spending proposals. For instance, the House Ways and Means Committee and the Senate Finance Committee have jurisdiction over most social spending bills. Yet the House Rules Committee can stall the discussion of these bills, and Appropriations Committees can cut the funding for programs. Unusual requirements such as the supermajorities required to close debate in the Senate also aid obstruction.[20] To stop such delaying tactics, proponents of social spending often must agree to the dilution of legislation. The constitutional separation of powers between the legislative and executive branches is compounded by the existence of courts with legislative and, more important, veto powers. Even when the president and Congress agree, the Supreme Court can spoil new legislation by declaring it unconstitutional, undermining the output of a reforming regime or causing delay.

As for the vertical dimension, subnational governments are more numerous and matter more in the United States than in federal polities elsewhere, such as Canada and Switzerland. American states with their police powers often have contended with the national government over public social provision. Perhaps more important, local governments have had great say over social policy. The relief of the poor was initially the responsibility of townships. Later, county governments gained influence over some social policies. Though often willing to accept funding, lower levels of government typically fight the loss of control over policy.[21]

The fragmentation of political institutions in America has more influence on the process of policymaking than on its final result. Because of the different constituencies of the various U.S. political actors, any truly national social spending politics in the United States has to be led by the president. Unlike other political actors, the president has a national constituency and can demand and direct the administrative means needed to run modern, national social policies. As Stephen Skowronek argues, the presidency is in part an order-shattering institution. To create national social policy, presidents must fight to create national bureaucratic authority and to wrest power or potential power from the Congress and state and local governments.[22]

With its conglomeration of local constituents, Congress must somehow be induced to go along. Because of its representative structure, its divisions of authority, and the need to construct coalitions for legislative action, Congress is inclined to promote divisibility in any benefits it legislates, through the time-honored practice of logrolling. Left to its own devices, a pro–social spending Congress is likely to provide money for subnationally controlled social policy and to promote incremental change. That route to national modern social policy is difficult and requires presidential leadership all the same. To induce subnational governments into simultaneous action on social spending programs, the national government has to provide powerful incentives and national bureaucratic authority to help induce sympathetic responses. Uniformly positive responses are unlikely, though, as states rarely find themselves in similar places, politically speaking. For structural obstacles to social spending vary greatly across the states, and there are strong vertical separations of powers in each state, with the corresponding obstructing effects.

Domestic Bureaucrats Promote and Shape Social Policy Reforms

Another influence on social policy concerns the capacities of bureaucracies in the executive branches. As Theda Skocpol in particular argues, state bureaucracies are potentially capable of autonomous action, for state officials can make binding rules over subjects and citizens, and they monopolize matters of social order and military policy. In democratic and capitalist societies, the state can be considered autonomous when it creates strategies of action independently of capitalists and organized business groups, political parties, interest groups, movement organizations, and public opinion. Autonomy in turn depends on far-reaching capabilities and unencumbered resources. One sort is a civil service not captured or susceptible to capture by political or social groups through selection or prospective employment. State officials must see themselves as state officials first and not as members of a class or political party. Money is the second key resource. In the twentieth century, states have enacted modern taxes, sales, payroll, and income taxes, without needing to dispatch the army to collect them.[23] Once enacted, these taxes provide dependable streams of revenue. Generally speaking, it is expected that the more autonomous the state, the faster the development of public social provision and the greater the spending on it.[24]

Largely autonomous states clearly do not always advance the cause of public social provision and defend citizens' rights. Neither the Soviet Union nor Nazi Germany—each with a highly autonomous state—promoted welfare states. Executive institutions can be constructed in different directions. To the extent that a state devotes personnel and revenues to military, incarceration, or policing purposes, its growth seems unlikely to augment public social provision. Historically, the American state has been distinguished by its weakness, but overall changes in bureaucratic development did not result in social spending changes. Although U.S. government employment did grow more rapidly during the New Deal 1930s than in the conservative 1920s, other facts conspire against this thesis. The American state also grew dramatically from 1901 to 1921, during the Progressive Era and the First World War, and from 1939 to 1947, during and after the Second World War. Indeed, the civil service grew more rapidly during these periods than during the New Deal, but national social spending policy did not make similar gains. What seems more plausible is that only specific types of state autonomy—in social spending bureaucracies—aid the development of modern public spending programs.[25]

For that reason, I argue that a fourth institutional condition that can aid or harm the proponents of social policy is the bureaucratic and programmatic equipment they have to work with. I expect that domestic bureaucracies—whether engaged in public spending or not—will generally aid proponents of public social provision. The greater the number of people in such bureaucracies, the more people working from within the government to promote social spending and to provide aid and information to reformers outside the government. The number and scope of programs also influence reform battles. A large number and variety of working programs provide an array of models demonstrating that similar programs might also work. A lack of working programs leads reformers and sympathetic politicians to diminish their expectations of what is possible—in their imaginations as well as in their proposals. On the positive side, an amorphous and underdeveloped domestic executive branch makes it more susceptible to new ideas and proposals provided by outside experts.[26]

Again, the United States found itself relatively lacking in domestic bureaucratic equipment and policy infrastructure in the early twentieth century. For that reason the government itself was unlikely to be an overflowing source of reform proposals and powerful proponents for reform. It was not as if American public spending advocates had a completely free hand in what they might propose, however. Although there were few national agencies and bureaus with the kind of staff and information-gathering abilities needed to implement or plan extensive social spending programs, there were some social spending programs and labor and safety regulations in the states and localities, and different bureaus administered them. Moreover, there were some long-standing domestic bureaucracies at the national level, and these were augmented by new ones in charge of providing and administering aid in the Depression. Given their positions, the existing actors had a distinct advantage in designing the permanent public spending policies of the New Deal. Policy designs would be colored by their missions and powers.

A lack of democracy in America remained in the middle of the twentieth century as the central structural obstacle for U.S. proponents of modern social policy. A second major obstacle was the entrenchment of a patronage-oriented party system. To different degrees, those conditions inclined political leaders against modern social policy. The division of authority in the polity and the relative lack of domestic bureaucratic machinery were additional hurdles, far from minor, but not as daunting as these others. Divisions of authority can be overcome and state domestic capacities can be constructed. Together, however, these conditions meant that coherent and national social spending reform was unlikely and could be expected only under unusual circumstances. For the better part of the twentieth century—an era in which welfare states were constructed around the world—American proponents of public social provision had the political playing field tilted against them.

REFORM-ORIENTED REGIMES, STATE BUREAUCRATS, CHALLENGERS, AND THE STRUGGLE FOR PUBLIC SOCIAL PROVISION

Institutional conditions do not often change quickly, however, and cannot explain the historical trajectories of social spending programs, the crucial periods of policy innovations, or the forms of these innovations. The "politics" part of the institutional politics theory addresses this gap in theorizing. I argue that political actors working through and around these structural constraints explain the rhythms and characteristics of social spending programs. Policy outcomes are due to political and social struggles, inside and outside the state, for and against public spending. I also argue that the most important actors are politicians who form what I call a reform-oriented regime and state bureaucrats in domestic agencies. The former are generally responsible for passing legislation that makes new social policy commitments. The latter have the greatest influence on the content of these commitments. In addition, challengers have an expansive influence on social policy—though only on specific issues and when political conditions are otherwise favorable.

My argument is that reform-oriented regimes and state bureaucratic actors work in an interactive way to produce specific policy outcomes. The combination of circumstances and activity matters. My central claim is that a combination of national state planning and implementation capacities in

FIGURE 1.2
Institutional Politics Theory: Short-Term Expectations for Policy Outcomes

National State Capacities
for Social Policy

	Strong	Weak
Strong	Adoption of national, collective social spending programs	Adoption of power-sharing programs, some national experiments
Medium	Extension of national experiments in social spending	Extension of power-sharing programs in benefits, coverage
Weak	Failed national proposals; rollback of social spending programs	No national proposals; rollback of social spending programs

Reform Group's Power

specific social policy areas and the rise to political power of a reform regime is necessary to produce nationalized social spending programs. Together I expect these conditions to be sufficient. If a reform regime rises to power without national planners in place, the result is likely to be legislation that provides financial support for "power-sharing" social spending initiatives. If national capacities are created in government bureaus in the absence of a pro-spending political majority, I expect far-reaching and coherent plans to be generated, but rejected.

Figure 1.2 indicates six combinations of state capacities and pro-spending political actors. Each combination is expected to bring specific policy outcomes. The best case for national social spending policies is a strongly reform-oriented regime in power in combination with centralized policy-making abilities in the state (upper left-hand cell). The worst case is when pro-spending political contingents are weak, leading to the rollback of existing policies (bottom cells). Those are not the only important cells, however. Another key combination is that of a strongly reform-oriented regime in power, without centralized state planning capacities (upper right-hand cell). Under these circumstances the national government is likely to commit itself to a variety of disjointed initiatives, building on and supporting state and local precedents. In policy areas where there are no state policy precedents, national experiments may be undertaken. Another important combination is moderate strength for the pro-spenders and centralized state planning capacities (middle left-hand cell). Under these circumstances, minor nationalizing amendments to previous reforms are expected. Let me unpack these analytical boxes and display how their contents apply in the American setting.

Reform-Oriented Regimes Encourage and Enact Social Spending Programs

The institutional politics theory holds that political party regimes greatly influence public social provision and owes much to theories of partisanship, such as the social democratic thesis. Introduced by John D. Stephens, that argument holds that the social democratic parties are central to the adoption and expansion of social policy.[27] Francis G. Castles amended this thesis by focusing on the discouraging impact on social policy of right-wing political parties, and Alexander Hicks has posited social democratic and center-party routes to the adoption of social policy. These arguments suggest that gains in U.S. public spending would result from the taking of power by the Democrats, considered a center party.[28] I also borrow from political coalition arguments about the adoption of social policy suggested by Gøsta Esping-Andersen and Ann Shola Orloff.[29] These coalitional arguments plausibly suggest that wider groups of political actors—including expert advocacy organizations, civic associations, farmers' organizations, organized labor, and social movements—matter in the making of public policy.

Neither standard partisanship nor coalition theses go far enough, however. Democrats held power throughout the Depression and wartime, but without completing American social policy. In any case, the rule of any party often does not reflect U.S. political reality. A president is often elected without a substantial majority or must coexist with a Congress divided along party lines.[30] The coalitional argument does not help to explain why some social programs were chosen and not others. There were few outside experts calling for the Works Progress Administration in the 1920s, and organized labor was never fully behind it. Also, during World War II, U.S. social spending policies were rolled back—despite the agreement of organized labor and policy experts on the need to complete the social spending system. Since the war, organized labor and social spending experts have been more often allied than not, but reforms have appeared only sporadically.[31]

What I call reform-oriented regimes are more broadly drawn than social democratic regimes, but more narrowly defined than expert-labor or farmer-labor political coalitions. These regimes include the political control of the instruments of government by centrist and liberal parties as well as left-wing parties. These political actors and parties are defined by their connection to pro-spending advocates, including expert, labor, and other organizations. Such regimes are expected to encourage spending legislation of all sorts to reach the political agenda and, more important, to *pass* public spending legislation.

Like those who consider the U.S. Democrats a center party, whose rule is expected to promote moderate social spending gains, I argue that pro–social spending or reform-oriented regimes are possible in the American setting and that the Democratic party is central to such regimes. Unlike the center-party hypothesis, however, the institutional politics theory holds that an American pro-spending regime requires more than Democrats controlling the White House and holding majorities in both the House and Senate. In the nonparliamentary United States, representatives can break from the party line without risking the fall of the government and the loss of their own seats. More important, though, even after its alliance with the labor movement, the Democratic party was not so much a unified center party as a hodgepodge of ideologically divergent organizations not all equally likely to favor social spending. For the party has never been centralized and has included sorts of legislators unexpected by partisanship hypotheses: representatives from undemocratic political systems and patronage-oriented party organizations. For the reasons I noted above, Democrats from undemocratic districts are likely to prevent or kill social spending proposals when they can, and when they cannot they are likely to try to stall or diminish these proposals. Democrats from patronage-oriented parties are likely to use their leverage to make programs more arbitrary and subject to manipulation. A reform-oriented or pro–social spending political regime can take power in the American setting, but it is not easy to do and the requirements are strict.

I expect a president's orientation toward reform to have a key impact on social spending and to be crucial for national social spending programs. Only the president has the incentive and ability to create the kinds of national administrative authority needed to forge and secure new relationships between all citizens and the state. Presidents can employ persuasion or favors or their influence over public opinion to convince wavering legislators to support a domestic program. But what is likely to make a president support social policy? A few things come to mind. First, a president is likely to be reform-oriented if affiliated with a party in favor of social spending or if lacking affiliation with a party that opposes it. Second, a president's orientation to reform depends on the number and degree of alliances with pro-spending organizations, ranging from professional reform organizations to the labor movement. Third, orientation to reform depends on a president's political history of supporting or opposing social policy. Finally, the president has to be oriented more toward domestic policy than foreign policy. Wanting to reform is not enough, though. Also needed are power and room to maneuver—which depend in turn on the degree of electoral support and the relationship of the president to his predecessors of the same party. The greater the electoral majority, the greater the influence the president can have over social policy. A president following a series of presidents from the same party is likely to have less policy room to maneuver, being constrained by previous policies. A president not so bound will be freer to move in new directions.[32]

Because presidents cannot legislate on their own, a reform regime requires the election of a large pro–social spending congressional contingent. I expect the most reliable representatives to be Democratic and third-party legislators from democratic political systems and non-patronage-oriented party systems. These legislators are central to the construction of a social policy coalition by a reform-oriented president, or during his tenure. To count as a reform-oriented regime, this contingent must be sizeable enough to overcome resistance from anti-spenders, including both Republicans and Democrats from undemocratic regimes. When led by a reform-oriented president, a large reform-oriented contingent will be likely to support a wide range of social spending proposals and will result in the greatest gains in social spending legislation. A reform-oriented president acting in conjunction with contingents of a medium size is expected to produce moderate gains in spending legislation. Specifically, I expect that existing programs are likely to be extended, augmented, or better grounded administratively speaking, but I expect no major initiatives to pass. I expect the rolling back of social policy when such contingents are small in size and greatly outnumbered by anti-spenders. The range of setbacks run from the retrenchment of existing programs to their elimination.

The election of a reform-oriented president and large contingents of reform-oriented legislators sends clear and persistent signals throughout the political system about social spending possibilities. Left-leaning political appointees in the administration are more likely to demand dramatic spending initiatives. Policy bureaucrats are more likely to press new or long-standing proposals. Reform-oriented members of Congress are likely to make renewed efforts on behalf of their own favored programs, devise new ones, or jump on the bandwagon of administration-sponsored programs. State-oriented challengers are likely to redouble efforts at collective action to promote programs that might benefit their constituents. The incentives to press for social spending efforts are high, because these efforts are more likely to succeed. The efforts are more likely to succeed because reform-oriented regimes can pass new legislation despite the opposition of right-wing political representatives, including Republicans and Democrats from undemocratic polities.

Reform regimes are rare in America because they are more difficult to assemble here, and partly for this reason they are faced with dilemmas that are unusually pressing. That that these regimes are not parliamentary majorities, that they must rally behind a given program, and that they always face sizeable contingents opposing national social policy—each of these circumstances provides pressure to strive for less than what is possible. If programs are designed to be short-term or stingy or locally controlled, they may pick up the support of undemocratic representatives. If programs are designed to provide spending without administrative authority, the pro-spenders might pick up the support of patronage-oriented representatives. Because battles over social spending are likely to be situated within the Democratic party, there are incentives to duck them and thus diminish social spending reform.

Another dilemma is whether to emphasize long-term state-building or short-term spending commitments. On the one hand, creating administrative capacities before making commitments to spend provides coherence in policy and the ability to build policy in the long run. So, too, does convening study commissions to devise new policies. But reforming in this way risks losing favor with the electorate, as potential beneficiaries are kept waiting, and missing a chance to make spending commitments before the regime loses power. On the other hand, making spending commitments by employing the typically flawed administrative machinery available provides immediate benefits, but risks incoherence and the eventual undermining of reform.

In short, reform-oriented regimes are central to the adoption of new public spending programs, and I expect the greatest reforms to take place when these regimes hold power. I also expect them to attempt and succeed in creating bureaucratic capacities to administer programs for the long run. For these reasons, reform regimes need to remain in power for a reasonably lengthy period—long enough to pass new spending commitments and to build bureaucratic capacities. In turn those running the programs usually try to expand social policy—in part to realize the missions that animated their creation—along the lines of the initial program.

State Bureaucrats and Experts Influence the Policy Agenda and Policy Content

According to the institutional politics theory, state bureaucrats and policy experts are expected especially to influence the *content* of social spending proposals and the political agenda. I expect that state domestic bureaucrats will try to fulfill the mission of their agency—typically underdeveloped in the American setting. Because they are strategically situated, though, I expect state actors to do much of the designing and planning of spending programs—more so than outside experts and more so than interest groups such as capitalist organizations. The likeliest sites of social spending innovations and improvements are the parts of the executive with powerful domestic bureaucracies. Domestic bureaucrats will also lobby for their proposals, deploy expert information in support of them, attempt to instill confidence in

their feasibility, and support groups whose goals are consonant with the
bureau's objectives.

Other scholars have of course focused on organizational and intellectual
capabilities in policymaking agencies and on the impact of programs themselves on later policy developments. "Political learning" arguments, such as
those of Hugh Heclo, hold that state administrators puzzle over the experiences of previous programs in devising new ones or augmenting old ones.
Along these lines social scientists argue that social policies may make their
own politics and engender specific political responses, or "policy feedbacks." For that reason, the process of social spending policy is path-
dependent. The initial form a program assumes may influence its political
future by determining whether groups will mobilize around it in support.[33]

Policy feedback arguments, however, do not often provide specific expectations for the adoption and early development of public spending policies,
let alone for the maturation of policies. For the former reason they cannot
account for why the modern American public spending was initially constructed as a work and relief policy. For instance, the corruption in Civil
War pensions from the nineteenth century did not prevent tremendous social spending in the Depression era, and a lack of public employment
programs did not prevent the construction of extensive ones. In other ways
the arguments are too rudimentary. Groups sometimes form in support of
programs, sometimes not. It is not always clear which programs will be
so favored and what the result will be. Those groups that supported
the adoption of mothers' pensions programs in 1910, for instance, had
lost interest in them by 1930. Moreover, need-based programs can have
generous standards and be politically popular, as they were during the
New Deal.[34] An important issue is how to make these arguments more than
heuristic.

Like the political learning and policy feedbacks theorists, I argue that
program content will be related to the efforts of state administrators and
reformers puzzling over social policy questions with the experiences of previous programs in mind.[35] I also argue, however, that the puzzling of domestic bureaucrats is highly structured. The perceptions of administrators
are typically limited by the programs and the configuration of bureaucratic
capabilities in existence. For that reason, I expect the type of planning and
implementation capacities, the sorts of people running them, and their distribution across state institutions to influence the type and character of
spending proposals. The fact that policies and people running them exist
prior to any new reform regime taking power influences the outcomes of the
policymaking process. But even so, the impact on social policy of the activity of state bureaucrats on policy is contingent on a reform-oriented political regime. Let me specify this argument.

First, the times and policy areas in which bureaucratic actors are powerful are more likely to produce reform proposals. For that reason, I expect
the most highly developed domestic bureaucracies to control the bulk of the

reform agenda—when reform regimes come to power. Proposals with high-level bureaucratic sponsorship will be more likely to get on the political agenda than programs without such backing and are thus more likely to be enacted. Those programs and risks related to bureaucracies that have already created a beachhead in the national domestic bureaucracy are likely to be central to the policy process when reform-oriented regimes take power. Not only can program administrators lobby for their favored proposals, they can also provide technical support for them. Their relative advantage in information increases the chances that their proposals will dominate the agenda and find favor over the proposals of outside experts, pro-spending groups, and challengers. To the extent that national bureaucracies do not exist in a given area, the opportunity for those outside the government is correspondingly greater.

Second, the overall configuration of bureaucrats, policies, and abilities will influence the nature and coherence of reform. A planning process dominated by competition among many bureaucracies is likely to produce incoherent proposals comprising different ideological and programmatic approaches to the hazards of everyday life. When state domestic planning capacities are centralized, ideologically and programmatically coherent proposals are more likely to result. But state bureaucrats cannot legislate, and thus the nature of policies depends on these planning capacities and the existence of a reform-oriented regime. This situation is indicated on the right-hand side of Figure 1.2.

Third, I expect the distribution of prior programs and those administering them to influence the form of innovations when reform-oriented regimes take power. In a federal system, polities and bureaucracies are likely to compete over social spending policy, and programs controlled by a lower level of government will be difficult to transfer completely to a higher level. For several reasons, power-sharing arrangements—in which the federal government supports state-level initiatives—are likely to result. Such programs will have developed their own government-sponsored expert support and are likely to find champions in Congress. More important, power-sharing arrangements constitute a safe retreating point for opponents of national social programs, which are typically more generous and standardized. Programs already in place in some states and localities are likely to be converted into power-sharing programs—not nationalized—when reform-oriented regimes rise to power.

Creating a nationally controlled program is difficult in a structural political setting like the U.S. polity, and prior state-level policy experiments make adopting a nationally controlled program more difficult. If a policy area is not covered by a program or a program is absent at a lower level of government, however, the way is open for national experiments. It is possible to develop new national policies even when planning capacities are not centralized. I expect that this might happen by a process of experimentation and then augmentation and extension during consecutive reform regimes.

However constructed, programs with only minimal commitments to them are likely to be boosted greatly when a reform-oriented regime comes to power. A small early commitment can often be transformed into a substantial one later on. Moreover, once policies are supported by the national government it becomes much easier for social policy advocates to expand them than to generate new ones. I argue that it does not take as strong a political reform grouping to augment an existing program as it does to create a commitment to a program for a new risk or group. Thus medium-sized reform contingents are likely to result in the augmentation of existing social programs, but not to new commitments in areas uncovered by social policy.

Creating strong social policies also means constructing much of the bureaucratic machinery needed to run them, and it takes political effort to do so. Pro-spending partisans can make commitments to fund programs without providing complete or suitable bureaucratic backing. That is an especially inviting option in a polity in which legislators will often seek to make spending commitments transitory or include patronage opportunities in them.

Creating a new spending commitment without commensurate bureaucratic authority, however, poses danger to a social spending program in the long run. On the one hand, ungrounded programs run partly by favoritism are more vulnerable to political attacks than programs that are bureaucratically well grounded and run according to well-defined principles. The opponents of social spending will have more ammunition to fight bureaucratically backward programs. In addition, if a social spending program is staffed in an incompetent way or in a way that allows discrimination against citizens who meet the criteria for spending, the program may alienate those who would otherwise favor social spending. On the other hand, highly powerful executive bureaucracies with great powers of discretion are also likely to be vulnerable. In any period of domination by anti-spenders, the programs administered in a partisan or idiosyncratic way are likely to suffer more radical attacks that those run under standard and routine procedures.

Under Favorable Political Conditions, Challengers Can Increase
Social Spending; Members of the Polity Can Dilute
Spending Initiatives, Regardless

The institutional politics theory also holds that challengers and organized interest groups influence public spending policies—a rapid way for democratic politics to affect social policy. Challengers are defined by their lack of routine access to polity and most seek to become "members of the polity," to use Charles Tilly's terminology, and have their interests privileged in everyday politics. Most challengers are state-oriented, in that they seek to alter state policies to the advantage of their constituencies.[36] Depression-era America saw the rise of groups as disparate as the unemployed, World War

I veterans, farmers, organized labor, and the aged. Researchers have debated, however, whether these movements had important impacts on New Deal social policy. The evidence suggests, as Doug McAdam argues, that the impact of challengers is conditional on other political circumstances.[37] But which circumstances matter for gains in social policy?

I argue that the main way that reform groups can promote public social provision is through alliances with political party actors—advancing the policy process by backing the proposals of reform administrations and their supporters in Congress. These pro-spending groups and challengers constitute an important part of these processes of ideological separation of parties.

In addition, state-oriented challengers not allied with reform forces can advance social policy under two conditions: if the challenger is highly mobilized and has established a political presence for itself, and if conditions are already favorable for social spending proposals. A highly mobilized challenger is one that has gained commitments from participants and resources at its disposal, and by political presence I mean devoting significant resources to influencing elections or legislation, or both. Under conditions otherwise favorable for social spending proposals—basically, the existence of a reform-oriented regime and powerful state actors in social spending areas—the constituencies of challengers with such a presence are likely to gain greater benefits in public policies than those groups unrepresented by challengers.

Independent challengers can have an impact in a number of ways. Well-mobilized groups may focus attention on an issue that might otherwise be eliminated from the agendas of administration policymakers, state actors, or legislators. I expect organized challengers to be able to induce state actors and legislators to alter proposals. State actors may sweeten their proposals to favor groups represented by well-organized challenges, and, more likely, political representatives will up the ante on the proposals of state actors. For these reasons, programs enacted to aid groups already organized are likely to have greater benefits in them than programs enacted to benefit groups not organized. Organized challengers with well-developed political resources—such as having worked for the election of legislators—may also aid the passage of new bills. For instance, insurgent movements and third parties might prevent Democrats in patronage-party organizations from defecting from the pro-spending line of the national party. They might also induce support from the occasional representative from the opposition party. In those ways challengers can help to create a reform-oriented coalition for their issues of concern when pro-spending forces are moderately well represented.

My arguments about challengers are interactive, and their impact depends on the strength of pro-spending political forces and previous policies and bureaucratic capabilities. Figure 1.3 indicates the situation when a reform-oriented regime is in power. Under these circumstances, challenger or

FIGURE 1.3
Expected Program Outcomes under a Reform-Oriented Regime, According to National Bureaucratic or Social Movement Influence and State-Level Precedents

<table>
<tr><td rowspan="2"></td><td colspan="2" align="center">Bureaucratic or Movement Influence</td></tr>
<tr><td align="center">Present</td><td align="center">Absent</td></tr>
<tr><td>Absent</td><td align="center">National experiments</td><td align="center">No action</td></tr>
<tr><td>Present</td><td align="center">Power-sharing programs</td><td align="center">Continued state or local programs</td></tr>
</table>

Prior State-Level Program

national bureaucratic support aids the creation of new national commitments, and areas and programs without such support will be less likely to see national action. The existence of previous programs at the state level influences the form of these commitments. If there are state-level precedents, national action will be likely to reinforce them, resulting in power-sharing programs. If there are no precedents, the way is open for new national programs or programs with less power sharing. In this way, challengers can influence the political agenda, as do state bureaucratic actors, but do not devise or greatly influence the form of program, as the latter do.

Independent challengers have other limitations as forces for social spending change. Even pro-spending regimes are likely to attempt to disorganize or contain movements and will not likely endorse their plans or leadership. Elected officials will try to appeal over the heads of the leadership of the challengers to win the allegiance of their followers or those the movement leadership hopes to represent. Moreover, the specific plans of challengers are likely to be rejected, and in any case to be influential the challenger's demands have to be broadly consistent with state proposals. Positive impacts of challengers—on the political agenda, the content of proposals, and their passage—are likely only if reformers already have considerable power. Mobilizations in the face of an anti-spending president or majority in Congress are unlikely to augment social policy.

I expect anti-spending groups and organizations to ally with politicians of the right to stall and dilute social spending. The most important of these anti-spending organizations in the American setting have been those of conservative businessmen. Groups such as the Chamber of Commerce and the National Association of Manufacturers had a strong motive to fight public spending. The benefits of public social provision would accrue to workers, and taxes—on employers' payrolls, in some cases—would be needed to pay for them. Moreover, public programs would not induce loyalty or prevent workers from joining unions, as private programs might. U.S. businessmen have often opposed social spending and have been the standard bearers of antistate values, and numerous business associations organized across the U.S. polity did their best to forestall the public spending programs of the New Deal.[38]

These groups have the best chance of defeating social spending and corresponding taxation by throwing in their lot with candidates for office who represent their preferences on social spending and taxation. Basically, though, anti-spending groups have an easier task than pro-spending groups—because of the numerous structural barriers to reform-oriented regimes. Because anti-spending organizations typically have greater resources and access to politics they will be able to dilute social spending—even during the rule of reform-oriented regimes. Membership in the polity has its privileges.

THE TERMINOLOGY AND CONCEPTUALIZATION OF SOCIAL POLICY

Analyzing the development and decline of modern American social policy requires making some terminological and methodological decisions. First among them is deciding what to analyze and explaining why it is worth it. In any study of social policy, moreover, conceptualizing the policymaking process is necessary.

What Social Policy Means Here and Why It is Worth Studying

I expand my focus beyond the Big Five programs of the welfare state and drop the standard terminology. I analyze something more general—state policy responses to basic societal risks to employment, income, and economic security. Social relations in the modern capitalist and democratic world produce a number of perils to income. These include growing old and infirm; being injured at work or at war; becoming ill, unhealthy, or disabled; becoming unemployed or underemployed; and being in a family where the principal wage earner or earners are incapacitated or eliminated by these other risks, or where there is no principal wage earner. To say that modern capitalist democratic societies have generated certain problems does not imply that these problems require or have generated specific responses. Some of these hazards have been covered by social insurance programs, others by need-based ones, or by social services or in-kind programs.

Frequently these social conditions elicited minor or no public or private programmatic responses. In the period between the world wars, it was uncertain how public social programs were going to be structured and how much spending countries were going to devote to them. What constituted a politically important threat to the incomes of citizens had not yet been decided. Countries took different approaches to protecting citizens from risks to income and employment. During the 1930s the world had not converged on specific policies to address these risks. For every hazard to income, universal social insurance programs or targeted and upgraded need-based programs—or neither, or both—have been employed.

Whatever one calls it, social policy is worth examining. Although the effects of different programs on income have been debated, these programs are undoubtedly egalitarian insofar as income inequality would be aggravated in their absence. Often they are the only thing standing between an individual and destitution. In this respect, social policy matters for political scientists and political sociologists because it bears on debates about power, as exercised through the state. If state power is defined as "the social capacity to make binding decisions that have major consequences over the directions in which a society moves," social policy is integral to it. For in modern social policy the state is making important and binding decisions about the life chances of large categories of citizens. In America, the beginning of the era of modern social policy augured the end of the era of the poorhouse. Identifying what causes social policy speaks to debates about who or what exercises power in capitalist democracies.[39]

The structure and array of programs also matter. In a democratic polity, social policy indicates what society considers legitimate roles for people of different ages, sexes, and group affiliations and also what counts as an appropriate departure from expectations. Well-funded and automatic programs suggest that the problems addressed are legitimate social problems, and those benefiting from such programs are considered worthy. Less well-funded programs indicate a grudging acknowledgment of the problems and the individuals suffering from them. Where funding is minimal or nonexistent, this suggests that society views the problems concerned as insignificant, or the fault of the individual, and those suffering from them as unworthy. As Theda Skocpol has argued, the groups considered worthy in American social policy have varied historically—from Civil War veterans in the nineteenth century to the aged today.[40]

I do not want to narrow my focus to the adoption and expansion of major social insurance programs—the typical purview of studies of social policy between the wars. The standard view is that the period between the wars saw the adoption of major social programs and the first decades of the postwar period witnessed an expansion of spending for them, whereas only the last decade and a half has been a time of retrenchment.[41] Although the standard view is in many ways right, the story of social policy between the wars was not a tale of unbroken victories for reformers. The formative years of modern U.S. social spending also resulted in the retrenchment of some programs. The work and relief policy was conspicuously diminished as other programs prospered.

Taxation policy has many connections to social spending policy and merits attention of its own. It is necessary to tax in order to spend, and taxation policy may influence the prospects and possibilities of social spending. What is more, spending programs are often packaged politically with taxes to pay for them, and the form and amount of taxation influences the overall degree of redistribution effected by a given program and fiscal system. Spending policies may be redistributive, but if they are financed by regressive taxes—payroll or consumption—the effect on income inequality is muted. The taxation system itself can redistribute income. Income lost due to unemployment, old age, poor health, and so on can be restored through taxation policy.[42]

And so I employ the terms "public social provision," "public social spending programs," or simply "social policy" and mean by them something more than the Big Five social insurance programs. I include all public spending programs that served to reduce risks to income, whether inspired by social insurance principles or otherwise. For these reasons I examine public employment programs along with unemployment insurance, need-based Old-Age Assistance along with Old-Age Insurance. Although public employment and Old-Age Assistance are no longer major parts of current U.S. policy, they might have been. Assuming otherwise would be reading history backward.

The Policymaking Process

Studies of social policy also need to work from a conceptualization of the policymaking process. Here is how I see it. Each social spending program involves at least three dimensions of state activity. Legislation must be enacted to make commitments to spend, bureaucracies must be set in place to administer the legislation, and money must be appropriated to fund it.[43] Because legislation typically is required for administration and funding, my emphasis is not on overall spending—the focus of much excellent research—but on the key legislation creating and expanding social spending and taxation programs and their bureaucratic infrastructure. What accounts for key legislative enactments stands as the top analytical priority. During bursts of legislation—such as the Social Security Act of 1935 or the Revenue Act of 1940—states make long-term commitments to large categories of citizens.

Enacting legislation can be divided into smaller events. As John Kingdon has argued, any successful policy requires the successful performance of three operations. It must get on the political agenda; it must have its contents specified; and it must be voted and signed into law. Varying groups and actors will have varying impacts on each of these steps of the policy-making process.[44]

Although the distinction between social insurance and assistance is important, other matters of form or policy content are crucial. Programs can assume a collective or distributive form or fall somewhere in between. Distributive benefits can be divided among recipients and can be granted or timed with political discretion. The smaller the group gaining the benefit and the easier it is to withhold the benefit from persons within the group, the more distributive the benefit. By contrast, collective benefits go to large categorical groups and are relatively automatic in action.

It also matters greatly whether a program is controlled by the national government or by subnational governments such as states and localities. Throughout U.S. history national government control over public spending policies has meant more generous, fairer, and better-run programs. The key U.S. national spending program is old-age insurance, and American spending for the aged places it in the middle of capitalist democracies. Food Stamps, a national need-based program, are more accessible than other need-based programs. Similarly, during the Depression, when America led all major nations in public spending efforts, its margin was built by the nationally funded WPA.

These issues might be combined and simplified in the following way. Each major public social spending program includes collective benefits for those who qualify for it. To create any new program, and thus deliver the benefits, requires the successful negotiation of all three parts of the policymaking process. Success in placing an issue onto the political agenda amounts to greatly increasing the probability that collective benefits, whose value is unknown, will be incorporated in legislation. By influencing the content of proposals, people can work to increase or decrease the value of collective goods. Once an issue is on the political agenda, more than one proposal is often entertained, but in the end usually only one is a serious contender for passage. Once that bill's content has been specified, it must be enacted by political representatives. After enactment, a law must be implemented. Institutionalizing public spending programs increases the likelihood of the continuation of benefits. Those institutions, groups, and individuals who influence these processes and outcomes thus influence the expected value of collective benefits in public social spending policy.

WHY YOU SHOULD BELIEVE ME: MATTERS OF METHODOLOGY

Anyone with the sorts of claims I am making needs to develop strategies to appraise them. Social scientists hoping to support their assertions about U.S. social policy often prime themselves to scale the interpretive Mount Everest that is the Social Security Act. The thinking goes something like this: If the act was the most momentous thing ever to happen in American social politics and if one's own argument explains it—what more is there to prove? That approach, though, would lead to explanatory trouble even if the Social Security Act had mattered as much as many seem to think. For analyzing one case means an inability to appraise theoretical arguments. Like other case researchers, I need to demonstrate that my explanation is more than just plausible. My problem is aggravated by the fact that one of my key research questions strays into the nether realm of the counterfactual—why no welfare state in America? Claims about "why the dog didn't bark" are always difficult to support.[45]

My approach is to go beyond explaining one piece of social legislation by confronting an entire terrain of policy differences. My argument has implications for the greatest periods of reform, but also for other social policy outcomes. And so the problem is reduced to specifying these implications and identifying appropriate research sites, often more commonplace ones, to appraise the claims. As I discuss below, my theoretical arguments have enough implications, and there are abundant research sites for appraisals.[46] Although not all of these sites are as celebrated as the Social Security Act, some of them, such as the political battles surrounding the WPA, perhaps ought to be.

Mapping and Analyzing Historical Trajectories of Social Policy

One way to appraise my theoretical argument and to expand a case study generally is to extend the range of the study beyond one episode of reform. This matters, as I expect variations in the reform-oriented nature of regimes to result in variations in overall developments in social policy. I do not want here to go into great detail in demonstrating the periods in which, according to my argument, the reform forces were greatest, but let me provide some sense of the variation in political alignments.

The fate of social spending legislation overall was tied to the fates of Democrats at the national level. After 1932, Democratic presidents held power until the 1950s. Both Roosevelt and Harry Truman were mainly oriented to policy reform, except when their domestic agendas were preempted by war. Roosevelt always had a strong mandate, though his support peaked in 1936. A reform-oriented regime was present only after the elections of 1934 and 1936. In the legislative sessions following these elections, the president was interested in and active on social policy, and Congress had an overwhelming Democratic majority—one in which Republicans and southern Democrats were a minority. Other periods were also favorable, if less so, for social policy advocates. Congress included a moderate-sized reform-oriented contingent after the elections of 1938 and 1940, and again after the election of 1948. By contrast, the period before Roosevelt's election was unfavorable, as were the two-year periods following the elections of 1942 and 1946.

I appraise these claims by comparing them to a detailed historical trajectory of U.S. policy in depression and war. I address the breakthroughs, to be sure. Also, though, I try to explain what happened at other times, most of which were less conducive to reform, but were important in the development of American social policy. Mapping its historical trajectory provides additional instances of reform to examine. Such a map appears in Table 1.1, which breaks the two decades into seven periods.

The table indicates that most policy breakthroughs came in the 1930s. However, the period from 1930 through 1932, which I am calling that of "misery," saw little action on short-term aid or long-term social spending policy. The years of "recovery" (1933–34), including the so-called First New Deal, were dominated by experimental and temporary aid programs, some of which had long-term effects. The next period, described as "reconstruction" (1935–36), included the Second New Deal and many breakthroughs in public social provision. Still, a number of these were federal or power-sharing programs. During the recovery and reconstruction years, new spending programs were part of a political package that also included taxation innovations and increases. The Third New Deal (1937–39) was a period of "consolidation" for social spending programs. During that time, some new social policy gains were made—especially the Fair Labor Standards Act of 1938—but for the most part these gains were minor.

By contrast, the 1940s were overall much less productive of social policy reforms, but there were also important exceptions to the rule. The early war years, lasting from 1940 through 1942, were those of the "taxation revolution." The income tax took its modern form, but proposed spending innovations were put on hold. By contrast, a sixth period running from the end of 1942 through 1944 saw the "rollback" of the New Deal, notably the demise of public employment programs and the removal of social policy from the political agenda. The final period, that of "muddling through," includes the immediate postwar years through 1950. Important extensions of social assistance and insurance were made in 1950, but innovations in new areas of policy were rejected. A split social security/welfare policy had crystallized.

Comparing the Development and Fates of Programs

Following programs over time can also aid in appraising the aspects of the explanation that are sequential.[47] I am arguing that the initial developments in programs and how they are run influence them at later times. My claims about state capacities and previous policies have implications for the forms of programs. The institutional politics theory expects different outcomes depending on whether a reform-oriented regime comes to power, for instance, before or after national state social spending capacities have been built. I expect the existence of state-level experiments to influence the form that programs will take when reformers come to power.

TABLE 1.1
Seven Periods of U.S. Social Spending and Taxation Policies, 1930–1950.

Social Spending Developments	Taxation Developments
MISERY: EARLY DEPRESSION (1930–32)	
Reconstruction Finance Corporation (1932)	**Revenue Act** (1932) **income taxes increased**
RECOVERY: FIRST NEW DEAL (1933–34)	
Federal Emergency Relief Administration (1933)	**Alcohol taxes** (1933)
Civil Works Administration (1934)	State-level sales and income taxes
RECONSTRUCTION: SECOND NEW DEAL (1935–36)	
Works Progress Administration (1935)	**"Soak the rich" taxes** (1935)
Social Security Act (1935)	State-level sales and income taxes
Old-Age Assistance	
Unemployment Compensation	Unemployment Compensation tax
Aid to Dependent Children	
Old-Age Insurance	**OAI payroll tax**
Social Security Board	
Veterans' Bonuses (1936)	**Undistributed profits tax** (1936)
CONSOLIDATION: THIRD NEW DEAL (1937–39)	
SSA found constitutional (1937)	*Undistributed profits tax repealed*
Fair Labor Standards Act (1938)	*(1937)*
SSA Amendments (1939)	
OAA increased, ADC extended	
Old-Age and Survivors' Insurance	*OASI payroll tax postponed* (1939)
Federal Security Agency (1939)	
WPA, NRPB reorganized (1939)	
TAXATION REVOLUTION: EARLY WAR YEARS (1940–42)	
	Income tax system transformed
NRPB Report (1941)	**Revenue Acts** (1940, 1941)
ROLL BACK: MIDDLE WAR YEARS (1943–44)	
WPA terminated (1943)	*OASI payroll taxes delayed*
NRPB killed (1943)	
Wagner-Murray-Dingell bill fails (1943)	
GI bill passed (1944)	*Revenue Act, over FDR veto* (1944)
MUDDLING THROUGH: POSTWAR YEARS (1945–1950)	
Second Wagner bill fails (1945)	
Employment Act (1946)	*Income tax cut* (1948)
SSA Amendments (1950)	**OASI payroll tax increased** (1950)
OASI extended, ADC extended	**Income tax restored** (1950)

Note: **Nationalizing reforms are in bold.** *Social policy cutbacks and failures are italicized.*

Policy will be made and unmade historically in a number of ways. If a program already has state-level predecessors, it is more likely to be incorporated in power-sharing legislation. Programs supported and overseen by national-level bureaucracies in power are likely to be aided by legislation, taking precedence over those not so favored. Small differences in programs are expected to widen as they are built. In addition to that, programs already created or supported at the national level are likely to be augmented during moderately reform-oriented regimes, favoring them as against programs not yet created. My argument also pertains to the retrenchment of programs. The most radical of the programs and those not run according to proper administrative standards are likely to suffer greater attacks when anti-spenders gain control of the government.

My claims about the role of challengers in social policy help to explain why some programs had greater benefits than others. I would expect that those groups, notably the aged, who were represented by challengers in the 1930s would likely have their interests realized to a greater extent than groups that were not so well mobilized. I would, however, also expect policy breakthroughs even in social areas where no challengers were present, such as was the case with programs for children and mothers. In addition, I would expect groups—such as the veterans' Bonus Marchers—with agendas that strongly opposed that of the administration to fail. Moreover, even well-organized groups such as the Townsend Movement and labor would be likely to be ineffective once congressional reform forces were weakened.

A way to appraise these claims is to compare the differences in form, size, and fate of the individual programs of New Deal social policy. Such comparisons can help uncover the reasons behind the divergent fates of programs—whether they become nationalized or power-sharing, whether they were well funded or poorly funded, whether they survived or were destroyed. The two programs that stand out as nationalized innovations are the WPA and Old-Age and Survivors' Insurance (OASI). The patterns of development for these national programs can be compared to the patterns for programs in which governments shared control, including both relief and social insurance programs, such as Aid to Dependent Children and Unemployment Compensation. Also, some otherwise similar programs were better funded than others—notably, Old-Age Assistance was privileged over Aid to Dependent Children. Finally, some programs did not survive at all—in particular, the work programs.

Variation in Federal Programs across States of the Union

Another explanatory terrain is provided by the social politics in individual states of the Union. As the historian James Patterson once put it, scholars almost invariably prefer "the excitement of Pennsylvania Avenue to the more prosaic events of Albany, Atlanta, and Santa Fe."[48] But important things were going on in state capitals, as each had considerable influence over social policy. Some states had much larger "little New Deals"—as state responses to New Deal social policy were called—than others. That is to say, some states provided much greater and more extensive benefits for citizens in their versions of social policy. State-level social policies also constrain and help to set the agenda for national-level social politics.

My arguments have implications for social policy developments in the states—which are especially well suited to examining simultaneously the institutional and political aspects of the theory. I expect combinations of institutional conditions and political actors to interact in producing social policy outcomes, and greatly varied configurations of institutions and actors appeared at the state level. Political institutions, which change only slowly over time at the national level, varied substantially across the states. So, too, did the strength of reform-oriented regimes, domestic bureaucracies, and social movements.[49]

When the national polity is providing incentives for the adoption of social spending programs, the greatest social spending progress will be found only where the institutional context is favorable—where voting rights are protected and patronage parties have been reformed, superseded, or eliminated. Such states would be considered likely candidates for far-reaching little New Deals, but a favorable institutional context would not be sufficient. Powerful political actors in favor of social spending would also be needed. Democratic or insurgent third-party regimes in these structurally conducive states would be considered to be analogous to reform-oriented regimes at the national level. The theory also expects that state bureaucrats will be important proponents of social spending change in states structurally conducive to reform. Bureaucrats will be effective, however, only if they have wide authority in administrative matters. Highly mobilized and politically resourceful social movements are also expected to influence state-level public spending policies. Well-mobilized and politically powerful challenges might constitute a functional equivalent to reform-oriented regimes or powerful bureaucrats at the state level. The impact of social movements will be localized. Although reform-oriented regimes will have an impact across spending policies, challengers will have an impact only on specific issues of concern—the Townsend Movement of the aged on old-age spending policy, for instance, or the labor movement on unemployment policy.

American polities across the states can be divided into profiles across the theoretical categories. In the states most likely to achieve reform, according to the argument, the political system was highly democratized and the party system open. In the best-case scenario for generous social policy, structurally open states will have a radical third party or a Democratic party in power, a tradition of administrative reform at the state level, and powerful social movements pushing for social policy. In the 1930s, as Table 1.2 shows, only seven states fell into this category, which I label "type I." Slightly less favorable for reform is the structurally open situation in which only one or two powerful social spending advocates were present. That was

TABLE 1.2
State Political Profiles According to Institutional and Political Categories

Type		Voting Rights[a]	Patronage Party[b]	Left/Center-Party Rule[c]	Administrative Powers[d]	Social Movement[e]
I.	Best-case scenario (7)	Yes	No	Yes	Yes	Yes
II.	Open, some forces for change (15)	Yes	No	—	—	—
III.	Open, but no forces for change (2)	Yes	No	No	No	No
IV.	Patronage, countervailing forces (9)	Yes	Yes	—	—	—
V.	Patronage, no countervailing forces (4)	Yes	Yes	No	No	No
VI.	Undemocratic, Democratic (11)	No	No	Yes	—	—

[a] Refers to the right to vote, as manifested in relatively high voting participation.

[b] Refers to whether a state had centralized, patronage-oriented electioneering organizations.

[c] Refers to whether the Democratic party or a radical third party controlled the state government for four years or more during the 1930s.

[d] Refers to whether the state labor commissioner had rule-making authority in safety issues by the end of the 1920s and is used as general indicator of power in domestic bureaucracies before 1930.

[e] Refers to whether the state had a powerful labor movement or Townsend Movement in the 1930s. See chapter 5 for complete definitions and measurements.

the case in fifteen states (type II). Less likely to witness reform were the structurally open states in which no pro-spending actors had a major presence. That was the case for the two states falling into type III. Further down the scale of expectation are states in which patronage-oriented parties dominated. Those with some countervailing influences, such as strong labor movements or traditions of independence in social spending bureaucracies, are expected to make moderate, but minor accommodations to New Deal social policy—the greater the countervailing forces, the greater the accommodation. Near the bottom are states in patronage-oriented states without countervailing forces for change—which was the case for four states (type V). At the very bottom of the table (type VI) are undemocratic polities, which, in the American setting, were typically dominated by one-party Democratic regimes. The eleven states of the former Confederacy fit here. There were no instances of highly patronage-oriented party systems coexisting with underdemocratized polities.[50]

I support my claims by tracking social policy in four states that I would expect to have reacted in divergent ways to the New Deal. I choose one state each with a particular institutional obstacle to social spending—a lack of democratic political practices and a dominant patronage-oriented party system. In the underdemocratized states I expect little New Deals of the stingiest kind, and in the patronage-oriented states, small-scale little New Deals focused on the programs with the greatest patronage opportunities. I also choose states in structurally favorable circumstances, but with different combinations of powerful pro-spending actors, and trace their responses. I expect more generous little New Deals in such circumstances, but slanted ones where only some groups are powerful, and more balanced ones where a reform-oriented regime takes power. These brief narratives also give a better sense of the actors involved, the decisions they faced, and the choices they made. Political leaders such as Senator Harry F. Byrd of Virginia, the La Follette brothers of Wisconsin, Governor Culbert Olson of California, and Mayor Edward J. Kelly of Chicago had different responses when faced with similar pressures and incentives.

A Cross-National Comparison

To be able to sustain more general claims, however, it is useful for a case study to have a cross-national dimension. Here I compare the United States with Britain—countries that were similar in important ways that might matter for social policy outcomes. America adopted British poor laws, providing similar starting points for and obstacles to modern social policy. Both were large capitalist democracies—and remained democracies despite the Depression. Although Britain suffered greater damage, both countries avoided invasion and were allied on the winning side of the Second World War.[51]

All the same, my argument would predict substantial differences in their social policies. Overall, it ought to be more difficult to enact social spending reforms in the United States than in Britain. The latter had eradicated its rotten boroughs long before the United States did so, and did not have as strongly patronage-oriented a party system. I would also expect the United States to see greater achievements in social policy during the Depression 1930s, when a reform-oriented regime held sway there. By contrast, because Britain was ruled by a Conservative-dominated national government in the 1930s, I would not expect any breakthroughs at that time. In the 1940s, though, Britain was ruled by a coalition and then a Labour government. I will argue that Britain found itself in the upper right-hand corner of Figure 1.2, where the prospects for nationalized social policies were the greatest, while the United States never found itself in that situation.

During the 1930s and 1940s the public policies of these countries moved in opposite directions. British social policy muddled through the Depression, but Britain enacted its "welfare state" after the Second World War— just the opposite of the United States. Especially because of its postwar policy successes, the example of Britain can help to indicate why U.S. social spending policies did not become similarly nationalized and completed. The dog in one country was barking, so to speak, while a similar one in another country was not. In this way I address more directly the counterfactual question of why American enacted no welfare state. The institutional politics theory suggests that the reasons for the American Depression-era breakthroughs and the British wartime and postwar innovations were similar, even if they took different forms and happened at different times.

I rely on a variety of evidence. Basic facts about the enactment of policies and political life are mainly gleaned from secondary sources—the excellent historiography on the period and social science research on social policy. Much of the evidence, however, comes from primary sources. These range from autobiographies and memoirs of participants in the policymaking process to governmental statistical output, from executive branch documents to congressional testimony.[52]

Conclusion

Institutional theories indicate the constraints on social politics, and political theories indicate the actors who struggle for social policy, but both are incomplete and neither has expectations for positive developments in U.S. social policy. The institutional politics theory addresses these gaps and has implications for differences in public social policy across industrial capitalist countries as well as for the United States across time and section. I am suggesting that the institutional barriers to national social policy are great in America, but also that it is possible to overcome these barriers.

I hold institutional barriers to social policy up to the following standard: To what degree do they motivate political actors to oppose or deflect collective social spending policy? Based on this standard, I expect deficiently democratized political institutions to damage the prospects of public social policy. Representatives from undemocratic polities have little motivation to aid those who would benefit from social policy and every reason to aid those opposed to it. I expect similar problems from leaders of patronage-oriented political party systems. They see politics and policy as means of promoting not programs and ideology, but the political organization and the careers of those connected to it. Such political leaders will see collective social policy as threatening to their prerogatives, as these policies cannot be used as individualized rewards, remove degrees of freedom from their action, and require taxes to be paid by potential allies. In the United States at the beginning of the twentieth century, the polity was relatively underdemocratized and patronage-oriented—harming the prospects of national public social policy.

Other institutional conditions are important, too. Like others, I argue that fragmented political authority will damage the prospects for public social provision by placing obstacles in the way of political actors favoring social spending. Majorities in favor of public social spending policy can be blocked where power is shared among the national and subnational governments in such settings. The American polity is greatly fragmented—beyond merely being nonparliamentary and federalized—and so these obstacles constitute another barrier here to social policy. But the peculiar fragmentation of American political institutions biases some institutions, such as Congress, against collective public spending policies. I argue that nationalized social policy is more likely to come from a reform-oriented executive branch, which has a national constituency and less institutional reason to create fragmented social policy. I also see domestic bureaucracies as important forces for social policy and their relative underdevelopment here as another barrier to reform. But the open nature of the U.S. bureaucracy makes it possible to use it for reform as well as patronage purposes.

Like the political theories, the institutional politics theory holds that political actors apply the pressure needed for the passage of social spending reforms. My arguments here are neither as strict as the social democratic thesis, nor as wide as the coalition thesis. My alternative is the reform-oriented regime thesis. In the American setting, I expect national social policies to be likely under a president with reasons of party situation, group alliances, and previous history to support social policy. Yet to head a reform-oriented regime, presidents need a strong mandate and have to take power in concert with a majority of representatives of left and center political parties in conducive structural settings—democratic polities with programmatic parties. Also expected to promote social policy are social movements and other organized groups. Such groups can ally with political actors and influence policy by adding to a reform group or by working from the outside. I expect these regimes to have their main impact by placing social policy on the political agenda and passing new social legislation. People situated in executive bureaucracies are expected to do most of the devising of reforms, though their impact depends on their powers and the outlook of their bureau, agency, or department.

Any study of social policy needs a focus. I emphasize the legislation creating new commitments between the state and citizens. In doing so I include but go beyond the Big Five social insurance programs and examine all manner of social policy and the taxation policies on which it was based. In doing that I want to go beyond analyzing the timing of adoption of legislation and examine the form it takes and its development over time. I analyze several aspects of the policymaking process. These include agenda setting, the specification of policy content, the passage of legislation, and its administration. Each matters in making or undoing state commitments to large groups of citizens.

My arguments may seem difficult to support. After all, this book is a case study asking questions that are sometimes counterfactual, such as why the bid failed to complete American social policy. Nevertheless, the theory has implications for a number of policy outcomes—including when social policy innovations are likely to be adopted, the form they take, and differences in spending and policy developments across states and countries. Although like other scholars of American public policy I closely examine the Social Security Act, I bring to bear other evidence. Fortunately most of it addresses important questions about the development of social policy in America. I compare the episodes of policy innovation with those of policy stalemate. I also trace the fates of different programs. In addition I compare the prospects and results of little New Deals across the country—exploiting the "natural experiments" of the American political system for social science purposes. Finally, I compare the fates of reform efforts in the United States and Britain. Although the United States did not complete its system of social policy, Britain did. And when the United States was building a work-relief state, Britain was not.

In the next chapter, I begin my account of American social policy and an appraisal of the institutional politics arguments. I discuss and analyze the decades from the late nineteenth century until the Second New Deal of 1935, which was a period of very limited development of modern social policy.

CHAPTER TWO

An Indifferent Commitment to Modern Social Policy, 1880–1934

> The Federal Government has sought to do its part by example in the expansion of employment, by affording credit to drought sufferers for rehabilitation, and by cooperation with the community, and thus to avoid the opiates of government charity and the stifling of our national spirit of mutual self-help.
>
> —*Herbert Hoover, February 1931*

> Nothing will contribute more to the return of prosperity than to maintain the sound fiscal position of the Federal Government.
>
> —*Herbert Hoover, November 1931*

> It is essential to our recovery program that measures be immediately enacted aimed at unemployment relief.
>
> —*Franklin D. Roosevelt, March 1933*

> It does not mean that because a person served in the defense of his country, performed a basic obligation to citizenship, he should receive a pension from his Government because of a disability incurred after his service had terminated.
>
> —*Franklin D. Roosevelt, October 1933*

THE STANDARD STORY about the history of American social policy is that little of note happened until the Social Security Act of 1935.[1] As the story goes, the act vaulted the United States into the world of modern social policy by enacting old-age and unemployment insurance and some other programs. American social policy before that time at best laid the groundwork for that breakthrough legislation.[2]

That account has been recently revised in two key ways by Ann Shola Orloff and Theda Skocpol. Orloff and Skocpol have demonstrated that the United States was no laggard in social policy in the late nineteenth century. Skocpol has argued, notably, that Civil War pensions of that era constituted a "precocious" welfare state that provided disability, retirement, and survivors' benefits to many Americans. She also shows that in the first decades of the twentieth century America went some distance toward creating a "maternalist" welfare state—labor regulations for women, pensions for widows provided by localities, and health benefits for pregnant women and young children encouraged by the Sheppard-Towner Act of 1921.[3]

In other important ways, though, the standard story is reliable. Although Civil War pensions made America a social spending leader in the late nineteenth century, they did not spur modern social policy. And despite the innovative programs for mothers, the United States did not go very far down the road toward modern social policy in the early twentieth century. Struggles by all manner of social progressives for modern social policy were confined to the state and local levels of government. There they typically foundered. Meager as it was, moreover, American social policy in this period was based on an idea of a family wage, the income necessary to support a nuclear family. Families were understood as having one breadwinner, expected in most instances to be male. Government programs were designed to uphold this wage and the social institutions standing behind it. Workmen's compensation typically went to men and mothers' pensions went to women, but both were based on stereotyped thinking about and images of gender roles. America's commitment to modern social policy was at best indifferent.

The standard and revised accounts are less reliable on other points, however. Both greatly discount the importance of emergency relief in the first years of the Roosevelt Administration. To be certain, emergency relief under the auspices of the Federal Emergency Relief Administration (FERA) was meant to be temporary and rightly has no place at the center of any account of permanent social policy. Yet the amount of emergency relief under Roosevelt was substantially greater than and different in form from what had been forthcoming under Herbert Hoover. It constituted the first major national effort in social spending since Civil War pensions. More important, emergency relief policy induced states to create new forms of control and oversight in social policy, in many cases wresting poor laws from townships, and led to the passage of new and modern forms of taxation. More important still, the FERA and other social policy developments during Roosevelt's First New Deal of 1933–1934 had a crucial impact on the deliberations for social policy in the Second New Deal of 1935.[4]

In this chapter, I address American social policy before the reforms of the Second New Deal. I argue that breakthroughs in premodern social policy in the late nineteenth century and the rejections and retrenchment of modern social policy in the early twentieth century were due to institutional and political conditions. The early extension of the franchise in America gave an impetus to the creation of policies for everyday people. Patronage-oriented political parties ran the state through Congress, and were well suited to provide discretionary programs like pensions and tariffs. Also, partisanship determined the pace of social policy in the nineteenth century, as Civil War pensions and customs tariffs made their most dramatic strides under Republican regimes and were generally cut back under Democratic ones.

For the most part, however, early twentieth-century America provided tremendous institutional and political impediments to modern social policy. America was no longer a democratic leader—just the opposite. Southern states had completed the disfranchisement of almost all blacks and poor whites, and stricter electoral rules in the North discouraged some poorer segments of the population from voting. The patronage-oriented nature of the party system and the discord between the parties and pro-spending groups also conspired against the creation of modern social policies. The easy money accruing from the customs tariffs—a policy that provided benefits coming and going—also ended. Creating social policies meant making difficult choices about financing them. The first decades of the century were dominated by the "system of 1896"—Walter Dean Burnham's term to describe Republican party hegemony at the national level.[5] This Republican regime was hostile to most modern forms of taxation, and to social policy that might require such taxation. As a result, America faced the Great Depression with little in the way of modern social policy.

THE RISE OF PREMODERN SOCIAL POLICY

In the late nineteenth century, American social policy centered on Civil War pensions and taxation policy centered on customs tariffs, and pensions and tariffs were tightly connected politically. The Republicans were in favor of strong tariff protection, especially for most manufactured goods, and soon jumped on the bandwagon for so-called dependent pensions. The Democrats favored lower tariffs and smaller pensions for fewer recipients. To the extent that they favored new taxes, the Democrats supported income taxes, a modern source of revenue that did not fall so heavily on the party's constituency. Also, the major parties used the national government as a kind of employment program. By the end of the century, Republicans controlled the government and their fiscal policy won out.

Civil War pensions initially benefited only war widows and injured veterans, and by the middle of the 1870s, the number of claimants had started to drop. In 1873, there were about a quarter of a million pension recipients. In 1879, however, the so-called Arrears Act authorized for the first time the payment of all the accumulated benefits due to an injured or widowed party from the time of the alleged war injury or death. A great rush for pensions began, for the act provided enormous incentives to press claims, including equivocal and false ones, on the government. Claimants provided their own evidence, and the primitive bureaucracy and its political operatives did not often have the ability or the desire to verify the stories. In 1889, the number of pensioners approached half a million. The benefits were nothing like automatic, however. There was always a waiting list of applicants, and politicians decided who would receive pensions, when, and at what rate. Additional legislation, especially the Dependent Pensions Act of 1890, added new groups of claimants and higher benefits.[6] The numbers of recipients peaked at nearly one million by the end of the century. Pension expenditures constituted more than 40 percent of government spending and 1.1 percent of GNP by the middle of the 1890s. It was a highly earnest effort in social spending for any country in the nineteenth century.[7]

Unlike modern social assistance, though, the program did not select recipients according to need, and unlike modern social insurance, it did not select according to work record. Civil War pensions provided benefits to an assortment of Northerners who could make a mildly plausible case for their role in preserving the Union. It helped to have a connection to a political organization, preferably Republican. All the same, a sizeable proportion of the American aged received a pension. The more than half a million elderly men on the rolls translated to approximately 29 percent of American men sixty-five years old and older in 1910. And the amount of benefits compared favorably to those given in Germany or Britain. The average pension for the disabled soldier in 1910 amounted to about 30 percent of average earnings, and for widows, 25 percent; in Britain, an old-age pension came to 22 percent of average annual earnings, and in Germany, about 17 percent.[8]

A second national public policy was the creation of jobs for people below the middle class and lacking professional credentials. Unlike Civil War pensions, this employment policy was not used by professional politicians to make rhetorical appeals to the electorate. Governmental positions went to party supporters, who gave the party political work and part of their salaries in return. Blatant use was made of the post office and the customs houses. In the late nineteenth and early twentieth centuries, there were more than 100,000 federal government jobs available. In 1891, of the 157,442 civilian employees of the federal government, more than 60 percent worked in the post office. Less than 22 percent of federal civilian employees were classified as part of the competitive civil service. There were many more patronage employees at other levels of government, especially in cities, not to mention those who were given jobs in businesses allied to local party machines or public works. The numbers of such jobs were inadequate and the choice of recipients biased, but in comparative perspective this ambiguous public employment program stands out.[9]

These premodern social policies relied on a premodern and relatively easy means of public finance—a complex assortment of customs tariffs. From immediately after the Civil War until the First World War, these taxes on imported goods generated about half the revenues of the U.S. national government. In 1890, for instance, customs provided 57 percent of national revenues, compared to about 21 percent in Britain.[10] Fiscally productive though they were, tariffs were much more than a means of revenue generation. Tariff protection constituted American macroeconomic policy.[11] Tariffs were used to defend established industries and protect infant industries. They were used rhetorically to merge the interests of capitalists and industrial workers—each group would be protected.[12] Much sought after by producers hoping to avoid competition, tariffs were also distributive benefits. They mattered greatly to the businesses benefiting from them, while diffusely taxing consumers who paid somewhat higher prices for imported products. Tariffs were devised within congressional committees and party caucuses, and attempts to rationalize their formation through tariff commissions failed. How did this fiscal system come about?

The story starts with the Civil War. Because of it, by 1865 the national debt had reached $2.7 billion, half of the GNP.[13] The government had resorted to the printing of $450 million worth of legal tender notes, or "greenbacks." The Republican party, which had led the Union to victory and claimed the presidency for a generation after its rise to power, wanted to retire that debt in a way that financial interests considered responsible. As a result, customs tariffs enacted in wartime were kept in service afterward to buy back greenbacks and speed the return to the gold standard.[14] Tariffs produced mounting surpluses—more than $100 million for each of the first three years of the 1870s—and by 1876 all the greenbacks had been redeemed. A new justification for the tariffs was needed, if they were to remain.

The Republicans linked the protection of economic enterprises and workers through tariffs to protection for veterans and their families.[15] As the Democrats and Republicans exchanged control of the national government, pension and tax policy changed accordingly. After his election in 1884, the Democratic President Grover Cleveland vetoed a dependent veterans' pension bill. He feared pension costs would preempt his proposed tariff reductions, underlining the tradeoff between them.[16] Led by Benjamin Harrison, Republicans fought the 1888 elections by taking issue with Cleveland's tariff reforms and his veto of the pension bill, and won handily. In one of the few periods when one party controlled the presidency and Congress, an outburst of legislation firmly established the Republicans as the party of protection. The so-called McKinley Tariff Act of 1890 undercut the reforms of the Cleveland Administration and increased government revenues to enable the funding of programs for other members of the political coalition. The Disability Pensions Act of 1890 provided benefits to veterans with ninety days or more of service and unable to perform manual labor for whatever reason, and to new categories of veterans' widows. In addition, the Republican Commissioner of Pensions promulgated Order No. 164, which increased payments for non–service-related disability pensions.

More political and policy flipflopping ensued. Upon returning to office in 1893, Cleveland and the Democrats passed the Wilson-Gorman Act, which slashed tariffs on manufactures and eliminated those on raw materials. The administration also introduced a personal income tax of 2 percent on incomes of four thousand dollars and more but the Supreme Court, consisting mainly of Republican appointees, quickly ruled it unconstitutional.[17] In addition, the Democrats abrogated Order No. 164, dropping or downgrading more than five thousand pensioners. Unfortunately for Cleveland and the Democrats, the Depression of 1893 ensued. During the elections of 1896, the Republicans portrayed themselves as the party of prosperity, with tariffs as the means to prosperity, and won handily. The McKinley Administration undermined the Wilson-Gorman reforms through the Dingley Tariff Act of 1897, which increased industrial protection across the board. Arresting the deficit was their top priority, though, as it had been after the Civil War. So the administration failed to reinstate Order No. 164—despite the denunciations of the Grand Army of the Republic, an organization of veterans allied with the Republicans that grew rapidly after the Arrears Act of 1879.[18] In 1899, moreover, the Republicans passed legislation restricting new pensions to those widows who had lived with their soldier-husbands from the war until their husbands' deaths. The deficit came first.

What accounts for the extent, form, and pace of this premodern fiscal and social spending system? Why could Civil War pensions be transformed in the ways they were, but without modern social spending policies getting a hearing in the American setting? The nature and extent of this premodern social policy related back to the nature of American political institutions. The early rise of mass democratic rights in America provided an impetus for policies benefiting people at lower income levels. This impetus was heightened by the mobilization needed to fight the first modern war.

The early development of democracy in America and the weakness of executive institutions meant that political power was centered in legislatures. The nineteenth-century American state has been characterized by Stephen Skowronek as consisting of "courts and parties." Political parties were an American invention, and the mass parties of the nineteenth century ruled through legislatures, whose powers dwarfed those of bureaucracies.[19] The fact that the democratization of politics mainly preceded the development of national bureaucratic institutions affected the nature of the party system and with it the types of policies that parties would pursue. Those two processes partly determined whether political parties were geared toward providing patronage—divisible and discretionary benefits to constituencies—or toward programs—collective goods to organized groups. Where democracy appeared much sooner than bureaucracy, as it did in the United States and Italy, political parties were disposed toward patronage—government positions and other benefits could be used as rewards to party workers. In countries such as Germany, the opposite occurred: bureaucratic standards preceded democratic practices. Because government positions were filled on the basis of professional credentials, parties were forced to appeal to the electorate with collective programs.[20] These processes predisposed American parties to individualistic, discretionary, and temporary benefits— such as government jobs and Civil War pensions—rather than collective, automatic, and permanent programs, such as social assistance and insurance. Because American legislatures controlled most important political decisions and legislators represented districts, the parties themselves were highly locally oriented. This reinforced their propensity to patronage.

The fact that neither party was a proponent of modern social spending reforms also related back to their origins. The American party system was settled during the second half of the nineteenth century—much earlier than European party systems, which were typically set in the first two decades of the twentieth century.[21] The American parties were split along two lines. One ran according to section. The Republican party won national power due to its strongholds in the industrial North and Midwest, which had opposed the extension of slavery. Although the Democratic party was competitive in these areas, it was hegemonic in the South, where Republican influence had dwindled at the end of Reconstruction. Black men won the franchise in Reconstruction-era reforms, but were almost completely disfranchised in the South, where most African Americans resided, by the beginning of the twentieth century. Party divisions split the upper classes: the industrial elites of the North stayed Republican, and landed elites of the South dominated Democratic parties.

In the loyalties of voters, the parties differed along ethnic and religious lines more than class ones. Men subscribing to "ritualistic" religions—Catholicism and Lutheranism—tended to vote Democratic. Men subscribing to "pietistic" religions—most strands of Protestantism—tended to vote Republican. The former included Irish and German immigrants, and the latter included native white Americans. The parties divided to some extent on issues involving alcoholic beverages with Republicans supporting "temperance" and northern Democrats "personal liberty."[22] Although U.S. national parties were little more than the outcome of the cyclical cooperation of state and local parties to win national elections, they were impressive in mobilizing the male electorate. Between 1876 and 1892, the heyday of American political parties, 77 percent of the eligible electorate voted in presidential elections, 82 percent outside the South.[23]

As the nineteenth century ended, both major parties had constructed political and discursive bonds between taxation and the premodern social spending of the Civil War pensions. The Republicans generally opted for the expansion of both, while Democrats pushed for their reduction. The pace and timing of adoption and augmentations of Civil War pensions were due to rhythms in party control of the national government. Neither party, however, was so concerned about the taxation or spending side of the equation that it would permit them to differ. The Democrats would not reform tariffs and thus cut taxation revenues without commensurate reductions in spending. The Republicans would not advance Civil War pensions without corresponding revenues being readily available. The Republicans did not consider expansions of domestic spending until the middle 1870s, when greenbacks had been repaid with gold. When depression caused revenues to drop in the 1890s, the Republicans held down pension spending and resorted to ideologically and politically unappealing taxation increases, such as levies on sugar. In short, the premodern social policies of the nineteenth century were undergirded by a taxation system that was unusual and highly productive of revenues in its heyday, but fundamentally weak. Tariffs eventually stopped generating great amounts of revenue. Politicians were forced to devise new types of taxes that could not be portrayed simultaneously as benefits to important groups.

The success of the nineteenth-century parties in winning voters promoted fragmented forms of political mobilization by other organizations. The parties split industrial workers along ethnic and religious lines. As Ira Katznelson has argued, American labor movements formed trade unions, mainly avoiding the creation of political parties. The early rise of locally based parties ensured that capital would organize politically in a fragmented manner, with a lack of control over policy outcomes. Partly because they were excluded from male-centered party politics, women formed self-conscious organizations that sought public influence over social policy. The winner-take-all electoral system and the sheer strength of the two major parties prevented additional parties from becoming permanent contenders—though it did not prevent new attempts at creating them.[24] Groups in favor of social policy had to work around the major parties in the early twentieth century to win social spending reforms. Given the strategically central position of the major parties, these groups faced an uphill climb.

ROLLING BACK PREMODERN SOCIAL POLICY WITHOUT REPLACING IT

The first two decades of the twentieth century were notable for attempts at bureaucratic, political, and policy reforms. A middle-class reform movement with adherents in both political parties, as well as a short-lived political party, the progressives attacked party machines and sought to create merit-based bureaucratic executive institutions at all levels of government. The reformers opposed the parties' often illegal methods and demanded political and civil service reforms. Social progressives favored modern social policies and other economic and social reforms. The progressives were only partly successful in breaking the hold of the major parties, threatening their state and local organizations only where they had been previously weak. Bureaucratic state-building efforts, too, achieved only partial gains. The social progressives fared the worst.[25]

One victory of sorts was their bid to halt the premodern public policies of the nineteenth century. Progressives opposed Civil War pensions on account of their corruption. Eliminating pensions was in part a one-sided war of attrition with the aging pensioners. Time was on the side of the progressives—they merely needed to deflect new legislation providing similar benefits to later veterans. All the same, the passing of Civil War pensioners brought no fiscal dividend because pensions paid to World War I veterans with service-related disabilities kept the total spent on military pensions at nearly a constant level.[26] The reformers also stopped the growth of the back-door system of public employment through government jobs. By 1916, the number of federal civilian employees had reached approximately 400,000, or about two and a half times the number in 1891. But nearly three-quarters of the appointments were on a merit basis.[27]

Another more substantial victory concerned a potentially vast new source of revenue. In 1913 the Democrats, under Woodrow Wilson, assumed national political power for the first time in decades, with their southern and western bases of support. Backed by the Progressive as well as the Democratic party, the Sixteenth Amendment to the Constitution, passed in 1913, made possible new income tax legislation. The individual income tax tapped the rich. Those making less than four thousand dollars a year—the vast majority of wage earners—were exempted. Although income taxes were increased during World War I, the personal income tax remained a "class" tax rather than a "mass" tax. Only about 13 percent of the labor force filed returns in 1920.[28]

The progressive social agenda was mainly confined, however, to the state and local levels. Initiatives in modern social policy were pushed furthest by various national reform organizations with chapters in states and localities. Among the social progressives were women's organizations, such as the National Congress of Mothers (NCM), the General Federation of Women's Clubs (GFWC), the Women's Trade Union League, and the National Consumers League, that promoted policies especially to aid women. There were also professional associations, notably the American Association for Labor Legislation and later the American Association for Old-Age Security, that promoted social insurance and old-age pensions. Another important group was the Fraternal Order of Eagles, which by the 1920s massed its membership behind old-age pensions. Organized groups of social workers, such as those connected to the National Conference of Social Work, and settlement house leaders also demanded the reform of poor laws. On some issues and in some places, these groups were joined by state and city federations of labor. The social progressives hoped to win in states, like Wisconsin, chosen for their record of receptivity to social reform, to publicize the victories, and to take the strengthened cause to other states.[29]

Those trying to secure categorical assistance to mothers or the aged or the temporarily unemployed as a matter of right had an especially tough job ahead of them, for they had to confront the traditional poor law with its maze of customs, laws, and institutions. Based on English precedents, American relief for those unable or unwilling to support themselves was historically controlled locally, in townships and municipalities. By 1930, there were more than twenty thousand American townships, along with more than sixteen thousand cities and incorporated villages. Responsibilities often overlapped in confusing ways. Twenty-seven separate political authorities, for instance, governed Chicago and its suburbs. In theory, townships were paradigms of democracy, in which citizens were presumed to convene, discuss, and decide all matters of local moment. In practice, townships were run haphazardly. Also, they relied on property taxes, whose assessment and collection were subject to politics and incompetence as well as being vulnerable to economic downturns.[30]

American townships were mainly responsible for the indigent, and the townships in turn held the indigent responsible for their misfortune. Those who could or would not support themselves, who had no relatives to do so, or who could gain no aid from private charities were typically declared paupers and committed to public "institutions." The unemployed faced the workhouse or the flophouse, and the parentless the orphanage. Dependent families and the aged, especially, faced the poorhouse, which was being transformed into the old-age home. Often run by counties, these institutions meted out a harsh brand of exemplary justice, designed to frighten people into embracing values such as the work ethic and thrift. Although "outdoor" relief was, in the historian Michael Katz's phrase, "as old as the colonies," few received it and fewer still received it in cash. Instead recipients were usually allocated in-kind benefits, such as coal, rent vouchers, clothing, and grocery orders. Indeed, a heavy reliance on in-kind aid constituted a form of American exceptionalism in social policy apparent to experts of the day. In-kind aid also provided patronage opportunities. Overseers of the poor often invested in or received kickbacks from grocery stores, for instance, and grocery orders made modern-day Food Stamps seem the height of convenience and dignity in comparison. Whenever work was provided, moreover, it was meant to be degrading, so as to discourage loafing. Localities would go to great legal lengths to avoid paying relief and fought one another in court in their attempts to evade responsibility. Social reformers typically wanted counties to gain control over the poor laws, so that state boards could then supervise them to ensure that more aid was distributed with greater fairness.[31]

The first categorical aid program attempting to loosen the hold of the poor law was mothers' aid or pensions, a means-tested allowance for families without fathers. Enabling legislation for mothers' aid passed in thirty-nine states between 1911 and 1919. The typical law allowed localities to provide pensions for widowed mothers to keep their children at home. Promoted by groups such as the NCM and the GFWC, these programs were staffed mainly by middle-class women, and most included strict rules of eligibility. In addition, state-level programs for infants and pregnant mothers were encouraged by federal grants-in-aid under the Sheppard-Towner Act of 1921. Like Civil War pensioners, these recipients were portrayed as exceptionally worthy of assistance. All the same, mothers' pensions were "county-optional" and underfunded by the end of the 1920s.[32]

Other lasting state-level reforms did not upset this pattern. Child labor and women's hours legislation was promoted by reformers and supported to some extent by organized labor because of the competitive threat posed by women and children. In addition, various health and safety laws were established.[33] One major risk, industrial accidents, was covered by a species of state-level regulatory policy. Workmen's compensation passed in forty-two of the forty-eight states between 1911 and 1921 and required businesses to insure, not necessarily through the state, their workers against industrial accidents. Workmen's compensation replaced liability laws that sometimes resulted in large settlements for injured workers. Many of these programs were administered by state-level Departments of Labor or Industrial Commissions, which were also in charge of enforcing other labor legislation. But an integrated department was more the exception than the rule.[34] Taking a "corrective response" to the problems of the handicapped, as the historian Edward Berkowitz has called it, state-level programs for vocational rehabilitation also were initiated in the 1920s, but faltered partly because of the lack of bureaucratic connection with workmen's compensation programs.[35]

Reformers and their supporters had uneven success in promoting other social policies in the states before 1930. In the 1910s, state-level movements for health and unemployment insurance and old-age pensions often made it to the study-commission stage of state politics, but no further. Before 1929 the movement for means-tested old-age pensions made advances, although the laws were always county-optional and were sometimes declared unconstitutional. California became the first state to pass a compulsory old-age pension program in 1929. Moreover, state governments made some effort to oversee poor laws. Some twenty-six states had developed departments of welfare, many of which had responsibilities for programs beyond running charitable and correctional institutions. New York, for instance, revamped its poor law in 1929. Working from its workmen's compensation law, Wisconsin was seriously considering unemployment compensation legislation at the end of the decade.[36]

In Britain, social policy had advanced much further. Like Imperial Germany before it, Britain mainly employed social insurance to combat threats to income posed by capitalist industrialization, through the impetus of Liberal governments. Workmen's compensation was adopted in 1897 and disability insurance in 1906. Although means-tested old-age pensions, not insurance, were adopted in 1908, they were followed by the breakthrough National Insurance Act of 1911, which added health and unemployment insurance. In 1924, old-age insurance was adopted. Yet social policy was far from comprehensive and did not end the need for the locally administered poor law—anathema to reformers there as well. One "insurance" program, moreover, took on a burden not previously anticipated. British unemployment insurance was intended to pay covered workers for up to twenty-six weeks. Yet after the Great War, the British economy did not rebound, and its unemployment rate hovered at about 10 percent throughout the 1920s. Unemployment insurance subsequently degenerated into a long-term unemployment relief program, as restrictions on the length of payments were eased. This system produced fairly stable efforts in social spending. Public social spending reached 4.6 percent of the British gross domestic product in 1921. By the end of the decade it was 4.4 percent.[37]

U.S. social policy was primitive by comparison. Numbers sometimes lie, but the following ones are so small that they provide little material for fabrication. State-level workmen's compensation, pension, and aid programs accounted for less than half of 1 percent of the GNP in 1929. That year U.S. veterans' pensions and compensation accounted for about the same amount. After three decades of the twentieth century, in short, America was putting less than half as much fiscal effort into modern social policy as it had expended for Civil War pensions more than a generation earlier. It is difficult to disagree with the historian Morton Keller's assessment that "it became clear over the decades from 1900 to the early 1930s that a greater interest in social welfare did not necessarily have sweeping policy consequences."[38]

The reasons for American backwardness in social spending in 1929 are closely connected to the reasons for American leadership in social spending in 1892. In the vanguard of suffrage extension in the nineteenth century, America greatly restrained suffrage near the end of that century and during the early part of the next. The historian Paul Kleppner refers to period from 1896 through 1928 as the "Era of Electoral Demobilization," so dramatic was the decline in voting. The political scientist Walter Dean Burnham estimates that 79.9 percent of the demographically or potentially eligible electorate voted in presidential elections from 1876 to 1896. By contrast only 59.9 percent of the eligible in this sense voted in presidential elections from 1900 to 1928.[39] It was mainly the less affluent portion of the electorate that was voting less frequently, and they were voting less frequently mainly because of greater restrictions on the franchise.

Nowhere were these restrictions more blatant than in the South. Opponents of the widespread franchise there had to contend with the Fourteenth and Fifteenth Amendments. The former restricted the representation in the polity for districts disfranchising people for reasons other than crime and rebellion, while the latter prohibited discrimination on the basis of race, color, or previous condition of servitude. For this reason, disfranchisers resorted to all manner of means to restrict the vote, typically legal ones, including the manner of conducting elections and limits on voter eligibility. Among the milder forms were voter registration procedures and the secret ballot, which hindered illiterates. Stronger restrictions included literacy tests and poll taxes. Literacy tests were meant to humiliate as well as exclude former voters, and the prospect of taking the test intimidated others. Poll taxes also greatly curbed the propensity to vote among the poorer segments of the electorate. The taxes were steep relative to the very low cash incomes among the poor in the South. What is more, the poll taxes were typically due months before election day. As an investment in democratic

Plate 2.1 "Pay Your Poll Tax Now" (Russell Lee). Poll taxes deterred many poorer people from voting in the South. In Virginia, for instance, the poll tax was $1.50. Poll taxes typically had to be paid well before the election, as this sign in rural Texas indicates. In some cases, people who had not paid the tax for previous elections would have to pay the accumulated "arrears" from those taxes in order to vote.

influence paying the tax was uncertain at best. Those in the vanguard of efforts to restrict the electorate were affluent whites in the so-called Black Belt region where many former slaves resided, and the disfranchisers knew electoral restrictions would reduce poor white as well as black voting. The results of their efforts were easily evident in 1904, the first presidential election since all the disfranchising projects in the South had been completed. That year only 27.9 percent of the potentially eligible electorate voted. In Mississippi and Louisiana, the figure was a tiny 15.6 percent.[40]

In the North, most restrictions were of a milder sort, notably stiffened registration procedures and changes in the way that elections were run. Almost all states had by 1896 adopted the secret or "Australian" ballot, which tended to discourage some voters and induce them to vote other than straight party lines. Personal-registration procedures were a more significant hurdle, placing the burden on individuals rather than the state. Many of these changes were a result of progressive mobilizations, which sought to limit the role of the party organizations that dominated American political life. A number of other states also increased residency requirements, imposed literacy tests—less damaging to the electorate in the North, but nonetheless discouraging—and abolished alien voting rights, which had permitted immigrants to vote once they declared their intention to become citizens. Also depressing voting rates, while increasing the number of voters, was women's suffrage, which was authorized in many states before 1919 and in all of them afterward in the wake of the Twentieth Amendment. Because politics had always been a man's world, it is not surprising that women at first voted less frequently than men. What is more, women from the poor and immigrant groups that were the targets of suffrage restrictions voted less frequently than other women, decreasing the electoral power of the less well off.[41]

Another key obstacle was the political party system. Patronage-oriented parties continued to thrive, especially in their strongholds in the Northeast and Midwest, and had little enthusiasm for the cause of modern social policy. Although they could support programs with patronage opportunities such as Civil War pensions, they had less reason to support social insurance and social assistance, which did not allow such opportunities. Moreover, politicians who benefited from the poor laws, through controlling the staffing of county institutions or profiting from in-kind aid, for example, had concrete reasons to fight movements for modern social assistance. The patronage-oriented politicians saw the progressives as their enemies, and rightly so. Progressive reformers ranged from those, such as the businessmen of the National Civic Federation, who merely wanted to keep everyday people as far as possible from political power, to those like the social progressives who advocated social policy and the rights of workers. Even among the social progressives, patronage politics induced divisions about first steps—to clean up politics or to create social policy. It was often thought that social legislation would do more harm than good if it were going to be overseen in the corrupt manner of the poor laws. Divided attention and confused priorities were only some of the problems faced by the progressives. Their political victories, notably instituting the secret ballot, sometimes proved pyrrhic as they undercut parts of the electorate with an economic interest in social progressivism. In any case, because of patronage-oriented parties, American social progressives had more formidable problems with which to cope than did their counterparts in other countries and experienced more difficulty coalescing.[42]

What is more, American federalism provided a rigorous obstacle course for the reformers. The reformers fought in individual states hoping for a domino effect—a form of politics with distinct disadvantages. Often, it was difficult to get the first domino to fall, as was the case with health, sickness, unemployment insurance, and old-age pensions. Some states, especially those in the South, seemed willing to stand firm against a social program even after other states had succumbed to it. And even when all the dominoes dropped, sometimes very little happened. County-optional programs provided little aid. Even the bid for compulsory old-age pensions at the state level had its limits. State governments, too, relied heavily on property taxes and license fees for their revenues, and thus were not likely to have the ready cash to answer the social question. Social policy advocates were fortunate that the flawed domino strategy was soon to be outmoded.

The underdevelopment of U.S. social policy in the first three decades of the twentieth century was due also to the dominance of the Republican party. The Republicans controlled the presidency for all but eight years of the period. Their only losses came in 1912 when Theodore Roosevelt's Progressive party split the vote among the Republicans and opened the way to Woodrow Wilson's election, and in 1916 when Wilson was reelected. Although the Democrats controlled Congress between 1913 and 1919, the Republicans dominated Congress for most of the rest of the time. That party's opposition to the income tax and its alliance with industrialists inoculated it against modern social spending programs. To keep pace with their Democratic competition in the South, moreover, the Republicans promoted electoral restrictions that consolidated their political hold over the North.[43]

The Republican dominance at the national level was part of the reason that struggles over social policy were confined to the state and local levels. Keeping income taxes low was at the top of their political agenda, and, unlike in the late nineteenth century, their tariff policies no longer generated significant revenues. Though central to the protective economic vision of the Republicans, customs tariffs constituted only 0.58 percent of GNP and less than 16 percent of federal revenues in 1929.[44] The Republican party, which had bound tariffs and Civil War pensions with a rhetoric of "protection," would not, however, countenance deficit spending or income taxes. There was no longer a politically easy way to finance social policy, so far as its corporate and upper-class constituents were concerned.

For that reason the Republicans capped government spending, even for veterans. The veterans of the Great War were not treated as generously as those of the Civil War, as they were granted so-called adjusted service or compensation certificates in 1924, scheduled to pay out in 1943. Needless to say, the Republicans did not call for national support for any modern social assistance or insurance programs. On the contrary, the little national executive power devoted to social spending policy was diminished. The main national spending bureau, the Children's Bureau of the Labor Department, was stripped of its maternal and child health programs when funding for the Sheppard-Towner Act was eliminated in the late 1920s.[45] Still, the Republicans could not afford to abolish income taxes, because, despite numerous rate cuts, by 1929 they were providing the bulk of national government revenue.[46]

The Democratic party, however, was only partly suited for modern public spending policies. Though committed to the income tax, a potentially far more productive source of revenue than tariffs, the party was strongest in the South—where most poor people could not vote and existing social programs were weakest. In the urban North, the party was making a comeback among industrial workers. This was seen especially in the elections of 1928, when the Democratic party nominated New York Governor Alfred Smith for president. Moreover, progressives constituted a significant fraction of the Democratic party. A drive for social policy led by the Democrats would depend on changes in the party's fortunes in the North.[47] In the meantime, the Republicans remained in power, as the stock market crashed in October 1929.

IMMEDIATE SOCIAL POLICY RESPONSES TO THE DEPRESSION

After the crash, economic activity in America went into a tailspin, as it did throughout much of the industrialized world. Not surprisingly, the public policies of the 1930s, under Presidents Hoover and Roosevelt, were dominated by attempts to return the economy to good health. Both thought industrial self-government would end the Depression. Hoover backed self-government with exhortation and information, Roosevelt with the law, but neither solution worked, as economic recovery proved elusive in the 1930s.[48] The economy did not return to the level of 1929 until the decade had ended. Although fiscal policies of both Hoover and Roosevelt were animated by a desire to avoid accumulating large deficits, they took greatly different approaches to the provision of unemployment aid.

Hoover and Unemployment

Herbert Hoover was in the forefront of innovative efforts to study and combat unemployment as Secretary of Commerce in the early 1920s, and as president he tried measures considered experimental and forward-thinking. Yet he stressed economy in government and hoped to keep the national government out of the business of unemployment relief. Hoover considered it the "American way" for communities to fight their own relief battles and preferred to oversee the exhaustion of the resources of private charities, community chests, and local governments before providing money from the national treasury. Although he created the President's Emergency Committee for Employment (PECE) in October 1930, Hoover did not heed its call the next year for federally supported public works. The more conservative successor to the PECE, the President's Organization on Unemployment Relief (POUR), led by Walter Gifford, president of the American Telephone and Telegraph Company, mainly urged industry to "spread" or "stagger" work. The POUR also sought to stimulate voluntary charitable activity, and to minimize the seriousness of unemployment. Hoover held fast to these views despite three winters of Depression.[49]

Some state governments attempted to fill the void. New York, notably, appropriated $20 million in aid to the localities in September 1931. Governor Franklin D. Roosevelt appointed a Temporary Emergency Relief Administration (TERA) to run the program, which received another $20 million after six months. In 1932, Roosevelt appointed as the TERA's chairman Harry L. Hopkins, a New York social worker who had been raised in Iowa. Hopkins sought to apply uniform standards in relief across the counties, to ensure the hiring of qualified staff, and to provide work relief with cash benefits rather than benefits in kind—for white-collar as well as blue-collar applicants. Honest, but impatient with standard casework practices, Hopkins sought to help as many as possible as quickly as possible, with the least loss in dignity to recipients. In some ways, the TERA constituted a model in the minds of many social workers. It was a strong state-level agency with state funding and oversight powers over counties, which in turn were wresting power from townships. Yet the TERA was only temporary and gained control completely only over work relief operations. And New York's lead was not followed by many. Only eleven states had instituted emergency relief operations before June 1932.[50]

Categorical aid programs were being easily outstripped by the social devastation of the Depression, which greatly aggravated the economic troubles of the indigent. Consider, for instance, county-optional mothers' pensions, on the books of most states by 1930. Few counties were able or willing to fund mothers' pensions at anything resembling an adequate level to allow poor women without male breadwinners to care for their children at home. The U.S. Children's Bureau, part of the Department of Labor, made a study of the programs in its 1933 report, *Mothers' Aid, 1931.* Although gains had been made, localities were not realizing the promise of the program. The bureau estimated that only about half of all counties authorized to grant benefits were doing so. Only a few—about 6 percent of female-headed families with children—were receiving mothers' pensions. Furthermore, the lucky ones were not chosen randomly from among the population at risk: about 82 percent of the recipients were widows, and only about 3 percent of recipients were African American. In some states, such as Louisiana and Mississippi, there were no black recipients. In an addendum to the report, the bureau found that programs did not expand much in 1932, despite greater need. A later Children's Bureau study indicated that payments in ninety-three cities and city areas were decreasing in 1933, the low point of the Depression, despite greater numbers receiving such aid.[51]

Old-age pension movements seemingly made dramatic gains during the early years of the Depression. California became in 1929 the first state to pass a compulsory old-age pension law, and by the end of 1934 some twenty-eight states had followed suit.[52] Yet the speed of passage of old-age pensions was belied by the grudging manner in which they were granted. In three states, the laws were inoperative because of a lack of funds, and where pensions were granted the amounts were far from adequate in most instances. Only in Massachusetts, New York, and California were the payments twenty dollars per month or greater. Most states granting old-age pensions paid less than ten dollars. The average in North Dakota was sixty-nine cents. In most instances the state government itself did not contribute to the financing of pensions, and the counties, with their property tax bases, could not fund adequate ones. A vast array of regulations—aside from a means test and budgetary analyses—prevented the aged from receiving aid and demeaned those who did receive it. All state laws had long residency requirements. Almost all states provided no grants if relatives could be located and made financially responsible. Almost all laws had strict "lien on estate" provisions—recipients would ultimately forfeit their property to the state as a kind of reparation. Almost all had "deserving" provisions, which denied aid to applicants for reasons ranging from having a criminal record to having abandoned a spouse. Of the more than 6.5 million people over sixty-five years old in the United States in 1934, less than a quarter of a million were receiving old-age pensions.[53] The crisis seemed to slow the progress of permanent social spending programs in the states.

Federal help came, eventually, but the impetus was not from the president. In 1931, emergency national relief bills were devised by Senator Robert Wagner of New York, Senator Edward Costigan of Colorado, and Senator Robert La Follette Jr. of Wisconsin. Wagner preferred an approach based on loans, while La Follette promoted grants-in-aid. In his subcommittee on federal aid, La Follette solicited the testimony of expert after expert that charity and local government efforts had failed, embarrassing the witnesses for the unhappily named POUR. Each of their bills, however, died in the Senate.[54]

In July 1932, Hoover finally conceded to sign a bill sponsored by Wagner. The Emergency Relief and Construction Act provided advances to states, to be repaid from future highway grants, and loans to localities for unemployment relief. These monies were to be granted through the Reconstruction Finance Corporation (RFC), an organization set up earlier in the year to extend credit to financial institutions. Some $300 million were appropriated, but only about $30 million were distributed by end of the year. The administration and the RFC moved slowly, some states refused to accept the terms, and others were not organized well enough to apply for the cash. The bulk of the aid was distributed in the period between the defeat of Hoover in November 1932 and the inauguration of Roosevelt in March 1933.[55]

To be fair, Hoover was even-handed in his fiscal vigilance—which was extended to veterans, a group that had historically relied on the kindness of Republicans. In 1932, the ragtag Bonus Expeditionary Force, or Bonus Army, as people liked to call it, marched on Washington. This impoverished group of World War I veterans was demanding the early payment of adjusted compensation certificates or "bonuses" granted in 1924, but due in 1945. These bonuses now appeared to veterans as untimely postdated checks and they encamped in the capital, often with families in tow. Instead of acquiescing in their request, though, Hoover called out the regular Army under General Douglas MacArthur to scatter the Bonus Army. As the one was well equipped and fed and the other was an army only in name, it was no contest.[56]

Also among the many things Herbert Hoover was unwilling to do was to run deficits without compensatory fiscal action. In the wake of the Depression, Hoover abandoned the long-standing tax-cutting program of Andrew Mellon, the secretary of the Treasury, in order to protect the reputation and value of American currency and debt. Although the administration and some of the Democratic leadership in Congress hoped to increase taxes by way of a new national sales tax, that plan was rejected by the bulk of congressional Democrats and some progressives. Anomalous from today's perspective, Hoover, an American president and a Republican at that, proposed a long-term increase in income taxation in order to arrest a deficit. The Revenue Act of 1932 constituted a complete and permanent reversal of the Republican income tax cutting initiatives of the 1920s.[57]

Roosevelt and the Emergency Relief Breakthrough

When he assumed the presidency in March 1933, Franklin Roosevelt, too, set his sights on economic recovery. Roosevelt's New Deal, like Hoover's attempts at recovery, first involved quasi-corporatism. The National Industrial Recovery Act (NIRA) of June 1933 put the authority of the national government and new bureaucratic means, the National Recovery Administration (NRA), behind the self-organization of industries. The NIRA provided legal backing to the price-fixing and market-setting activity of capitalist trade associations, which had been encouraged to coordinate under Hoover. But Roosevelt's view of the political economy was more balanced. The law also invited labor to organize with its Section 7a, which guaranteed collective bargaining, though without enforcement mechanisms. The NIRA also authorized $3.3 billion in public works expenditures, through the newly created Public Works Administration (PWA). Still, the PWA never got entirely under way, and the NRA caused more problems than it solved for most industries. It probably would have been abandoned if the Supreme Court had not declared it unconstitutional in 1935.[58] Approach after approach to economic recovery was tried throughout the remainder of the decade, but without great success.

Meantime, matters of social policy were pressing. When the Bonus Army rallied again in Washington in 1933, Roosevelt was seemingly conciliatory. As one veteran famously put it, "Hoover sent the Army, Roosevelt sent his wife," as both Eleanor and Franklin Roosevelt met with the protestors. But the new president's approach to veterans was economically more brutal than the old one's. In the nineteenth century, non-service-related disability pensions for veterans constituted a selective form of addressing the risks of disability and old age. Roosevelt wanted instead to bring American spending policies into the modern world of social assistance and insurance and rejected the elevation of veterans into a group with rights greater than those of other citizens. To do so required recasting old policies. One of the first pieces of legislation of the First New Deal was the National Economy Act of 1933, which gave the president temporary power to issue executive orders to regulate veterans' benefits—which he did, to the detriment of many veterans. Veterans with service-related disabilities had their compensation lowered, and almost all veterans with non–service-related disabilities were removed from the pension rolls. As if these orders were not explicit enough, Roosevelt made a speech before the American Legion that told veterans not to expect pensions for disabilities incurred after their service.[59]

In the area of employment policy, the United States Employment Service (USES) was reestablished in 1933. Although this agency had received government funding during the world war, it was cut back afterward. Making the USES permanent was part of the reform agenda of Senator Wagner. Under the so-called Wagner-Peyser Act, the federal government provided grants-in-aid for states to set up employment offices, and the USES attempted to coordinate their efforts. Although the new USES gave few powers to the national government, this service was viewed as an integral part of any national employment policy. The employment offices were also considered necessary for the provision of unemployment compensation.[60]

A far greater break with political orthodoxy and with Hoover's policies was coming. After his message in March 1933 on "Relief of Unemployment," Roosevelt created in May 1933 the Federal Emergency Relief Administration. The FERA constituted the first major grant-in-aid program for social policy. Based on the grant-in-aid proposals of Senator La Follette and modeled on New York's relief operations, the FERA began life with an appropriation of only $500 million, from the RFC, in 1933. Initially, a large proportion of the money was to be provided by matching grants—three parts state funding to one part national. Harry Hopkins, the newly appointed Federal Emergency Relief Administrator, would try to do for the nation what he did for New York. Each state was required to set up an emergency relief administration, like that of New York, to handle, oversee, and distribute its own and federal funds to localities. The localities were to continue to provide both cash aid and aid in kind to all manner of needy family heads and individuals. By the time it wound down its operations at the end of 1935 the FERA had distributed unprecedented sums, more than $3.25 billion in less than three years, including most of the money appropriated for the PWA.[61]

Although the FERA was granting great sums, it was making little progress in promoting work relief for wages. Two other programs were devised to do so. One of them addressed the President's desire to conserve both human and natural resources. In his March relief message, Roosevelt called for the creation of a Civilian Conservation Corps (CCC) to employ young

Plate 2.2 Receiving a Relief Check from the FERA (Ben Shahn). A woman receives a relief check from the Federal Emergency Relief Administration in 1935. Aid by the FERA for women without male breadwinners had eclipsed aid from county-optional mothers' pensions. The FERA was terminated at the end of 1935.

men in forestry, erosion, flood control, and other conservation projects. Enrollees were to enlist for a year, report to camps, receive thirty dollars monthly, and remit money home to dependents. The program was to be funded by unobligated funds for public works. Although initially attacked by William Green, president of the AFL, for its low wages and seeming regimentation of workers, after amendments the bill passed by the end of March and gave great powers to the President to run the CCC through existing departments of the government. Led by Robert Fechner, a former vice president of the AFL, the CCC divided powers over the selection, enrollment, and supervision of the enlistees among the departments of Labor, War, Agriculture, and Interior, with the Army central to mobilization of the recruits. By July 1, the quota of 275,000 men had been reached and they were engaged in conservation projects in camps around the country.[62]

Another program was more ambitious, but also more temporary in aspiration. On November 9, 1933, the president created by executive order the Civil Works Administration (CWA) and diverted some $400 million from the PWA budget to finance it. The CWA was designed to provide work for the winter to those on emergency relief and those unemployed workers too proud to apply for it. According to the plans of Roosevelt and Hopkins, who was also placed in charge of the CWA, the program was to employ in one month's time the staggering number of four million. Almost immediately, some two million FERA "clients"—being provided aid by way of investigation though the intrusive budgetary-deficit method—became CWA "wage earners." The rest were recruited through the USES, or by way of labor unions or professional associations. A Public Work of Arts project was among the initiatives. Even dentists sought and gained relief. Some nine million people applied for two million positions by the end of the year and those chosen were compensated at the relatively high PWA wage rates, which were meant to match the wages "prevailing" in the area.[63]

Unlike the Public Works Administration, the CWA was to encourage smaller labor-intensive projects that did not need to rely on the extensive planning, engineering, and private bidding involved in large-scale public works. Yet the CWA also tried to avoid useless "made work." It had to devise projects falling somewhere between the construction of sewage disposal systems and the collection of garbage. Although most often the CWA workers found themselves building roads, a wide variety of workers with varied skills were employed. Local governments usually suggested the projects. Using the administrative structure of the FERA, the disbursement powers of the Veterans Administration, the employment offices of the USES, and its own engineering staff, the CWA was successful according to the terms that Roosevelt set for it. By New Year's Day, as advertised, four million were working for it.[64]

Public employment under the CWA embodied many of the attitudes about gender and family relationships that animated New Deal work and relief policy. Work was mainly provided to men, of all class backgrounds, and these men were expected to earn a wage high enough to support a family. The idea was for men to reestablish themselves as heads of households. Although there was no regulation that prevented more than one family member from getting CWA work, it was expected that married women should not take work. Women were not expected to lead families, and if in the absence of husbands they were doing so, they were expected to take a more standard sort of relief. For that reason, women were not highly represented in the CWA. Women constituted about one-quarter of the labor force when the Depression began, but constituted only about 13 percent of the applicants for CWA wage positions. Of the approximately four million receiving work through the CWA in the spring of 1934, only about 300,000 or 7.5 percent were women. The women fortunate enough to find CWA work were mainly confined to sewing projects, receiving the minimum wage allowable, and were often subject to means tests.[65]

Though a qualified success, the CWA was conceived as an experiment. By the spring, the relief burden was returned to the FERA, which had changed and expanded its operations. After the first year, most of the FERA's disbursements were provided at Hopkins's discretion, giving it leverage over the relief policies of various states and localities. Although it continued to fund cash and in-kind aid, it also now included work projects like those of the CWA. Of the approximately 5 million being aided by the FERA at the end of 1934, some 2.3 million, most recipients considered "employable," were receiving some form of work relief. Recipients of work relief almost invariably were paid a wage. The program, in short, stood somewhere between the public employment of the CWA and other forms of relief. In most places work relief recipients now had to submit to a means test, but were paid in money and avoided the stigma of in-kind aid and intrusive, repeated estimations of the family budget. Some 4.4 million of the 5 million receiving aid at the end of 1934 were considered to be "family cases" for whom one relief recipient was considered the head. These families were receiving about twenty-eight dollars in aid per month, as compared to about fifteen dollars during the middle of 1933.[66]

Moreover, the FERA had almost nationalized—in terms of funding at least—assistance to special groups who were not considered to be merely unemployed. For some groups the FERA preempted "special" assistance programs. The FERA funded many a recipient elderly enough for an old-age pension. The results were even more dramatic for families without male breadwinners. By the end of 1934, county-optional mothers' pensions had experienced something akin to a total eclipse by the FERA. By the middle of 1934, the FERA shouldered the burden of 719,000 of the approximately one million dependent children receiving aid. Most of these children lived in households headed by a separated or divorced woman.[67]

Roosevelt broke with economic orthodoxy by running deficits with emergency relief, but he, like Hoover, hoped to coordinate spending and taxing policy. The President aimed at balancing the "non-emergency" budget, which excluded expenses related to the slump. The First New Deal typically financed progressive spending measures by way of regressive taxation. Ending Prohibition in 1933 was partly a fiscal policy, producing a windfall for the treasury. Legalizing the sale of alcohol permitted the levying of heavy excise taxes—five dollars per thirty-one gallons of wine or beer.[68]

A major breakthrough in taxation, though, took place in the states, which were under pressure to raise revenues to pay for emergency relief. Although the matching formula for FERA grants had been dropped, Hopkins frequently withheld emergency funds from states until they showed good faith in generating their own monies. And although the federal government shouldered most of the costs of relief, the results in state-level taxation were impressive, as eighteen states responded with new sales taxes, and states also began to compete more closely with the national government in income taxation.[69]

The results of all this effort were impressive and indicate the difference between aid under the Hoover and Roosevelt regimes. By fiscal year 1932, including the last half of 1931 and the first half of 1932, only 1.34 percent

Plate 2.3 Waiting for Work at a FERA Office (Ben Shahn). The Federal Emergency Relief Administration of 1933–35 also provided work programs, especially after the termination of the experimental Civil Works Administration in the spring of 1934. Here workers in New Orleans apply for employment at FERA offices—most likely for WPA jobs.

of a greatly reduced U.S. GNP went to social policy. By fiscal year 1934, by contrast, almost 5 percent of GNP was social spending. Yet the programs of the early Roosevelt years were meant to be temporary. If the Depression had miraculously ended in 1934 and the emergency programs immediately disbanded, modern social policy would have remained close to the depressed state it had assumed in the 1920s. But Roosevelt and the social progressives who became New Dealers had other plans.

CONCLUSION

American social policy was not always as backward as has been claimed. In the late nineteenth century, social policy to deal with the various risks to income for veterans was well established. In a less well-publicized way, politicians of both parties continued to use positions in governmental bureaucracies around the country as a kind of jobs program. Veterans' benefits and other government expenses were mainly paid for by an assortment of tariffs. Yet this premodern scheme of social policy was not to last. Reformers struggled to stop corruption in public policy and to promote the use of merit standards in government employment. Veterans died off, and tariff revenues dried up.

Modern social policy did not replace these programs, however, and advanced very slowly through the first three decades of the twentieth century. Social progressives allied with labor and fraternal organizations fought for modern social policies ranging from health insurance to workmen's compensation, from old-age pensions to mothers' pensions, but did not get very far. Only one significant spending program was supported through national legislation. Furthermore, maternal health grants under the Sheppard-Towner Act were stopped before the Depression hit. Other drives for social spending were confined to states and localities. Even when nationwide campaigns succeeded, as they did for workmen's compensation and mothers' pensions, they did not constitute great advances. Workmen's compensation took the place of legal settlements won by injured workers through the courts. Mothers' pensions were a step up from restrictive poor laws, but were granted to only a few white widows. Old-age pensions merely scratched the surface of poverty among the aged.

Modern American social policy had many circumstances working against it in the early twentieth century. One daunting obstacle was that the influence of everyday people in politics had been dramatically decreased through restrictive electoral rules and practices. In the South, poorer people, black and white, were disfranchised, and the Democratic party gained a monopoly on politics. In the North, the Republicans followed with less restrictive, but far from negligible means to prune the electorate. Moreover, despite the efforts of progressives, patronage-oriented political parties continued to hold sway in the Northeast and Midwest. The leaders of these parties were not going to run interference for modern social policies and instead did what they could to keep them off the political agenda. After all, social assistance and insurance did not promise many new patronage opportunities and threatened to dry up existing ones. Those who promoted social policy, moreover, typically included the same people attacking the means by which parties controlled political life.

On top of these structural political restrictions were partisan ones. The Republican party held tight control over national politics after 1896. In the twentieth century as in the nineteenth, it still promoted protection through tariffs, but tariffs were no longer bringing in much revenue. By contrast, the Republican party was wholly opposed to the income taxes enacted in 1913 and augmented during the Great War, for income taxes fell heavily on the upper-class and industrial backers of the party. For these reasons, the Republicans sought to keep government spending low and in doing that they kept modern social policy off the national political agenda. The one major social spending bureaucracy at the national level, the Children's Bureau in the Department of Labor, was harmed by the Republican agenda in the 1920s. Indeed, if the Republican regime had retained power during the

1930s, mothers' pensions doubtless would have remained a source of aid to only a fortunate few, and the movements for old-age pensions and unemployment compensation would have continued to make fitful progress.

Innovative as he was for a Republican president, Herbert Hoover was greatly constrained by the policies and program of his party and did little even to provide temporary relief in the Depression. Following the lead of northern Democrats and progressives in both parties, Franklin Roosevelt broke the pattern of Republican relief policy. He provided large sums to aid those in need during the Depression, which hit bottom at the time of his inauguration. He also rejected the elevation of veterans over other Americans in the provision of aid. Roosevelt, however, was soon to reject the policy of cash relief for the able-bodied—or "the dole" as he disparagingly called it. It was unclear whether the relief policies would be transformed into something permanent.

A number of circumstances suggested that they might. The FERA brought many policy advocates to work for the government, set some important precedents, and taught lessons to proponents of national reform. The FERA induced the creation of agencies at the state and county levels that served as models of what modernized relief administration might become. The adoption of sales and income taxes placed states in a stronger position relative to local governments that controlled poor relief. The CWA, the first program of national public employment, was followed by FERA's own work programs, which held out promise for later initiatives. The FERA was aiding not only unemployed men of working age, but also families without breadwinners and the aged, preempting the state and local programs for those purposes. These programs were soon to be incorporated in a policy that overshadowed them in making a genuine bid to uphold the family wage.

CHAPTER THREE

America's First Welfare Reform, 1935–1936

> Boys—this is our hour. We've got to get everything we want—a works program, social security, wages and hours, everything—now or never. Get your minds to work on developing a complete ticket to provide security for all the folks of this country up and down and across the board.
>
> —*Harry L. Hopkins to his aides, after Democratic victories in the congressional elections, November 1934*

> To dole out relief in this way is to administer a narcotic, a subtle destroyer of the human spirit. . . . Work must be found for able-bodied, but destitute workers.
>
> —*Franklin D. Roosevelt on the FERA's open-ended cash payments to the unemployed, January 1935*

> [Public employment] should be recognized as a permanent policy of the Government and not merely as an emergency measure.
>
> —*Committee on Economic Security, January 1935*

> Don't do it, Mr. Hopkins!
>
> —*Edith Abbott, University of Chicago, on his proposal to return responsibility for general relief programs to states and localities, January 1935*

AFTER THE ELECTIONS of 1934, a tremendous sweep for the Democrats, reformers knew they had a rare opportunity.[1] The plain-spoken Hopkins put matters bluntly after the people had seemingly ratified the president's approach and program: Government-based reformers should devise permanent versions of New Deal social policy experiments and congressional reform proposals and induce the president to place them before Congress. From his position as federal emergency relief administrator, Hopkins saw a special need for public employment.

During the Second New Deal of 1935, the United States entered the modern social spending world with dispatch—in keeping with Hopkins's now-

or-never sentiment. Franklin Roosevelt pressed forward in earnest on his agenda for permanent reform or "reconstruction"—to use his term. He wanted to distance himself from his own emergency relief policies of the early 1930s, with their open-ended grants of cash aid and halting attempts to provide work. In their place he wanted to substitute a modern social policy destined to outlive the Depression. He considered social policy the right thing to do and calculated that it would be popular among the increasingly urban and working-class constituents of the Democratic party.

When Americans today think of the policy breakthroughs of 1935, we are most likely to remember the Social Security Act and "social security"—the national old-age insurance (OAI) program. We may also recall that the central "welfare" program of recent memory, Aid to Dependent Children (ADC), was part of the package. The taxation initiative that Americans are most likely to remember is Roosevelt's "soak-the-rich" proposal of that same year. The period of legislative action that comes most readily to mind is the "second hundred days" that began in June 1935. At that time, Roosevelt declared that five bills, including the security legislation, were on his "must" list. All soon passed.[2]

These recollections, however, miss the central meaning and result of American social politics in the Depression. The program that absorbed the greatest amount of both public spending and public attention was the "Works Program"—public employment mainly through the Works Progress Administration (WPA). Its priority was so great that it was brought before Congress ahead of the Economic Security Act, as the security bill was initially called. As for the latter legislation, moreover, the program attracting the greatest public interest was means-tested Old-Age Assistance (OAA), not OAI. The resulting Social Security Act created only one national spending program and mainly funded and encouraged programs controlled by the states and localities, mostly means-tested, "special" assistance programs, such as OAA and ADC. Also, Roosevelt's taxation proclamation resulted in perhaps more bombast than revenue. The legislation that resulted had far less fiscal impact than did payroll taxes for social insurance, which soaked a decidedly less-than-rich group.

Almost never remembered is that the Second New Deal social policy came in part at the expense of previous commitments. It was in that way America's first effort at welfare reform. In adopting a work program and security measures, Roosevelt and Hopkins declared that the federal government would end its support to those not fitting a special category, such as the aged or dependent children. That decision came much to the dismay of social reformers such as the University of Chicago's Edith Abbott. She warned Hopkins against abandoning general relief when the proposal first transpired, arguing instead that the federal government should not withdraw just as the efforts of the Federal Emergency Relief Administration (FERA) were forcing locally controlled poor laws to the verge of extinction.

In this chapter I recount the story of the creation of a modern American social policy, based on work and relief. I want, however, not only to recast perceptions, but to explain what happened. I argue that the institutional politics theory provides the best explanation of these initiatives. But let me start with the legislative developments that mattered most.

Launching a Work and Relief State in the Second New Deal: Employment, Stipends, and the Retirement Principle

The making of the Social Security Act is a tale often told before, by both participants and scholars, but it is worth placing the project in perspective. The best known account is *The Development of the Social Security Act*, the book-length memorandum of Edwin Witte, the executive secretary of the Committee on Economic Security (CES).[3] According to Witte, the catalyst was congressional deliberation over bills for unemployment compensation and old-age pensions. The Wagner-Lewis bill of 1934 envisioned using the taxing powers of the federal government to induce states to pass unemployment compensation laws of their own design. Another piece of Senator Robert Wagner's reform agenda, this bill had many members of Congress and experts behind it, but not Roosevelt, and it died in committee. The old-age proposal, known as the Dill-Connery bill, appropriated $10 million in federal matching aid to states with old-age pension programs—two state dollars for every national dollar. By the middle of 1934, most states already had enacted means-tested old-age pension programs, but could not fund them at all adequately. The Dill-Connery bill passed the House in 1933 and 1934 and very nearly the Senate in 1934.

With his own reform plans still lacking focus, Roosevelt announced on June 8 the creation of the Committee on Economic Security (CES) and charged it with constructing a comprehensive economic security policy.[4] A cabinet-level group chaired by Frances Perkins, the secretary of labor, the CES also included the secretary of the treasury, Henry Morgenthau, the secretary of agriculture, Henry Wallace, the attorney general, Homer Cummings, and the federal emergency relief administrator, Harry Hopkins. The committee's deliberations were framed by the Technical Board and the staff of the CES. Although the CES addressed the sorts of programs that Congress was entertaining, the committee also saw public employment and other relief issues as part of its mission.

A University of Wisconsin public policy expert, Witte was appointed at the end of July—only four months before the committee's report was due. Few academics ever faced a semester so daunting. The committee was allotted a mere $87,500, which came from the Federal Emergency Relief Administration (FERA), making the committee itself a work project.[5] The Technical Board formed five subcommittees of policy experts inside the government, and the staff went to work. Late that autumn, once the deliberations of the Technical Board and staff committees were nearly completed, an Advisory Council of prominent businessmen, labor representatives, and citizens supposedly representing the public was convened. By the end of the year, ready or not, it was time to turn in the final reports and a proposal. Its authors hopefully labeled it the Economic Security Act.

So far, so good. But Witte's account has one important gap in it—the administration's most pressing concern, its "Works Program," as it was called. The program is missing because soon after the CES convened, the group working on "public employment and relief" was separated from the CES proper and from the economic security legislation. Thus it was lost from Witte's sight, and his disregard of the works program was not due to its lack of importance—just the opposite. The works program was Roosevelt's top priority in social policy. The idea that national employment was an essential part of guaranteeing economic security insinuated itself forcibly into the thinking and declarations of the CES. "Employment assurance" was the first topic in the committee's report, which stated that public employment should be permanent social policy.[6]

The First Campaign for Welfare Reform: Work Relief for the "Employable"

In introducing the works program and the other economic security measures on January 4, 1935, Roosevelt inaugurated what appears in retrospect as America's first effort at welfare reform, for as he advanced his program, Roosevelt also signaled the end of the FERA. In denouncing "dole relief," Roosevelt was referring, ambiguously, to two unpopular aspects of recent policy: the open-ended provision of cash payments to the able-bodied unemployed and the demeaning and often corrupt provision of grocery orders and other forms of in-kind aid to those employed on work projects. In place of the dole, Roosevelt's frequent shorthand for that assortment of aid, he offered work, or what was sometimes called "work relief."[7] The works program committed the national government to providing jobs—and wages. To gain support, Roosevelt attempted to put rhetorical distance between the FERA's temporary, but outmoded activities and the new works program.[8]

The joint resolution authorizing the appropriation for the works program was drafted in late December 1934 and placed before Congress on January 21, 1935—well before the second hundred days of June 1935. With an initial appropriation of approximately $4.9 billion, an enormous sum for that time, the resolution gave the president authority to fund all manner of work projects and public works. Based on the powers given the president through the Emergency Relief Act and the public works titles of the National Industrial Recovery Act, the resolution was enacted eleven weeks later and approved by the president on April 11. Exactly how the works program was to be run was up for grabs. By way of an executive order in May, authority to spend the appropriation was granted partly to

Harold Ickes, the secretary of the interior and head of the Public Works Administration (PWA), who was named to head an Advisory Committee on Allotments. Hopkins shared power over the program. He was placed in charge of what was called the Works Progress Administration, which oversaw the works program as a whole, but had only limited authority over project choice. There was a brief, but one-sided competition, with Hopkins, a poker enthusiast, holding most of the cards—his willingness to spend money, his vast knowledge of labor-intensive work projects, and his still persisting FERA program which continued to fund and oversee the Depression-era "welfare" population. Hopkins and the WPA were freed from Ickes's committee by September and work relief took off.[9]

Drawing on the Civil Works Administration (CWA) experiment of 1933–1934 and work relief under the FERA, the Works Progress Administration (WPA) also differed from these programs. Whereas the CWA was closely tied to the FERA and state-level emergency relief organizations, the WPA was entirely a Washington operation and initially under the control of the president. The WPA brought national control over the selection of labor-intensive works projects, which were to be proposed mainly by state and local authorities. By law, WPA projects could not compete with private business. The works program was to employ almost exclusively able-bodied workers, one per family, who had applied for and were receiving means-tested aid. Some 90 percent of the workers were to be taken from the relief roles, in keeping with Roosevelt's goal to move the "employable" from the dole to work. The new works program resembled FERA work-relief projects more than work projects run by the CWA, in that the latter employed both those on relief and those who did not seek it. WPA wages were generally lower than those of the CWA as well. Unlike the FERA, however, the WPA paid cash wages in standardized amounts—not sundry cash and in-kind aid attempting to fill a "budget deficiency."[10]

The WPA paid a combination of a "security" wage and a "prevailing" wage. WPA work was to be paid with a monthly, security sum, and the number of hours worked to receive it were determined by the wages prevailing for the type of work. This prevailing wage rate was necessary to win the support of organized labor, which did not want to be undercut by low-wage WPA labor. The sums varied according to the location and skill-basis of the job.[11] Because of the energy of Hopkins and his experience with administering work programs, the WPA was employing more than three million workers by February 1936.

The WPA was supplemented by the National Youth Administration (NYA), created by an executive order in June 1935. Led by Aubrey Williams of the FERA, the NYA was designed to provide employment and job training to youths, and encouraged college education. Also, it was supposed to delay the entrance of the young into the labor market. The appropriations for the works program also were to bolster the operations of the Civilian Conservation Corps. The CCC was to remain committed to the

Plate 3.1 Lineup of WPA Workers (Russell Lee). The Works Progress
Administration, part of the Roosevelt Administration's plan for "reconstruction" or permanent reform, was aiding more than 3 million people
in its first year of operation. Here workers line up for WPA jobs in
Cairo, Illinois.

national conservation projects it had begun in 1933 and to the employment
of young men in its rural work camp outposts.[12]

Earnest though it was, the commitment to the WPA and the works program was somewhat equivocal because of how they were funded and administered. Initially funded by way of a joint resolution, the WPA was sustained by appropriation acts that invariably included the word "emergency"
in them. The WPA itself was created by an executive order. In addition, there
was no legislation establishing an entitlement to jobs for individuals meeting
standard criteria, and there were no standards setting the number of jobs per
year or their allotment across political units. For the time being, the WPA
relied on the administration's desire and ability to gain funds for it, and a
sounder administrative setup would be necessary for the program to become
the permanent commitment envisioned by the CES.[13]

As it stood in 1936, however, the WPA held a radical promise. By law it
could not discriminate against racial or ethnic groups. Unlike social insur-

ance, it was not limited to industrial workers. Unlike social assistance, it could not be readily undermined by state-level funding or staffing practices. The ultimate authority for the program was the president's, and he delegated it to people like Hopkins who believed that work should stand as an essential and permanent commitment of the state. The WPA was soon to become a central issue in the 1936 presidential campaign as Roosevelt supported the idea of government-provided work and the Republicans rejected it.[14]

Relief for the Deserving "Unemployable"—the Aged and Dependent Children

The administration's "Economic Security Act" that followed the works program was also part of a welfare reform strategy, for it was designed to upgrade and make permanent some of the FERA's commitments, while dispensing with others. All in all, the security bill provided a mix of means-tested relief and social insurance programs, but was more weighted toward relief programs, nowadays disparaged as welfare. Notably, the bill included titles for national grants-in-aid for a number of groups deemed "unemployable" but deserving by New Deal planners—in particular the aged and families without breadwinners to which Congress added the blind before the bill became the Social Security Act. But the two most fiscally consequential programs were Old-Age Assistance and Aid to Dependent Children.[15]

Little remembered today, OAA was the selling point of the economic security bill to Congress. Old-Age Assistance, Title I of the bill and act, provided that the federal government would match state and local spending for old-age pensions, up to fifteen dollars per month, and appropriated approximately $30 million for the first year. It is no surprise that this part of the omnibus bill achieved the most support in Congress. After all, the similar Dill-Connery bill had almost reached passage the previous year without the administration's encouragement.[16] Meantime, an old-age pension insurgency led by Dr. Francis E. Townsend demanded pensions of two hundred dollars per month, and a Townsend-inspired bill appeared in Congress soon after the economic security bill.[17]

The matching funds proposed by the CES for Old Age Assistance would not permit pensions nearly as generous as those envisioned in the Townsend Plan, however. What is more, although the committee stipulated that states must provide OAA pensions at a level allowing "a reasonable subsistence compatible with decency and health," Congress eliminated this provision. Whether the loss of this provision was the cause, the legislation gave states the option to keep benefit levels low and eligibility standards high, yet still receive matching national funds.[18] In addition, members of Congress objected to the creation of civil service standards in administering the program and eliminated these as well. And although the CES called for this program to be run by the powerful FERA, Congress created the Social Security Board to administer OAA.[19] For all these reasons state-level legislation for OAA was far from standardized. Rules of eligibility varied enormously, and benefits varied much more widely than regional differences in the cost of living warranted.

All the same, Old-Age Assistance constituted a major social spending breakthrough that soon swept the nation. Every state with previous old-age pension legislation quickly replaced it with OAA legislation. States like California, with relatively well-established old-age pension programs before the Depression, saw great increases in average benefits and overall coverage of pensions.[20] And the twenty states without old-age pensions by 1935 had adopted OAA by 1939. OAA meant a new commitment to the aged, but the program was extremely contentious, and its boundaries would have to be settled in the various polities with authority over it.

The new special assistance program of the act best known today was Aid to Dependent Children. Its status as the core of welfare, however, was far from determined in 1935. It is ironic that the program Americans were to associate with welfare was created by an act called "social security." It is even more ironic that ADC was a somewhat higher congressional priority than old-age insurance—the program now known as social security. The CES wanted to upgrade and make permanent the FERA's support for children without breadwinning fathers to replace the inadequate mothers' pensions. Marking the break, the legislation emphasized "children" rather than mothers.

Like OAA, however, ADC was also meant to remove permanently a category of people from the labor market and to provide cash for them. Odd though it may seem from today's perspective, mothers without male breadwinners were deemed unemployable by New Deal planners. Such women were considered as unlikely candidates for wage employment as aged men, or the blind. Everyone would be better off if such women avoided paid labor, the thinking went. The sponsors of the bill were clear on this point. As Grace Abbott, the former long-term chief of the Children's Bureau and Edith's younger sister, put it in testifying in support of the bill before Congress, a "mother's services are worth more in the home than they are in the outside labor market. . . ." And, she argued, aid should be sustained not just until the children were ready for school, but until they left home. In their bid to end this commitment, those who claimed in the 1990s that welfare through AFDC was not meant to be permanent could not have been more wrong.[21]

Aid to Dependent Children drew only little attention, as Congress was more concerned with OAA, and as ADC's supporters were eager to avoid scrutiny. The latter portrayed the program as little more than federal backing for already existing and traditionally "American" aid. Title IV of the Social Security Act established ADC as a federal-state grant-in-aid program that required states to make benefits available statewide and designate a single agency to administer the program or supervise local administration.

The act specified that states be reimbursed for one-third of their expenditures up to eighteen dollars per month for the first child and twelve dollars for each additional child, with the limits decided by the House Ways and Means Committee. No grant was proposed for the caretaker, and the federal commitment to ADC compared unfavorably to the one-half reimbursement for OAA, up to a maximum of thirty dollars per month per recipient. The Social Security Act defined dependency in a broad fashion and marked a great departure from mother's pension programs limited to small categories of widows. ADC applied to all children under the age of sixteen deprived of "parental support or care by reason of the death, continued absence from the home, or physical or mental incapacity of a parent." As with OAA, the House of Representatives assigned the program to the newly created Social Security Board and its Bureau of Public Assistance. As with OAA, too, stipulations about meeting standards consistent with decency and health were removed. Most states passed a qualifying ADC bill by the end of the decade.[22]

With the new emphasis on work and on special categories of public assistance and with the disbanding of the FERA, a major gap, however, opened in public assistance. The administration placed the responsibility for others with inadequate incomes onto states and localities. Left out of consideration were those considered "unemployable," but not fitting any special category. Also left out were the "employables" passed over by the underfunded WPA. Administration reformers hoped that the states would use the experience of the FERA to upgrade their relief systems for this "general" category. Because of everything the national government was proposing to do, though, administration reformers thought that states and localities had a moral obligation to assume this responsibility. Such was the implicit bargain of the federal government in advancing the works program. But the CES proposed no assistance or incentives to the states to do so, and Congress did not volunteer such support.[23]

Unemployment Compensation: Strong Incentives
for State-Level Programs

One social insurance proposal overshadowed all others among social policy experts. This proposal was not old-age insurance, but Unemployment Compensation (UC), a program currently with an ambiguous status, neither social security nor welfare. Experts were exercised over several issues, most of them obscure. Before the CES took up the issue, proponents of the so-called Wisconsin and Ohio schools debated whether to have a pooled fund or individual employer reserves, and whether to tax the payrolls of employers alone or to tax employees as well.[24] The debate about UC that had the greatest ramifications, however, was whether to have a national program or one controlled mainly by state governments. At the one extreme was a "tax offset" program—embodied in the 1934 Wagner-Lewis bill—which removed most reasons for states not to enact their own legislation. At the other end was a proposal that offered strictly national insurance. In between was a federal subsidy program. In the end, the committee endorsed the tax offset scheme to promote state-level experimentation.[25]

Like the Wagner-Lewis bill, the Unemployment Compensation titles of the administration's economic security bill gave states an overwhelming incentive to pass their own legislation.[26] There was a separate federal payroll tax—1 percent of employers' payrolls in 1935. It was scheduled to increase to 3 percent in 1937, 2 percent lower than the original Wagner bill. Because the federal tax was credited to the employer once a state had passed a plan meeting the minimal national standards—the so-called tax offset—the only tax that mattered was the one enacted by the state government. The payroll taxes for the state programs were in turn subject to lowering by what was known as "merit rating." That is, employers who did not frequently lay off workers would pay less tax—an idea from the Wisconsin school. Regardless of the form that such compensation might take, the program was connected in the president's mind with his works program. He expected that in the future those whose unemployment insurance benefits ran out would be automatically certified for government-supplied work.[27]

When the economic security bill was introduced only Wisconsin had passed Unemployment Compensation. Some other states followed in 1935, but the legislators in many states waited to see if the national legislation might be ruled unconstitutional. Late in 1936, the New York law survived a state Supreme Court challenge and eighteen states quickly passed legislation. By the middle of 1937, after the Social Security Act won a final Supreme Court challenge, all states had bowed to the extreme incentives and passed legislation, and most states enacted some form of merit rating.[28] Some states, such as Illinois, the last one to pass a program in 1937, allowed companies to pay nothing if their employment record was deemed acceptable.[29]

An Uncertain Start for "Social Security"

Integral to our understanding of social security today, old-age insurance was at the margins of the Social Security Act. "Federal old-age benefits," as OAI was originally called, was not at the center of the CES's project and found little resonance in Congress. OAI was funded at a lower level than UC and was not scheduled to pay benefits until 1942. What is more, OAI was far from inclusive. Congress amended the security bill to exclude agricultural laborers and domestics and accordingly most African Americans, especially in the South. Only the intercession of Roosevelt himself prevented this program from being deleted or further crippled by amendments.[30] Although the program was designed to pay recipients according to previous earnings, other aspects of the program conflicted with the insurance model and imagery that the Social Security Board would later elaborate to justify the program's expansion.[31] The spending and taxation titles of the bill had to be separated to avoid provoking a fatal Supreme Court ruling, and Congress added a provision that the recipient must retire in order to receive the benefit. By proposing a national program—with the greater likelihood of its being found unconstitutional for that reason—the administration signaled that OAI was of a lower priority than UC.

In 1935, old-age insurance was little more than a special tax or, really, a promise to tax, for Congress had time to change its mind, and the Supreme Court seemed likely to declare it unconstitutional. Like Unemployment Compensation, OAI included a payroll tax on employers, but also included a tax on employees. Though compulsory, this tax was called a "contribution" by the social insurance proponents on the CES. The rhetorical sleight of hand was a bid to bolster the commitment between taxpayer and recipient and to make it seem as if the administration were not really raising taxes. The tax was scheduled to go into effect in 1937, at 1 percent of payrolls and wages, and was to increase by increments to 3 percent in 1949. On the recommendation of Morgenthau, the secretary of the treasury, and in opposition to the CES staff, Roosevelt insisted on a stringent tax schedule to make sure that paying benefits would not mean spending any general revenues.[32] Later, as we shall see, Roosevelt did not hesitate to undermine the self-supporting aspect of OAI when it suited his purposes.

Soaking the Rich or Inundating the Forgotten Man?

Like those of the First New Deal, the social spending innovations of the Second New Deal were accompanied by increases in taxation. However, not all were national, few were progressive, in the sense of taking higher proportions from higher incomes, and together these tax initiatives were not enough to balance the budget. As the historian Mark Leff has put it, Second New Deal fiscal policy centered on "taxing the forgotten man," the struggling worker who was the supposed beneficiary of the New Deal.[33] Notably the payroll taxes for social insurance are generally considered regressive, for taxes on employers are probably taken from what would otherwise be wages and taxes on employees almost certainly are. Also, the rates were flat rather than progressive. Moreover, the old-age insurance taxes, on employers and employees, were designed to apply to yearly incomes only up to three thousand dollars.[34] Although this "wage base" has risen over time—approaching sixty thousand dollars in the late 1990s—this ceiling adds to the regressiveness of the tax. The payroll tax for Unemployment Compensation, levied solely on employers, was higher, but did not accrue to the national government. States also targeted the forgotten man, by continuing to pass regressive sales taxes as well as progressive income taxes to pay for power-sharing, means-tested programs.

Although the relief or public assistance titles of the Social Security Act had no corresponding taxation titles, the final congressional push for the bill was accompanied by Roosevelt's drive for "soak the rich" taxation. The administration began to explore new sources of revenue in 1935. In June, Roosevelt unexpectedly demanded the passage of a Treasury Department proposal to tax extremely high incomes at a stiff rate, to raise inheritance and gift taxes, to tax undistributed dividends of corporations, and to increase and make more graduated the corporation income tax. The taxes were designed in part to break up large corporations. They also provided some new revenues, opened the door to later taxation increases, and won the praise of one of the administration's left-wing critics, Louisiana Senator Huey P. Long. This soak-the-rich legislation may have been largely political theater, however, for higher taxation rates on the incomes of the super-rich did not translate into greatly increased revenues.[35] In any case, the legislation did not provide revenues commensurate to its rhetoric and did not secure a stable fiscal footing for the work and relief policy.

Paying Out and Paying For the Veterans' Bonus

A final spending program with great immediate fiscal significance ran outside the boundaries of New Deal reform. Despite Roosevelt's opposition to the use of veterans' benefits as a backdoor relief policy, Roosevelt found his administration paying $2 billion in adjusted compensation certificates or "bonuses" to World War I veterans. These bonuses were enacted in 1924 and were due to be paid in 1945. In the Depression, however, many veterans sought to forge a separate peace with their pecuniary struggles—through the immediate payment of the bonus. Veterans' groups began demanding this as early as 1930, and the Bonus Army massed in Washington in 1932 and 1933. In Congress, their cause was led by Wright Patman, a Texan who labored in vain for several years. When Congress finally passed an early payment bill in 1935, however, Roosevelt vetoed it—with a stinging speech delivered before Congress for emphasis. His point was that veterans' benefits should not be confused with economic security for all Americans. When the early payment bill passed again the next year, Roosevelt again vetoed it. This time, though, he indicated that he would not fight a bid to override—which Congress quickly did.[36]

THE ORIGINS OF THE WORK AND RELIEF POLICY

The above account outlines what happened. After all, by definition Congress must pass legislation to create and fund social policy and the executive branch must effect this action. But the account does not answer why the events happened or happened as they did. Why was an American work and relief state launched in the 1930s, especially after 1934? What conditions and actors were responsible for the form that it took? What accounts for the differences in form across the programs?

Here I want to show that the timing and character of these public policy breakthroughs follow the expectations of the institutional politics theory. American political institutions structured what was possible in public spending. Because the polity was only partly democratized and because the political parties were mainly patronage-oriented, it was difficult to gain new national commitments to social spending in America. The numerous veto points in the system also made innovations difficult, and the divisions of authority in the polity tended to be reproduced in policy. Yet breakthroughs were possible, and divisions of authority differed across programs. Both these facts require explanation.

I argue specifically that the nature of U.S. public policy and the configuration of policy abilities in the national state and across the country greatly influenced the form of New Deal social policy. U.S. public policies were devised mainly by state actors and experts, who reacted to these previous programs in predictable ways. This influenced the nature of reforms proposed. Because the main state domestic bureaucracy was the FERA and because of previous state-level experiments in new means-tested social programs, the CES produced a work and relief policy. Otherwise, though, the committee's blueprint was messy. Other bureaus had a hand in it; where there were openings outside experts also insinuated themselves into the process. As a result, social insurance programs were included with means-tested programs, and national programs with those that extended control to states and localities. Yet previous policies and the degree of centralized planning did not account for the adoption or rejection of plans.

Those matters were decided by the existence of a reform-oriented president and the configuration of political forces in Congress. The existence of a Democratic administration committed to social policy reform, based on a national coalition of support from less well-off voters, was central. Moreover, the emergence of a large pro–social spending or reform-oriented contingent in Congress provides the best proximate answer for why the Roosevelt Administration succeeded and why breakthroughs in social spending were enacted when they were. A reform-oriented regime, in short, took power in the middle 1930s. Congress was willing and sometimes eager to support programs embracing abiding commitments to large groups of Americans. Similarly, the waning of this reform regime provides the best answer for why the work and relief policy was eventually stopped and reversed.

Furthermore, social protest movements and capitalist organizations had important, though secondary, influences on the work and relief policy. Some social movements—notably organized labor—mainly supported the efforts of the president, New Dealers within the administration, and social policy advocates in Congress. In this way they advanced the process by which state actors and reform-oriented politicians constructed and passed social policy innovations. Movements challenging the New Deal from the left also stimulated social policy in various ways. Notably, they helped to keep specific issues from leaving the political agenda and placed pressure on policy experts and legislators to augment the collective benefits in their proposals. Some challengers, notably veterans' movements, largely failed, however, and some new programs, notably Aid to Dependent Children, were passed in the absence of movement support. Organized capitalists sought to mobilize money, and secondarily people, and to exploit open lines of communication to prevent the legislation of the Second New Deal. In that they failed. But organized capitalists were able to dilute some of this legislation, and later their alliance with the Republican party helped eventually to stop the New Deal. Before I make these points, though, I want to address one argument sometimes made about the causes of U.S. social policy.

WHY THE DEPRESSION DOES NOT EXPLAIN NEW DEAL SOCIAL POLICY

Some analysts of American public programs argue that it took the Depression to jolt the U.S. political system into action on public spending. It has also been argued that generally economic crises give political and state actors in capitalist societies more room to maneuver than usual.[37] The public spending breakthroughs of the New Deal occurred during the Great Depression, and the breakthroughs and the Depression are difficult to consider in isolation from each other. The crisis sucked dry the treasuries of states and localities—key political actors in relief—and politician after politician went hat in hand to Washington seeking loans and grants.

All the same, the formation of an American work and relief policy cannot be attributed to this economic crisis. For one thing, the slump was severe in many industrial democracies, but few of them saw their public policies restructured. Britain, for instance, was a world leader in public spending on the eve of the Depression and there were various gaps in its social policy, including a restrictive Poor Law and no programs targeting families with children. The year 1929 saw the rise to power of a Labour government, which ruled in coalition with the Liberals. Despite the new government, British policy during the Depression broke very little with political or economic orthodoxy. There were no public works programs, not to mention public employment programs, no nationalized social insurance innovations, and not even much deficit spending.[38]

For another, the pace of permanent U.S. policy reform did not closely track the rhythms of the crisis. The Depression quickly forced millions of people out of work and steadily worsened until the inauguration of Franklin Roosevelt in March 1933. At that point more than one-quarter of the work force was unemployed, and the gross national product had dipped almost one-third from 1929 levels.[39] Despite the desperation surrounding it, however, the Hoover Administration dragged its heels on short-term relief. The Roosevelt Administration, moreover, did not propose permanent reforms until the worst of the Depression was over.

The main trouble with the thesis, though, is that there is no necessary connection between economic crisis and permanent public spending reform. After all, the social emergency of the Depression might have been addressed solely by way of temporary relief funds provided to states and localities. If Hoover had remained in power he might have merely upgraded the Reconstruction Finance Corporation and kept it going until the worst of the crisis was over. Similarly, Roosevelt might have extended some version of the FERA.[40]

That said, that the Great Depression happened when it did had an indirect impact on the character of U.S. public social provision. Permanent social policy proposals were more likely to find themselves on the political agenda and win support if they also addressed social problems—especially unemployment—due to the Depression. The dire economic situation biased all public spending breakthroughs toward permanent means-tested relief programs, which were well known among experts and politicians and were a plausible way to address both immediate and chronic problems. Weakening private business as a contender for adequate provision against some risks, such as poverty in old age, the Depression also helped to clear the way for public efforts.[41] Most of all, the Depression helped to discredit the Republican party and its policies, but this was at least in part fortuitous.

State Actors, Experts, Previous Policies, and Spending Proposals

Experts situated within the state developed the social spending programs of the New Deal. These experts ranged from the former social workers of the Federal Emergency Relief Administration who devised the Works Progress Administration to the members of the Children's Bureau who devised Aid to Dependent Children to the university-based members of the Technical Board of the Committee on Economic Security which devised old-age programs and Unemployment Compensation. These proposals made their way onto the political agenda.

Planning the Spending Programs of the Second New Deal

To address these issues it is useful to return to Edwin Witte's account. In it planning for New Deal social policy centers on the Technical Board and the CES staff. The board and its committees, nominally directed by Arthur Altmeyer, an assistant secretary of labor also from Wisconsin, included political appointees and policy experts from inside the government. There were four substantive Technical Board committees—for unemployment insurance, old-age security, medical care or health insurance, and public employment and public assistance. The staff, overseen by Witte, included policy experts and was authorized to gather the facts regarding economic insecurity in America, to study the programs here and abroad dealing with insecurity, and to suggest legislative proposals. Staff committees were to study each of the subjects corresponding to the board committees. In principle, Witte was to gather these staff recommendations and pass them on to the relevant committees of the Technical Board, which were in turn to make recommendations.[42]

All of this calls to mind nothing so much as a conference of academic experts planning a welfare state on the basis of knowledge and brainpower, with like-minded political officials endorsing the best of their studies. But the image is misleading. The staff filed its reports, but the Technical Board committees of governmental officials had to pass on all recommendations. Only their votes counted, and many Technical Board members had their own ideas for social policy. Moreover, the staff did not have much time to do its studies and thus to influence the Technical Board. The staff made its preliminary recommendations on September 26, a scant six weeks after Witte had outlined its work. As a result the recommendations were made well before the completion of the studies that were supposed to generate the recommendations. In any case the Technical Board made its preliminary decisions, the ones that really mattered, by October 9.[43]

What is more, many staff members were far from disinterested experts. Crucial staff efforts were dominated by experts already working for the government, especially the FERA and the Department of Labor. The operation of the CES as a whole was overseen by the FERA and the federal emergency relief administrator, Harry Hopkins, who was soon to be in charge of the WPA. The CES was financed by FERA funds, and Witte was housed in the FERA office building. Moreover, three FERA members held positions on the executive committee of the Technical Board. A second center of policymaking was the Children's Bureau of the Department of Labor. The bureau, the longest-standing social policy bureaucracy in the executive branch, had run grant-in-aid programs for maternal and child health through the Sheppard-Towner Act in the 1920s and had monitored state and local mothers' pensions programs since their inception.[44]

Given the high priority of the works program, the deliberations over it preceded those over the economic security legislation and were removed from the control of the CES proper before the committee had much say in the matter. The planning of the program was dominated by FERA officials. Roosevelt met informally on this issue over the summer with Hopkins and Henry Morgenthau, secretary of the treasury, and their discussions were aided by FERA staffers.[45]

Questions of work and relief were central to the initial thinking of the CES. Indeed, "guarantee of work," "relief," "social insurance," and "annuity" were the four approaches suggested by Witte for the committee to adopt in its overall vision of economic security. Coordinating, funding, and promoting means-tested programs across the country, the FERA staff had an excellent overview of the advantages and disadvantages of these pro-

grams and definite views about how to address them. They also had substantial control over the issue in the CES. Aubrey Williams, an assistant
administrator of the FERA, was named the chairman of the Technical
Board committee on public employment and assistance. Also included were
Corrington Gill, another assistant administrator of the FERA, and Howard
B. Meyers, of the FERA's Division of Research and Statistics. FERA Assistant Administrator Jacob Baker also made a number of proposals for a
work program. The FERA's Emerson Ross was placed in charge of staff
studies and was aided in turn by a considerable FERA-financed staff. He
produced a report entitled "A Permanent Program of Public Employment
and Relief." FERA officials soon had the issue to themselves, as the committee on public employment and assistance was removed from CES auspices,
much to the dismay of Witte. In late November 1934, a memo to the president was drafted by the FERA staff, making recommendations for the public employment program.[46]

Also working somewhat outside the formal structure of the staff committees of the CES was a contingent from the Children's Bureau. The CES
charged central figures in the bureau with making studies and recommendations for programs in a number of areas concerning children.[47] Katharine
Lenroot, acting chief of the bureau, took the lead in researching and proposing a program, with the assistance of the bureau's Martha Eliot. The
Children's Bureau's previous research on mothers' pensions, especially its
1933 report, *Mothers' Aid, 1931*, had indicated their failure. The bureau
diagnosed the problem with mothers' pensions as primarily one of inadequate coverage and lack of funding and concluded that leaving such matters
wholly up to states and localities was a mistake. The bureau's prescription,
however, continued to be to provide mothers without breadwinning husbands with continuous aid, not jobs. The problem was devising a means
of providing the aid to all who needed it. Following the vision of Grace
Abbott, former chief of the bureau—who later surfaced as a "public" member of the CES Advisory Council—the Children's Bureau wanted to support
dependent children being aided through the FERA, but to make the aid of
children a separate mission employing casework methodology and adequate long-term benefits. The bureau also wanted to reinstate the federal
grant-in-aid for programs for maternal and child health previously funded
through the Sheppard-Towner Act.[48]

Among the issues confronted by the CES staff committees, Unemployment Compensation had the longest history and provided the greatest
constraints. The Wisconsin school, following in the tradition of John Commons, saw in UC a means to make capitalism work better and included such
policy academicians as John Andrews, Elizabeth Brandeis, and Paul
Rauschenbush. The Wisconsin reformers expected that individual employer
reserves would give employers incentives to minimize unemployment, just
as workmen's compensation, by making employers pay more for accidents,
could prevent them. In contrast, the Ohio school stood for the pooling of

risks and secure and generous benefits, and hence the most productive sources of taxation, including taxes on workers. This line of thinking, associated with Abraham Epstein (the head of the expert reform organization the American Association for Social Security), Isaac Rubinow, William Leiserson, and Paul Douglas, saw in Wisconsin-style programs a potential limitation of benefits. Benefits for workers in a firm would be only as secure as the employer of that firm. If a company went bankrupt its unemployed workers would be out of luck, as far as unemployment benefits were concerned, as well as out of work. Also, the Ohio school believed that business cycles and unemployment were systemic features of capitalism and thus not subject to the control of individual employers.[49]

Witte discussed unemployment compensation extensively with numerous experts inside the government and in universities before devising a staff group to study the issue. Bryce Stewart of Industrial Relations Counselors, a New York firm, was chosen to head the group. He used his own staff and remained in New York. Merrill G. Murray, the director of the Minnesota Unemployment Service, represented the group in Washington. It had to contend with a Technical Board committee comprising Alvin H. Hansen, the chairman and a famous University of Minnesota economist, Jacob Viner, and William Leiserson—all with experience in studying this issue. These planners in turn had to contend with the support in Congress for the Wagner-Lewis bill, whose taxation provisions would allow states to choose between Wisconsin-style unemployment compensation and Ohio-style unemployment insurance.[50]

The other staff committees of the CES included outside experts, some based in universities, others not. The studies for old-age security were headed by Barbara Nachtrieb Armstrong, professor of law at the University of California and the author of *Insuring the Essentials*, a 1932 study of social insurance and assistance around the world. The monograph revealed Armstrong as a forceful advocate of social insurance. This committee devised proposals for both Old-Age Assistance and old-age insurance—a distinction that Armstrong made in her monograph. Murray Latimer of the Railroad Retirement Board and J. Douglas Brown of Princeton were chosen to advise her. Latimer was also the head of the Technical Board committee for this subject.[51] The staff committee in charge of studying medical care was headed by Edgar L. Sydenstricker of the Milbank Memorial Fund, assisted by I. S. Falk, also of the fund. This committee also worked in New York, in the Milbank offices, but its efforts did not figure in the economic security legislation.[52]

In short, the planning for social policy in the Second New Deal was done mainly by social policy experts—social workers, scholars, private economists, actuaries, and the like. The vast majority of them, moreover, were government employees, with a stake in existing programs and ideas about what to do next. The planning for the WPA, for public assistance, and for programs for children, was carried out by people already working in the federal bureaucracy. Other studies and proposals were undertaken by the staff committees of the CES. Often these were led by tenured academicians. Only rarely were these planners employed by foundations or by private businesses, and those most closely connected to foundations did not have much impact on social spending proposals that found their way into CES recommendations.

If the CES staff deliberations had been an academic semester, most of the projects would have earned a grade of "I" for incomplete. Not that all that much mattered—as the reports were designed to provide evidence in support of proposals decided by Roosevelt Administration officials near the beginning of October and would be needed once the proposals were to face congressional scrutiny in 1935. In the end the relevant committees of the Technical Board and the cabinet members of the Committee on Economic Security decided what would constitute the committee's official recommendations.

The Impact of Previous Policies and National-Level Planning Capacities on New Deal Proposals and the Political Agenda for Social Policy

The fact that the formulators of New Deal social spending programs were state actors or independent experts does not say much about why these proposals took the forms that they did, however. A number of issues stand out. An important one is why so few of these programs were nationally controlled. Another is why some programs were better funded than others. Other issues concern the nature and coherence of overall social spending plans. The proposals tilted toward work and means-tested principles, but also included social insurance, and addressed some risks to income, but not others of equal importance, such as health, workers' compensation, and programs for families generally.

The structure of the U.S. polity influenced these outcomes. The underdemocratized nature of the polity meant that the committee was unlikely to propose an entirely national system. The committee was concerned with getting its proposals past Congress, and Congress always had a contingent of undemocratically chosen representatives who could be counted on to oppose national social policy. Moreover, much of the bureaucratic abilities to run these programs would have to be built. Where there were state-level efforts underway, there would be pressure to build on them instead of over them.

The underdevelopment of democratic institutions and domestic capacities at the national level did not make national social programs impossible, so much as it made them unlikely—especially where state-level alternatives had been passed. These power-sharing alternatives were likely to get on the congressional agenda. Moreover, programs with institutional sponsors in the federal government were more likely to get on the agenda. The nature of national state planning capacities for social policy had a greater impact on the nature and coherence of social policy proposals. During the develop-

99

ment of the Second New Deal, these abilities were widely scattered—a situation that changed little until the end of the decade. As a result, planning in the Second New Deal was relatively incoherent. To the extent there was a central planning agency in 1935, it was the FERA. The FERA set the tone for the work and relief policy, but the limitations on its outlook and the pressing nature of its mission meant that other proposals could be only loosely connected to it. Only later, in the late 1930s, were domestic planning capacities centralized.

Though working with a comprehensive mandate, the CES was assembled hastily and was unable to devise a coherent system of social policy. It referred accurately to its proposals as "piecemeal."[53] The staff studies were provoked by political recommendations that preceded them. Starting somewhat late in the debate, the CES often found itself reacting to rather than shaping political developments. The committee's planners relied heavily on social spending proposals before Congress. The CES was also at a disadvantage with respect to the planning and designs of islands of strength in the domestic bureaucracy. The CES did little more than endorse their various initiatives. Those proposals that had received prior study and national bureaucratic backing had the best chance of reaching the policy agenda of the CES and thus of the Roosevelt Administration. These conditions—prior study and bureaucratic backing—reinforced each other, as the reform proposals benefiting from the greatest previous analytical attention also had support in the FERA and the Children's Bureau. The main exception to this rule was old-age insurance, a program in which the president took a special interest, and which began life as an adjunct to Old-Age Assistance.

Tardiness in beginning the deliberations and divisions among the experts produced recommendations that often constituted uneasy compromises. The plans of action were divided by relief and insurance principles and by national and state-level control. Even the recommendations for relief did not propose a wholesale reorganization of means-tested programs. Instead they provided for the creation of special assistance programs around which state and local relief efforts would revolve. Differences remained among the special assistance programs. Some long-term programs, such as health insurance, that were deemed necessary were left out of the final recommendations.

The forms of programs that the committee endorsed and that Roosevelt proposed reflected bureaucratic and policy facts. The CES and Roosevelt extended and ratified legislative proposals developed in Congress, and these proposals were designed in turn to buttress existing programs controlled at the state and local levels of government. Members of Congress, especially from states that had already adopted programs, in turn were aided and advised by state-level administrators. Wherever states and localities had begun to develop programs, legislation devised in Congress, before the creation of the CES, recognized the developments and sought to support them. Many of the programs proposed by the administration in 1935 gave the lower levels of government large degrees of bureaucratic and fiscal control despite the national standards proposed by the CES.

Consider the case of Old-Age Assistance. Most states had passed compulsory old-age pensions by the end of 1934—a culmination of professional reform movements such as those led by Abraham Epstein. The Roosevelt Administration's economic security bill took these state laws into account and attempted to improve on them. The administration's bill borrowed heavily from the Dill-Connery bills of 1933 and 1934. Like that legislation, the administration's proposal merely granted aid and incentives for states to pass their own programs, with some minimal national standards.[54]

By the end of 1934 unemployment compensation had been passed only in Wisconsin. In crucial ways, however, unemployment compensation was similar to state-level old-age pensions and led to states gaining great control over the program, through the tax offset provision. The issue had been formally debated in many states beginning in 1932, and compensation proposals neared passage in some of them at the beginning of 1935. When the Social Security Act became law, some eight states had already passed their own plans.[55] The administration's bill and the act were influenced by these developments. There were other reasons that pushed the CES to give states control over unemployment compensation—worries about the constitutionality of a national program, disagreements among policy experts, and the influence of Wisconsin reformers, like Witte and Altmeyer, on the committee.[56] All the same, national old-age insurance was just as likely to be declared unconstitutional as national unemployment insurance and other reforms were far from matters of consensus. The existence of one state plan, the formation of political compromises in other states on different plans, the drafting of a bill by Congress, and the support gathered behind it prior to the forming of the CES, are probably more important. As in the case of Old-Age Assistance, a precursor of the administration's program had been drafted and supported in Congress and had reflected existing policy debates at the state level.

Like Old Age Assistance, Aid to Dependent Children was constructed as a means-tested grant-in-aid program. This also was due in part to programs in existence. Because of mothers' pensions, with their state enabling laws and state and local administration, the proposals for ADC were designed with the best state mothers' pensions laws in mind. What is less apparent is why ADC, a program without previous support in Congress, found itself on the agenda at all. The reason is the existence of the Children's Bureau, which had studied inadequate mothers' pensions. Compare workmen's compensation, a state-level program that was far from perfect. That program was not being studied by the CES or overseen by any national-level bureau and was left out of the reform plans altogether. So, too, were proposals developed by the CES's medical care staff committee. The fact that the Children's Bureau researchers working on ADC were separated from the group working on OAA also led to some inconsistencies between otherwise similar "special assistance" proposals. The federal government was to match state-level OAA spending dollar for dollar, but was to provide only one-third of ADC grants.[57]

These state-level programs can be contrasted with the two major national innovations of the Second New Deal: old-age insurance and public employment. Although many states had developed means-tested old-age pensions by the middle of the 1930s, none had adopted old-age insurance. Public provision for the aged on the state and local levels of government was strictly a means-tested affair. The national government was free to experiment with an old-age insurance program. If it had failed, a means-tested system would have remained. The lack of controversy surrounding OAI allowed the CES experts to dictate the form of the program.[58] National old-age insurance had the same potential constitutional obstacles as national unemployment insurance, but the difference was that OAI was such a low priority that the Supreme Court was not an issue. Indeed, Witte himself was willing to sacrifice OAI in Congress, in order to smooth the passage of unemployment insurance. To uphold his end of a bargain he even prepared arguments against the OAI program for Senator William King of Utah![59] The person who cared most about the program was Roosevelt. The president demanded that the proposed taxes would pay for outlays. He also prevented Congress from removing the program from the security legislation and from crippling it with unfriendly amendments.[60]

In addition, permanent public employment programs were never part of policy makeup of states and localities. Although states and localities had been involved in cyclical, cost-effective public works in the nineteenth and early twentieth centuries, these programs focused on the content of the projects more than the employment they generated.[61] States and localities, moreover, had developed various works projects during the Depression, but these were stopgaps and not matters of permanent public policy, and by the time Roosevelt took office these units of government had reached their fiscal limits.[62] Thus the way was paved for the large scale experiments in national public employment that began with the Civil Works Administration in the winter of 1933 and 1934. These experiments in national public employment were followed by the more elaborate and institutionally stronger Works Progress Administration.

Reform-Oriented Regimes and the Enactment of the Work and Relief Policy

Political theories sometimes consider the U.S. Democrats to constitute a party of the political center, whose rule is expected to provoke moderate spending increases. I agree, but because of institutional variations across American polities, taking power in the American context usually means more than having a Democratic executive and a mere Democratic majority

in the legislature. At the national level, a pro–social spending regime requires the election of a president allied with the labor movement and other
insurgent political groups *and* a pro-spending majority in the legislature.
This group must be large enough to overcome resistance not only from Republicans, typically characterized as a party of the political Right, but also
from Democratic representatives of undemocratic regimes.[63] The group
must also overcome the indifference of Democrats from patronage-oriented
organizations.

For a number of reasons it was unlikely that Herbert Hoover would be
closely aligned with the reform of social policy. He was philosophically opposed to many forms of aid from the federal government, which he felt
squelched local and personal initiative. For him structural circumstances
dovetailed with personal philosophy. Hoover was long associated with the
low-tax policies of the Republican administrations of the 1920s and was
not closely aligned with either the labor movement or professional social
reform associations. Although like most American presidents of his era he
was more concerned with domestic than foreign policy, he had no previous
political record as being in favor of modern social policy, as he held no
previous elected political office. As secretary of commerce in the early 1920s
he had explored modern and moderate means to fight short-term unemployment, but his inquiry stopped short of unemployment insurance or any
large increases in expenditures to promote direct employment. Hoover was
also elected with the support of most states from the former Confederacy.[64]

Roosevelt has always been more difficult to figure out, and his personality comfortably embraced many a contradiction. He was the consummate
political artist, with an unnatural ability to envision the reactions of everyday people. But he was not temperamental; on the contrary, he maintained
an outwardly sunny disposition despite the enormous burdens of being a
political leader in a time of crisis. He seemed to care about people, but
harbored unlimited ambitions for himself. He went well out of his way to
avoid personal conflict, but once engaged in a struggle he could be ruth-
less. He was at once accessible and remote. He listened to many people
and seemed to agree with most of them, collecting their ideas like the stamps
in whose company he would spend hours. He considered friends many
people whom others might view as mere acquaintances. But he resisted inti-
macy with anyone—including his partner-wife Eleanor—and in the end
kept his own counsel. He reasoned more from the particular to the general
than the other way around. And so it was not always clear how any one
connection might be made. Anyone attempting to follow his reasoning over
a sustained period confronts inevitable questions: What was he thinking?
Was he thinking? It is in keeping with his character that he was an enthusiast for solitaire. Playing by himself, he still kept his cards close to the
vest. For him, the "New Deal" probably evoked the image of shuffling the
cards after a game had not come out, but the prospects for the next one
remained uncertain.

Perhaps all that means, though, is that as a leader he was probably un-likely to balk from personal conviction at structural situations. And these indicated that Franklin Roosevelt was going to be more favorably disposed to social policy reform than his predecessor. One reason was that he was the nominee of the Democratic party. To be sure, that party had not been in the vanguard of national and permanent social spending reform, but it did have its advantages. Democrats in Congress led the fight for emergency relief during the waning years of the Hoover regime. The nation's strongest social policy advocate, Senator Robert Wagner, was a New York Democratic leader. The party, too, supported unemployment insurance and old-age pensions in its 1932 platform. Most of all, the Democratic party was not the Republican party and thus not wedded to its policies of low taxation and to industrial and financial interest groups. Roosevelt, moreover, was an ear-nest champion of social policy reform as the governor of New York, follow-ing in the tradition of his predecessor Al Smith. Roosevelt had presided over the passage of New York's old-age pension legislation and the reorganiza-tion of its department of welfare. He also was in the forefront of providing emergency relief through the Temporary Emergency Relief Administration. For these reasons, he received support from many pro-spending people and groups. His philosophy of government as it developed in New York was that state and business should become and remain separate, in contradis-tinction to what he perceived to be happening under Hoover. Finally, he was not the choice of the conservative, business-oriented wing of the party, led by Jouett Shouse and John J. Raskob.[65]

Social spending results depend not only on the strength of the reform impulse of a president, but also on the mandate received. And Roosevelt was authorized by the voters to act on his agenda to a extent that probably exceeded his substantial orientation to reform. He was only the second Democratic president of his century and followed twelve years of Republi-can rule—freeing him from the policies of predecessors. And he won land-slides from the start, amassing in 1932 some 57.4 percent of the vote re-ceived by himself and Hoover. Roosevelt lost only six states in running up a victory in the electoral college victory of 473 to 59.[66]

The president needed, however, pro-spending congressional majorities to support his social legislation—or to force his hand by proposing some of its own. Not working in a parliamentary system, the Democratic party, a hodgepodge of local organizations, did not need to vote together to remain in office. Two sorts of Democrats were likely to defect from administration-sponsored social spending proposals. The segments of the party most likely to oppose national social policies were likely to be found in the South—where politics was largely undemocratic and there was little electoral reason for politicians to promote policies to aid the less well off. In the 1930s, for instance, 102 House seats were held by the South. A second group likely to defect were Democrats from patronage-oriented parties. In the thirteen states where these party organizations flourished, Democratic congressional

representatives might back social spending, but were unlikely to be enthusiastic supporters of the administration's reform proposals and might require
further inducements to grant their support.

Southern Democrats were basically unfriendly to social spending legislation that sought to grant nationally ensured rights to income to individuals
and often sought to stop or dilute it, including the Social Security Act.
Although in the end most southerners voted for the act, it was only after
significant changes had been made in it. The administration's security bill
had national generosity standards removed from it at the initiative of southern Democrats, notably Senator Harry F. Byrd of Virginia, in the House
and Senate spending committees. According to Witte, all southern members
of both committees opposed national standards in Old-Age Assistance.
Both Virginia senators sought to reduce appropriations for the WPA and
argued in favor of a less expensive and more locally controlled and degrading relief policy.[67]

Political Contingents for Reform

Despite Roosevelt's victory, the possibilities for social policy rested in
Congress, and the requirements for reformers or pro-social spenders to
dominate Congress were exacting. For those in favor of national social
spending policy with national standards to control the government a number of things had to happen simultaneously. First, it required effort from the
president, who could employ persuasion or favors to convince patronage-
oriented Democrats or moderate Republicans to support his domestic program. It was also necessary for Democrats, especially in the agrarian and
non–patronage party West, and third-party candidates to establish a strong
presence in Congress. It was helpful, too, for Democrats to win the House
districts where organized labor had a substantial electoral presence.[68] For
patronage-oriented Democrats with a well-organized labor constituency
might overcome their natural indifference to programmatic public spending. These contingents had to be large enough to overcome opposition to
social spending proposals—notably from Republicans and from southern
Democrats.

The unusual nature of the Congressional alignment in 1935 stands out
when seen in the context of the makeup of Congress from 1929 through
1936. Although the Democrats dominated for most of the period, party fortunes varied. The strongest Democratic representation in the Congress came
after the elections of 1934 and 1936. At the beginning of 1935, the Democrats had a majority of 216 in the House and 44 in the Senate. This result
belied the usual electoral principle that the president's party loses seats during the off-term election.

It is worth taking a closer look at the House, not because it was more
important intrinsically than the Senate, but for analytical purposes. To my

TABLE 3.1.
U.S. National Election Results, 1928–1934

	House			Senate			President
	Dem.	Rep.	Dem. Margin	Dem.	Rep.	Dem. Margin	
1928	167	267	−100	39	56	−17	Hoover, Republican 58.2%, 444–87 electoral
1930	220	214	6	47	48	−1	
1932	310	117	193	60	35	25	Roosevelt, Democrat 57.4%, 472–59 electoral
1934	319	103	216	69	25	44	

Sources: Congressional Quarterly, Guide to U.S. Congress (Washington, D.C.: Congressional Quarterly, 1985), p. 896. U.S. Bureau of the Census, Historical Statistics of the United States From Colonial Times to 1970 (Washington, D.C.: U.S. Government Printing Office, 1975), series Y 79–83, p. 1073.

way of thinking, a Democratic majority in the House does not mean a pro-social spending majority, for I expect the solidly Democratic southern delegation to Congress to be mainly unfriendly to generous national social spending proposals. Democrats from patronage party organizations might also defect from the administration's spending line, especially those from districts without countervailing influence from organized labor or mobilized challenges. Members of Congress elected by way of radical third parties are expected to champion spending initiatives, but were few in number.

The potential of reform forces in the House can be traced first by isolating Democratic representatives from democratic political systems and programmatic, "open" parties and representatives from radical third parties or endorsed by them. According to the institutional politics theory, a sizable contingent of these legislators is key to innovations in public social provision. Labeled "very probable pro-spenders," these legislators are posited to be steadfast in support of new permanent national commitments to citizens in social spending legislation. They are arrayed appropriately on the left side of Table 3.2. On the right side are Republicans from traditional, patronage party systems and Democrats from the nondemocratic South. These groups—"very probable anti-spenders"—are expected to be the least likely to support new national commitments in social spending and most likely to fight them. Also included in the category are representatives of conservative third parties or endorsed by them. In the middle left side of the table are less reliable allies of public spending. Patronage-oriented northern Democrats are counted as "probable pro-spenders," as are representatives running on both Democratic and Republican party lines. Northern Republicans from

TABLE 3.2
Pro– and Anti–Social Spending Contingents in the U.S. House of Representatives,
1931–1936

	Pro-Spending Members		Anti-Spending Members		
	Very Probable[a]	Probable[b]	Probable[c]	Very Probable[d]	Size of Pro-Spending Contingent[e]
1931–32	28	90	108	206	Small
1933–34	95	127	52	161	Medium
1935–36	99	135	44	157	Large

Source: Congressional Quarterly, Guide to U.S. Elections (Washington, D.C.: Congressional Quarterly, 1985), pp. 766–85.

[a] Includes radical third-party representatives, Democrats elected in open polities, and Democrats or Republicans affiliated with radical third parties.

[b] Includes Democrats affiliated with the Republican party and Democrats from states dominated by traditional patronage parties.

[c] Includes Republicans from open polities and Republicans affiliated with the Democratic Party.

[d] Includes Republicans from the South and from states dominated by traditional patronage-party organizations, Democrats or Republicans affiliated with conservative third parties, and southern Democrats.

[e] The size of the pro-spending contingent is a judgment based on the relative sizes of each grouping. See text for discussion.

open party systems, in the middle right part of the table, are counted as "probable anti-spenders." I envision these representatives as being susceptible to influence from the administration or insurgents, or both.

Given a reform-oriented president, the best case for social spending innovation is for a large very probable pro-spending contingent to coexist with a sizable probable pro-spending contingent. A moderately sized pro-spending group, when faced with less than an overwhelming anti-spending contingent, is also expected to produce significant if less dramatic gains in social spending legislation. When very probable anti-spenders are in a majority I expect no social policy or anti-spending legislation.

As Table 3.2 shows, the very probable pro-spenders never outnumbered the anti-spenders, but sometimes rivaled them in size. In 1935 through 1936, the high point of the period, the pro-spenders had 99 seats, as compared to 157 for the conservatives. Moreover, if one adds the probable pro-spenders to the reform group and the probable anti-spenders to the anti-reform group, the pro-spenders held a majority after 1933, though only a narrow one. By contrast, in 1931 through 1932, the right-wing combination numbered more than two hundred, almost a majority in themselves, and held office simultaneously with an anti–social policy president. It is no surprise that Hoover dragged his heels, even on short-term national relief with no permanent implications for social policy.

The final column of Table 3.2 provides a summary of the extent of the pro-spending forces, based not only on the makeup of the House of Representatives, but also on the existence of a reformer in the White House and the composition of the Senate. Accordingly, the period after 1935 is rated as having the largest pro-spending contingent. The period from 1933 through 1934 is judged to have been of moderate size, partly because the Senate had only a twenty-five-member Democratic majority. After the off-year 1934 elections, Roosevelt and proponents of spending reform inside and outside his administration were in an extremely favorable position. After 1935, pro-spenders and their likely allies numbered more than the 218 House members required to sign a discharge petition to bring any proposed bill to the floor of the House. With this sort of political configuration, the Roosevelt Administration and its supporters could overcome the opposition of Republicans and southern Democrats—on most social spending issues. It is therefore no surprise that the far-reaching Works Progress Administration was created and the Social Security Act was passed in 1935.

I am not trying to explain individual votes and voting records. The best evidence for my arguments is the pattern of social spending legislation—not specific votes on specific bills. Legislators can indicate lack of support by way of proposing unfriendly amendments, attempting to table legislation, speaking against it, and the full range of parliamentary maneuvers. Anti-spending members might in the end vote for a bill whose passage was inevitable, once they had done everything possible to stall or dilute it.

All the same, some evidence is consistent with my categories. Notable here was the formation of a thirty-five-member "liberal bloc" in the House in 1935. At the core of this bloc was the Wisconsin-Minnesota Progressive Group, which was led by Wisconsin's Gerald Boileau and included the seven-member Wisconsin Progressive delegation as well as three Minnesota Farmer-Labor representatives. The latter had been elected on the basis of a radical platform that called for the end of capitalism and very high social spending. The final member of the Progressive Group was Vito Marcantonio of New York, a Republican who also ran on the American Labor party line. The rest of the liberal bloc included mainly northern and western Democrats as well as a handful of progressive Republicans from the North and West. One of its most publicized leaders was Maury Maverick of San Antonio, Texas—the only southern member. The liberal bloc was especially cohesive on relief issues.[69]

The Democratic party controlled Congress for all but two years of the two decades. Because most southern congressmen had to die or lose interest to forfeit office, many were able to gain committee chairmanships and exercise power disproportionate to their numbers because of seniority. Southerners chaired, for instance, the crucial House Ways and Means Committee and the Senate Finance Committee. Such control colored the deliberations over and the pace of legislative developments. It gave southern Democrats opportunities to dilute the benefits in any social spending legislation and to limit national control in social policy, by providing a plausible threat to delay legislation and to stall the legislative machinery generally.

However, ensconcing southerners in important congressional chairmanships did not inoculate the polity against spending innovations. Some national proposals did make their way through Congress. After all, it took only a majority in the House to discharge a bill from committee during this period. When such threats were plausible, as they were when the Democrats so thoroughly dominated Congress, the anti–social spenders in leadership positions mainly tried to amend and modify legislation they could not stop. In any case, conservative leadership of many committees was basically *constant* from 1930 to 1950 and thus cannot explain why sometimes New Deal legislation advanced, and—the subject of later chapters—why legislation sometimes stalled or was reversed.[70] The structure of Congress provided anti-spenders with strategic positions from which they might fight the New Deal, but tremendous reform occurred all the same because it depended on the fates of reform-oriented representatives, notably radical third party representatives and Democrats from the nonpatronage north.

Social Movements and New Deal Policy

Social movement organizations and more spontaneous protest campaigns were rampant in Depression-era America. The unemployed, the aged, veterans, and workers were among the many groups that engaged in political action that challenged institutional politics and sought to influence public policy—joining already organized interests in this pursuit. But what was the impact of these movements and groups? To support a claim for a challenger's impact, one must be able to make a case that the innovations or changes in public policy would not have come about in the challenger's absence.

My institutional politics argument expects the impact of this collective action to be significant, but limited. Those groups that backed the New Deal would have to rely on the fate of the reform wing of the Democratic party for the passage of legislation. Those that worked outside and opposed the Democrats and the New Deal from the left had more localized effects. They might boost benefits in social spending policies to the constituencies of organized groups, but would have little say in the overall construction of policies and could not directly influence the passage of legislation. In addition, the influence of the challengers depended on the existence of strong or moderately powerful reform-oriented regimes. In the absence of such political formations, challengers would be expected to be less than influential.

Below I examine some of the more important movements of the 1930s and 1940s: the labor movement and the "money radical" challenges led by Senator Huey P. Long and Dr. Francis E. Townsend. I also discuss the implications of the failed mobilization of veterans and the passage of programs in the absence of social mobilization. As expected the impact of these groups depended on whether they supported or opposed the New Deal, whether their plans were consistent with the New Deal, and the existence and the strength of the reform-oriented regime.

The Labor Movement and Its Alliance with the New Deal

Before the Great Depression, American labor movements sought innovations in public spending policy, such as workmen's compensation in the 1910s and old-age pensions afterward. State federations of labor lobbied and sought to aid friends and punish political enemies. Moreover, the AFL supported compulsory state-level old-age pensions in 1929 and state-level Unemployment Compensation in 1932. Organized labor grew hand in hand with the New Deal.[71] But what impact did labor have on social policy in the New Deal and how was this impact felt?

The New Deal witnessed a labor upsurge, but the New Deal had as much influence on the upsurge as the latter had on the New Deal.[72] The early years of the Depression saw union members dropping to about 2.7 million in 1933 and isolated in large cities and in the railroad, printing, building, coal, and clothing industries. During the Roosevelt era, this trend was reversed and the labor movement prospered, despite the fact that economic hardship tends to weaken the bargaining power of workers. Section 7a of the National Industrial Recovery Act gave symbolic governmental sanction for unionization and collective bargaining, and these rights were made enforceable by the National Labor Relations Act of 1935 with its National Labor Relations Board.[73]

Organized labor at first had only minor influence. Key labor leaders were included on the twenty-three-member Advisory Council on Economic Security, which counted as members William Green, president of the AFL, and Henry Ohl, the president of the Wisconsin State Federation of Labor. The labor representatives were not major influences on the council, however, and they played little part in the shaping of the economic security bill. At the time, there were no experts on social policy in the employ of the AFL. When the bill was introduced, labor was not among its sponsors, but labor leaders had been consulted, were in favor of the bill, and aided its passage.[74] Though favorable to the idea of work relief, moreover, leaders of the AFL criticized the proposed Works Progress Administration because of the "security" wages it would pay. The AFL much preferred the CWA, with its nonrelief workforce and its "prevailing" wages. With others, labor successfully sought amendments to provide prevailing wage rates in the WPA.[75]

The rise of the labor movement made it a force to be reckoned with in politics. Labor's alliances with the Roosevelt Administration, the Democratic party, and New Deal administrative agencies constituted the most important way labor aided social spending reform. Section 7a of the NIRA and the National Labor Relations Act cemented the alliance between labor and the national Democratic party. The AFL in turn supported the economic security bill and helped its cause by opposing alternatives, such as the so-called Lundeen bill, which called for expensive relief provisions to a wide segment of the unemployed, and the Townsend bill. Although labor did little in the way of formulating policy, its support for the Roosevelt Administration's programs made it more likely that they would prevail. It helped that labor's champion, Senator Wagner, was the cosponsor of the economic security bill, as well as other initiatives in employment policy and public spending.[76]

The Roosevelt Administration encouraged both unionization and public spending in order to build a long-term, winning electoral coalition. The organization of workers in turn helped to provide support for the administration's public policy objectives, but most of this support was to come after 1935. For the most part strikes of workers were designed to achieve organization, and labor's organizing did not advance in earnest until after Wagner Act. Labor did not seriously bid to organize industrial workers until the creation of the CIO in 1936—after most of the Second New Deal reforms.[77]

Huey P. Long's Share Our Wealth Movement and
"Soak-the-Rich" Taxation

Other challengers took a more defiant stance toward the New Deal and hoped to push it further left. In 1934, Senator Huey Long, a radical critic of the New Deal, began to promote his Share Our Wealth plan in earnest over the radio and declared the inauguration of a society of the same name. By February 1935 Long claimed that more than 7,500,000 people had joined more than 27,000 Share Our Wealth clubs. A folksy political operator who had enhanced his natural rhetorical endowments by selling cooking oil and fighting workmen's compensation cases, Long had gained political control in Louisiana. In April 1935, the Democratic National Committee (DNC) conducted a secret mock presidential poll, and the chairman of the DNC, James Farley, thought Long might win "three or four million votes" in the 1936 election. According to Raymond Moley, a probusiness adviser to Roosevelt who eventually broke with the New Deal, the president supposedly said that the Second New Deal was devised to "steal Long's thunder."[78]

Ascertaining the accuracy of that claim requires further consideration of the man and his movement. Share Our Wealth had two goals. It sought to redistribute income from the rich to the poor. The program, also known as Share Our Wealth or the Long Plan, limited wealth to $3 million through direct taxation. With the revenues so generated, every family would be staked to what Long liked to call a "homestead": about five thousand dollars to purchase a house, car, and radio—the necessities of middle-class life as redefined by the 1920s. To secure these claims, Long also guaranteed an annual income of two thousand dollars to three thousand dollars. Those sixty-five years and older would receive pensions of thirty dollars a month or more, and World War I veterans' "bonuses," due in 1945, would be immediately paid. The Long Plan would increase the minimum wage and limit hours for workers, purchase and store agricultural goods from farmers, and provide scholarships to students.[79]

Share Our Wealth also shouldered the ample ambitions of Long, who hoped it would carry him to the presidency. The organization was based in Louisiana, and the clubs there—perhaps as many as one-fourth of the total— resembled local political machines. Through fund-raising in Louisiana— mainly mandatory deductions from the paychecks of state employees—the senatorial frank, radio speeches, and the road trips of his confederate Rev. Gerald L. K. Smith, Long was able to spread his message to other states. Elsewhere Share Our Wealth was less well organized. Any two people could begin a "society," and members were not required to pay dues and received for free the movement newspaper, the *American Progress*. The largely autonomous clubs had many potential uses: a center to protest Roosevelt Administration policies, a lever to install Share Our Wealth planks in the Democratic platform, or a springboard for a third-party challenge.[80]

Roosevelt monitored these developments closely—thus the secret poll. Emil Hurja, the DNC pollster, saw a tight race: Roosevelt with 49.3 percent of the vote, the Republican 42.5 percent, and Long 7.4 percent. Roosevelt would win in thirty-three states with 305 electoral votes, and the Republican would win in fifteen states with 226 electoral votes. If Long was drawing support only from the left, as everyone from Hurja to *Time* speculated, the poll suggested that he would transfer five states, including New York, and 122 electoral votes to the Republican candidate. According to these results, it would take only the defection of Michigan, Iowa, and Minnesota—where Roosevelt held a lead of 7 percentage points or less—to swing the election.[81]

To check Long the president may have adopted some parts of the Long Plan or similarly redistributive programs. Yet Long and Share Our Wealth had little influence on the planning and content of the economic security bill—which took place before the polling. And most historical accounts agree that Long and Share Our Wealth did not place these programs on the political agenda.[82] T. Harry Williams, Long's biographer, and the historian Arthur Schlesinger, Jr., however, see the influence of Long on Roosevelt's tax message of June 19.[83] At that time the president unexpectedly demanded the passage of a Treasury Department plan to tax extremely high incomes at a stiff rate, raise inheritance and gift taxes, tax undistributed dividends of corporations, and increase and make more graduated the corporation income tax. In addition, though, Schlesinger argues that the character of the taxes owed more to Louis Brandeis than Long, because of their bids to slow the growth of large corporations. Another part of the Share Our Wealth program—the early payment of veterans' bonuses—had to wait, however, until Roosevelt ended his fight against it. By then Long had been dead for a year.

All in all, Share Our Wealth had a stimulant influence on Second New Deal policy, but one that was limited and contingent. No Second New Deal proposal resembled closely any part of the Long plan. But Roosevelt did advance something unexpected—the tax proposal. Although this so-called "soak-the-rich" tax measure did not threaten the truly wealthy and the revenues from it could not finance Long's ambitious program, the measure broke the pattern of regressive New Deal taxation initiatives.[84] Share Our Wealth could not have had much influence, however, without the existence of a reform administration and a pro-spending Congress. Under most other circumstances, a president might have had neither the inclination nor the power to preempt a challenger bidding for economic redistribution. Long began making his demands when Hoover was president. But Roosevelt was a reformer building a new coalition for power and thus willing to bend in the direction of redistribution, and he was backed by a decisively Democratic Congress, and so his proposals resulted in new laws. Such were the politics of stealing thunder.

The Townsend Movement and the Politics of Old-Age Pensions

Francis E. Townsend and his aged followers also challenged the New Deal. On one level, the Townsend Movement was an utter failure. The movement was centered on the so-called Townsend Plan: two hundred dollars per month for any Americans sixty years or older, so long as they did not work and spent the money within the month. But the plan never passed. A physician who had migrated from Illinois to California and was left unemployed by the Depression, Townsend seemed the embodiment of the rootlessness and despair critics detected in participants in feckless collective behavior. All the same, the Townsendites, as they sometimes called themselves, have been acclaimed by scholars and contemporaries as having a major effect on American old-age spending. Townsend agreed. After a decade of organization and agitation, he claimed that because of his Movement, "the aged people of this nation today are receiving millions of dollars annually in old-age pensions. . . ."[85] Did his Movement have such a great impact on New Deal social policy? Was he the hero for the aged that he claimed to be?

In September 1933 Townsend revealed his plan, which braided recovery, relief, and reform around a homespun supply-side and demand-side economics. The plan would solve poverty in old age by throwing money at it. It would reduce unemployment by removing the aged from the job market, while stimulating the economy with enforced spending. In January 1934 Townsend created the not-for-profit "Old Age Revolving Pensions Ltd." (OARP), run by himself known as the "founder," and the Movement's self-styled "cofounder," Robert Clements, a real-estate agent. At the beginning of 1935, as the Committee on Economic Security finished its deliberations,

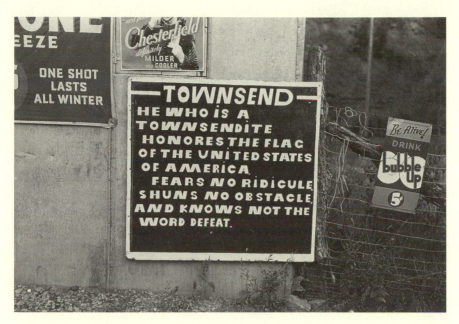

Plate 3.2 "He Who Is a Townsendite . . ." (Russell Lee). The Townsend Movement promoted old-age pensions of two hundred dollars per month. More than a million of the American elderly, men and women, joined Townsend clubs by the beginning of 1936. A homemade Colorado sign indicates some of the principles espoused by at least one "Townsendite."

a Townsend bill was written, calling for the pensions to be funded by a "transactions" tax, which amounted to a multiple sales tax.[86]

The Townsend Plan had many critics. The political Left argued that the transactions tax was regressive. The Right feared that the plan would undermine profits and the incentive to work. Scholars and policy experts felt that the tax would not produce enough revenue to fund large pensions.[87] Witte of the CES wrote a report entitled "Why the Townsend Old-Age Revolving Pension Plan is Impossible" and provided members of Congress with statistical ammunition against it.[88] The 1935 Townsend bill was rejected handily in the House, mainly along partisan lines, Democrats in opposition, 206–56. Many western members wanted neither to support the bill, nor to go on record opposed. Representatives from other parts of the country were not so obliged.

One sign that the Townsend Movement cannot be held to account for Second New Deal social policy is the pattern of its membership and political activity. The first club appeared in August 1934, and Movement membership made its greatest leap in the second half of 1935, *after* the passage of the Social Security Act. Also, it was only that summer that OARP began to spread significantly beyond the West. In early 1936 its paid membership

peaked, probably at about one million of the aged. The Townsendites' political action centered on endorsing congressional candidates—Republicans
and Democrats—in favor of the plan. Chosen by the national leadership,
the selections were publicized in the *Townsend National Weekly* and
backed in rallies. In 1934, however, the policy was far from systematic, and
in 1936 the strategy was so ineffective that the movement failed to endorse
even half of those who voted for the plan in 1935.[89]

Tallying the balance sheet on the Movement's early impact may be aided
by comparing its impact in three different areas—the political agenda of
old-age policy, the content of proposals, and support for them in Congress.
The Movement may have prevented old-age security from leaving the
agenda of the CES by protesting a statement by Roosevelt in November
1934 that hinted that old-age proposals were going to be delayed.[90] It also
seems likely that Old-Age Assistance was made more generous by Movement activity. The OAA provisions of the economic security legislation
compared favorably to the Dill-Connery bill of the previous year in the
amount of money and in the matching formula. Because of the Townsend
mobilization, moreover, members of Congress probably were more willing
to support the Social Security Act generally. The Movement may also have
made the Roosevelt Administration more determined to force the passage of
the less popular old-age insurance program. There is little doubt that the
Movement speeded the process by which the Social Security Board approved state plans for OAA in early 1936.[91]

Nevertheless, the Movement was not the main force behind putting old-
age legislation on the political agenda, on specifying the content of legislation, or in getting it passed in Congress. The Movement appeared after the
first Dill-Connery bill placed, in 1933, means-tested old-age pensions on the
national political agenda, and the CES had planned at the outset to address
old-age spending. The old-age spending programs that passed corresponded
only marginally to the Townsend Plan: old-age insurance was to be based
on previous wages; OAA was means-tested. The Movement opposed old-
age insurance, but neither the Movement nor other opponents could remove it from the bill. The Townsendites did not mobilize in earnest until
after the Social Security Act, and their regional isolation meant that only
western representatives feared opposing the Townsend bill. Townsend himself was treated roughly in Congress. In the *New Yorker*, E. B. White wrote
that the way that the doctor came undone during questioning called to mind
an "inexpensive toy."[92]

Matters were soon to get worse. In early 1936 Congress convened a
Special Committee to Investigate Old-Age Pension Organizations and
aimed it directly at Townsend. His supporters were shocked to learn that
the *Townsend National Weekly* was run by a for-profit concern, the unfortunately named Prosperity Publishing Company, owned by Townsend and
Clements. The "cofounder" cleared seventy thousand dollars from it at the

expense of the loyal Townsendites. Another unhappy revelation for this quasi-religious crusade was that the northern California organizer had been indicted for bootlegging and pimping. Membership drives stalled, and the OARP's income plummeted. Convinced that the president had ordered the investigation, Townsend joined the former Long associate Reverend Smith and Father Charles E. Coughlin in a campaign to unseat Roosevelt in 1936. But the resulting Union party candidacy of William Lemke was a disaster.[93] In its salad days, then, the Movement helped to keep OAA on the administration's menu, to whet congressional appetites for OAA, and to provide more for the aged and more rapidly than was the case with other "deserving unemployables." As with Share Our Wealth, the Townsend Movement's actions were intensified by a favorable political alignment. In claiming all that he did, Townsend may have given himself and his eponymous challenge too much credit. Still, in 1936 he was far from finished.

Aid to Dependent Children, the Bonus Army, and the Limits to Social Mobilization

If widespread social mobilization is always expected to affect public policy and if public policy changes are expected to be due to social mobilization, the New Deal provides two anomalies. The first is the adoption of Aid to Dependent Children. This program did not have any movement or organized group outside the state demanding it. Even labor stayed out of the fight. If social protest were the only route to public spending innovations, ADC would not have happened. By contrast, a well-organized and highly threatening protest movement worked to little effect—the crusade of World War veterans. The creation of ADC suggests that a reform-oriented regime and state policy administrators can effect social policies even without widespread social protest to back them up. The failure of the veterans' protest suggests that well-mobilized challengers demanding benefits inconsistent with the president's plans are likely to be resisted during the rule of a reform-oriented regime.

Two groups that might have had an impact on the debate over ADC were the General Federation of Women's Clubs (GFWC) and the National Congress of Mothers (NCM). These women's organizations supported and may have effected the passage of state-level mothers' pensions legislation in the Progressive Era.[94] However, these organizations were mainly demobilized on this issue during the 1930s, and what little support they provided came at the urging of the Children's Bureau. For example, when the NCM, known by 1935 as the National Congress of Parents and Teachers (NCPT), was prevailed upon by the Children's Bureau to testify in the House of Representatives, the organization's representative admitted that none of its state branches had called for a national program to aid children without breadwinning fathers.[95] All in all, very little about the creation of ADC can be

Plate 3.3 Applications for the Bonus (Dorothea Lange). World War I veterans were finally granted the early payment of their adjusted compensation certificates, or bonuses, in 1936, after the Roosevelt Administration had cut veterans' benefits in the Economy Act of 1933. Here veterans pick up applications for their bonus payments at a local American Legion post on New York's Lower East Side.

explained by group mobilization. There was no strongly mobilized group outside the state actively promoting ADC or anything like it.

By contrast, World War veterans were highly mobilized across the country, but were mainly thwarted by social policy in the Depression. Veterans formed the Bonus Expeditionary Army in 1932 to demand the early payment of Adjusted Compensation Certificates, which were passed in 1924 and due to be paid in 1945. The Bonus Army, which included many veterans' families, encamped in Washington in the spring of 1932, but Hoover sent the army under the command of Douglas MacArthur to scatter the protestors. When the Bonus Army massed again the next year, Roosevelt may have sent his wife to greet it, but he also called for the passage of the Na-

tional Economy Act of 1933, which gave him the power to implement severe cuts in existing veterans' benefits. When veterans received at long last
the "early" payment of their bonus in 1936—nine years before the bonus
was due to be paid—it was already seven years into the Depression and five
years after they had begun to demand it. The cuts in long-term military pensions courtesy of the Economy Act remained policy.[96]

BUSINESSMEN'S FAILED QUEST TO STOP THE SECOND NEW DEAL

Businessmen also moved to influence the New Deal.[97] They had greater access to the state than did challengers, and, unlike them, capitalists and their
organizations had vast economic resources to sway policy debates. Roosevelt was far more likely to consult business officials, such as the ubiquitous
Gerard Swope of General Electric, than protest leaders, such as Townsend,
whom Roosevelt slighted. There were various governmental institutions—
the Business Advisory Council (BAC) of the Department of Commerce and
the Advisory Council on Economic Security—through which businessmen
might gain influence over public policy. Furthermore, there were long-
standing national- and state-level peak associations of businessmen, as well
as trade associations, each of which had applied pressure in the past. In
addition, some prominent industrial leaders also inaugurated a mass organization, the American Liberty League (ALL).

The inside track did not help much. Neither the Business Advisory Council nor the capitalists on the Advisory Council on Economic Security had
much effect on the Second New Deal. BAC proposals were "habitually dis-
regarded."[98] The capitalists on the twenty-three-member Advisory Council—Swope, Morris E. Leeds of Leeds and Northrup, Walter Teagle of
Standard Oil, and Marion Folsom, of Eastman Kodak—were indeed more
active than the labor members. Yet the Advisory Council was consulted
near the end of the CES's deliberations to provide the appearance of widespread public support and had little impact on the capitalists' main concern:
the unemployment compensation provisions in the security bill.[99] A term
sometimes used for failures in the more difficult struggles of social movements seems to apply here: cooptation.

Did capital influence the formulation of proposals through their funding
of private foundations and research? It seems highly unlikely. The experts
involved in studying and drafting legislation were not reliable allies of
capital and had positions that provided protection from retribution.[100] In
any case, as we have seen the staff experts themselves were invited to
participate relatively late in the proceedings, by Roosevelt Administration
officials who devised plans first and sought academic support for them
later. More important than that, American policy experts in the 1930s did
not have to invent social insurance or public assistance, exploiting an ad-

vantage of backwardness—the ability to study the more advanced programs of other countries.[101]

At the other extreme in the spectrum of influence, the bid to mobilize the masses against the New Deal through the ALL was a failure as pathetic as it was extravagant. Formed in 1934, the ALL included among its founders James M. Beck, a House representative, Will Stayton, the head of the Association Against the Prohibition Amendment, and Pierre Du Pont. Other members included conservative Democrats Al Smith, John W. Davis, and Jouett Shouse, each estranged from the New Deal. The ALL national advisory council included Du Pont, Alfred P. Sloan, and Ernest Weir, and the Du Ponts and General Motors backed the ALL, which spent more than one million dollars. The league, with its quixotic acronym, aspired to win four million members from the general public. Suggesting that liberty meant freedom from the sort of governmental aid on which many Americans were relying, its message was poorly received. The ALL gained only about 150,000 members at its peak. It reached the front page of the *New York Times* some thirty-five times, but the coverage was mainly unfavorable.[102] The League closed up shop for good in 1940 having profited little from its imprudent investment in mass organizing.

Organized capital's offensive against the economic security bill in early 1935 revealed its relative helplessness against a reform-oriented regime. In February 1935, representatives of peak and trade associations converged on Washington to attack the security bill before the U.S. Senate Committee on Finance. These groups ranged from the National Association of Manufacturers to the National Metal Trades Association to the Ohio Chamber of Commerce to the Laundryowners National Association. L. C. Morrow, who opposed the bill for the National Publishers Association, produced letters he solicited from trade association leaders. His summary of the results of his research could not have been more pointed: "[that] any sudden imposition of a pay-roll tax up to 5 percent, which is proposed by the bill, would retard recovery [and] that industry and the business [sic] should appreciate very much, very slow action in regard to the bill, particularly old-age pensions and unemployment security." H. Walter Forster opposed old-age insurance taxes on behalf of four hundred companies with pension plans—supposedly the most liberal of capitalists. The only trade group in favor was the transparently motivated National Retail Dry Goods Association.[103]

Because of the access of organized capital and its superior command of organizational resources, it was able to influence the Second New Deal at the margins. The lobbying and congressional counterattack was influential in diluting the security legislation—notably, through the lowering of payroll taxes for Unemployment Compensation from 5 percent to 3 percent and the inclusion of "merit rating" to make possible the further lowering of those taxes.[104] Other efforts were effective only up to a point. A proposal, written by Forster, to exempt from the OAI taxes companies with pension plans was embodied in the so-called Clark amendment, which passed the

Plate 3.4 "Less Taxes = More Jobs" (Marion Post Wolcott). The Chamber of Commerce opposed, unsuccessfully, most of Roosevelt's Second New Deal because increased social spending implied higher taxes. The chamber and the National Association of Manufacturers took their case to everyday people through billboards such as these that appeared across the country.

Senate. All in all, though, the impact of organized capital's offensive was minor. The Clark amendment was deleted in the conference committee, at the instigation of Roosevelt, and the attempt of organized business to remove the security legislation from the political agenda—what Morrow of the publishers' association meant by "very slow action"—was rebuffed.[105]

CONCLUSION

The Second New Deal of 1935 is often considered *the* social spending reform period in U.S. history, because of the Social Security Act and its old-age insurance and Aid to Dependent Children programs. But the social policy of the Second New Deal was centered neither on social insurance for the aged, nor on welfare for dependent children. Nor was New Deal social policy designed to combine the two in an explicitly two-track scheme. What was built instead was an incipient work and relief state. U.S. social policy centered on means-tested work programs, mainly for able-bodied men, and federal-state public assistance programs for special categories of Americans, deserving of aid, but presumed to be of limited economic usefulness. The latter were to be provided stipends and removed or retired from the labor force. The United States was spending unprecedented sums, but not on OAI, which had yet to pay out benefits. The money mainly went to the unemployed through the WPA and to the aged through OAA, the means-tested program. All of this came at a cost, as general relief was turned back to the states and localities.

Although the Depression colored the New Deal work and relief policy, the proximate causes of it were state actors and previous policies and a re-form-oriented political regime. State actors planned reforms, studied their ramifications, and justified them before Congress. For these reasons these actors spurred social spending and had a great impact on the content of policy. Yet they could not create a new public spending system from scratch. Previous policies and a lack of centralized planning abilities both limited and channeled these actors. The Committee on Economic Security was greatly fragmented and had to contend with a congressional agenda for social spending as well as with state-level initiatives. Programs at the state and local levels of government, such as means-tested old-age pensions, had already gained political support and proposing to nationalize them was not feasible. Which programs reached the agenda of planners also depended on national-level bureaucratic capacities. Without the Children's Bureau, notably, Aid to Dependent Children would not have been included in the security legislation.

Whether social policy innovations would be enacted depended on the existence of a reform-oriented political regime. Enacting social policy depended on the efforts of the president and congressional Democrats, mainly those from the North. The president, a former New York governor in the forefront of social policy, was leading a Democratic party that had been out of power for most of the century. He had beaten the representative of a dominant Republican regime based on its alliance with industrial interests and its long-standing opposition to the income tax. During the middle 1930s, Democrats from outside the undemocratic South mainly controlled Congress and oversaw the enactment of the initial legislation of American social policy and some extensions of it. Despite the efforts of the new regime to include previously excluded or ignored citizens, America's status as a democratic laggard made it difficult to construct and maintain a pro–social spending regime. But that is getting ahead of the story.

Social movements ranging from unemployed workers to the aged pressed demands on the government and also influenced the New Deal work and relief policy, but their impact was indirect. The impact of organized labor on aiding the passage of New Deal reforms was perhaps the most crucial and was realized mainly through an alliance with the administration. Labor supported the administration and its Democratic allies and the fate of social spending depended on the fate of the Democrats. Other movements, more critical of the New Deal, had varied impacts. In advancing legislative proposals that stood to the left of administration-backed or congressional alternatives, these movements drew attention to their issues and often induced the upgrading of proposals. As a result, the value of new reform legislation was greater for groups well mobilized than for groups less well mobilized or demobilized. Nevertheless, it seems likely that reforms would have been adopted in the absence of these protest groups. Major protest movements, such as the Bonus Army of World War I veterans, worked to little effect, and some major reforms of the New Deal were adopted in the absence of sustained protest. Notably, the Works Progress Administration emerged largely after the demobilization of the unemployed workers, and Aid to Dependent Children, the eventual centerpiece of welfare, emerged in the absence of societal collective action for it.

No coherent fragments of U.S. business systematically planned or supported the New Deal relief state. Just the opposite was true. Through trade associations, peak organizations, and the heavily funded but ill-fated American Liberty League, capital threw its economic might against the New Deal, including its social spending programs. But these programs were enacted anyway. However, organized capital diminished the worth of New Deal proposals in 1935. It would try for more later.

The work of the reformers was far from complete, however. They needed to place the programs on a sounder administrative footing. Authority for social spending was scattered in bureaus and agencies throughout the executive branch. Also, the removal of merit standards in administration of grant-in-aid programs was a potentially serious problem. The Social Security Board also had to monitor and assess how the states of the Union responded to the myriad incentives and exhortations to support adopt social policy. This would have been necessary even if the "decency and health" standards had remained in the legislation. It also remained to be seen whether the deal of ending general relief in exchange for providing work relief at the national level would work. What is more, social policy needed to be placed on a sounder fiscal footing. Reformers hoped that the president and his congressional allies would be reelected in 1936 to make good on the promise that was the New Deal work and relief policy.

CHAPTER FOUR

Consolidating the Work and Relief Policy, 1937–1939

> I see one-third of a nation ill-housed, ill-clad, ill-nourished. It is not in despair that I paint you that picture. I paint it for you in hope—because the nation, seeing and understanding the injustice in it, proposed to paint it out. . . . Overwhelmingly, we of the Republic are men and women of good will . . . [and] will insist that every agency of popular government use effective instruments to carry out their will.
>
> —*Franklin D. Roosevelt, January 20, 1937*

> I am as anxious as any banker or industrialist or business man or investor or economist that the budget of the United States Government be brought into balance as quickly as possible. But I lay down certain conditions which seem reasonable and which I believe all should accept. . . . The first condition is that we continue the policy of not permitting any needy American who can and is willing to work to starve because the Federal Government does not provide the work.
>
> —*Franklin D. Roosevelt, January 5, 1938*

FRANKLIN ROOSEVELT was reelected in 1936, but soon afterward it seemed as if the Roosevelt magic had evaporated.[1] His first major initiative in 1937 was a failed bid to transform or "pack" the Supreme Court. In the fall an economic downturn began that the president's critics labeled the Roosevelt Depression. In 1938 Congress rejected legislation to give the president a free hand to reorganize the executive branch of government. Congressional elections that year began with Roosevelt's failed "purge" of anti–New Deal Democrats and ended with a big swing in seats to the Republicans. Afterward, it is argued, congressional power was grasped by a conservative coalition of Republicans and Southern Democrats with one objective: to stymie the New Deal. For all these reasons, this period is viewed as relatively unproductive of reform. In his political biography of Roosevelt, for instance, the political scientist James MacGregor Burns refers to this chapter of history as the "Deadlock on the Potomac." The historian William Leuchtenburg calls it "Stalemate."[2] Roosevelt's second term is also sometimes called the "late" New Deal—with its connotations of defeat and demise.

The Supreme Court and reorganization battles did reveal Roosevelt to be a political mortal, and his second term was not the unbroken string of triumphs that was his first. All the same, social policy reform in the second Roosevelt term can easily be overlooked by comparing it too closely to the Second New Deal—which was unprecedented in American history for its productivity in social legislation. In comparison to almost any other period in the century, the end of the 1930s remains remarkable for its social policy achievements. During this time, moreover, Roosevelt's brand of progressive liberalism changed. As the historian Alan Brinkley argues, the New Deal after 1937 centered on social policy and its residual economic benefits, not the industrial planning of the First New Deal or the trust-busting of the second.[3] Losses over some issues translated into lost prestige for the president and count against his lofty legislative record. But those failures did not necessarily mean harm to social policy.

Just the opposite was true. What the historian Barry Dean Karl calls the "Third" New Deal was no stalemate with respect to new social legislation and institutional reform.[4] Wages and hours legislation helped to inform and reinforce the president's idea of a national minimum income and an American standard of living. The administration, moreover, reaffirmed its commitment to its work programs, and amendments to the Social Security Act strengthened programs for the "unemployable." By any quantitative measure, moreover, social policy was on the rise. The number of WPA recipients jumped over 3 million in 1938. Near the end of the decade, the United States became a world leader in social spending.

Even the failures were not entirely in vain and resulted in developments more mundane but necessary for the progress of social policy. The attempt to pack the Supreme Court ended with its acquiescence to the New Deal. The permanent reforms of the Second New Deal were not going to be ruled unconstitutional as the more experimental legislation of the First New Deal often had been. Roosevelt's bid to shift power within the national state made possible the fight for wages and hours legislation—which was passed. The failed reorganizational legislation, moreover, was followed by a less radical bill that succeeded and was far from insignificant. To secure legislative commitments between the state and citizenry though social policy requires administrative machinery. That is what the president meant by "effective instruments." In 1939, these were readied to allow Roosevelt, political artist that he was, to paint out the pecuniary problems of one-third of a nation.

The Third New Deal, in short, expanded and consolidated the work and relief policy of the Second New Deal. The period witnessed not the death or decline of New Deal social policy, but its maturation. To be sure, social policy reform did not move at the same rapid pace that it had during the

Second New Deal—especially after 1938. And the Third New Deal also saw the beginning of the separation of taxation and spending policies—as the administration sought spending increases without worrying about budget balances. But the advances were far more significant than the declines.

In this chapter I explore the extension and consolidation of American social policy in the late New Deal. I argue, too, that the institutional and political factors that help to explain the origins of social policy also matter here. The processes by which the New Deal social policy was expanded and consolidated resembled the processes by which it was created. I also want to analyze the nature of this social policy, based on work and relief. Like the economy, social policy had seemingly stabilized by the end of the decade. It is worth inquiring further into the types of support this social policy provided, the kinds of people and groups that were privileged by it, and the images and sorts of social relations it sanctioned for Americans. The work and relief policy provided protection from markets that had radical possibilities. At the same time American social policy was underfunded and could not make good on its promises. What is more, despite attempts to the contrary, the policy did little to undermine unequal gender relations and was far from completely fair in its differential treatment of groups.

THE EXTENSION AND CONSOLIDATION OF THE WORK AND RELIEF POLICY

The Lost Battle over the Supreme Court and the Fair Labor Standards Act

Soon after his second inauguration Roosevelt took on the Supreme Court, attempting to enhance its efficiency, as he saw it, or to "pack" it with New Deal supporters, as opponents viewed it. Most historians agree that Roosevelt's bid to reconfigure the court was disingenuous at best and cynical at worst. Most also agree, however, that the attempt was rooted in the president's frustration over the court's eagerness to overturn the New Deal. The National Recovery Administration (NRA) was thrown out in 1935, as was the Agricultural Adjustment Administration. The next year saw the rejection of the Guffey Coal Conservation Act and soon after that a New York state minimum wage law. The Committee on Economic Security had worried that the social insurance parts of its economic security bill would be subject to rejection by the court, and these decisions seemed to confirm these fears. According to Leuchtenburg, these decisions also "suggested that the Wagner Act would not survive a test in the courts, and that a wages and hours law was out of the question."[5]

The Supreme Court, especially Justice Owen Roberts as it happened, seemingly reacted to the political pressure. After Roosevelt announced his plan, Roberts began to rule in favor of New Deal legislation. In March, he joined the opinion to uphold a Washington state minimum wage law, ensuring a five-to-four victory. Soon afterward the Wagner Act was declared constitutional by the same margin with the same divisions of opinion. In May, two decisions similarly validated Unemployment Compensation (UC) and old-age insurance (OAI). Roberts's switch may not have been due to Roosevelt's plan and may not have doomed the president to a political defeat. But in the absence of Roosevelt's bold but ill-conceived plan it seems possible that much of the Second New Deal would have been wiped out, going the way of much of the First New Deal. It may also be true that Roosevelt's move crystalized opposition among conservative Democrats that might have remained dormant. But given the president's goals, it seems highly likely that organized opposition was coming sooner or later. What is certain is that by the middle of 1937 judicial obstacles to the completion of an American welfare state were removed for good. Never again would the Supreme Court strike down a significant piece of social legislation.[6]

The administration followed quickly on these decisions to introduce national wages and hours legislation. This legislation resulted in protracted struggles. The key one was between southern legislators who demanded that the minimum wage provide a "differential," or a lower standard, for the South and organized labor which would not stand for one. Opponents of the bill managed to dilute the legislation in various ways, including the exception of numerous industries from the law. Nevertheless, in the spring of 1938 the Fair Labor Standards Act passed without the wage differential.[7] Although the forty-cent-per-hour minimum wage was low and many industries could avoid it, the wage rate provided an immediate raise to 12 million Americans and, just as important, constituted the first official commitment to an American standard of living. This standard could be used as a baseline for social spending programs—a possibility that was not lost on its opponents.

The Triumph of the Spenders and Social Policy Progress in the Third New Deal

Social policy progress was promoted by the Roosevelt Administration's new approach to government spending. Although Roosevelt had reluctantly adopted deficit spending as a temporary expedient, through 1937 he continued to balance the "nonemergency" budget annually and made progress in balancing the overall budget. In the midst of an economic downturn on his watch, however, Roosevelt reversed course to follow a policy of government spending and the deliberate creation of deficits.

Although these ideas were associated with the recent theories of the English economist John Maynard Keynes, Roosevelt was far from a convert.

His meeting with Keynes in 1934 had gone badly, with Keynes questioning Roosevelt's economic literacy and Roosevelt dismissing Keynes as an impractical mathematician. The president was convinced more by administration "spenders"—who were mostly unfamiliar with Keynes—who thought that government spending would provide people with money to buy things, which in turn would reverse the downturn. The spenders' stronghold was an unlikely one from today's vantage point—the Federal Reserve Board, led by Marriner Eccles, a Utah businessman, and his assistant Lauchlin Currie. A more important advocate was Harry Hopkins, whose Works Progress Administration (WPA) had previously taken the brunt of Roosevelt's sacrifices to the idol of fiscal orthodoxy. The president's tilt toward the spenders in April 1938 came much to the dismay of his old friend Henry Morgenthau, the secretary of the treasury and a believer in balanced budgets. Something new was needed, though, as four million rapidly joined the ranks of the unemployed during what the administration termed a "recession," a euphemism of a euphemism.[8]

One program that seemingly gained from the political economics of Roosevelt's new fiscal thinking was the WPA. Public employment policies were pursued with renewed vigor as Roosevelt reversed course to give the WPA a role resembling the one originally envisioned for it by the Committee on Economic Security (CES). In his fiscal program of April 1938, Roosevelt's first demand was for an additional $1.25 billion for the WPA, and he also called for additional funds for the National Youth Administration (NYA), Civilian Conservation Corps (CCC), and Farm Security Administration. Appropriations for the WPA increased sharply in 1938. Employment under the WPA reached 3.35 million in November.[9]

This policy turn was ratified by a more unlikely source. A 1938 Special Senate Committee to Investigate Unemployment and Relief led by Senator James F. Byrnes of South Carolina, no friend of Hopkins and the WPA, also endorsed the program. The committee justified the centrality of the WPA, despite the first payments being made through the unemployment compensation programs. The committee's report suggested that the two programs would work together, as in Roosevelt's initial conception of them. Unemployed workers whose benefits were running out would be provided work.[10]

Social Policy Advances Despite the 1938 Elections

Even after the seating of the 1939 Congress, with its additional Republicans, social spending progress did not grind to a halt. In appropriations bills for the WPA, Congress was emboldened to attach some punitive restrictions, such as ending the controversial Federal Theatre Project and writing a provision that anyone employed on the WPA for eighteen consecutive months be laid off for thirty days. All the same, the administration received almost all of the supplemental appropriations it requested for the

WPA in fiscal years 1939 and 1940.[11] Roosevelt's endorsement of spending also seemed to imply a more stable funding basis for the WPA. In his budget message of 1939, the president now employed a distinction between "extraordinary" and "ordinary" expenditures. Funding for the works program as well as some new appropriations for defense purposes fell under the former. More important, the president asserted that the extraordinary category was to be a permanent part of the budget.[12]

In other ways social policy made moderate progress in 1939. In August, the president signed a bill of amendments to the Social Security Act, mainly to aid those considered unemployable. Some changes concerned old-age insurance, the main concern of the Social Security Board (SSB), and were in accordance with the new "spending" philosophy of the administration. Retirement benefits were scheduled to begin in 1940 rather than 1942 and were increased. In addition, survivors' insurance was established to pay benefits upon death to the dependents of eligible workers. Wives of "primary insurance beneficiaries" were also entitled to benefits, and the program was now known as Old-Age and Survivors' Insurance (OASI). To offset in part these increased, expanded, and accelerated benefits, lump-sum death benefits were eliminated. The legislation also postponed a payroll tax increase that was to have taken effect in 1940.[13]

More significant for the short term, categorical assistance programs were also augmented by these amendments. Congress increased the maximum for federal matching payments per Old-Age Assistance (OAA) recipient from fifteen dollars to twenty dollars. The amendments also raised the federal share of Aid to Dependent Children to the one-half level of OAA, improving the prospects for increased coverage. However, the ADC maximum benefits subject to reimbursement were not increased—leaving ADC still one step behind OAA. The amendments also strengthened the means-tested aspects of both programs by requiring states to consider all of an applicant's assets when determining eligibility. Finally, the bill required that state agencies administering special assistance programs be subject to merit hiring procedures.[14]

Health policy, an issue discussed but put aside by the Committee on Economic Security, had to wait, despite new plans for it. The Interdepartmental Committee to Coordinate Health and Welfare Activities, a group set up by the CES filed its report at the end of 1938. It called for increases in federal public health expenditures, expansion of maternal and child health services, grants to build and expand hospitals, aid to state medical programs for the needy, grants-in-aid to establish temporary disability insurance at the state level, and a general program of publicly supported medical care. Attempts to legislate a new system of public health programs failed. Roosevelt limited his health initiatives in 1939 to a WPA hospital-construction project, a prerequisite to any national health policy, but that, too, failed to pass.[15] A run of new legislation to cover the risks left unaddressed by the CES was not in the cards.

Consolidating the Work and Relief Policy

As social policy legislation made significant if marginal gains, public social provision was fortified by way of administrative reorganization. The reorganization legislation that passed in 1939 was not as dramatic or controversial as the 1938 legislation that had failed. Notably, the 1939 legislation exempted some regulatory agencies from reorganization and denied the president the power to create executive departments at will and to remake the civil service system. Still, the Executive Reorganization Act of 1939 gave Roosevelt the ability to gain easily much of what he wanted to rationalize social spending. All reorganization plans submitted by the president, under the new law, would go into effect unless explicitly rejected by both houses of Congress.[16] Soon national administrative practices began to catch up with national spending initiatives, and these organizational changes mattered. Not only did new administrative structures and arrangements ease the implementation and planning of social policy. The reorganization maneuvers also signaled a long-term commitment to the programs of the incipient work and relief state.

Using this new authority, Roosevelt placed four reorganization proposals before Congress in 1939. His first allowed him to strengthen a president's capacity to plan social policy. The Executive Office of the President was created, and Roosevelt named Currie to head it. The Bureau of the Budget was moved from the Treasury to this new office, and it was joined by a revamped National Resources Planning Board (NRPB). It was a substantial promotion for a board that had begun life in the Department of the Interior and later had fallen under the control of a cabinet-level group. The NRPB was now the president's personal planning organization and soon began to turn its attention to social policy reform.[17]

In the same reorganization plan, the WPA, renamed more mundanely the Work Projects Administration, was incorporated as a permanent bureau. With the Public Works Administration (PWA), the WPA was placed in the newly created Federal Works Agency. Another change indicated the routinization of the WPA. A lightning rod of criticism in the formative years of the WPA, Hopkins was nominated in 1939 to become secretary of commerce. In his place Roosevelt promoted the inoffensive army engineer Colonel Francis Harrington rather than the ardent New Dealer Aubrey Williams. The Social Security Board lost its independent status, as it was placed in the Federal Security Agency—not a cabinet-level department as originally hoped.[18]

The WPA itself underwent significant centralizing changes and rationalization. In the early years of the program, state and local relief agencies had complete responsibility for certifying workers as eligible. That power introduced much inequality and some corruption into the program, as relief agencies did not always have the same goals as the WPA and were subject to the pressure of local political figures. In the Emergency Relief Act of

Plate 4.1 Local Funding for the WPA (Russell Lee). In 1939 Congress established that states or localities had to contribute 25 percent of the cost of WPA projects. Before that the local amount was at the discretion of the national WPA. In this photograph, citizens of San Augustine, Texas, hold a mass meeting to formulate means to raise funds for the local share of the WPA.

1939, the WPA gained somewhat greater authority. The process of certifications of need for WPA work were confined, by law, to the purview of the WPA and public relief agencies authorized by it. In turn, the public relief agencies could now only refer workers to the WPA, with the latter having the final responsibility for certification. The agencies cooperating with the WPA had also rationalized their procedures. By 1940, only in six states was the WPA dealing with local agencies. Congress also removed some other arbitrary aspects of the program—not at the request of WPA officials, but probably to the long-term advantage of their program. Congress established a formula for the contribution of project sponsors—25 percent of the cost of the project—and set the hours of WPA work at 130 per month per worker. These standards helped to deflect the criticisms that WPA officials favored some towns, cities, and states over others, that WPA workers were slackers, or that WPA projects produced few useful results.[19]

The Third New Deal is sometimes seen as a stalemate in social policy because of the failure in 1939 of the administration's so-called spend-lend proposals. Approximately $3 billion would have been subject to lending through the Reconstruction Finance Corporation, for public works among other things. The economist Herbert Stein calls this failure "The Last Spending Effort."[20] To focus merely on the failed spend-lend bill, however, is to become preoccupied by Keynesian theory and to miss progress in social spending legislation. The failed bill was merely the last spending effort for spending's sake. There were gains in specific programs, which were typically supported by the public, as opposed to spending in general, which had less support as policy.[21]

The Spending Philosophy and the Decline of Taxation Innovations

Helpful as it was to advocates of social policy, the tilt toward spending had a deflating effect on proponents of national taxation. Although some voices on the left called for increases in business and income taxes, Roosevelt was no longer willing to fight for tax increases. Indeed some New Dealers thought that increased taxes, especially for social insurance programs, provoked the recession and that tax increases might slow recovery. Some of the appeal of the new thinking to the president was probably that it gave ideal economic grounding for ducking new political battles over taxes.[22]

Trying less hard on taxes had a notable impact on the long-term outlook for the program later known as social security. Whereas in the 1939 amendments survivors were included into the program's coverage and benefits were speeded up, the schedule of payroll taxation was lowered to make the program no longer self-financing. The legislation postponed until 1943 a tax increase that was to have taken effect in 1940. According to the amendments, the payroll tax was scheduled to rise, in delayed steps, to three percent of employers' and employees' wages up to a maximum of three thousand by 1949. According to the new schedule of taxes and benefits, policymakers projected that the program would eventually require heavy subsidies from general revenues.[23] In the bargaining for the new benefits their supporters jettisoned the self-financing aspect of the program that had seemed so crucial only four years before. This new taxation strategy loosened the connection between the payroll tax and benefits and thus subverted the insurance imagery with which the Social Security Board sold the program. Things were going to get worse before they got better. During the Second World War these taxes, and with them the future of OASI, were placed in real jeopardy.

WHY SOCIAL POLICY WAS EXTENDED IN THE WAY THAT IT WAS DURING THE THIRD NEW DEAL

As was the case with the creation of American social policy in the early 1930s, the expansion of social policy was largely a result of institutional and political forces. Institutional obstacles to reform remained. Among these were the severe separations of powers in the American polity. Perhaps more important was the continuing deficiency of democratic practices in the polity, despite the many new voters encouraged by the administration. Policy planning was now more tightly controlled within the administration and the proposals of these agencies dominated the political agenda. Yet planning remained scattered across different social spending agencies and thus pushed in different directions. Legislation achievements, moreover, still depended on the fate of the reform-oriented regime that grasped power in 1935.

The Recession and Social Policy in the Third New Deal

Before I discuss these conditions and processes, though, it is worth entertaining again the impact of economic decline on public policy. The recession beginning in the fall of 1937 had effects in some ways similar to if less dramatic than those of the Depression beginning in 1929. Each created social dislocations. Each made the issue of unemployment more pressing. Each played into the hands of those who proposed means-tested public assistance. Yet there were differences, too. The recession happened when durable public programs had already been fashioned. They were automatically expanded and proved their usefulness, and in that way the recession bolstered these programs. The fact that social spending had only begun to get under way and had been cut back before the recession had effects that were fortuitous and fortunate. Social policy as a whole was not blamed for the recession and could plausibly be advanced by its supporters within the administration as needed to stop the slide.

That the economic downturn took place on Roosevelt's watch, however, had repercussions less favorable for social policy. Unlike Hoover's Depression, Roosevelt's recession partially discredited Democratic rule. The recession undercut Democratic representatives in Congress, typically those from democratic districts and thus more likely to be social spending advocates, to the disadvantage of social policy. Their replacements were more likely to support alternative economic analyses and lines of action, such as the anti-tax and anti–New Deal prescriptions of organized business. In short, the impact of economic downturns depended greatly on the situation during which the downturn occurred and, as I show below, had an indirect impact on more crucial political conditions.

Institutional Conditions and Social Policy Revisited

The American polity remained fragmented and the main force for social policy change came from within the Roosevelt Administration. Policymaking was slowed by the extensive horizontal separations of power in the national American state. The battles over the Supreme Court and executive reorganization were between branches of the government and unique to the American setting. Although in each case the administration made blunders, some version of these battles was likely required to safeguard social policy. The battles used up valuable political energy that might have been deployed on social policy itself. Separations of power did not stop the progress of social policy, but certainly slowed it down and otherwise diverted the reformers.

The social policy of the Roosevelt era also depended on democratic practices. In many ways social policy was spurred by a wave of democratization. As we have seen many potential voters in the North had been discouraged by way of restrictions on the franchise during the Republican-dominated era beginning in 1896. Others, immigrants and their children, had been ineligible to vote. The elections between 1928 and 1936, however, were ones of democratic upsurge. Most of the electoral realignment in favor of the Democrats beginning in 1928 and culminating in the overwhelming majorities of 1936 was due not to voters switching parties, but to the previously discouraged or ineligible voting Democratic. The increased voting of these groups was animated in large part by New Deal social policy. Between 1930 and 1940, some 400,000 black Americans migrated from the South to the North. By voting with their feet, they added themselves to the electorate.[24] The substantial barriers to voting in the South remained, however, and continued to slow political support for American social policy. Since the poorer people there were not a substantial part of the electorate, politicians had no incentive to appeal to them, and thus had little reason to support New Deal social policy. For the same reason it was difficult for Roosevelt to appeal over the heads of southern political leaders as those most likely to answer the call had no electoral say.

Southern Democrats were in the forefront of the conservative revolt against the New Deal beginning in 1937. Leuchtenburg lists Vice President John Nance Garner, the Texas Democrat, and Josiah Bailey, a Democratic senator from North Carolina, as the ringleaders of the anti–New Deal coalition.[25] When Roosevelt attempted to "purge" four conservative senators in the primary elections of 1938, two—Walter George of Georgia and "Cotton Ed" Smith of South Carolina—were from former states of the Confederacy. A third, Milliard Tydings, was from Maryland, a state with restricted voting rights. Of the fourteen most conservative Democratic senators, only two were from democratic or open party systems.[26]

A less dramatic, but still substantial hurdle was the patronage orientation of many American political parties. Patronage-oriented party leaders hoped to use social policy for narrow political ends and in the process corrupt it. In the initial appropriations bill for the WPA, a provision was added that required Senate approval for all state WPA heads. Through standard senatorial prerogatives this meant that an appointment would have to find favor with at least one of the state's senators. In one study of twenty-two of these appointments, it was found that some twelve were made for political reasons, and of those only four were competent administrators. Although Hopkins was explicit about keeping politics out of the WPA, in the sense of local politicians inducing WPA workers to contribute to local campaigns,

such charges dogged the program throughout its life. These charges culminated in investigations of the WPA in 1939 and 1940. The problem was in
a sense one of lacking state capacities—the inability to administer programs
fairly. Yet it was not as if there were a sheer lack of ability—things worked
fine in the states where Hopkins was able to avoid senatorial confirmation
by choosing the state head of the FERA to run the WPA. Such was the case
in Ohio, which had been upbraided for using the FERA for narrow political
purposes.[27] The problem was in the nature of the party system.

Similar trouble was faced by the special assistance programs. In the debates over the security bill in 1935, Congress had removed the provision
that cooperating state agencies had to be staffed according to civil service
criteria. When SSB officials went to examine the administrative practices for
new grant-in-aid programs in 1936 and 1937, they uncovered numerous
problems in the northeastern and midwestern states. The biggest trouble
was in Missouri, where the Kansas City political machine of Thomas J. Pendergast controlled the appointments. The western states, with their lack of
patronage-oriented parties, presented fewer problems and better candidates. Although no state agencies had the capacities to run these programs
properly at their inception, such abilities could have been easily constructed. The board was willing to help, and qualified people to run the
programs were abundant. In many places the social security programs were
up and running quickly. In some others like Missouri, though, administrators did not get the chance. Merit provisions were written into the law in the
1939 amendments, but political effort had to be expended and valuable
time had been lost.[28]

Planning Social Policy in the Third New Deal

Despite various problems in the states, the planning of social policy extensions during the Third New Deal came mainly from the two main centers of
policymaking in the administration—the national organizations of the
WPA and the Social Security Board. Unlike the previous wave of policy,
during which Congress induced the administration to back its proposals,
Congress was now reduced to skirmishing on the margins of the process. As
was the case in 1934–35 with the CES outside experts were again introduced in ways that supported the goals of government agencies, and social
policy planning again came from a number of directions. As a result, the
thinking behind social policy remained somewhat scattered. The administration pressed ahead in the directions advocated by its best-positioned social policy administrators—those in the WPA and the Social Security Board.

The WPA was a world of policy planning and implementation unto itself.
It had separate divisions for matters of finance, research, investigation, information, and law. On average there were more than two thousand employees of the national WPA organization from its inception through the
end of the decade—a number that dwarfed the total of state and district

office employees. Once sufficient money was appropriated to the WPA it
worked more or less as it saw fit. The WPA itself researched economic conditions and set its wage rates in accordance with what it thought reasonable. Congress decided merely whether to grant the funding requested for
the program or to attach various restrictions to funding requests. It did the
latter with increasing regularity, especially after 1938.[29]

The SSB, with its control of the special assistance and social insurance
programs, took the lead after 1935 in devising improvements in them. The
SSB mainly wanted to rationalize, standardize, and upgrade the programs
of the Social Security Act. The planning for the Social Security Act amendments of 1939 began in the middle of 1937, when Arthur Altmeyer, chairman of the SSB, wrote a memo to the president suggesting changes. After
1937, when the old-age insurance and Unemployment Compensation titles
were found constitutional, the SSB assessed the effects of its programs. In
1937–1938, an Advisory Council, convened by Altmeyer and reporting
to the House Ways and Means Committee and the SSB, made detailed
recommendations, most of which found their way into legislation that
passed in 1939. An increase in the federal share of funding for Aid to Dependent Children (ADC), for instance, was proposed by the board's Bureau
of Public Assistance, led by Jane Hoey, to make it conform with the bureau's better-funded Old-Age Assistance program. The bureau was also behind the proposal detailing regulations behind means testing, partly as a
way to protect old-age insurance, the program favored by SSB administrators, and partly as a matter of equity. The board also suggested the improvements in old-age insurance. It was far from the extremely powerful
"tool" depicted by Jerry Cates, however.[30] To get what it wanted in this
case the board had to bargain away some of the taxes for the OASI program. Even then, larger political circumstances determined whether amendments extending the relationships between state and citizens would be advanced and passed.

Legislating Social Policy Progress in the Third New Deal

As with the creation of New Deal social policy, its consolidation was due to
the existence of a reform-oriented regime. At the center of this regime was
the president, whose alignment with social policy became closer before his
second term. He employed the Social Security Act and the WPA as issues
defining the differences between the parties. The 1936 Democratic platform, written by Roosevelt and his team, took the Republicans to task for
their neglect of "aid to the destitute"—employing the preamble that "We
hold these truths to be self evident. . . ." Behind Roosevelt, the Democratic
party advanced a kind of Declaration of Independence for American social
policy and the Americans benefiting from it.[31]

Roosevelt was aware that he was gaining the allegiance of those who
benefited from New Deal policies. It was no secret that industrial workers,

many of them naturalized immigrants or the children of immigrants, supported New Deal labor policy. Because of New Deal social policy, moreover, African American voters abandoned the party of Lincoln and joined the party of Roosevelt in the 1936 presidential election. The secret polls taken by the administration beginning in May 1935 suggested that those on relief favored the president much more strongly than those not on relief.[32]

Roosevelt also sought and gained the support of progressive organizations in his bid for reelection in 1936 and to remake the part of the Democratic party controlled by him. Roosevelt ran for reelection not so much as a Democrat, but as the embodiment of the New Deal, and conducted the campaign that way. James Farley, the chairman of the DNC and an opponent of New Deal social policy, was removed from a position of prominence in developing the campaign's message. Encouraged by his wife, the redoubtable Eleanor Roosevelt, the president built up the Women's Division of the DNC, led by Mary Dewson, and sought the support of feminists such as Carrie Chapman Catt. The campaign reached out to African Americans via the Good Neighbor League and won the support of NAACP President Joel E. Spingarn, a lifelong Republican. The administration created an informal Black Cabinet, led by Mary McLeod Bethune of the National Youth Administration. The Labor Division of the DNC was led by Daniel Tobin of the Teamsters. The CIO created organizations of its own to aid the president's reelection. Roosevelt made electoral agreements with the Farmer-Labor party in Minnesota and the Progressive party of Wisconsin and backed the progressive Republican George Norris of Nebraska.[33]

And the electorate remained committed to Roosevelt, whose electoral support peaked in the 1936 elections, as Table 4.1 shows. He won with 60.8 percent of the two-party vote and captured all states but Maine and Vermont.[34] After his electoral landslide, it is no surprise that Roosevelt interpreted it as a call to "paint out" the ill-situated one-third of a nation. His mandate could not have been clearer. After the election, Roosevelt moved further to the left, culminating in the attempted purge in 1938 of anti–New Deal elements in the Democratic party. Another sign of his dedication to social policy was the rise of Hopkins, who symbolized the work program. Kept partly on the sidelines in 1936, he was being groomed by Roosevelt to become the Democratic nominee for president in 1940, and his elevation to secretary of commerce constituted a course of cosmetics meant to preen him for his run.[35]

What is more, the pro–social policy group in Congress was never more dominant than it was after the 1936 elections. In Roosevelt's wake, the Democratic majority in the House rose to 242 and the majority in the Senate to 60. Also in the House were representatives of the Farmer-Labor and Progressive parties. To use the concepts and language of the previous chapter, the very probable pro–spenders in the House reached 106, seven more than after the 1934 elections, and the very probable anti–spenders dropped by 14. (See Table 4.2.) In the Senate, too, the pro–spenders increased their

TABLE 4.1
U.S. National Election Results, 1936, 1938

	House			Senate			President
	Dem.	*Rep.*	*Dem. Margin*	*Dem.*	*Rep.*	*Dem. Margin*	
1936	331	89	242	76	16	60	Roosevelt, Democrat 60.8%, 523–8 electoral
1938	261	164	97	69	23	46	

Sources: Congressional Quarterly, *Guide to U.S Congress* (Washington, D.C.: Congressional Quarterly, 1985), p. 896. U.S. Bureau of the Census, *Historical Statistics of the United States From Colonial Times to 1970* (Washington, D.C.: U.S. Government Printing Office, 1975), series Y 79–83, p. 1073.

margin over the anti–spenders. Again, this structural situation was reflected to some extent in coalition formation. The "liberal bloc," referred to by one political columnist as the "shock troops of the New Deal," expanded to 46 members of the House in early 1938. The building blocks were there for extensions of New Deal social policy.[36]

However, the period immediately after the elections of 1936 saw few new legislative successes for the administration, and, according to the usual story, the bids to transform the Supreme Court and to grant greater powers to the national executive were conspicuous failures. Those failed attempts and the relative inaction on social policy stand apparently in contradiction to the expectations of the institutional politics theory.

The conflict is more apparent than real. The Supreme Court and reorganization gambits were viewed as crucial to the extension and consolidation of social policy. The move against the court was provoked by its likely rejection of the Second New Deal, given its previous decisions, and resulted in its accepting the new measures. Similarly, although the bill to remake the national executive fell short of passage by a few votes in 1938, soon afterward significant reorganization legislation passed that allowed the consolidation of the work and relief policy. In any case, the administration's losses were not explicitly about social policy, but about the balance of power between the executive and the other branches of the national state. The battles also served as diversions from social policy, which had been hotly contested and had room to grow as new conflicts raged around it.

Social policy made gains that went beyond benign neglect. The wages and hours bill was social legislation that mattered, and during this battle the potential power of the administration and its pro–spending allies in Congress was realized. Although the administration rarely attempted to circumvent congressional committee processes, it did so on the wages and hours bill. In 1937 this bill was tied up in the Rules Committee by southern Democrats. Employing the rule that a majority of House representatives could

Table 4.2
Pro– and Anti–Social Spending Contingents in the U.S. House of Representatives, 1935–1940

	Pro-Spending Members		Anti-Spending Members		
	Very Probable[a]	Probable[b]	Probable[c]	Very Probable[d]	Size of Pro-Spending Contingent[e]
1935–36	99	135	44	57	Large
1937–38	106	142	44	143	Large
1939–40	90	86	73	186	Medium

Source: Congressional Quarterly, *Guide to U.S. Elections* (Washington, D.C.: Congressional Quarterly, 1985), pp. 776–90.

[a] Includes radical third parties, Democrats elected in open polities, and Democrats or Republicans affiliated with radical third parties.

[b] Includes Democrats affiliated with the Republican Party and Democrats from states dominated by traditional patronage parties.

[c] Includes Republicans from open polities and Republicans affiliated with the Democratic Party.

[d] Includes Republicans from the South and from states dominated by traditional patronage-party organizations, Democrats or Republicans affiliated with conservative third parties, and southern Democrats.

[e] The size of the pro-spending contingent is a judgment based on the relative sizes of each grouping.

sign a petition to free the bill from this committee, the administration led the successful fight for its discharge.[37] In doing that, the president demonstrated his ability to prevent the killing of social legislation by his southern and Republican congressional opponents. The administration also received its appropriation for relief, and the Senate Committee to Investigate Unemployment and Relief endorsed New Deal social policy.

The ability to force the issue on social policy ended after the elections of 1938, however, when the pro-spenders lost their majority. According to James T. Patterson's famous thesis, a conservative coalition supposedly came to power in Congress after the elections of 1938, signaling the end of the New Deal.[38] And there is no doubt that the congressional alignment in 1939 was less favorable to social spending advocates than the previous one. The Democrats dropped seventy seats in the House in 1938, and none of the losses were from the pool of anti-spenders. Much of the liberal bloc was eliminated, including 4 of the 5 Farmer-Labor members and 5 of 7 Progressives. But the Congress that resulted was far from dominated by conservatives. The Democratic majority in the Senate fell only to 46, an extremely high level for any period in U.S. history, and the Democratic majority in the House was almost 100 despite losses. To put it a different way, the very probable anti-spenders in the House increased only to 183—short of the 218 needed to control it. The very probable pro-spenders in the House remained numerous at 90, and overall the partisan alignment was more favorable than the one Roosevelt had faced in 1933.[39]

This medium-sized pro-spending contingent produced the expected moderate gains in social policy. Notable here were the secondary, but significant social policy successes of the late 1930s—the 1939 amendments to the Social Security Act and the high appropriations for the work programs. These gains were possible because the administration pressed for them and because the political Right was not in a majority in the House or Senate.

The lack of a reform-oriented majority like the ones of 1935 through 1938 undermined efforts to act in new areas of social policy, however. That was demonstrated by the fate of the administration's health proposals. Despite plans generated in connection with the CES, health policy was placed on hold. The "spend-lend" bill, a more difficult sell, was also doomed. Also, the power of anti-spending members of Congress to dilute legislation increased. Although Congress gave Roosevelt the bulk of his demands for WPA funds, he had to ask more frequently, with greater exertion and lesser results. Congress applied increasingly severe restrictions on the money.

The Impact of Labor and Social Movements

The resolve of the administration and its congressional allies was stiffened by other groups, most notably a burgeoning labor movement. The alliance between the New Dealers and labor culminated in unprecedented labor contributions of money and manpower to the Democrats. In 1936 Roosevelt was richly rewarded for his support. Organized labor gave financial assistance of approximately $770,000 to national campaign organizations. More than $200,000 of this went to the DNC and the Roosevelt Nominators' Division. The most prominent union contributor was the United Mine Workers of John L. Lewis. Large sums also went to New York's American Labor Party, an electoral vehicle used to steer voters around Tammany Hall toward New Deal candidates, such as Mayor Fiorello LaGuardia. These funds amounted to a significant proportion of the $5.2 million that the DNC spent on the campaign.[40]

In the wake of the National Labor Relations Act, the industrial unions of the 1936 Congress of Industrial Organizations (CIO), led by Lewis, seized the initiative in organizing. The CIO targeted the auto, steel, and rubber industries. Meantime the American Federation of Labor (AFL) redoubled its efforts in its traditional centers and challenged the CIO in some industries—with, for instance, the International Association of Machinists. As a result, unionization jumped from about 11.3 percent of the nonagricultural labor force in 1933 to 28.6 percent in 1939. The approximately 8.7 million unionized workers that year were divided almost equally between the AFL and CIO.[41] The increased numbers lent additional authority to labor's demands.

Labor in turn stood as a bulwark of support for social policy in the Third New Deal. Organized labor supported the amendments devised by the SSB

Plate 4.2 Pickets outside a Textile Mill (Jack Delano). Workers engaged in numerous strike and job actions in the late 1930s and early 1940s. Most strikes were
designed to induce businesses to recognize unions and sign union contracts. In
this photograph, workers attempt to unionize a textile mill in Georgia on the
eve of World War II, claiming that the U.S. government backs their efforts—"100
percent."

to upgrade the security programs. Some labor organizations, especially in
the CIO, also fought cuts in the WPA, and some CIO unions demanded
old-age pensions beyond what the SSB proposed. Nonetheless, labor was
still mainly concerned with organizing workers. Most of its strikes, including the strike wave beginning in 1937, were designed to force businesses to
recognize the right of workers to organize as provided in the Wagner Act
and to win recognition of unions as bargaining agents, not to influence New
Deal social policy. One of labor's social policy campaigns did not prevail.
Labor was unable to prevent Congress in 1939 from undermining the prevailing wage rates in the WPA by way of the 130-hour rule, despite generating protests and legislative proposals to reverse it.[42]

More challenging social movements continued to influence social policy,
mainly reinforcing directions it had already taken. The Townsend Movement was notable for the productiveness of its efforts in behalf of its aged
constituency. After the disastrous 1936 congressional investigation, the
Movement put its operations on a more supportable financial and administrative footing, having unseated its profiteering "cofounder" Robert Clements. Led now solely by the incorruptible, if often illogical, Dr. Townsend,

TABLE 4.3

The Townsend Movement: Membership, Resources, and Political Activity, and Democratic Majorities in the U.S. House of Representatives, 1934–1939

	Paid Members (thousands)	Gross Receipts (thousands of dollars)	Membership as Percentage of U.S. Population 65 and Over	Townsend-Backed House Candidates (Percent Elected)	Democratic House Majority (Size)
1934	—	84	—	—	216 (large)
1935	—	905	—		
1936	—	562	—	72 (28.8)	242 (large)
1937	—	369	—		
1938	612.5	453	7.20	147 (55.7)	97 (medium)
1939	761.6	622	8.69		

Source: Edwin Amenta, Bruce G. Carruthers, and Yvonne Zylan, "A Hero For the Aged? The Townsend Movement, The Political Mediation Model, and U.S. Old-Age Policy, 1934–1950," *American Journal of Sociology* 98 (1992): 308–39.

the Movement rebounded to claim approximately 750,000 members by 1939. More important, perhaps, its congressional endorsement strategy started to pay off. That year saw the seating of 147 Townsend-endorsed members of the House, more than twice the previous total, as Table 4.3 indicates. Many of these candidates were Republicans, blunting their anti-spending propensities so far as old-age pensions were concerned. Prominent among those winning with the Townsend seal of approval were three members of the House Ways and Means Committee.[43]

Although Congress again rejected the Townsend Plan in 1939, the Movement's fingerprints were all over the legislation to increase the matching payments for Old-Age Assistance that year. More concerned with its fledgling old-age insurance program, the SSB and its stacked Advisory Council were calling for no new increases in OAA—perceived as a potential competitor to OAI. The SSB and the Advisory Council proposed "variable grants" for OAA, in order to appease southern Democrats. By paying a higher proportion of the first segment of the pension, these grants would keep pensions low in the South, but place their fiscal burden almost wholly on the federal government without increasing federal spending elsewhere. Instead, however, the maximum federal matching payments for OAA were increased from fifteen per person to twenty dollars. Testifying against the increase, Abraham Epstein noted the influence: "If you . . . raise the Federal grant to $20 . . . they will say 'It is Dr. Townsend that did the job,' and the Dr. Townsend movement will grow." In doing so, the Townsendites foiled the SSB's plans to promote ADC, a program without social movement support, to equal status with OAA.[44]

Also important was the unemployed workers' movement, which had

Plate 4.3 The Workers Alliance of America Protests WPA Cuts (Dorothea Lange). More than 200,000 workers on the WPA were mobilized in the Workers Alliance of America. Here WPA workers in San Francisco protest cuts in WPA funding by Congress in February 1939 and demand an increase to 4 million WPA jobs—a total that was never reached.

been rejuvenated by New Deal policy to organize almost exclusively workers on the WPA. Led by David Lasser, the Workers' Alliance of America (WAA) had 200,000 members at its peak. The alliance engaged in job actions to improve the wages of WPA workers and protested funding cuts for the WPA. Although it had not won as many political allies in Congress as the Townsend Movement had, the WAA was far from negligible. The administration was on friendly terms with the WAA, and its activity reinforced the president's appeals for increased WPA appropriations in 1938. The administration called for $2.75 billion and the WAA called for $3.5 billion. The alliance probably also helped to prevent further congressional cuts in WPA funding in 1939. It was unable, however, to prevent restrictive congressional action aimed squarely at it—the eighteen-month rule for laying off WPA workers.[45]

Well-Situated Opposition to the New Deal

From the other side, in their relatively privileged position of access, organized businessmen regrouped. Their sentiment ran strongly against the New Deal. An October 1935 Chamber of Commerce survey of one thousand five hundred members found them opposed to the philosophy of the New Deal by a margin of thirty-five to one.[46] They soon put their money where their mouths were, and capitalist cash tilted heavily to the Republicans in 1936. Campaign contributions show that finance and heavy industry provided little support to the Democrats in 1936. Among organized and individual capitalists, only tobacco and liquor interests gave consistently and readily.[47]

With the restoration of the Republicans in 1939, organized business's mobilization began to pay dividends. As was the case in 1935, the fiscal policy agitating businessmen was taxation, especially the undistributed profits tax. Of secondary importance were the Social Security payroll taxes. In a repeat of their 1935 performance, representatives of organized business appeared in Congress for hearings on the amendments to the Social Security Act. This time they were fighting proposed increases in the OAI tax and were successful in having it delayed. In addition, the WPA remained a sore spot among businessmen, and organized business was in support of bids to cut WPA appropriations.[48]

Organized business had money and access, and its Republican allies had picked themselves off of the political floor. Access would have got their mobilization some distance, and it helped to have supported members of a renewed party. All the same, changes in legislation that business demanded came only partly as a result of its actions. Organized business and the Republicans could not have been as effective as they were without the aid and leadership of southern Democrats, unconstrained as they were by electoral sanction to support programs to aid the poorer members of their districts. The advantages of polity membership are magnified when the polity is significantly underdemocratized. More important, the benefits won by businessmen were only minor, as the political situation was aligned mainly against them. Their day was yet to come.

A Brief Comparison

That American social policy was making remarkable strides throughout the Third New Deal, and largely for the reasons given above, can be seen by a brief comparison across the Atlantic Ocean. In Britain, the Labour party gained office briefly in 1929, but by 1931 was out of power. Conservative-dominated national governments ruled until the eve of the next world war. In Britain, moreover, throughout the 1930s the key national bureaucracy in social policy was the Treasury, a site of orthodox economic thinking based on London's role as the financial capital of the world. Fiscally conservative, the Treasury opposed social spending innovations and insisted on balanced

TABLE 4.4.
U.K. and U.S. Social Spending Efforts, 1929–1938

	United Kingdom[a]	United States
1929	4.41	0.53
1930	5.36	0.74
1931	6.33	1.34
1932	6.59	1.98
1933	6.30	4.95
1934	5.90	5.10
1935	5.76	4.70
1936	5.35	4.73
1937	4.94	4.79
1938	5.01	6.31

Sources: Peter Flora, Jens Alber, Richard Eichenberg, Jurgen Kohl, Franz Kraus, Winfried Pfenning, and Kurt Seebohm, *State, Economy, and Society in Western Europe 1815–1975: The Growth of Mass Democracies and Welfare States* (Chicago: St. James, 1983), pp. 442, 446. U.S. Bureau of the Census, *Historical Statistics of the United States From Colonial Times to 1970* (Washington: U.S. Government Printing Office, 1975), series F 1–5, H 32–47, pp. 224, 341.

[a] For the United Kingdom, the data are from Flora et al., *State, Economy, and Society*. Social spending, which they call "social security," is defined as public money expended on social insurance and social assistance programs. U.K. spending is taken as a percentage of gross domestic product.

[b] The data for the United States are from columns 33, 34, 39, 41, 42, 47 of the "H" series of *Historical Statistics*. These columns include spending from all sources on "social insurance," "public aid," and "other social welfare." U.S. spending in any year is taken from the following fiscal year, running from July 1 to June 30, as a percentage of average gross national product in the two calendar years that the fiscal year spanned. For instance, the figure for the calendar year 1938 is from fiscal year 1939 and is divided by the average GNP in 1938 and 1939.

budgets. The National governments of the 1930s followed the lead of the Treasury, as social spending programs were targeted for cutting rather than improvements and increases.[49]

Britain's conservative approach to public social provision in the Depression provided a sharp contrast developments in America, where reform-oriented regimes dominated political life by the middle 1930s. The social spending efforts of the two countries stood similarly in bold relief. As can be seen in Table 4.4, the share of "social security" spending, as Peter Flora and colleagues refer to spending for social insurance and assistance, in British gross domestic product peaked at approximately 6.6 percent in 1933.[50] By the end of the decade, though, Conservative cost-cutting measures led to social spending to drop to approximately 5 percent. American efforts went in the opposite direction and dramatically so. In America, social spending went from almost nothing—about 0.5 percent of the GNP in 1929—to surpass British spending efforts by 1938. That year the U.S. figure was greater than 6 percent—quite a turnabout no matter how one looks at it.

AMERICAN WORK AND RELIEF POLICY AT THE END OF THE 1930s

Counting the money devoted to social policy is important, but how the money is spent matters at least as much. The possibilities for social policy suggested by Edwin Witte, the executive secretary of the CES, focused on four areas—work, relief, social insurance, and private annuities. By the end of the 1930s, American social policy constituted an amalgam of these elements: works programs offering publicly funded employment, power-sharing special assistance programs and employment services, two incipient social insurance programs, and state- and locally-controlled general assistance. Some elements, though, were more conspicuous in the mix than others. Work and relief predominated, social insurance was present on a smaller scale, and annuities were almost completely absent. This incipient work and relief state was designed to confront failures of capitalist industrialization at their source and to meet the needs of those who would be destitute without employment, but whom the Roosevelt Administration considered employable. Efforts centered on employment programs—to redress the main failure of capitalism—and means-tested public assistance—to support those considered economically extraneous. The programs were aimed at the unemployed and those of limited means, especially the aged poor, but were designed to reach a wide spectrum of Americans, not merely a few selected groups.

A Programmatic Accounting of Depression-Era Social Policy

At the end of the 1930s, America's most significant social policy efforts were in works programs. Some 2.1 million workers were on the rolls of the reorganized WPA in December 1939. The WPA remained concerned with its labor-intensive undertakings, mainly constructing or rehabilitating highways, roads, streets, and public buildings and making garments of various kinds. All told, the WPA itself accounted for about $1.57 billion in 1939, amounting to about 46 percent of social spending and 1.7 percent of GNP. In addition, 1 million young Americans were working for the NYA and CCC. The cost of all national public employment programs excluding public works projects was approximately $1.87 billion, or about 55 percent of social spending and about 2.1 percent of GNP in 1939. These pro-

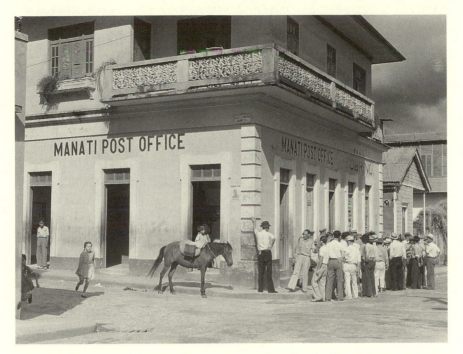

Plate 4.4 The WPA Arrives in Puerto Rico (Jack Delano). The WPA was not confined to the U.S. mainland. In 1939 Puerto Rico began to participate. Here some of
the first WPA workers in Puerto Rico wait outside the local post office for their
paychecks.

grams employed less than one-third of the approximately 10 million unemployed that year.[51]

This left a wide range of activity for need-based public assistance. For the
largest group of the formerly able-bodied, older workers who retired or
who could not find employment, the federal government had brought
greater funding to spending programs, with the 1935 Social Security Act
and its 1939 amendments. By the end of 1939, 1.9 million people—about
one-fourth of the aged population—were receiving means-tested OAA.
That constituted almost a tenfold increase over the 200,000 that had received old-age pensions at the end of 1934. OAA accounted for $430 mil-
lion, about 13 percent of social spending and one-half of 1 percent of GNP
in 1939.[52]

In four years of operation ADC had also marked a fundamental break
with mothers' pensions. By the end of 1939 some 760,000 children, about
three times as many as during the peak of mothers' pensions in the early
1930s, were receiving ADC. If heads of families are included, ADC reached
more than 1 million. By 1940, 16 percent of female-headed families with
children received ADC, a proportion almost three times as high as the 1931

figure. In 1939, spending for ADC constituted 3.4 percent of social spending and about 0.12 percent of the GNP, four times the effort dedicated to mothers' pensions in 1931.[53]

Much of the relief burden remained entirely in the hands of states and localities. When the Federal Emergency Relief Administration concluded its operations at the end of 1935, national support for general relief ended. That left state and local officials to provide general relief or assistance to both "unemployables" not aided by special assistance programs and the numerous "employables" not aided by the WPA. Unlike the special assistance programs, general assistance was left without federal controls or standards. Its administration varied widely, with some states providing it through the supervision of state-level Departments of Public Welfare, while others delegated local authorities great control in the manner of the old poor laws. Average benefits varied more widely than for the special assistance programs and had dropped since the FERA days. Still, general relief was substantial. Approximately 1.6 million people were receiving general assistance in 1939, accounting for about 14 percent of social spending and more than one-half of 1 percent of GNP. The federal government was no longer running a dole, but the dole nonetheless remained in states and localities as most people on assistance were employable by even the strictest standards.[54]

The social insurance programs of the Social Security Act were only beginning to have an impact. Many state-level Unemployment Compensation programs began to pay benefits in January 1938, soon after the beginning of the recession. However, the tax offset plan did not work entirely as the CES imagined it. Merit rating allowed for wide differences in taxation rates and thus opened the way for states to diverge in the construction of their compensation programs. Very few states taxed corporations at the full 3 percent rate, and the average taxation rate was approximately 1 percent. Because the state unemployment insurance funds were designed to function without help from other state revenues or from federal general revenues, there was concern about the ability of these trust funds to survive high unemployment. In 1939, the program accounted about 13 percent of social spending and one-half of 1 percent of GNP, about the same as for OAA.[55] OASI was not yet paying benefits.

There was one set of spending programs the Roosevelt Administration discouraged—benefits for military veterans. The nineteenth-century military pension policy for aged Northern veterans and their widows was far removed from the vision of the New Dealers. The former soldier had his place in this vision, but in the ranks of the citizenry. In 1933 nearly 750,000 veterans were receiving benefits for service-related and non–service-related disabilities. These pensions cost about $825 million or 1.4 percent of GNP. By 1939 the federal government was only spending about 0.67 percent of GNP, or somewhat more money than for OAA or UC. Administered by the Veterans Administration, veterans' benefits went mainly to those with ser-

Plate 4.5 Unemployment Compensation Begins (Dorothea Lange). Unemployment compensation received its first test during the "recession" of 1937–38. Despite this new program, the administration thought that work would continue to be needed to aid the unemployed. Here unemployed workers in San Francisco mass for their checks in January 1938.

vice-related disabilities.[56] New Dealers hoped that spending exclusively for veterans would eventually end, as would the separate administration of veterans' benefits. After all, sooner or later the veterans from the Great War would pass away—just as the Civil War veterans had. The battle was uphill, but the administration was winning it.

Despite the lack of tax increases in the late New Deal, the 1930s witnessed dramatic changes in the structure of U.S. taxation. National taxation "efforts" from the seven largest sources in 1939 almost doubled relative to their size in 1932, growing from about 3.3 percent to 6.1 percent of GNP. One notable increase was in excise taxes, which accounted for almost 2 percent of the GNP in 1940, about two-and-one-half times the size of their contribution during the last year of the Hoover Administration. The other main increase came in social insurance payroll taxes, which did not exist in 1932 and accounted for about 1 percent of GNP in 1939. Yet taxation policy did not mainly follow spending policies in the direction of progressiveness. Excise taxes fell harder on those with smaller incomes. According to most analyses of tax "incidence," moreover, payroll taxes ultimately fall on the wage earner. For payroll taxes are treated by the employer as part of the wage bill, drawing from wages that workers might otherwise have received. The taxes nowadays considered the most progressive, corporate and personal income taxes, were by 1940 only marginally greater than in the last year of Hoover's presidency. These moves toward progressiveness were augmented by higher estate and gift and capital stock taxes.[57]

Contemporary Social Science and Depression-Era American Social Policy

Since Witte's day social scientists have gone beyond matters of form in analyzing differences in the type and nature of social policy. According to Gøsta Esping-Andersen's well-known classification of "welfare state regimes," the "social democratic" type affords the best position for workers. It is based on the principles of universalism and "decommodification"—the latter meaning that private markets play a minimal role in workers' lives. Universal Scandinavian social insurance programs are considered by Esping-Andersen as archetypical of this regime. The second best, "conservative corporatist" regime is also universal, but solidifies status distinctions between groups and upholds the traditional family, with one male breadwinner bringing home a family wage. The "liberal" welfare regime, the most inferior, is designed to make labor markets run smoothly—at the expense of people by forcing them to take what the market offers. Current American policy is deemed to approximate the liberal type, especially because of its relatively heavy reliance on need-based programs.[58]

One problem with that analytical model is that it relies too much on existing programs in which the scope and generosity of benefits are closely related to the type of program. Nowadays need-based programs are currently among the poorest-funded programs around the world, and countries that rely on them provide the stingiest aid to their citizens. Need is typically defined strictly, often by intrusive methods, and income and wealth tests are set at low thresholds, reducing both the number of recipients and the potential political support for the programs. For all these reasons, programs based on need are considered by most scholars to be only halfhearted commitments.[59] By contrast, social insurance programs, such as American "social security," are much wider in scope, are often universal, and have relatively high benefits.

Need-based programs may nowadays provide poor support for poor people, but that does not have to be so in principle, which is what analytical types are supposed to address. To the contrary, in theory a need-based policy based on the rights of a potential recipient, understood as a citizen and an honored member of a national community, is most likely to challenge or subvert the market. For such programs "need" would be interpreted in a liberal way—and in the extreme case by the individual. Benefits would also be high and adequate. Such a policy would correspond, moreover, to a common understanding of freedom—to be able to do what one wants. Citizenship would likely include specific responsibilities and among these would doubtless be work. But citizenship might comprise a wide range of work considered socially desirable, not merely full-time work for whatever jobs might become available on the market. Need-based programs that were guaranteed as a right for all citizens, with inclusive standards of need, with adequate benefits, and with impartial administration, would provide great freedom from market pressures. Even the relatively stingy current programs provide some relief, as was implied by the opposition to recent American welfare reforms. For the alternatives are to receive nothing—the market solution—or to be subject to incarceration, loss of political citizenship, or both in the manner of the old poor laws.

Because they are state interventions that provide payments to those who would not otherwise get them, social insurance programs also provide aid that is superior to the market alternative. But such programs have less potential to challenge market decision-making. People gain access to a social insurance benefit by earning it in a relatively narrow sense—by compiling an extensive work record in the private market or by being closely related to someone who does. What is more, social insurance benefits are typically geared to private wages and sometimes are justified on the basis of taxes paid, as in the case of American social security. At its best, social insurance can free selected groups of those socially defined as no longer likely candidates for work.

A scheme reflecting those analytical possibilities is arrayed in Figure 4.1, which divides the types of programs, need-based or social insurance, according to their scope and generosity.[60] A policy or program with the greatest potential to subvert unequal market relations—the shaded area in the upper left-hand corner of the figure—grants generous benefits to citizens who need them, for whatever reason, across the economic spectrum. No current program fully fits the type. As I noted above, current programs tend to fall into the upper right or bottom left of the figure. The distinction between "welfare" and social security is of this sort. American welfare programs are need-based, are generally confined to the very poor, and provide relatively stingy, though not insignificant benefits. They appear at top right, in the category labeled "failed market-subverting." For the programs like New Deal–era Aid to Dependent Children and Old-Age Assistance, designed to suspend market forces, the right to the benefit was usually undermined by the terms of the benefit. Low benefits provide some incentive to take what the labor market offers. Such failed attempts at market subversion differ in intent and outcome from American poor laws, which were designed for degradation and were more closely akin to policies of incarceration than to any current social spending policies.

By contrast, many current social insurance programs are often extensive and generous. Gaining access to them, however, requires a lengthy work

FIGURE 4.1
Public Policy's Influence on Markets According to Type, Scope, and Benefits

Scope and Benefit Levels

	Extensive/Generous	Exclusive/Stingy
Need-based	Market-subverting: WPA (1930s) OAA (some states) ADC (as planned)	Failed market-subverting: ADC (in practice) OAA (most states)
Social Insurance	Generous market-related: OASI (after 1972)	Limited market-related: OASI (before 1950) UC (most states)

Policy Type (label at left, vertical)

record or a close familial connection with someone with such a record, and so they fall into the category "market-related." Perhaps some old-age insurance benefits, such as those through social security since 1972 and in Scandinavian countries, approach the market-subverting category at top left. Most other social insurance benefits would not. In the lower left-hand corner is a box—"limited market-related" benefits—that includes social insurance benefits that are limited in coverage and paltry in amount. Although there are few such programs nowadays, in their early years both UC, especially in states with limited payroll taxes, and OASI were relatively restricted in both benefit levels and scope. Perhaps the initial Imperial German social insurance programs also fit here. Like the failed market-subverting programs, however, both forms of market-related programs ameliorate market forces to different degrees, as those benefiting from them would be worse off under purely market conditions. The relative quality of the programs would depend on their generosity and extensiveness.

During the 1930s, however, American social policy, in conception and sometimes in practice, did not always tend toward the current polarization between the generous market-related and the failed market-subverting types. Some programs at least attempted or tended to provide significant autonomy from the market. The WPA was a case in point. It was designed to replace the wages of anyone who became unemployed, from professionals to unskilled workers, and where wages were below the "American standard of living," the WPA was to provide that higher wage. It was only partly successful, but more about that later. In some states at the end of the 1930s, moreover, need-based OAA programs paid high benefits relative to current incomes and had few restrictive provisions. ADC was also supposed to provide adequate benefits, but did not come as close in any states as OAA to doing so. Though never enacted, the Townsend Plan provides another example. The plan promised great sums to aged people who agreed not to work for the market and presumably would need the money, although need would have been self-defined.

Any analytical typology of social policy based on markets makes an error of omission by failing to address gender inequality. As Ann Shola Orloff has argued, market-based schemes ignore domestic and caregiving work, typically performed by women, and women's connections to the state through marriage or motherhood. Policy that challenges the market does not necessarily address gender inequalities, unfairness, and stereotypes. For one thing, access to paid work for women in capitalist societies promotes the financial autonomy of women from men. Policy that "commodifies" women by supporting equal participation in the paid labor force, as through antidiscrimination and comparable worth programs, tends in that way to free women. For another, market-related ideas of autonomy ignore the capacity to maintain an autonomous household—another issue with a great impact on women. Analysts therefore need to take into account the degree to which programs subvert or ameliorate unequal gender relations.[61]

And so I provide a preliminary design that addresses both market and gender inequalities, by arraying whether policy ameliorates or subverts the market against whether it ameliorates or subverts unequal gender relations and stereotypes. Policy might be "doubly subversive," as in the shaded upper left-hand box of Figure 4.2, in that it subverts both unequal market and gender relationships by providing autonomy from each. Policy might ameliorate both sorts of social relationships, as in the lower right-hand corner, labeled "doubly ameliorating." Policy might also subvert one form of inequality and pressure. So the "gender inequality–subverting only" and "market-subverting only" categories round out the analytical possibilities.

Varied as they often are, most current social programs doubtless fall somewhere in the doubly ameliorating category. That category would include both social security and general assistance, despite the fact that the one is far more generous and less degrading than the other. However different, neither program challenges markets, as we have seen. Both at best do not challenge gender inequality and may to some extent reinforce it. Social security is currently gender-neutral in its provisions. Because of differences by sex in work force participation, however, social security may tend in its effects to reproduce gender inequality, and it certainly provides incentives to prolong marriages.[62] General assistance programs, available to employable men facing long-term unemployment, support the male breadwinning role; their low benefits provide few alternatives. By contrast, access-produc-

FIGURE 4.2
Public Policy According to Influence on Market Forces and Unequal
Gender Relations

Gender Inequality

	Subverted	Ameliorated
Subverted	Doubly subversive: WPA (as planned) Townsend Plan ADC (as planned)	Market-subverting only: WPA (in practice)
Ameliorated	Gender inequality– subverting only: Comparable worth Antidiscrimination ADC (in pracitice)	Doubly ameliorating: OASI Mothers' pensions General assistance

Market Forces (left axis label)

ing programs, like comparable worth and antidiscrimination programs, challenge or subvert unequal gender relations. Although they do contest some decisions made by the private market, access-producing programs tend at best to ameliorate market relations, as they integrate women into it. The former AFDC freed some women from reliance on a man for a paycheck, but was undermined in part by the low funding for it in many places and by its reinforcement of stereotyped gender roles. All the same, in its long-term support of separated, divorced, and never-married mothers AFDC diverged from the widows-only program it replaced and the temporary benefits that replaced it.

As I noted above, there are few examples of programs that tend to undermine the market, and they might or might not undermine unequal gender relations. Some U.S. Depression-era programs, however, did tend to be doubly subversive—at least in intention and principle. The WPA might have subverted both market and unequal gender relations by providing jobs impartially and by easing the way for women with children to take WPA jobs. It was the official view of the WPA that it should provide jobs to all men and women who wanted them—if funding was available. But funding was not available, and, as I detail below, women lost out as a matter of policy. A kind of two-way autonomy was also the hope of the early proponents of ADC. They wanted it to provide an adequate if modest stipend—one that promoted decency and health—to make it possible for a single parent, whether widowed or not, to raise a family but avoid wage labor. Such a program would do little to shatter stereotypes, as it tended to confirm gender roles. Yet ADC also defined raising children as a socially desirable activity worthy of reward, and a mother supported adequately—and most beneficiaries were women—would need neither job nor husband. The meager national commitment to ADC and the way it was administered, however, cut short that potential. Finally, the Townsend Plan would have treated aged men and women as citizens of equal stature, freeing women from men and each from the market.

These typologies and analytical criteria beg a number of questions about New Deal social policy. How closely did New Deal social policy approximate the types? Did the policy enhance autonomy from unequal market and gender relationships? How did specific programs vary across the types? Those same criteria of autonomy might also be extended across age, race, and ethnic relations. Other questions, though, go beyond those criteria: Did New Deal social policy undermine or uphold economic and status distinctions among groups? What sorts of social relations did it legitimate and support by way of official state action? And, more generally, how fair was it? In addressing these questions I consider official statements of policy through legislation and administrative rulings. But officially mandated fairness can be undermined by administrative practice, such as state and local officials with great control over the certification process for potential WPA workers, or the eligibility process for means-tested public assistance, or the funding of unemployment compensation. So I also examine who exactly was benefiting from the programs.

New Deal Social Policy as an Alternative to Markets

Though never reaching the standards set by the New Dealers, work and relief were designed by them to be provided as a matter of right, and thus constituted a challenge to markets and promoted autonomy. The state took a great measure of responsibility to employ citizens when the private market failed them.[63] Other citizens were also to have a right to a stipend if they needed it and fit standard criteria—such as being aged or the head of a family without a breadwinner. Though based on need, moreover, the work and relief policy was not designed to punish or stigmatize its beneficiaries or to force them to take low-paying work, or any combination of the above. In that way the work and relief programs diverged from the locally funded and controlled pre-Depression relief system they were designed to replace. There is reason to believe that the work and relief programs of America in the 1930s were as challenging as current ones anywhere are.

The claims by policymakers about employability, moreover, constituted a discourse of "decommodification" that divided those who should work from those who should not. In American social policy a line was drawn among citizens between those considered high priorities for paid work, known as the "employable," and those not, known as the "unemployable." The WPA was to provide work and wages for the employable. Others were to receive stipends that were expected to sustain the person or household, but were not as generous. In this way, the policy officially legitimated the idea of work for some groups and honored their role generally, while discouraging work by others.

The WPA program, the centerpiece of the policy, sometimes provided an alternative to menial and poorly paid labor through the private market. The WPA set its monthly wages according to the "decency and health" standard that had been deleted from the special assistance programs and according to region, size of community, and skill rating. The highest wage, the $94.90 per month for professional and technical workers in the most expensive, urban wage region, was more than three times higher than the lowest, the $31.20 received by the lowest category of unskilled worker in the least expensive, rural wage region. But the latter figure was not vastly less than the $52.00 received by the lowest category of unskilled worker in the most expensive, urban wage region. Wages for WPA were largely in line with those on the private market. When WPA workers were required to work 130-hour months, in September 1939, average wages dropped to 44 cents per hour. Still, the lowered rate was not greatly less than the 51 cents per hour that was the average hourly entry-level pay of common laborers in 1940. About 70 percent of all WPA employment in 1939 provided work designated as "unskilled." The WPA also included many workers who had previously held middle-class occupations. Professional work was more highly represented among WPA work than the usual occupations of WPA recipients would warrant. WPA work was far removed from the degradation rituals that had accompanied work relief throughout American history. According to the Emergency Relief Act of 1939, moreover, workers were required to accept offers of private employment only if that employment paid prevailing wages.[64]

Unemployment compensation was a limited market-related program. It typically paid about one-half of wages for regularly employed workers for relatively large industrial employers. Among those excluded from coverage were agricultural workers, domestics, maritime workers, and government workers. In 1940, the average benefit amounted to about $10.50 per week. But these benefits lasted for only very brief periods of time—thirteen weeks at best in most states—and were typically subject to two- or three-week waiting periods. If the taxes for the program ran out, so, too, would the benefits. All in all, however, New Deal unemployment policy incorporated elements that subverted markets, especially in the WPA program. But because the policy was incomplete and underfunded the reality only approximated the model.

Little Impact on Unequal and Stereotyped
Gender Relations and Roles

New Deal policy did not go far in addressing gender inequality. The policy was based on the desirability of providing a minimum household or family income for all, and on the concept of the family wage—one worker's wage was expected to support an entire family. The expectation of policymakers was that satisfactory jobs in the private economy were likely to be scarce. This concept was underscored by the stricture that only one family member could receive WPA employment. This family member was expected in most instances to be a man. In this way the program by design fortified power relationships within a standard nuclear family, in which the husband was expected to be the breadwinner and the wife to take charge of home life.[65]

Who, exactly, gained the privilege of WPA employment, the principal and most beneficial form of aid in New Deal social policy? How were other programs related to it? Did groups fare better by way of social policy than they would have fared in the private labor market? Or with the policy system prior to the New Deal? Did women do as well as men under the work and relief policy? Did different age groups do better or worse? Did social policy promote the capacities of women and groups of the young and old? Did it undermine or uphold stereotypes of men's and women's work? One way to approach the issue is by way of demographics and the ideas, regulations, and practices that led to the results.

Mainly, WPA jobs went to men of a certain age and family status. Men on the WPA were slightly older on average than those in private employment. The median age of men on the WPA was 39.4 years in February 1939, more than three years higher than the median age of men in the labor force. In 1938, moreover, legislation stipulated that a recipient had to be at least eighteen years old. The preference of the WPA for older men had its limits, however. Until legislation in 1939 prohibited the exclusion of people above sixty-five years and older, older men were routinely purged or "separated," according to the official euphemism, from the WPA's rolls. WPA officials viewed the aged as eligible for and more suited to old-age pensions. Although older workers could not be summarily dismissed after 1939, they were not encouraged. In 1939, men sixty-five years and older constituted 4 percent of the labor force, but only 1.6 percent of WPA employment. In addition, heads of families were given preference for WPA work over single men. All the same, wages were not in any way adjusted for dependents. In short, the WPA supported and elevated through its aid the status of men leading families. But the WPA designated some others, such as older men, as not desirable for employment, and yet others, young men and those without families, as not suitable for employment through the WPA.[66]

Older men and women were consigned to the category of unemployable by American policy makers. At the end of the 1930s, only OAA of the

U.S. old-age programs was providing regular pension benefits. Although these payments varied widely across the states and localities, as did restrictions and guidelines behind need, these pensions averaged about twenty dollars per month by the end of 1939. The state with the most generous payments, California, was paying about five times as much as the state with the least generous ones, Arkansas, a much wider range in benefits than those for the WPA.[67]

Programs for younger people, the NYA and CCC, were designed to provide aid and training, to keep students in school, and to delay the movement of young people into the paid labor force. The CCC was for younger men, between the ages of seventeen and twenty-three. A successful CCC applicant typically had "dependents"—either a wife and children or a parent or parents on relief—and the program upheld the male-breadwinner role with a vengeance. From the CCC stipend of thirty dollars per month—lower than WPA wages—twenty-five dollars were typically remitted to the family. The young men of the CCC had to withstand the trials of separation from home and army-enforced discipline during their conservation missions. All the same, CCC recipients were often referred to as "CCC boys," perhaps because the vast majority were under twenty-one years old. The NYA provided less total control in its work and training programs. Designed for high-school and college students, NYA in-school programs averaged only about eight dollars per month for part-time work. Designed to train young people for work in the private market by imparting skills and work habits, the out-of-school programs had wages that were not even half as high as those in the CCC. There was little difference by sex in the recipients for either NYA program. Often, though, NYA out-of-work programs for young women were designed to inculcate in them skills more suited to homemaking than to paid employment.[68]

Though not denied WPA work, women received it at a much lower rate than men and lower than one would expect given women's representation in the labor force. This was due mainly to the restriction on WPA employment to one family member and the WPA's vision of what constituted employability. In 1940, for instance, women constituted one-fourth of the private labor force, but in 1939 they constituted only 13.1 percent of WPA's certified work force. Like their male counterparts, the women on the WPA tended to be heads of households. WPA women, moreover, were clustered in the Division of Service and Professional Projects. And most semiskilled and unskilled women working on service projects were engaged in so-called welfare projects. The most significant welfare project, in turn, was the sewing project, which produced garments and household items. Sewing projects were such an important part of the WPA that they were submitted at the state level, not the local level. Sex-segregated, the sewing projects reinforced the distinction between men's and women's work. Like aged men, women with children but without men were not encouraged to take WPA jobs and were presumed by WPA officials to be better candidates for categorical assistance than for WPA work. As it did with aged men sixty-five years and older, Congress provided that women with dependent children were not to be barred from WPA employment. The WPA sometimes provided employment in cases where states or localities did not provide ADC, but that was not the WPA's preference.[69]

ADC was the policymakers' preferred program for women without husband-breadwinners in the home. By law the program was not explicitly for women, but for a wide range of families in which children were dependent. Although one-fourth of ADC households were two-parent families by the end of the 1930s, in the others the head of family who was issued aid was a woman. In aiding women family heads, ADC was a big step up from the mothers' pension programs it had replaced. The mothers' pension recipients were overwhelmingly widows, but only 49 percent of children accepted for ADC in 1937–38 lived with widowed mothers, and this percentage dropped to 20 percent by the early 1940s. This suggests that ADC programs were increasing access greatly beyond the few widows previously considered deserving. But the programs were funded, as we have seen, at a lower level than OAA. The average payment per child was about thirteen dollars in 1939. Worse, the disparities across states and localities were even greater than those for OAA. The average payment per child per month ranged from approximately $2.50 in Arkansas to $24.50 in New York. In short, ADC was far better that what had been available before its existence. The wide way that the law was drawn held out the potential to provide greater autonomy than WPA or other forms of work. But this potential was largely unrealized because of the relatively low and highly variable payments under it.[70]

The OASI program wrote its age and gender expectations explicitly into the legislation. The categories for insurance benefits included "primary," "wife's," "child's," "widow's," and "parent's." The benefit of the primary beneficiary's wife was set at one-half his benefit. She was entitled to it only if she remained married to the "primary," however. Widows could receive benefits, too, only if they did not remarry. Women could of course be primary beneficiaries, but given the labor market were not as likely to be. Nor were there were corresponding husband's or widower's benefits. Various dependents were also specified, including parents.[71] Of all the programs, the one that was paying no regular benefits made the most explicit case for the family wage and set out the greatest expectations for social roles and work.

Race and Fairness in New Deal Social Policy

Whether the New Deal social policy served to ameliorate race stratification and whether the program was "fair" in that sense depends on what one means by that word. Some of the questions and issues suggested above, with suitable alterations, are applicable. Did African Americans fare better by way of social policy than they would have in the private labor market? Or with the policy system prior to the New Deal? Did African Americans as group do as well as white Americans under the work and relief policy? Did social policy promote segregation or integration? Did it undermine or uphold racial stereotypes? Did the WPA fundamentally challenge the racial caste system of the South, as its radical eligibility criteria and relatively high wage rates might lead one to believe? Needless to say, the answers to these questions are not all the same.

The official policy of the WPA was adamantly opposed to discrimination of most kinds. Throughout the 1930s, the no-discrimination pledge was made explicit for a number of potential sources, including "race, creed, color, or any political activity." Yet some official restrictions and favoritism did find their way into law. Over the course of the life of the WPA, various emergency relief acts applied restrictions on employment to aliens, and in 1939 even legal aliens were barred from WPA jobs, despite the objections of the Roosevelt Administration. In contrast, the emergency relief acts increasingly provided preferences for veterans or their wives.[72]

Figures suggest that American social policy served to ameliorate racial stratification. African Americans were more highly represented on the WPA than in the general population. Black Americans constituted 14 percent of WPA employees in 1939, whereas the proportion of nonwhite persons in the labor force was about 11 percent in 1940. The wages that African Americans received through the WPA, moreover, were likely to be higher than what was available to them on the private market. Blacks, moreover, constituted a higher percentage of WPA workers than relief recipients in the South. That suggests that the WPA was providing a better deal than what otherwise would have been available. Furthermore, African Americans were very highly represented in the WPA labor forces of southern cities, receiving a greater share of employment in relation to their share of the population in fourteen of twenty-two large southern and border state cities in 1941. In outdoor WPA projects in the South, black and white men worked together.[73]

All the same, these figures mask other ways that New Deal social policy failed to reduce inequalities and in some cases reinforced them. Blacks tended to suffer higher rates of unemployment than whites, so that their overrepresentation in the WPA work force with respect to population did not mean overrepresentation with respect to need. In northern cities, African Americans received work at a higher rate than their share of the population in every recorded instance. Blacks earned less than whites generally speaking, because they lived in low-wage counties, and only rarely found work on the higher-paying professional projects or supervisory positions. African Americans in the rural South did far worse than their counterparts in the urban South. In that region, moreover, the proportion of African Americans receiving WPA work relative to their representation in the population fluctuated wildly, indicating obvious discrimination. In the rural South, African American women were doubly disadvantaged, suffering racial discrimination as well as the program's biases against female family heads. Southern sewing projects, moreover, combined sex segregation with race segregation.[74] All in all, the WPA was by far fairer than what was available previously, and it eased some racial inequalities. But the program also included some inequalities, sometimes reinforced race distinctions, and did not greatly challenge the racial order in the South.

African Americans did less well in other New Deal programs. In the special assistance programs, their representation was similar to that in the WPA program. Black Americans constituted about 11.2 percent of those accepted for OAA in 1939–40, whereas nonwhites constituted only 7.1 percent of those sixty-five years of age and older in 1940. Yet African American recipients of OAA were on average older and received less per month than white recipients, especially in the South. Like OAA, ADC was a breakthrough in fairness compared to what was previously available. Although only 3 percent of recipients of mothers' pensions were African American, black children comprised 16 percent of all children accepted for ADC in 1939–40. However, the same problems of discrimination applied to ADC as to OAA.[75]

The social insurance programs were unfair in a different way. OASI was a national program and thus the prospects of racial discrimination within the beneficiary group were nil. Impossible, too, was discrimination against immigrants such as had been added by Congress to WPA work. Yet prominently excluded from its taxes and coverage, as was also true for Unemployment Compensation, were agricultural and domestic workers. As has been widely noted, in the 1930s two-thirds of African Americans were working in these occupations. Yet large numbers of whites and immigrants were also in the excluded categories of work. In 1937, for instance, African Americans constituted about 7 percent of covered workers in OAI.[76] Making social insurance programs fair across races would thus require the inclusion of more categories of workers.

CONCLUSION

Although the period after Roosevelt's reelection in 1936 is often considered one of political stalemate, it witnessed the augmentation and consolidation of modern American social policy. The Third New Deal provided at the very least a period of benign neglect. Opponents of social policy were engaged in other battles while new programs reached out to vast new constituencies. Moreover, the Fair Labor Standards Act of 1938 helped to legitimate the minimum American standard of living promoted by New Deal policymakers. More than that, administrative reorganization and legislative amendments helped to reinforce the programs of the Second New Deal. Executive reorganization also promised to provide more central planning in social policy than had been previously evident. As a result of all these changes, American efforts in social policy led those of major industrial nations.

The same sorts of forces that discouraged or encouraged the enactment of social policy also influenced its augmentation and consolidation. Southern members of Congress elected from undemocratic districts headed the opposition to New Deal social policy. Patronage-oriented legislators tried to use the new social policies for organizational purposes and made them more difficult to implement. The federal nature of the American polity made the president engage in battles that would have been unnecessary in other polities, delaying the progress of social policies.

The main burden of planning social policy remained within the social spending agencies of the administration. This time the important actors were within the new agencies created during the Second New Deal: the WPA and the SSB. Proposals for changes and expansions of social policy typically reflected their views. Whether social policy would progress in these directions depended on the orientation and power of the president and his backing in Congress. Roosevelt made a strong commitment to New Deal social policy in his reelection campaign and was returned with another Congress favorable to social spending. After the elections of 1938, the reform-oriented contingent in Congress was smaller, but still sufficient to press through augmentations of social policy. As was the case during the period of enactment, programs backed by social movements did better than those not so backed. The less well-mobilized Townsendites had notably channeled their political energies in such way as to make the most of the situation. Their efforts were not enough to pass the Townsend Plan, but did plenty to advance OAA.

The policy resulting from these breakthroughs had a number of distinctive characteristics. It was based mainly on work and means-tested relief programs and was supplemented by social insurance. The private component of social policy was small. This policy took many market pressures off workers, especially through the provision of work at reasonable wages for a relatively long period of time. The policy, too, sorted groups into the employable and the unemployable. In doing so, it tended to reinforce unequal and stereotyped gender relations. Racially speaking, the policy was much fairer than any previous American policies had been. Still, discrimination remained in the operation of programs, especially in the South and especially in programs with greater local influence in them.

The last half of the 1930s had witnessed impressive breakthroughs in social policy, and in the eyes of the reformers American public social provision was off to an excellent start. However, a number of problems remained. New Deal reformers saw the redressing of these problems in the relief state as the next challenge in social politics. With Roosevelt hinting that he might try for an unprecedented third term—Hopkins being removed from the running by radical surgery—it seemed as if the reformers would get their chance. Before I discuss these developments, though, it is worth examining social policy at the state and local levels of government. New Deal social policy had centralizing tendencies and moved far past the locally controlled poor laws it meant to replace. Yet the policy was predicated on the cooperation of states and localities. In many cases, as the next chapter shows, this cooperation was not forthcoming.

CHAPTER FIVE

Some Little New Deals Are Littler than Others

The General Assembly of 1936 will go down in history as one of the most reactionary legislatures which has sat in Virginia since the first parliamentary gathering the New World convened at Jamestown in 1619.

— *Richmond* Times-Dispatch, *after Virginia's failure in 1936 to adopt legislation to conform to the Social Security Act*

There will always be a measure of larceny in our state and urban politics, just as there is in business. Show me an administration that is one hundred percent pure and I will show you a new species of human being.

— *Edward Kelly, mayor of Chicago, May 1947*

In order that we may discontinue, as soon as possible, the maintenance of employable people in idleness, I submit . . . that we should substitute for the present policy of paying niggardly cash doles for unemployment relief, a new policy of placing the unemployed at work to support themselves.

— *Culbert L. Olson, governor of California, January 1939*

I know that this [Wisconsin Works] program will be attacked by those who say we cannot "spend" our way out of the Depression. But we most certainly cannot starve ourselves out of the Depression.

— *Philip F. La Follette, governor of Wisconsin, May 1935*

You fellows out West can do things I can't do. My hands are tied. I have the reactionary South on my hands and I cannot go into my own state, New York, and make the same appeal that you can make out West.

— *Franklin D. Roosevelt to La Follette, after learning of his plans to travel to promote political realignment, June 1937*

INNOVATIONS at the national level constitute only part of the story of American social policy in the Great Depression.[1] Any account that ignores the responses of states and localities would be deficient. For New Deal social policy provided inducements and incentives for states and localities to assume a fair share of social and fiscal responsibilities, and these responses mattered. National policy gave states fiscal incentives to pass programs for Old Age Assistance (OAA), Aid to Dependent Children (ADC), and Unemployment Compensation (UC), among others, but left up to the states if, when, and how they would participate. For the "unemployable" outside special categories and for those waiting to receive Works Progress Administration (WPA) work, the states were on their own. Even the WPA, run by a national agency and funded mainly with national money, required state and local cooperation to achieve its goals: to provide as much work with as little discrimination as possible to as many unemployed people deemed employable as possible. Each of these new obligations in social policy required states to raise funds.

The architects of New Deal social policy hoped that the states would join in the spirit of national reforms. They wanted the incentives of the Social Security Act to provoke broadly similar and adequate programs. They also wanted the states to hold up their end of the implicit deal over work and relief. That would mean instituting standards of general relief similar to those set by the defunct Federal Emergency Relief Administration (FERA). That would also mean cooperating with the WPA by designing programs and choosing fairly those who would get work. The Roosevelt Administration expected that states would secure their commitment to the new policy order by breaking new fiscal ground—revamping their taxation structures and eclipsing property taxes with modern sources of revenue. The administration hoped that the states would emulate the national government in adopting little New Deals.

By 1940 the states and localities were involved in social policy in ways that would have been difficult to imagine a decade earlier. Each state had some version of a little New Deal, and because the New Deal emphasized work and relief, each state created something of a "welfare" state in the American sense of the term. But the reactions to the New Deal's fiscal incentives, implicit bargains, and moral suasion were greatly different around the country. The states differed in their degree of cooperation with the WPA. Some states quickly legislated programs encouraged by the Social Security Act, while others took their time. Only few provided adequate payments to the bulk of the population targeted by the programs. Without any fiscal incentives, almost all states did a poor job in general assistance. Finally, almost all the states moved to modernize their taxation systems, but some adopted regressive sales taxes, while others adopted potentially progressive income taxes. As the decade ended, some little New Deals were littler than others.

Worth understanding in themselves, the experiences of the states also provide a means to appraise the institutional politics theory. The states varied quite a bit in their political institutions and actors. For instance, the states included polities only minimally democratic as well as polities in which patronage-oriented political parties were dominant. Progressive and Farmer-Labor parties took power in some states; other states had left-leaning Democratic regimes. States varied in the degree of domestic bureaucratic development, and the strength and collective action of challengers varied greatly across the country. I expect that states in different institutional and political situations would react differently, and I follow the responses of four such divergent states—Virginia, Illinois, California, and Wisconsin.

Overall, these case studies illustrate how a federal system with highly diverse polities within in it constrains social policy. Those fighting in national politics for greater state and local control over programs often did so because such control would produce lower benefits and greater opportunities for discrimination in choosing beneficiaries and the grants for them. Although some states were restrained in the development of their social programs by federal standards, for the most part greater federal control produced more generous, extensive, and fairer programs. States molded their little New Deals in ways mainly determined by the incentives and pressures applied by the federal government. But the states typically grew attached to their little New Deals, no matter how little they were. By 1940, states were far more powerful forces in social policy than when the 1930s began. Their decisions redefined social politics and constrained national reformers in the 1940s and beyond. The states could never again be taken for granted by the federal government.

FEDERAL STIMULI AND STATE RESPONSES IN SOCIAL POLICY

The programs of the Second New Deal provided different sorts of incentives and stimuli to the states for action on social policy. Very strong inducements were provided by the WPA. Because the federal government picked up the vast majority of the costs of the WPA, it would have been foolish for states and localities not to cooperate in some minimal fashion. And although WPA wages for specific types of work were set by the national government, state and local governments could affect these wages by their control over the design of WPA projects. For instance, lower levels of government might devise projects only for the greatly unskilled. States and localities could resist the WPA in other ways, notably by discrimination in choosing applicants for relief. Some states, moreover, were unable or unwilling to run the program. In such cases, the WPA assumed responsibility for operations.

The Social Security Act gave the states overwhelming incentives to pass their own UC programs by legislating an "offset" of the payroll taxes for unemployment compensation. If a state passed its own tax, the federal tax was null. Businesses, the main opponents of the program, were going to be taxed regardless, and the only way to ease their burden was for the state to pass its own program. National legislative action not only placed the issue on the political agenda of the states. Barring Supreme Court nullification, the legislation ensured that some program—whatever its quality—would pass in all of them.

The incentives for the grant-in-aid programs of the Social Security Act provided strong, but less compelling incentives to act. The OAA program provided one-to-one matching funds. By holding out, states would forgo federal monies. But even those states with old-age pension programs by 1935 had to make considerable changes to conform to federal standards. Thus the act placed OAA on the political agenda of each state—to decide whether and to what degree to take advantage of the federal offer. The national OAA provisions greatly increased the odds of individual legislators supporting a bill. The ADC program had a largely similar impact, but because the states had to put up two dollars for every federal dollar, the incentives were less forceful. In either case, states with the most advanced old-age or widows' programs had the strongest incentives to act.

Much lower on the scale of political priorities was general assistance. The federal government quit the business of general relief when it created the WPA and ended the operations of the FERA in 1935. Without incentives, save the unwieldy and potentially self-defeating one of withholding WPA jobs, the national government hoped that states and localities would fund the many people waiting for WPA work, as well as the unemployable. The best case would be for the states to create their own "little WPAs," as they were inevitably called, with work relief for those unable to receive Works Progress Administration funding. The burden-sharing implied by the creation of the WPA—a national work program in exchange for the states taking over general assistance—was only implicit, however. The federal government constrained the states to do little in providing relief. Changes in taxation policy were fostered by the adoption of these other programs, and in that way taxation policy followed spending policy. Yet new social policy left leeway in deciding the form of taxation.

As a result of national incentives and internal forces for change, some states made notable breakthroughs in public social provision. Wisconsin passed an unemployment compensation law before the Social Security Act and anticipated the WPA by presenting a works program before the national one was ironed out. California enacted one of the nation's most generous programs of Old-Age Assistance by the end of the 1930s and also attempted to create a state WPA for the unemployed unaided by the national one. In Minnesota the Farmer-Labor party took office and advanced programs to benefit its cross-class coalition of supporters. Huey P. Long and his followers reversed decades of old-guard rule to create one of the strongest tax systems in Louisiana, one of the nation's poorest states. Many states of the West, including such states as Montana and Idaho, ranking relatively low in income and industrialization, were nonetheless leaders in work and relief programs by the end of the 1930s. Other states held back. Illinois, one of the nation's richest and most populous states, with the nation's second largest city, was pushed mainly against the will of its political leaders into the world of modern public policy. Similarly, much of heavily urban and industrial New England only gingerly embraced New Deal reforms. The Louisiana of Long and his successors was anomalous. Most states of the former Confederacy were hostile to the New Deal. Virginia, as we shall see, was in the equivalent of open revolt.[2]

Greater national control and incentives resulted in greater benefits and less variability in relief programs. WPA wages were much higher than the payments received for OAA and ADC and the differences across states were greater in those programs. Still, there were some differences in average wages for the WPA. For the fiscal year ending June 1940, the wages ranged from about 55 cents per hour in New York to about 32 cents per hour in Mississippi.[3] If workers in those states logged the required 130 hours per month, this would mean about $71.50 per month in New York and about $41.60 in Mississippi—less than a two-to-one ratio. OAA was the most expensive grant-in-aid program and one of the hottest political issues in state-level politics during the Depression. Although each state had adopted a federally approved OAA program by 1939, these varied widely in generosity. In 1940 California was spending approximately $38 per month on each OAA pensioner, more than four times as much as Arkansas, which was spending about $9.[4] In part because of lesser incentives, states took more time in adopting legislation to qualify for federal matching ADC payments. At the end of the 1930s, only forty states had qualifying ADC programs. Each holdout still had a mothers' pensions law on the books, though, and was providing in a general sense aid to dependent children. In 1940, ADC and mothers' pensions benefits ranged from an average of about $23.50 per child per month in New York to about $4.67 in Alabama—more than a five-to-one ratio. Moreover, unlike for OAA, state-to-state differences in coverage were extreme for ADC. In 1940 Idaho provided benefits to 57 percent of female-headed families with children, while Texas covered a paltry one-tenth of 1 percent of such families with its outmoded mothers' pension program.[5]

Such disparities could not be accounted for by differences in incomes or the cost of living. It has always been more expensive to live in New York or California than in Mississippi, Arkansas, or Alabama, but never five times more expensive. To get a sense of the real significance of these differences in policy decisions, though, I rank the generosity of WPA and OAA programs in ways that takes into account income differentials. Because of greater variations in coverage for ADC programs, I take into account both income-corrected generosity and coverage in ranking states.[6]

The top ten states for each program are presented in Table 5.1. Many of the top states were from the West, including Utah, Idaho, and Colorado.

TABLE 5.1
Top Ten States in WPA Wages, OAA Pensions, and ADC
Programs, 1940

Rank	WPA Wages[a]	OAA Pensions[a]	ADC Programs[b]
1.	Colorado	Colorado	Utah
2.	Utah	California	Idaho
3.	Arizona	Arizona	Nebraska
4.	Oregon	Idaho	North Dakota
5.	New Mexico	Utah	Wisconsin
6.	New York	Massachusetts	Indiana
7.	Minnesota	South Dakota	Kansas
8.	Idaho	Kansas	Oklahoma
9.	Washington	Wyoming	Minnesota
10.	Montana	Wisconsin	Colorado

[a] Based on the standardized residuals of a regression of the average wage
or pension in 1940 on per capita income in 1940.
[b] Based on the 1940 ADC quality index, which includes benefits and
coverage and takes income into account.

Several, though, were from the upper Midwest. Wisconsin and Minnesota
each appear on two top-ten lists. Some eastern states appear on one list or
another, such as New York and Massachusetts. For the WPA, the states
with the highest wages were western ones, with Colorado, Utah, and Arizona near the top. For OAA the most generous states, also typically from
the West, were Colorado, California, and Arizona. They no doubt provided
pensions that might be fairly described as adequate. As for ADC, most of
the top ten states were from the West and upper Midwest, too, this time
with Utah at the very top.

Southern and border states were typically laggard in work and special
relief programs. As Table 5.2 shows, most of the bottom positions were
held by states of the former Confederacy. In terms of WPA wages, five
southern states were among the bottom ten, with Delaware at the very bottom, and near the bottom were the western state Nevada and the northeastern state Connecticut. The southern domination of the bottom ranks of
OAA pensions and ADC benefits was even greater. The least generous efforts in OAA pensions appeared again in Delaware, whose high income
contrasted with its stingy pensions, and seven of the bottom ten were from
the former Confederacy. The OAA programs of the bottom ten doubtless
did little more than stave off starvation or poorhouse institutionalization.
As for ADC, among the bottom ten were six southern states; also appearing
among the bottom ten were five of the eight states without federally sanctioned ADC programs. The only northern states on the list, Illinois and

TABLE 5.2
Bottom Ten States in WPA Wages, OAA Pensions, and ADC
Programs, 1940

Rank	WPA Wages[a]	OAA Pensions[a]	ADC Programs[b]
39.	Kentucky	Tennessee	Florida
40.	North Carolina	Arkansas	South Carolina
41.	Tennessee	Maryland	Delaware
42.	Florida	Kentucky	Georgia
43.	Oklahoma	Texas	Connecticut
44.	Texas	Florida	Illinois
45.	Connecticut	South Carolina	Virginia
46.	Virginia	Georgia	Mississippi
47.	Nevada	Virginia	Kentucky
48.	Delaware	Delaware	Texas

[a] Based on the standardized residuals of a regression of the average wage or pension in 1940 on per capita income in 1940.

[b] Based on the 1940 ADC quality index, which includes benefits and coverage and takes income into account.

Connecticut, had not passed ADC legislation by 1940. By their inaction on ADC, these states had made a political decision to rely on meager mothers' pensions programs dating from the Progressive Era.

As for general assistance, where they had the greatest power and the fewest incentives, states generally fumbled the issue. Work relief programs at their peak of efficiency hired only about 40 percent of the unemployed, but general relief programs did not come close to picking up the slack. Some did try, as about half of the states had little WPAs of some variety. Even the larger among them, however, rarely provided work for even a quarter of the general relief caseload. Work relief usually meant more money, but that was not always the case. A telling sign of their efforts appears in Table 5.3, which ranks states according to the ratio of WPA recipients to general relief recipients in 1940. A low ratio indicates that the state was picking up the slack left by the WPA, aiding relatively many by way of general relief, and a high ratio indicates the opposite. The top four states included New York, Maine, Iowa, and California. Each had about three general assistance recipients for every two WPA recipients. New York paid about thirty dollars per month in general assistance in 1940. On the other hand, some states were barely trying. Mississippi had more than twenty-nine WPA workers for each general relief recipient, and the ratios for the Alabama and South Carolina were around twenty. Mississippi also paid about three dollars per month. In short, almost no one in these states was being accepted for general relief unless he or she was on the way to being transferred to the WPA's rolls. Many of the bottom ten were also among the

TABLE 5.3
Ratio of WPA Workers to General Relief Recipients, 1940:
Lowest and Highest States

Rank	State	Ratio	Rank	State	Ratio
1.	New York	0.56	39.	Kentucky	5.36
2.	California	0.56	40.	North Carolina	5.36
3.	Maine	0.62	41.	Texas	5.80
4.	Pennsylvania	0.65	42.	Tennessee	5.89
5.	Iowa	0.65	43.	New Mexico	5.97
6.	New Hampshire	0.83	44.	Georgia	6.37
7.	Illinois	0.93	45.	Arkansas	11.41
8.	Kansas	0.93	46.	South Carolina	19.71
9.	Connecticut	0.94	47.	Alabama	21.77
10.	Wisconsin	1.00	48.	Mississippi	29.16

Sources: U.S. Federal Works Agency, Final Report of the WPA Program (Washington, D.C.: U.S. Government Printing Office, 1943), Table 2, p. 111. U.S. Federal Security Agency, Social Security Yearbook, 1940 (Washington, D.C.: U.S. Government Printing Office, 1941), pp. 283–84.

Note: The WPA data are from December 1939. The general relief data are from January 1940.

bottom in the generosity of general relief grants, even with per capita income taken into account.[7]

Social policy legislation spurred the states into action on taxation. State government revenue more than doubled between 1927 and 1940, jumping from $2.15 billion to $5.74 billion. In the same period, state taxes grew from $1.61 billion to $3.31 billion, or from about 1.7 percent of GNP to about 3.3 percent. Between 1929 and 1940, the median state had increased its taxes by about $16.50 per person—and that despite basically stagnant incomes. States did not move, however, in uniform or consistent ways on the issue of taxation. By the end of the 1930s some twenty-nine states had passed individual income taxes, and thirty-one had corporation income taxes. States such as Wisconsin and Massachusetts merely buttressed individual and corporate income taxes dating from before the Depression. States such as California waited until the Depression to adopt income taxes. Many states went the opposite direction, adopting regressive sales taxes, an innovation of the Depression. As the 1930s ended, some twenty-three states had adopted general sales taxes. Eight states adopted general sales taxes while avoiding income taxes during the Depression, including Ohio, Illinois, Indiana, and Michigan. Some states, including Arizona, Colorado, New Mexico, and Utah, had adopted both income taxes and general sales taxes by 1940. Other states, including Texas, Florida, Rhode Island, and Maine, ended the 1930s without either modern source of taxation. In short, some states reinforced their spending systems with progressive taxation and others muted the impact of spending with regressive taxes.[8]

THE INSTITUTIONAL POLITICS THEORY: EXPECTATIONS
FOR SOCIAL SPENDING IN THE STATES

What accounts for these different social and fiscal policy responses to
the Depression and the New Deal? My institutional politics theory suggests
that *combinations* of institutional and political conditions will predict
spending outcomes and that there is more than one way to achieve adequate
social spending. According to the theory, one of the most basic characteristics of political institutions is whether and the degree to which they are motivated by democratic practices of selection and recruitment. Can people
assemble and exercise free speech? Is voting widespread or discouraged by
poll taxes or violence? Is there more than one choice among parties? The
existence of democratic political institutions is expected to promote greater
spending efforts for programs benefiting everyday citizens and its absence
the opposite. A lack of democracy, working especially through restrictions
on the franchise, is expected to prevent pro-spending outcomes, and thus I
consider democratic rights to be a necessary condition for adequate little
New Deals.

Another important institutional influence on policy concerns the nature
of political party organizations. I expect patronage-oriented parties to regard programmatic spending policies as threats to the individualistic rewards upon which such parties thrive. They are expected to be willing to
adopt and spend on programs with patronage opportunities, but not to do
so with automatic or entitlement programs that cannot be easily divided
with discretion among constituents. Similarly, patronage politicians hope to
keep taxes down or hide them from voters—a conflict with social policy.[9]

These conditions are also expected to influence the presence of actors in
favor of social spending. Notably, I expect a denial of democratic rights to
discourage greatly the emergence of social movements. Under such circumstances any mass political activity is difficult, and so mounting challenges
will be especially trying. I also expect the entrenchment of patronage parties
to deter though not prevent social movements and administrative authority.
For the leaders of these organizations would likely to find both to be threatening to party prerogatives.[10]

If these structural doors are open, powerful pro-spending political actors
are still needed to urge new spending policies through them. One set of
these political actors includes reform-oriented or left-leaning regimes, with
right-wing regimes bringing the opposite. The most left-leaning parties are
expected to be those Democratic or third parties outside the nondemocratic
South that are not organized on patronage-oriented lines. When such parties gain power, I expect them to promote social policy. The theory also
expects policy innovations and more generous programs where domestic
bureaucrats are influential. Those agencies whose missions embrace social

spending are expected to become advocates and forces for public policies — by lobbying for and providing information about them. At worst they may simply provide the general public with confidence that new programs will be run fairly. I also expect social movements to spur social spending. Because organized labor has promoted social policies especially as they concern workers, a strong labor movement might form a functional equivalent to a pro-spending party in power or to strong domestic administrators. By strong I mean organizing a large percentage of workers and devoting considerable resources to political collective action. The same is true for the Townsend Movement on the issue of OAA. Other challengers might have an impact on issues of concern, if they were both well supported and politically mobilized.

In what follows, I divide the states of the Union according to these different institutional and political situations. These categorizations are often judgment calls and are based on indicators that do not entirely capture what I am arguing. All the same, doing so greatly clarifies matters. Dividing states into these all-or-nothing categories is simple for the main institutional features of the polity. To ascertain which states were democratized and which were underdemocratized, I examined voting behavior and party systems. A natural break in the data on the degree to which demographically eligible voters actually voted appeared between the eleven former states of the Confederacy and the rest. In the southern states voting was discouraged through violence, intimidation, and taxes. Each of these states, moreover, was characterized by one-party rule or one-party dominance.[11] To separate states according to the patronage bases of their party systems, I rely on David Mayhew's study, which categorizes each system according to the degree to which it is dominated by patronage-oriented parties. In many states across America, both major parties had been organized on such principles since the nineteenth century and had not changed much since then. Some thirteen states can be broadly characterized as having patronage-oriented party systems.[12] I consider the rest to have relatively "open" party systems.

The strength of political actors can also be broken down into straightforward "presence" or "absence" categories for purposes of simplification. There was no dearth of Democratic regimes in the 1930s. In some states, radical third parties also were strong. In Minnesota, the Farmer-Labor party won office behind Floyd Olson. In Wisconsin, the Progressive party, led by Robert M. La Follette's sons, Robert Jr. and Philip, briefly ran the state. All in all, some thirty states had either a Democratic-party regime or a third-party regime for four years or more in the 1930s.[13]

To summarize the strength of domestic bureaucracies, I am focusing on industrial commissions and departments of welfare. In some states industrial commissions had rule-making authority in the administration of safety laws and also had oversight power over workmen's compensation — the only major social insurance program in existence throughout the United

States before the Depression. One notable case was Wisconsin's powerful Industrial Commission, which was the site of that state's breakthrough Unemployment Compensation legislation in 1932. On the eve of the Depression, though, only fifteen states that had industrial commissions with rule-making powers in labor safety issues. More states, twenty-six all told, had created centralized departments of welfare. Most of these ran relief programs that went beyond charitable and correctional institutions. Most of the states with revamped domestic bureaucracies were outside the underdemocratized and patronage sector of the U.S. polity, but some were not.[14]

The presence of Depression-era social movements also varied across the states. Because I am arguing that their impact is a function of large followings and political presence I focus on each of these characteristics for the labor movement and the Townsend Movement. For labor, fourteen states scored high in *both* unionization and political resource mobilization through state federations of labor.[15] To divide states into ones with powerful Townsend Movements and ones without them, I also examine membership and political presence. Political presence can be ascertained broadly by examining the degree to which Movement-endorsed House of Representative candidates won office—the Townsendites' main form of political action. Some seventeen states, mainly in the West, had in this sense powerful Townsend Movements.[16]

FOUR STATES RESPOND TO THE NEW DEAL

I illustrate the argument by choosing states in different institutional and political situations and following their responses to the New Deal. My decisions combine theory and expediency. The states vary along the dimensions I identify as important and their Depression-era politics and social policy experiences are well documented, easing discussion and evaluation. These accounts suggest why some states went far down the road with New Deal social policy and why others held back.

My institutional politics argument suggests that various categories of states would respond positively to the New Deal. These states would be outside the underdemocratized and patronage-oriented sector of the polity and include one or more main forces for change: either a left-wing regime, an empowered state bureaucracy, or politically powerful social movement actors. In the best case for social policy, all three would be present. The theory also suggests three sorts of negative cases. The first is any state with an undemocratic political system. The second is a state from a patronage-oriented party system, but with limited countervailing forces for social policy. The third is a state with a democratic political system and an open party system, but with no powerful actors for change. In Table 5.4, I summarize

TABLE 5.4
Political Profiles of Four States According to Institutional and Political Categories

	Voting Rights[a]	*Patronage Party*[b]	*Left/Center Party Rule*[c]	*Administrative Powers*[d]	*Labor Movement*[e]	*Townsend Movement*[f]
Wisconsin	Yes	No	Yes	Yes	Yes	Yes
California	Yes	No	No	Yes	Yes	Yes
Illinois	Yes	Yes	Yes	No	Yes	No
Virginia	No	No	Yes	No	No	No

[a] Refers to the right to vote, as manifested in relatively high voting participation.

[b] Refers to whether a state had centralized, patronage-oriented, electioneering organizations.

[c] Refers to whether the Democratic party or a radical third party controlled the state government for four years or more during the 1930s.

[d] Refers to whether the state labor commissioner had rule making authority in safety issues by the end of the 1920s and is used as general indicator of power in domestic bureaucracies before 1930.

[e] Refers to whether the state had a powerful labor movement in the 1930s.

[f] Refers to whether the state had a powerful Townsend Movement in the 1930s.

See the text for complete definitions and measurements.

the characteristics for the four states—Virginia, Illinois, California, and Wisconsin, which I follow below.[17]

Two of them had structural blocks to reform. Like other states in the South, Virginia had representative government in which voting and other democratic rights were severely restricted. In the 1932 and 1936 presidential contests, only 22.1 and 23 percent of the demographically eligible voters actually voted, as compared to 56.9 and 61 percent in the nation as a whole. Virginia makes a good case for discussion, as it was not part of the Deep South, where cotton tenant farming was central to the economy. Instead it was part of the Peripheral South, as Earl and Merle Black call it. Also, Virginia had a relatively well-organized polity, with a coherently organized Democratic party receiving some competition from a small Republican party. These characteristics were chosen by V. O. Key as ones that mitigated against the South's characteristically disorganized politics, which he claimed hampered social spending for have-nots.[18] Illinois provides an example of a patronage-oriented party system. Mayhew characterizes Illinois as a "regular organization" state, scoring highest on his measure of traditional party organization. A highly industrialized state, Illinois also had some potentially countervailing influences on its party system, notably its historically strong labor movement, buttressed by the gains of the CIO at the end of the 1930s.[19]

The other two states were in democratic and open political systems, and thus had, to my way of thinking, more potential for big little New Deals. But each had different configurations of powerful pro-spending political actors. Although it had no Democratic or third-party regime during the 1930s, California was the site of previous progressive reforms and relatively powerful social movements, especially on the issue of old-age pensions. My expectation is for solid progress in social policy generally, but especial progress in areas of strong social movements. Wisconsin constitutes perhaps the best-case scenario. It was in the forefront of administrative reform before the 1930s, had powerful social movements, and was led by a Progressive party during the middle of the 1930s. There I expect the greatest gains in social policy, across the board.

The Virginia Political Oligarchy and the Thwarting of New Deal Social Policy

Described by Key as a "political museum piece" with a polity reminiscent of England's before its 1832 electoral reforms, the Old Dominion was dominated by a political oligarchy. The oligarchy was led by Harry F. Byrd, who served as governor in the 1920s and ran the state from the Senate after 1932. Although there was in existence a liberal, anti-Byrd faction of the Virginia Democratic party, it was effectively disfranchised. The result was a political regime that resisted entrance into the world of modern social policy. In terms of thwarting the social policies of the New Deal, Virginia constituted a model of the politically possible.[20]

As Key summarized the situation in 1949, the pro-New Deal faction of the party "cannot carry their case to the people; the people do not vote." Virginia poll taxes were unusually high and inhibiting. To vote in a primary cost $1.50, to be paid six months in advance. Worse than that, those who did not pay to vote in one year would have to pay the accumulated arrears to be able to vote in the future. Because of the stringent tax and the dominance of the regular Democratic regime, fewer people voted in Virginia than in many Deep South states. As Key notes, only 11.5 percent of those twenty-one years and older actually voted in gubernatorial elections from 1925 to 1945. He called Mississippi "a hotbed of democracy" by contrast. Unlike the subjects of Virginia, moreover, political officeholders enjoyed considerable security. During the 1930s, Virginia's delegation to Congress was not only solidly Democratic, but also was constituted of the same members each term.[21]

By all accounts the Virginia regular Democratic organization was not venal. It generally provided honest, good government. As governor in the 1920s, Byrd was responsible for the consolidation of more than one hundred bureaus, boards, and departments into fourteen departments centralized under the control of the governor. Among these was its department of welfare. The machine showed little sign of a traditional patronage orientation.[22] Administrative consolidation was, however, more a cost-cutting device than a means to provide better service. Good as far as it went, government in Virginia was extremely constricted. Although Virginia's mothers' pension program gave average monthly grants of about $16.50 per family in 1931, only somewhat below the median, only about four families in every ten thousand received grants, placing Virginia in the bottom ten. Virginia managed to make it into the middle 1930s without even a county-optional old-age pension program.[23]

The generous social policies of the New Deal came in direct conflict to the "no relief" policies of Byrd. The state fought Harry Hopkins during the period of emergency relief, setting up restrictions on relief much higher than its neighbors did. All the same, Byrd and Virginia's senior senator, Carter Glass, thought the FERA better than the works program, because the former was less expensive and presumably more degrading. Byrd and Glass led the charge against the WPA in the Senate. Byrd himself was the author of a failed amendment to reduce the works appropriation by $1.9 billion. Virginia wanted to keep strict control over its work relief operations and had among the lowest wages for WPA workers. Virginia had about three persons on the WPA for each one on relief, the fourteenth worst performance among states.[24]

Virginia also resisted the Social Security Act programs—which had greater implications for state finances. Byrd spoke against the bill in Congress, and when it passed his state-level supporters ignored the incentives in the act. In 1936, the Virginia General Assembly, labeled reactionary by the Richmond *Times-Dispatch*, passed "not one social security or labor bill of importance." The Virginia Manufacturers Association agreed to an unemployment compensation bill only after Roosevelt's overwhelming electoral triumph in November 1936. Virginia did not legislate an OAA bill until 1938—making it the last state to do so. When it finally adopted OAA, Virginia provided benefits that were very low given its income, ranking forty-sixth of the forty-eight states. Its mothers' pension program did not qualify for federal matching funds until the 1940s, leaving Virginia at forty-fifth in generosity and coverage in 1940.[25]

If the Virginia Democratic oligarchy was not going to press for social policy neither were there powerful movements to do so. The labor movement had not made much progress before the New Deal in Virginia and did not make much progress during the 1930s either. Virginia ended the decade with only about 10 percent of its nonagricultural labor force in unions. Pension movements did not gain a foothold. Partly because of perceived difficulties in organizing the South, the Townsend Movement turned to this region last. Southern states took nine of the bottom ten places in terms of the number of Townsend Clubs per capita, Virginia placing next to last. At least as important was the fact that none of the Virginia House delegation was supported by the Townsend Movement, nor did anyone from the delegation seek Townsend support.[26]

By every possible measure, good-government but underdemocratized Virginia placed itself near the bottom of states in social policy. Virginia's experience suggests the lower limit of the New Deal's national-level incentives for social policy. As one study of Virginia and the New Deal concluded, "Virginia's 'little New Deal' was very little indeed."[27] No doubt this had much to do with the fact that Virginia was a political oligarchy with only trappings of democracy. No doubt, too, the similarly unenthusiastic responses to the New Deal among politicians throughout the undemocratic South also owed much to the fact that everyday people could not easily participate in politics.

Democrats, Patronage, and the Conflict Between Clout and Reform in Illinois

In Illinois, proponents of social policies faced problems with its Democratic party that were far different from those in Virginia. Upstate Chicago Democrats had begun to build "the machine," as it came to be called, a political organization based on patronage and issue avoidance. The growing strength of the Chicago machine and the improving fortunes of Democrats nationally led to political dominance by the Illinois Democrats for the bulk of the Depression era. The machine cooperated with the Roosevelt Administration's work program—the aspect of the New Deal with the greatest patronage opportunities. The Democrats of Illinois, however, mainly deflected the programs of the Social Security Act. Its poor record was generated despite the fact that the state was among the most industrialized and urbanized in the nation, despite the fact that Illinois had a strong labor movement comprising Chicago industrial workers and downstate coal miners—and despite the fact that the Chicago machine had the backing of the Roosevelt Administration.[28]

The Chicago Democratic machine was a long time in the making, but the Democratic party in Illinois was far from an unformed shell which New Dealers might fill with like-minded leaders and constituents. Anchored by their control since the turn of the century over the vice wards, as well as by such colorful boss-hoodlums as Michael "Hinky Dink" Kenna and John J. "Bathhouse John" Coughlin, Chicago Democrats did not exit the political wilderness until the election of Anton Cermak as mayor in 1931. Cut down in 1933 by a bullet meant (probably) for President-Elect Roosevelt, Cermak gave way to Edward J. Kelly. Enlisting the talents of the behind-the-scenes operator Patrick A. Nash, Kelly led the Chicago regulars until the end of the Second World War. The machine wielded its "clout"—a Chicago coinage—for several purposes: to install Democratic loyalists on the city payroll, induce other city employees to work for the party, and manipulate city contracts to sustain the machine and some of its operators. According to one standard count the regular organization controlled some thirty-thousand jobs. The Chicago Democrats had great control over the slating of candidates for a number of offices, including statewide Democratic candidates.[29]

Perhaps because of the patronage orientation of both of the major parties, civil service reform made only sporadic gains in Illinois prior to the

Depression. When merit-based civil service was introduced in 1917, it was undermined by the practice of installing "temporary" appointees who did not need to take examinations, but who stayed in office for long periods nonetheless. In the same year, the Illinois Industrial Commission was created, but without jurisdiction over workmen's compensation.[30] The policy experts of Chicago, including the University of Chicago luminaries Charles Merriam of political science and Edith Abbott of social services, did not have much access to state administrative bodies, and they did not provide much impetus to reform.[31]

Illinois Democrats took power in the 1930s by combining dominance in Chicago with pockets of support downstate. Unlike at the national level, however, Illinois Democrats were slow to ally with the labor movement, which had supported mainly Illinois Republicans in the 1920s. In any case, the Illinois State Federation of Labor was not greatly independent of the national American Federation of Labor (AFL) and thus was not in the forefront of agitation for social legislation. And the Chicago Democrats took a live-and-let-live attitude to businessmen such as those represented by the right-wing Illinois Manufacturers' Association. They drew the line only at Al Capone, and only then because his operations threatened the Democrats' stand against Prohibition. The machine did not want to alienate businessmen with new income or payroll taxes or social programs that might require such taxes. Mainly, the Democrats hoped to be bailed out by the federal government. That was Mayor Cermak's purpose when he went to Washington in 1932 and demanded federal relief monies—or troops.[32]

The Illinois Democrats' lack of desire to pay for emergency relief led to well-publicized battles between Governor Henry Horner and Harry Hopkins in 1935. As he did in many other relatively rich states, Hopkins threatened to cut off Federal Emergency Relief funds in Illinois in 1935 unless it put forward more effort of its own. Horner balked, but Hopkins was not bluffing, and the governor reluctantly agreed to the passage of a sales tax.[33] Detached from the anchor of ideology, Governor Horner and Mayor Kelly were free to battle over such "issues" as the creation and control of off-track betting parlors. Perhaps there is larceny in all politics, as Kelly claimed, but the impulse was more freely expressed in Illinois than elsewhere. Looking to 1936, James Farley, the head of the Democratic National Committee, convinced Roosevelt to tilt toward Kelly, who had amassed a huge majority in his 1935 election. Yet Horner secured a downstate base of support and remained governor through 1940.[34]

Kelly and the Chicago machine were willing to cooperate with Hopkins on the WPA, and Hopkins, unimpressed by Horner, reciprocated. Kelly enthusiastically proposed projects. After all, his ally Robert Dunham was placed in charge of the program in Illinois and oversaw approximately 200,000 WPA workers, a bonanza that by far eclipsed the jobs available in the state's various municipalities. There was little hard evidence that the

Plate 5.1 The WPA in Chicago (Russell Lee). The New Deal social program that most interested Illinois politicians was the WPA, depicted here in a Chicago project. Illinois paid a small percentage of project costs, and an ally of Chicago Mayor Edward Kelly headed the state WPA organization. African American workers were highly represented on projects in northern cities, but rarely found work in professional projects or in supervisory roles.

Chicago Democrats greatly contaminated the processes by which workers were declared eligible for or were granted WPA jobs. Lorena Hickok, Hopkins's roving relief scout, gave a favorable rating to the WPA in Chicago. Still, the machine did what it could to take credit for the jobs and was not indifferent to all the political possibilities inherent in so many positions. Before elections, Kelly added workers to the WPA rolls to canvass in behalf of the Democratic party. In 1936, for instance, two-thirds of machine ward-heelers had held jobs as welfare and employment brokers.[35]

Kelly and his allies ran the WPA in a way that cost the state and localities little. Chicago Democrats typically chose highly labor-intensive projects for the WPA, minimizing the contribution for capital typically made by the sponsor. In 1938, before sponsors were forced to pay one-fourth of the cost of projects, Chicago was paying about fifteen times less than New York for its share of WPA projects. Although the WPA program in Illinois did not pay particularly high wages, Illinois found itself among the top ten states in the ratio of general relief recipients to WPA workers, with about one recipient per worker. Kelly did not want to jeopardize a good thing by skimping on general assistance—which had no federal standards in it. And Illinois was notable in employing about twenty thousand people through "little WPA" work relief in November 1939. Wanting to ride the coattails of Roosevelt's WPA and local popularity, the mayor exalted the president in a way that bordered on the slavish. Kelly's standard stump speech was entitled "Roosevelt Is My Religion."[36]

The Chicago machine and thus Illinois took a more aloof attitude to the programs promoted by the Social Security Act. For these programs called for standard and routine, rather than specialized and idiosyncratic, treatment of recipients, as well as required larger contributions from state funds or new taxes. Most northern states had adopted old-age pension legislation prior to the Social Security Act. Illinois waited until after the act to debate pensions in earnest. Even when it passed an OAA bill in 1936, over Horner's veto, the Social Security Board disapproved the plan on the ground that it lacked state supervision of county administrators, sending Illinois back to the drawing board. After Illinois delayed in responding it earned the distinction of being the first state to have its grant suspended. Once its OAA program was up and running, Illinois was not near the bottom in generosity—most places there having been secured by southern states—but it was nowhere near the top. Illinois showed even less enthusiasm for other programs encouraged by the Social Security Act. Waiting until the last moment to see if the act would be found unconstitutional, as urged by the manufacturers' association, Illinois was the last state in the nation to adopt UC, in 1937. Even then it provided the most extreme "merit rating" provisions—loopholes through which businesses might slip out of paying UC taxes altogether. That was not all. As we have seen, Illinois was one of eight states that had not adopted by 1940 an ADC program, and its mothers' pension program dropped it to the bottom ten in ADC. To finance these new programs Illinois chose to rely on regressive sales taxes and avoided passing income taxes.[37]

If Roosevelt was Kelly's religion, it was more like a cult of personality than a devotion to doctrine. The Chicago Democratic regime embraced only those New Deal tenets that provided many jobs at minimal cost. All in all, Kelly's and Horner's responses to the New Deal were not dissimilar to those of many other Democrats who gained power in state politics. These regimes were, in the words of James Patterson, "practical and uninspired . . . [and] looked on the New Deal less as a means of liberalized state policy than as a way of keeping themselves in power."[38] Part of the reason that the Illinois Democratic party was unmoved by most New Deal programs was that it was inspired by an opposing principle of organization—the perpetuation of the party through patronage rather than by way of the class issues of the New Deal.

Social Movements and Social Policy: A New Deal
for the Aged in California

California was politically open and had powerful political forces in favor
of social policy in the 1930s. In the forefront of the Progressive movement,
California had instituted a number of political and administrative reforms
before the 1930s and spawned numerous challenges during the 1930s.
Foremost among these was the one led by the muckraking novelist Upton
Sinclair, who ran on a platform to End Poverty in California (EPIC) that
advocated economic reforms based on "production for use," a kind of
home-grown American socialism. Having a longer life was the aforementioned Townsend Movement, born in Long Beach in 1934, and a number
of other old-age pension groups, including the California Life Retirement
Payments Association, which originated in the Bay Area in 1938. Commonly known as "Ham and Eggs," this challenger called for "thirty [dol-
lars] every Thursday" for everyone in California over fifty. Both the AFL
and the Congress of Industrial Organizations (CIO) wings of the labor
movement were powerful in California, as was the Workers' Alliance. Although some social progressive forces, including many former EPIC members, found a place within a reformed Democratic party, it was unable to
take power during the Depression decade. By the early 1940s California
was in the forefront of old-age pension politics, but did not develop a more
encompassing little New Deal.

California politics defined American progressivism. Hiram Johnson, a
Republican, won the governor's mansion in the election of 1910 by cam-
paigning against the Southern Pacific Railroad. In the following legislative
session he pressed the nation's most radical progressive agenda and secured
many constitutional amendments, including the provision of the initiative,
the referendum, and the recall. In 1913 he further promoted nonpartisan-
ship by the technique of "cross-filing" in primary elections—to allow the
new Progressive party, which he led, to contest Republican nominations.
But Johnson also moved on the agenda of social progressivism by promoting mothers' pensions, restrictions on child labor, an eight-hour day for
women, workmen's compensation, an Industrial Welfare Commission, and
a centralized Board of Charities and Corrections. Johnson was sympathetic
to labor unions, which were particularly powerful in San Francisco, and
was opposed by the conservative wing of the Republican party, led in the
southern part of the state by the antiunion Los Angeles *Times*.[39]

Less progress was made in social politics in the 1920s, during which
conservative and liberal wings of the Republican party vied for control of
California. The Fraternal Order of Eagles (FOE) combined with the California State Federation of Labor and the American Association of Labor Legislation to promote means-tested old-age pensions. Although a bill on these
lines was vetoed by the conservative Governor Friend Richardson in
1923, their efforts met with success in 1929. That year a bill sponsored by

William B. Hornblower, a prominent member of the FOE, made California the first state with mandatory old-age pensions. In the meantime, California had centralized its department of welfare and passed a corporation income tax. By the end of 1934, California stood in the top ten of the twenty-four states with compulsory old-age pensions in terms of average pension and coverage. All the same, California granted only about twenty dollars on average to old-age pension recipients and covered only about 9 percent of those aged sixty-five years and older. These pensions were tightly means- and property-tested and restricted to those seventy years and older, long-time state residents, and non-poorhouse inmates, with strict "relative responsibility" clauses. Embryonic as they were, California's old-age pensions had outgrown its mothers' pensions, which remained county-optional. The number of California families aided by mothers' pensions per ten thousand of population in 1931, for instance, was at the national median, and California's per capita expenditures were only slightly above the median, the average pension standing at about thirty-one dollars per family.[40]

The 1930s saw the resurgence of the Democratic party throughout the nation, but California Democrats were unable quickly to capitalize on it. Having switched his registration from Socialist to Democrat in 1933, Sinclair contested the Democratic nomination in 1934 on his EPIC platform. Among its twelve points were proposals to put to use idle factories and farm land by means of scrip, the adoption of progressive taxes, the repeal of the sales tax, and high old-age, disability, and mothers' pensions. His main primary battle was with George Creel, the candidate of the stalwart Democrat Senator William Gibbs McAdoo. Having benefited from McAdoo's aid in the 1932 convention and uncertain of the untried Sinclair and his EPIC scheme, Roosevelt tilted to Creel in the 1934 primary. Roosevelt withheld support from Sinclair as the election neared, for Sinclair had filled the California Democratic platform with EPIC planks and would not temper the "production for use" topic in the campaign. That further alienated McAdoo and the right-wing Democrat William Randolph Hearst. They were joined by unlikely accomplices. Sinclair's program was described as absurd by the Socialist standardbearer Norman Thomas, and in keeping with their line of the times official Communist organs labeled Sinclair and his program as fascistic.[41]

Worse, Sinclair was the victim of a scurrilous general election campaign in which he was assailed by all manner of conservative and business leaders, through all forms of mass communications media. Their attacks ranged from the slanted coverage and condemning editorials in Hearst's San Francisco *Examiner* and the *Times*, to the radio jeremiads of Aimee Semple McPherson, to the deceitful short subjects produced by MGM's Irving Thalberg. The latter depicted a California under Sinclair rule as the destination point for the nation's hobo population. Among the least malignant attacks were parodies of his program's name, such as "End Property, Introduce Communism" and "Easy Pickings in California." Sinclair also mishandled Townsend. Sinclair demanded fifty-dollar pensions per month from California revenues for everyone over sixty years old, but thought, out loud, that the Townsend Plan was unworkable. In contrast, Governor Frank Merriam, the conservative Republican nominee, skillfully if cynically played to the burgeoning Townsend Movement. He supported legislation "memorializing" Congress to pass the Townsend Plan—a step that would cost California nothing. Townsend in turn denounced EPIC and Sinclair and endorsed Merriam. Sinclair was beaten by 250,000 votes in the general election, even though a number of EPIC supporters, including the candidate for lieutenant governor, Sheridan Downey, twenty-two of the eighty-member Assembly, and State Senator Culbert L. Olson, were elected to office.[42]

As was the case in other states, the Social Security Act and the WPA put social policy on California's political agenda. And despite the loss of Sinclair and the Democrats, California responded vigorously—at least on the issue of old-age pensions. When John B. Pelletier, an EPIC assemblyman from Los Angeles, proposed to increase the monthly pension maximum to the EPIC sum of fifty dollars per month, he lost only narrowly. What became law instead was an act sponsored by Hornblower that raised the maximum grant to thirty-five dollars per month—five dollars beyond what would be matched by the national government. The act also reduced the minimum age of recipients to sixty-five years—five years before that step was required by national law. In 1936, as EPIC Assembly members dropped production for use and focused mainly on their old-age pension plank, another Hornblower proposal became law, converting the thirty-five dollars maximum benefit into a requirement. In 1937, Pelletier and Hornblower played off each other again, producing a law to discount some income in assessing need and to outlaw liens against the property of pension recipients—though the latter provision was eventually thrown out by the state Supreme Court. California was one of a few states that had abandoned the "family budgetary" method of determining grants for the more generous method of granting flat payments, after subtracting income. By the end of 1937 California had the second-highest average OAA benefit in the country. A combination of long-term interest-group activity and EPIC support, with the Townsend Movement constituting a backdrop, had much to do with that result.[43]

In other ways, though, California's reaction to New Deal social policy was somewhat sluggish. The State Relief Agency (SRA), established in California after the end of the FERA, was run by a board almost wholly appointed by the governor. Other positions in the SRA were not filled according to civil service standards. As a result of conservative Republican control, SRA cases were sometimes closed when strikebreaking work became available, as in the Bakersfield cotton fields in 1938. California also ran its own work camps. In 1939 only about eight thousand general assistance recipients received work relief, most of them in Los Angeles county. In contrast to the great attention policymakers paid to the aged, moreover, California's

ADC program advanced slowly, dropping the state to among the bottom twenty in generosity and coverage.[44]

In 1938, Culbert Olson, erstwhile EPIC supporter, won the Democratic nomination for governor and the support of the Roosevelt Administration as well as various California social progressives. Among the latter were the CIO-led Labor's Non-Partisan League (LNPL) and the Workers' Alliance. Labor organizations including LNPL and the California State Federation of Labor also had to fight an initiative outlawing most forms of picketing. Having learned from Sinclair's missteps, Olson hedged on whether he would support a Ham and Eggs initiative and gained some support from its enthusiasts. Olson survived the general election, while Ham and Eggs lost narrowly, 1,143,670 to 1,398,999. At his inauguration on January 2, 1939, Olson elaborated what he called his New Deal for California, demanding among other things increased taxation, a revamped relief program embodying production for use principles, protection for organized labor, and higher old-age pensions with a lower age requirement of sixty years. California seemed well on its way to legislating a more balanced little New Deal that would serve as a model for other states—as the state's Progressive movement had done a generation earlier.[45]

But Olson could not realize his California New Deal. The center of the resistance to it was in the Senate, which Republicans controlled by a margin of twenty-three to seventeen. In 1940, Olson also lost control of the Assembly, in which Democrats had a nominal majority, when some conservative Democrats joined with Republicans to choose leadership positions. Olson was stopped at almost every turn. His tax proposals were defeated and, far from increasing, relief expenditures were cut from the sum that the previous governor Merriam had projected. California now had more recipients on the SRA than workers on the WPA, but relief appropriations were allocated in such small amounts over such brief periods that Olson's work relief proposals were not workable. The SRA itself was attacked, perhaps inconsistently but nonetheless effectively, as simultaneously a hotbed of Communist activity and a cornucopia of patronage. Moreover, proposals to raise OAA grants to the fifty dollar EPIC standard and to lower the minimum age to sixty years were defeated. All the same, the maximum grant was increased to forty dollars, and in 1940 Olson finally was able to prohibit liens on pensioners' property—after a rejuvenated Townsend Movement concentrating on California politics had joined the issue.[46]

By the early 1940s California had in some ways moved beyond the federal government in public social provision—only, though, on the matter of Old-Age Assistance. OAA was pressed forward by all manner of pension advocates, including old-age pension organizations such as the Townsendites and Ham and Eggs, but especially by EPIC Democrats. The challengers were aided by the existence of a department of welfare that was revamped and professionalized in the 1920s. By contrast, in promoting a work program, Olson, the Workers' Alliance, and others had to work

Plate 5.2 "Olson Spending Plan Blocked" (Dorothea Lange). A head-
line from William Randolph Hearst's San Francisco *Examiner* an-
nounces the stalling of a supplementary relief appropriation backed by
California Governor Culbert L. Olson soon after his inauguration in
January 1939. The headline accurately foreshadowed the blocking of
Olson's New Deal for California by a Republican-controlled Senate.

through the compromised SRA. The Democratic party in California, moreover, was only partly reformed, did not do well until the Democratic support was waning nationally, and never completely gained power. Olson's
purge of anti-New Deal Democrats failed in 1940, and Olson himself was
cashiered by the voters in 1942. With him went his dreams of a California
New Deal.

Wisconsin: A Well-Balanced Little New Deal

Like California, Wisconsin had a strong progressive tradition and was
structurally open to reform. And the forces for social policy were as great in
Wisconsin as in any state. The labor movement was particularly powerful,
with a highly socially progressive state federation of labor, and in Milwau-

kee the Socialist party was a significant force in politics. The Wisconsin Industrial Commission was a center of social policy activity. The commission promoted a close connection between academic policy experts and the state government, both conveniently located in Madison. The Democratic party was largely conservative and had been out of power for most of the twentieth century. But the progressive faction of the Republican party was so large that it was able to split off, join with labor and farmer representatives, and launch in 1934 a Progressive party that immediately bid for power. Although Progressive party victories seemed to suggest that Wisconsin would move far ahead of the national New Deal, instead the state enacted a well-balanced little New Deal. It was a model of what national reformers hoped for in state reactions to national legislation, but little more than that.

As in California, the Progressive Era was highly productive of economic and political reform in Wisconsin. In 1910, notably, the progressive faction of the Republican party, led by Robert M. La Follette, was able to elect to the governor's mansion Francis E. McGovern, who was also supported by the Milwaukee Socialist party under Victor Berger. A period of reform ensued. Proposals for constitutional amendments on the initiative, referendum, and recall were approved. So, too, was much economic and social legislation, including a law regulating working hours for women and children, a workmen's compensation program, an income tax, and a law creating an industrial commission. In 1913, a mothers' pensions bill passed. The workmen's compensation law was inspired by Wisconsin economist John R. Commons, who saw it as a way to bring together industrialists, workers, and citizens and to wield state incentives to reduce industrial accidents. The commission was granted great powers of enforcement over workmen's compensation and other labor laws. Its employment of nonpartisan academic expertise made the commission the embodiment of the so-called Wisconsin Idea—the "expert on tap, not on top," as the Idea was once described. The University of Wisconsin brought a number of institutional economists trained by Richard Ely and Commons into state service, and later the Roosevelt Administration drew from that pool of talent.[47]

As in most of the nation, social progressive reform made slow progress in Wisconsin in the 1920s. Yet a unique coalition of the progressive faction of the Republican party, the state federation of labor, socialists, and the Industrial Commission kept the issue of unemployment compensation alive in Wisconsin. Coming close to passage was a bill embodying the idea that state incentives could induce employers to prevent unemployment in the way they inhibited accidents though workmen's compensation. This proposal, known eventually as the Wisconsin Plan, included employer reserves, individual accounts through which employers would compensate their laid-off employees. In 1932, Unemployment Compensation was passed under the regime of the progressive Republican governor Philip La Follette, although it was not put into operation until after federal legislation in 1935. Also passed was a unified state labor code that barred the use of some injunctions to stop strikes and anticipated the more powerful Norris-La Guardia Act passed by Congress in 1933. Although Wisconsin had relatively well developed old-age and mothers' pensions programs for the time, on the eve of the New Deal the programs covered very few at a very low rate of benefits. They were not destined to improve immediately as La Follette was defeated by Albert B. Schmedeman during the Democratic sweep of 1932.[48]

In 1933, Wisconsin was the site of a movement to create a left-wing political party inaugurated by the Farmer-Labor Political Federation (FLPF), an organization formed in 1929 by left-wing intellectuals such as John Dewey and Paul Douglas of the University of Chicago. For many reasons this movement took root in Illinois's neighbor to the north. Rejuvenated by the editors of *Common Sense*, the FLPF was led in Wisconsin by the former Republican Congressman Thomas Amlie. Also calling for a new party were the Madison *Capital Times*, the state federation of labor, and a radical group of farmers with an innocuous name, the Wisconsin Milk Pool. A statewide conference to this end was held in early 1934. Jumping into the driver's seat of this bandwagon were various progressive Republicans, notably Senator Robert M. La Follette, Jr., and his brother Philip, the former governor. In May 1934, the Progressive party was formed, despite FLPF sentiment for giving it the class-based Farmer-Labor label, after the Minnesota party that was created in 1918 and took power during the 1930s. The Progressive party quickly became a contender and was mildly encouraged by Roosevelt, who visited the state in August to support his ally Senator La Follette. In November, the electorate returned Robert La Follette to the Senate and Philip to the governor's mansion, sending with him to Madison forty-five Progressive members of the Wisconsin Assembly and eight senators.[49]

It seemed as though Wisconsin might provide a model for the national New Deal. Notable here was the attempt by Governor La Follette to create a Wisconsin works program, which was designed to go into operation in May 1935—before the WPA. According to the plan, to which Roosevelt agreed, Wisconsin was going to be granted $100 million from the federal works appropriation, but be exempt from the national WPA. The program was to aided also by a Wisconsin Finance Authority, modeled on the Reconstruction Finance Corporation. Although the works program overshadowed all other political issues in Wisconsin in 1935, it was defeated by a coalition of conservative Republicans and Democrats. Elected with only a narrow plurality, La Follette had a Progressive majority in the Assembly, but could count on only fourteen votes in the thirty-three-member State Senate. Wisconsin continued to employ some people on work relief and was home to a highly productive WPA program, but it was a WPA program nonetheless. The only disagreement between Senator La Follette and President Roosevelt on that matter was that the senator thought that the works appropriation should have been doubled. That, though, was the sort of dis-

pute that Roosevelt was happy to entertain, as it provided ammunition
against the Byrds and Glasses of the Senate.[50]

In 1936, the Progressives allied themselves closely with Roosevelt and
vice versa, and both won handily. The Progressives also benefited from the
cooperation of the Socialist party, which did not run candidates in its Milwaukee stronghold, in deference to Progressive ones. This time forty-eight
Progressives were elected to the State Assembly, and all told sixteen Progressives were in the State Senate. Finally in charge of the state government,
La Follette and the Progressives adopted a little New Deal that branched
out in all directions. In 1937 new legislation passed for OAA and ADC,
placing Wisconsin near the top of states in each program. In addition, Wisconsin was one of five states passing legislation to buttress the National
Labor Relations Act—a law called, unavoidably, a "little Wagner Act."
Edwin Witte was chosen to sit on the labor relations board. Like President
Roosevelt, Governor La Follette also demanded changes in the Wisconsin
Supreme Court and won a reorganization of Wisconsin government. In a
special session that fall, La Follette's Progressive coalition was strong
enough that he was able to pass with little debate eleven bills, including
taxation and relief legislation. Only Wisconsin's UC law, with its employer
reserves, was not at the cutting edge of social policy thinking. Almost all
other states had adopted the Ohio model of pooled funds, which were
deemed safer to unemployed workers.[51]

In the spring of 1938 Philip La Follette hoped to take his act to a larger
stage by founding the National Progressives of America (NPA). Not at all
modest, La Follette asserted that the NPA was not meant to be a third party,
but "*the* party of our times." Though designed to capture the support of all
progressives and New Deal Democrats and to effect the realignment in
American politics also being pursued by the president, the NPA was a celebrated failure, turning Roosevelt and even many Wisconsin Progressives
against La Follette and his pretensions. Although the president was in favor
of previous efforts by La Follette for ideological realignment, Roosevelt
also wanted any future realignment to be on the basis of his New Deal, not
La Follette's personality. Also dismaying to the Left were La Follette's turn
against economic redistribution, his party's cross-in-circle insignia, which
Roosevelt referred to as "a feeble imitation of the swastika," and the possibility that the NPA would split the votes of the Left and return a Republican
to the White House in 1940. Established Farmer-Labor organizations and
other left parties refused to sign on. The only exception was the moribund
Progressive party of California—which the Left had already abandoned and
whose only prospects were to upset EPIC Democrat Culbert Olson's gubernatorial bid. Only conservatives were enthusiastic about the NPA, although
they were not joining either.[52]

The NPA's failure also impaired the Wisconsin Progressives, as La Follette was their standardbearer in his bid for a fourth term in November

1938. This time they faced many conservative candidates who had sought and won Democratic and Republican nominations. La Follette was defeated by the Republican Julius Heil on an election day that also saw losses for New Deal Democrats nationally. Progressives remained strong, however, in state politics. The labor movement had grown to more than 26 percent of the nonagricultural labor force. Completing its comeback in the nation, the Townsend Movement had endorsed six of the ten-member Wisconsin House delegation. Wisconsin's New Deal was not going to be undermined, but was not again going to attempt to provide a model for national social policy. In 1946, the Wisconsin Progressive party disbanded, and most of its supporters migrated into the Democratic party, though not the La Follettes, who returned to the Republican fold. Neither held office again after Senator La Follette lost his primary battle that year. The process of realignment took time, and a more liberal Democratic party did not elect a governor until 1958.[53]

CONCLUSION

When the United States took world leadership in public social provision in the 1930s, it was not entirely by way of national-level politics and policy. The states, too, gained power and authority in funding and administering social policy. What was different from the 1920s and the early 1930s, when states moved slowly on social policy, was that the national government had spurred them into action. The FERA, the Social Security Act, and the WPA placed relief and security issues on the political agendas of the states and for some programs provided even stronger influences on action. The national influence ranged from the assumption of costs for WPA job quotas and the extreme pressure of the UC "tax offset," to the variable fiscal enticements of OAA and ADC matching payments, to the moral suasion to pass better general assistance programs. By 1940, as a result of these influences and their own actions, most states of the Union had adopted little New Deals, and their operations were for the first time significantly devoted to social policy for those in need.

Getting the states involved, however, also meant giving them important influence over the form and course of supposedly national policies. The result was forty-eight "laboratories" performing separate "experiments" for each program. This constituted a serious problem for poor people in states whose political leaders were dispensing the social policy equivalent of placebos—programs lacking adequate funding or coverage, or both. Poor programs were in greatest evidence where incentives were weakest, as in the case of general relief and, to a lesser extent, ADC. Five years after the creation of the WPA and the adoption of the Social Security Act, the states had constructed a greatly variegated social spending system. There were genuine little New Deals in some states, and very little New Deals in others.

These natural experiments also resulted in well-defined patterns, suitable for analysis and for the appraisal of the contextual aspects of the institutional politics theory. My theoretical expectations find support in the narrative case analyses of four states, chosen on the basis of their variation in institutional and political circumstances. As expected, institutional conditions worked as gatekeepers—undemocratic polities preventing adequate social spending programs and patronage-oriented parties forming somewhat less formidable barriers. Where the institutional gates were open, moreover, powerful political actors, including Democratic or third-party regimes, domestic bureaucrats, and labor and other social movements, were able to advance public social provision. The efforts of reform-oriented regimes, social movements, and domestic bureaucrats at the state level are no doubt more productive when the national regime provides the sorts of strong incentives that it did during the Second New Deal.

Two states had structural barriers to social policy. In Virginia, an under-democratized polity deflected and slowed much of the social policy impetus of the New Deal. This happened despite the fact that Virginia was relatively rich for a southern state and had previously modernized its administrative apparatus. In Illinois, the dominance of patronage-oriented Democrats, especially powerful in Chicago, skewed the regime's approach to New Deal social policy. These Democrats found much appeal in the jobs provided by the WPA and funded by the national government, but were not much interested in committing Illinois funds to the grant-in-aid programs of the Social Security Act. When the Democrats took power, social policy reflected those interests.

By contrast, California and Wisconsin were institutionally open to reform, but the configuration of politically organized actors was different within them. California was home to powerful social movements, especially concerning old-age pensions. In combination with a number of legislators elected behind the EPIC program, these movements advanced California's OAA program even beyond what the SSB wanted. In this they were aided by California's department of welfare. Yet the California Democratic party did not regroup quickly enough to take advantage of the president's popularity, and the opportunity for a wider California New Deal was missed. In Wisconsin, another institutionally open state, the political forces for reform were stronger. Notable among these was a Progressive party that had the support of social policy advocates and the labor movement and was able to take power completely during the two years following 1936. As a result, Wisconsin was able to enact a little New Deal that was among the state leaders across the gamut of New Deal spending programs.

It was not the federal nature of the American state that held back social policy. What mattered more was that states were in such different institutional and political situations. Federalism in turn allowed those institutional and political differences to play out in social policy struggles across the country—at the expense of consistent policy across the nation. If all states had faced institutional circumstances similar to those in California and Wisconsin it seems likely that the results of the experiments would have fallen within a range acceptable to New Deal policymakers. In the absence of the underdemocratized and patronage-oriented states, no doubt the national government would have gone further, too. Even in the structurally open states, however, political realignment took time to develop and did not happen concurrently with the New Deal. In California, EPIC supporters and followers of the New Deal did not transform a moribund Democratic party until after the national New Deal had passed its peak. In Wisconsin, progressives were able to create a new party that was able to take power when the New Deal was also strong. But the situation was not a stable one. As was the case in California, Wisconsin social policy advocates eventually coalesced in the Democratic party—a process that lasted more than a decade.

Discussing what happened in the states with the imagery of laboratories and experiments goes only so far and after a certain point is misleading. For these terms suggest that states were independently, but diligently searching for the best possible social policy, with a desire to converge on it, as research teams testing, say, drug treatments against a disease might try various compounds before focusing only on the most effective one. Before the New Deal, these laboratories proceeded at a leisurely pace. Anyone running a real lab that way would have been fired or run out of business. Because of the incentives of the New Deal, interest intensified. But instead of converging, states became attached to their experiments—regardless of how ineffective they might have been. States with minimal social policies showed no sign of abandoning them in order to replicate the results of the few states with adequate social spending systems. Also, states stopped experimenting once the incentives to do so subsided. None of that went unnoticed by reformers within the Roosevelt Administration. To their way of thinking the only way to move states to more equal and adequate social policies was to alter the incentives provided by national law.

So New Deal planners went to work, hoping to displace what they saw as failed experiments by creating and enacting new legislation to induce national standards in the state-level spending programs. As war broke out in Europe, the New Dealers thought they would be able to use the crisis to their advantage, to complete a work and relief state for a postwar America. As the next chapter shows, however, state-level divergences in social policy were there to stay.

Redefining the New Deal, 1940–1950

> The one thing which must be extended if we would help the young men
> and women of the nation, is to give them the opportunity to work. We
> have recognized that to the right to vote, the right to learn, the right to
> speak, the right to worship, we, your Government, add the right to work.
>
> —*Franklin D. Roosevelt, October 23, 1940*

> I. There must be work for all who are able and willing to work.
> We all accept this principle.
>
> —*National Resources Planning Board Committee on Long-Range*
> *Work and Relief Policies, December 4, 1941*

> I am proud of the Work Projects Administration organization. It has
> displayed courage and determination in the face of uninformed criticism.
> The knowledge and experience of this organization will be of great
> assistance in the consideration of a well-rounded public works program
> for the postwar period. With the satisfaction of a good job well done
> and with a high sense of integrity, The Work Projects Administration
> has asked for and earned an honorable discharge.
>
> —*Franklin D. Roosevelt, December 4, 1942*

HOPES WERE HIGH among reformers in the Roosevelt Administration that
the New Deal work and relief policy, which had come so far in the 1930s,
might be completed in the 1940s.[1] The president was still popular and signaled his intention to lead the nation during the world crisis by running for
a third term. Policy experts situated in the National Resources Planning
Board (NRPB), the Work Projects Administration (WPA), and the Federal
Security Agency were documenting problems in the social spending system
and ways to address them. New Dealers also were planning to alter the
nature of American taxation, whose provisions had evolved haphazardly in
the Depression.

As American participation in the European war loomed, the hopes of the
reformers seemed on their way to being realized. Roosevelt ran the 1940
campaign mainly as a referendum on his domestic policy and the need to

complete the New Deal, and he won handily. Preparation for war and then war itself required increased revenues, and the administration immediately started to put into effect a fairer and more progressive taxation system. Given the task of planning postwar social policy, moreover, the NRPB responded with an investigation into American policy with detailed recommendations for reform. When released in 1943, *Security, Work, and Relief Policies* was hailed by its supporters as the American Beveridge Report, after the wartime document that became the blueprint for the British welfare state. The NRPB called for a guarantee of work and a guaranteed minimum income. New York Senator Robert Wagner, central to so many laws constituting New Deal social policy, wrote a bill including many of the report's recommendations. The completion of a work and relief state seemed at hand.

But it was not. The reformers did not get anything resembling what they wanted and, worse, lost much of what they had gained. The conventional wisdom is that what took place during the war and afterward consolidated the New Deal.[2] In the realm of social policy, however, the New Deal failed and was redefined, as the work and relief policy of the 1930s was mainly dismantled. Notably, work relief through the WPA was ended, as Roosevelt, under pressure, gave the program an "honorable discharge." By the end of the decade, "the right to work" meant not the right to a job, provided in the last instance by the government, but the "right" not to join a union. Other means-tested programs, notably Old-Age Assistance (OAA), became marginal. In addition, a policy was enacted that Roosevelt and the New Deal planners had fought: veterans' benefits as a separate and unequal system of public social provision. The health, education, and housing benefits granted to World War II veterans through the so-called GI Bill of Rights were denied the rest of the citizenry. Mainly because of the decimation of the work and relief policy, by 1950 Old-Age and Survivors' Insurance (OASI) found itself at the center of American public social provision. The one major reform was the building of a mass, progressive income tax.

Here I outline this destruction and redefinition of New Deal public social provision. From the beginning of 1940 until the end of 1942, reformers began to plan for the postwar world. At the same time, a new system of taxation was introduced and enacted. A second period, comprising the middle of the war to its end in 1945, saw the rolling back of the incipient work and relief state. By contrast, the immediate postwar period through 1950 saw some minor gains in social spending. But that period did not serve to consolidate New Deal public social provision. By the end of the 1940s, only remnants of the work and relief policy remained. OASI had managed to survive the period, and OAA persisted, too. But only Aid to Dependent Children (ADC) emerged unscathed from the relief-based system of public social provision devised in the Depression.

I also want to explain why New Deal social policy failed and was redefined. Although much of the New Deal was lost during wartime and the war contributed to those losses, the war itself was not mainly the cause of them. What mattered more was the decline of the reform-oriented regime that had held strong from the middle 1930s and into the early war period. That decline owed much in turn to the structural barriers to reform in the American political system—especially in underdemocratized districts. Although that explains the general decline in New Deal social policy, the nature of the programs best explains why some survived and some did not. In opposition to the conventional view that means-tested programs are most likely to be retrenched, I argue that the most radical programs with the greatest executive discretion in them were targeted. Their elimination was due not so much to the mobilization of those opposed to them, as to their sources of power in the American political system.

Planning Public Spending and a Revolution in Taxation, 1940–1942

In June 1940 with the fall of France, Roosevelt became preoccupied with the Second World War and began to plan for the American entry into it.[3] Planning also began in earnest for postwar public social provision. In November 1940, Roosevelt instructed the NRPB to focus its attention on planning national social and economic policies for postwar America. Reformers based in the NRPB and also in the Social Security Board (SSB) undertook or sponsored a number of investigations of the social spending system and proposed changes in it. Their reports indicate what New Deal reformers hoped and expected U.S. public social provision to become.

The NRPB Proposes Revamped Works and Nationalized Relief Programs

Security, Work and Relief Policies, the most important NRPB report on social policy, was written by the Committee on Long-Range Work and Relief Policies. This committee was led by William Haber, a professor of economics at the University of Michigan, and Eveline Burns, of the Economics Department of Columbia University, was the director of research. The committee included representatives from many of the governmental agencies and bureaus in charge of social spending, such as the Federal Security Agency, the Work Projects Administration, the Children's Bureau, and the Farm Security Administration. The committee was charged to survey work and relief programs and redesign them. Begun in June 1940, *Security, Work, and Relief Policies* was submitted three days before the bombing of Pearl Harbor in December 1941. Unlike the 1935 *Report of the Committee on Economic Security*, the NRPB committee's report could reflect on the nation's recent experience with an array of social spending programs. Most of the 640 pages of the NRPB report were devoted to a study of the American social spending system. That left, however, plenty of room for recommendations to reform it.[4]

In the report, public employment, relief, and social insurance programs were all considered to be components of what the committee called "public aid." In using this term the committee blurred distinctions between the social insurance and means-tested programs of the New Deal and certainly had no intention to marginalize the latter. In keeping with its concern for "long-range work and relief policies," the committee provided a number of recommendations to upgrade public assistance. Echoing the sentiments of the Committee on Economic Security (CES), the NRPB committee called for the assurance of an "American standard" of economic security as a *right* of every citizen. By this the committee meant that all should receive at least the minimum wage as legislated in the 1938 Fair Labor Standards Act—in essence, the fifty-two dollars per month received by the most unskilled WPA workers in the highest-cost region.[5]

The committee's first recommendation was that there must be work for all Americans able and willing to work. Everyone who needed a job and could not find one should be provided one by the government, as a matter of right. That was the main road to economic security, and so the committee concerned itself foremost with measures to guarantee full employment. Following the conventional economic thinking of the day, the committee expected that high unemployment would reappear after the war. Like Alvin Hansen, the Harvard economist whose "stagnationist" Keynesian ideas inhered in other NRPB documents, the committee anticipated that business activity alone would not provide full employment. Left to itself the U.S. economy would follow a downward trajectory, and only vigorous and sustained government spending would counter that tendency. The NRPB committee did not think, however, that undirected government spending—a completely "demand-side solution"—would be sufficient. The NRPB committee saw direct public employment, as well as public works, as the best way to combat unemployment. Employing the unemployed would take some doing, however. For, as the committee documented, the WPA left millions of the unemployed uncovered.

The work and relief committee's vision of the American employment policy of the future was a strengthened and rationalized version of the WPA. The committee proposed the permanent planning of projects, mainly the labor-intensive WPA kind of project, but also the capital-intensive Public Works Administration kind. However, the work on these projects was to be given without a means test—unlike with the WPA—and was to resemble private employment in wages, hours, and work conditions. The committee proposed to pay the so-called prevailing wage where wages were high, as in the industrial North, and the so-called security or minimum wage where wages were substandard, as in the South. State and local general relief systems, the source of much discrimination and unfairness in the WPA, would not be the entry point for the new system of public employment, however. The committee wanted a nationalized United States Employment Service (USES) to provide the workers for public employment. The committee also proposed keeping those between sixteen and twenty-one years of age off the job market and in school, supplementing their educational aid with work programs in the manner of the National Youth Administration.[6]

For public assistance or "relief," as the work and relief committee called it, employing the vocabulary of the day, the report called for a rationalization of the programs and for the setting of national standards in them. The committee opposed the continued reliance on the special assistance programs, such as OAA and ADC. Although the committee wanted the states to continue to contribute financially to administer programs with the help of localities, the committee called for the end of the ability of states to set high eligibility hurdles and low benefits. Moreover, general assistance, the program with the least national influence in it, would become a much higher priority. All public assistance would be run by one agency in each state, similar to state-level emergency relief administrations in the early 1930s. To show that it meant business about national standards, the committee proposed that the federal government administer general assistance until each state proved able to do so. The committee was proposing, in short, to force the expansion of the tiny little New Deals enacted in many states.[7]

The committee was also committed to upgrading and revamping social insurance, but not to the disadvantage of relief. In using the term "social insurance," the committee did not mean by it what people mean nowadays by "social security." The committee saw no analogy to private insurance, according to which people supposedly pay premiums through taxes in order to receive an annuity upon retirement. To the contrary, the committee thought that social insurance programs and means-tested relief programs should accord to American citizens the same sort of rights. To that end, the committee sought to loosen the connection between taxation for social insurance and benefits from it. Like other Keynesians, the work and relief committee thought that building large trust funds aggravated unemployment by lowering current spending on consumption. Like others on the political left, the committee viewed the regressiveness of payroll taxes as undesirable. For these reasons, it called for a small payroll tax, chiefly for the sake of political appearances—as a tangible sign of the state's commitment to a group of citizens—and wanted the bulk of funding to be provided by more progressive means, notably by income taxes. Because of the perceived urgency of employment issues, the committee called for the nationalization of Unemployment Compensation (UC) programs and the conversion of them into true unemployment insurance providing standard benefits for twenty-six weeks.

The committee did not concern itself as much with national health policies, which had been omitted from the Social Security Act. The only program it was able to study and evaluate was the means-tested grants-in-aid to the states for maternal and children's health. The NRPB committee, however, endorsed national health insurance, and the Interdepartmental Committee to Coordinate Health and Welfare Activities set the tone on this issue.

Only secondarily, too, did the NRPB address the problems of veterans. Its members followed New Deal precedents in seeing veterans not as a kind of privileged group deserving benefits beyond what other Americans should get. Significantly, previous veterans' programs were not included under the NRPB committee's definition of "public aid." The board wanted to avoid doing what America did after the Civil War: setting up a separate and better scheme of public social benefits for veterans. Like the president, the board thought the war effort was expended by the entire society, in the factories at home as well as in the battlefields abroad.

The NRPB wanted to devise plans to address veterans' problems of readjustment without undermining social policy for all citizens. To accomplish these ends, it set up the Postwar Manpower Conference which first met in July 1942. Like the NRPB Committee on Long-Range Work and Relief Policies, the manpower conference included members from most of the departments and agencies concerned with veterans' policies, including the departments of Labor, Agriculture, the Navy, and War, as well as from the Federal Security Agency, the Veterans Administration, the War Manpower Commission, and the Selective Service System. The conference stressed aid for education—entirely consistent with the NRPB's concerns over high postwar employment. Veterans were to be kept out of the labor force for as long as possible. Other proposals for veterans accorded with planned changes in social insurance. For time spent at war, veterans were to be given credit toward OASI. Moreover, veterans were to be given USES-administered unemployment compensation for up to twenty-six weeks—exactly what the board was hoping to legislate for all the unemployed. In addition, veterans were to be provided three months' furlough pay of no more than one hundred dollars per month.[8] The reformers specifically wanted to avoid anything resembling the "bonuses" granted to World War I veterans and certainly did not want to grant the kind of separate rights for veterans that were the hallmark of Civil War pensions.

The Social Security Board and the Elevation of Social Insurance

The Social Security Board (SSB), led by its chairman Arthur Altmeyer, was also pushing for the improvement of social spending policies. In many areas its proposals paralleled those of the NRPB committee. The committee and the board agreed on the desirability of improving existing social insurance programs, especially Unemployment Compensation. That program, the centerpiece of social insurance in the Social Security Act, was not living up to reformers' expectations. Similarly, the SSB wanted to make OASI more inclusive—only slightly more than half of workers were in covered industries by 1940—notably by extending coverage to agricultural workers. The board was also in favor of improving public assistance programs—up to a point. Like the NRPB committee, the SSB felt that ADC was insufficiently funded and that federal matching funding for general assistance should be approved. The board mainly wanted new social insurance programs, notably health and hospitalization insurance, as well as temporary and permanent disability insurance. In the board's view temporary disability was considered akin to unemployment, permanent disability akin to old age.[9]

There was, however, a key difference in vision between the SSB and the NRPB committee, mainly over the status of public assistance. The SSB was convinced that social insurance was the best way to protect against risks in a industrial capitalist society and that public assistance should have a fundamentally secondary role. For that reason, public assistance was described by the leaders of the board as a "life net" under the social insurance system. The SSB's endorsement of an additional grant-in-aid for general assistance rather than a completely revamped public assistance system reflected this view of relief as residual. Perhaps because of its limited bureaucratic reach, moreover, the SSB was much less concerned than the NRPB about employment policies. In addition, the SSB did not consider the regressive nature of the payroll taxes for social insurance to be problematic. The board saw the program as a progressive combination of taxation and spending. Orthodoxy at the board held that payroll taxes should pay for social insurance benefits, to make plausible the private insurance analogy, which in turn could be used to promote advances in social insurance to the public. The SSB's idea of a right to a benefit because of previous "contributions" or payroll taxes was at odds with the idea of rights held by the NRPB—the right to a job for those citizens deemed employable, or to an income for those citizens considered unemployable but socially valuable.

The SSB hoped to use the wartime emergency to increase social insurance payroll taxes. The board called for payroll taxes to increase from the 3 percent on employers for UC and the 2 percent shared by employers and employees for OASI to 10 percent altogether. This plan glossed over the fact that the federal payroll tax for Unemployment Compensation was credited to employers in all states where UC was in effect. Because of so-called merit or experience rating provisions in most states, employers were paying on average less than half of the 3 percent. In any case, the board wanted to capitalize on the earmarking of the tax in order to make it easier to legislate greater benefits later—precisely the reason conservatives wanted to prevent such a payroll tax increase. Altmeyer justified the taxation as part of the wartime fight against inflation, and the increase was embodied in the so-called Eliot bill, sponsored by the American Federation of Labor.[10]

Both the National Resources Planning Board and the Social Security Board wanted to use the war to upgrade New Deal social policy, but there were some differences in emphasis. The NRPB took a more holistic approach to the problem of social policy, wanted to combat a potential relapse into postwar depression, and sought to complete the work and relief state as it had been begun in the New Deal. By contrast, the SSB placed an emphasis on social insurance policies under the control of the board. Still, the SSB planned and pushed for major innovations in health and unemployment policies and reforms in public assistance.

The early wartime period saw much planning, but little new social spending legislation. One gain in social policy was the exception that proved the rule. At the end of 1941, the control of the USES was taken from state-level commissions and placed on a national footing, a move dictated by the need to coordinate the movement of war workers to munitions factories.[11] It remained to be seen whether this wartime expedient could be turned into a permanent postwar reform. The reformers realized that the political struggles for these changes would have to wait until victory overseas was in sight.

The Remaking of American Taxation

As the war approached, the political situation was reversed with respect to taxation and social policy. Taxation increases and changes became possible, while social policy augmentations were not. Social policy advocates could not help being heartened by the changes in income tax policies. Most of the funding for war came through income and excess profits taxes. The Revenue Acts of 1940, 1941, and 1942 lowered exemptions and increased the progressiveness of personal income tax rates, increased corporation income taxes, and added a number of wartime emergency taxes, such as the excess profits tax, a World War I expedient, and individual and corporate income tax surcharges. Avoided was a national sales tax, which conservatives, notably the National Association of Manufacturers, hoped to enact to finance military expenditures. The 1941 Revenue Act was designed to add about $3.5 billion in revenues and about five million people to the rolls. The Revenue Act of 1942 was supposed to produce about $7.6 billion. At the top end of the income tax, marginal rates were increased. In addition, corporation taxes and a stiff excess profits tax were added. In 1942, exemptions were lowered, subjecting some 20 million additional people to income taxation.[12] The personal income tax became for the first time the mass tax that it has remained throughout the postwar period. Although some personal income tax increases, such as the "Victory" and excess profits taxes, were designed to end after the war, most of the changes in the income tax were expected to remain.

Not all types of taxation increases were so easy to achieve. The administration proposed that social security contributions be increased by $1 billion. Congress rejected that and instead put on hold scheduled increases for OASI payroll taxes that had been legislated in the 1939 amendments.[13] In doing so, Congress acted to prevent tax increases that would have become law automatically had the issue merely been ignored. Altmeyer's strategy, to hike social security taxes as a patriotic way to fight inflation, similar to purchasing war bonds, was off to an unpromising start.

ROLLING BACK THE NEW DEAL, 1942–1945

After the elections of 1942, social spending programs and initiatives suffered worse fates than merely having to wait until victory overseas was at hand. This period, which ran from the end of 1942 until the beginning of 1945, was the most ineffective and damaging of any of the Roosevelt administrations, as far as social spending policies were concerned. Far from being advanced, as the reformers wanted, and far from being consolidated, as some have argued, the New Deal was rolled back by Congress as America gained in its struggle against the Axis powers.

The earliest and most devastating assaults on New Deal social policy concerned longstanding public employment programs. According to the plans of the New Dealers, the national public employment system was to be strengthened and rationalized after the war. How else to deal with the expected high unemployment? Even if unemployment dropped to the level of the 1920s, New Dealers expected that there would still be a need for three or four million people on national works programs. Yet as the war absorbed almost all of the unemployed and drove people who had been retired from wage work back into the labor market, the public employment system was dismantled. This movement began in 1942 when Congress ended the Civilian Conservation Corps (CCC), a youth employment and conservation organization run by military officers.[14]

The attack on public employment gained real momentum in the wake of the 1942 congressional elections. Soon afterward Roosevelt appeased congressional conservatives by agreeing to the termination of the WPA. With other battles to fight, Roosevelt gave the WPA its honorable discharge. The National Youth Administration (NYA) seemingly had a stronger case for its continued existence. It funded training and work programs for the young to help them acquire jobs or to pursue higher education and began to provide training for military production. But the NYA, too, could not escape the anti-spending spree and was abolished in 1943.[15]

On taxation, the one domestic arena in which the New Dealers were winning at the beginning of the war, Congress now became intransigent. The fiscal demands of war-making were insufficient to salvage the administration's taxation proposals. Roosevelt lost his ability to gain from Congress increased revenues for the national government and to make the tax system more progressive. With the addition of so many new income tax payers, revenues became difficult to collect. In 1943, Beardsley Ruml, the chairman of the Federal Reserve Bank of New York and a liberal businessman who had served on the NRPB, proposed that in exchange for the prior withholding of income taxes, the government would forgo a year's worth of personal income taxes—a decided benefit for those with high incomes. The administration favored prior withholding, but opposed such inequit-

Plate 6.1 NYA Students Learn Forging (Gordon Parks). During the war, American work programs geared themselves to the war effort. Here National Youth Administration students at Bethune-Cookman College learn forging skills, useful in the making of war materiel as this Office of War Information photograph suggests. Nonetheless, the NYA was liquidated by Congress in 1943.

able tax breaks. In the end, though, approximately three quarters of 1942 taxes were forgiven.[16]

At least the Ruml plan had some long-term benefits. That was not true, however, of the Revenue Act of 1944, which decimated what remained of the administration's plans for wartime taxation reform. In the middle of 1943, the administration wanted about $12 billion in revenue, focusing on increased income taxes on individuals and corporations. The administration's bill, however, was entirely rewritten by Congress, which offered instead about $2 billion, mainly through increases in regressive excise taxes, but also including tax breaks. In February 1944 Roosevelt vetoed Congress's legislation, an unprecedented action on a revenue bill, calling it tax relief for the "greedy, not the needy." Congress promptly overrode him.[17]

What seemed perhaps worse for social spending advocates, Congress continued to delay scheduled increases in the social insurance payroll tax, preventing about $1.4 billion in additional revenue from accruing to the trust fund. The success of this freeze movement, led by the Republican Senator Arthur Vandenberg, jeopardized the future of OASI. By 1944 the SSB was desperate enough to drop the fiction that the program was a self-financing government annuity. It cooperated with Vandenberg on an amendment to back the program with general revenues if the trust fund were to come up short—an increasingly likely scenario.[18] Relying on general revenues ensured that OASI's obligations would be met, but came at the cost of the social insurance analogies that the board hoped to employ to expand the program and extend social insurance to other risks to income.

After the demise of so much of the New Deal, it was seemingly an inauspicious political moment to introduce the nationalizing social policy initiatives devised by New Deal planners. All the same, during the spring of 1943 Roosevelt transmitted to Congress *Security, Work, and Relief Policies* as well as other NRPB reports, including Alvin Hansen's *After the War, Full Employment*. Soon after their release, the far-reaching Wagner-Murray-Dingell bill was introduced into Congress.[19]

The bill drew on ideas promoted by both boards, including the nationalization of UC and its conversion into unemployment insurance, and the creation of national health insurance. To fund these programs, the Wagner bill tilted toward the views of the Social Security Board, calling for a stiff increase, to 10 percent, in the payroll tax. Under the bill, this increase in taxation would go the full distance toward funding all the main social insurance programs and thus would keep intact the social insurance relationship. Like the NRPB committee, Senator Wagner did not ignore the public assistance system, however, and he called for one grant-in-aid for all programs benefiting the needy. The enactment of this provision would end special assistance categories and, the senator hoped, raise benefits for all those receiving assistance to the level received by the aged. A single grant-in-aid would also promote the reorganization of state welfare departments. Wagner's bill also provided for the end of the ceiling on "matching" reimbursements by the federal government—ending the incentive to keep benefits low. For instance, if California wanted to increase OAA grants to sixty dollars per person monthly, the federal government would be required to pay thirty dollars, not twenty dollars. To ensure that poorer states would not be short-changed, the bill called for a weighted matching formula benefiting such states.

Wagner's bill did not escape from committee, however, and the Roosevelt Administration did little to promote it. But the bill was expected to resurface after the next presidential election and after the war.[20] It seemed possible that this legislation might follow the route of Wagner's other successful social bills, such as the landmark labor and unemployment legislation of the 1930s: initial rejection, growing support, and finally backing by the administration and passage.

What happened immediately, though, was the death of the NRPB. In June 1943, Congress appropriated only enough money for the board to end its operations. The NRPB was ordered to surrender its papers to the National Archives to ensure that no other agency would inherit its functions. The board, like the WPA, was seen as central to the social mission of the New Deal and therefore was targeted by conservative members of Congress. They disliked its planning for national social policy and for government influence over the investment activities of businesses. Before 1939, Cabinet members constituted the executive board of the NRPB. Once the board was placed in the Executive Office of the President, Cabinet department members became less closely attached to it. Once the president refused to fight for it, there were few others to stand up for it. Afterward, the Bureau of the Budget was the only nonemergency agency in the Executive Office of the President.[21]

The one social policy victory of the middle war years, if it could be called that, concerned veterans. The GI Bill of Rights, as this proposal was named by the American Legion, was largely consistent with the recommendations of the NRPB Postwar Manpower Committee. That was because the legion merely assembled in one bill the various proposals relating to veterans that the administration had forwarded to Congress in 1943—and then lobbied to convert them into law. This bid succeeded in 1944. The GI bill avoided large bonuses for able-bodied veterans. A measure sponsored by other major veterans' organizations calling for a maximum of five thousand dollars in payments to qualified veterans was defeated. Instead the GI bill offered "readjustment allowances." These allowances were nothing more than the UC benefits suggested by the committee, though the bill provided for a year's worth, rather than half a year's worth. More important, the bill provided generous benefits for vocational or college study. All those veterans whose education was "interrupted" by the war—defined generously as any veterans honorably discharged with six months' service and aged twenty-five years and younger—gained three years' worth of tuition at accredited colleges or vocational schools, plus a modest stipend.[22]

All the same, new rights for veterans tended to undermine the possibility of comprehensive social policy for all citizens. Partly the problem was a matter of administration, for veterans' programs were generally kept separate from other social programs. Although New Dealers won the battle of keeping veterans' placement services within the USES, otherwise the Veterans Administration controlled the implementation of the law, denying the U.S. Office of Education the administration of veterans' educational benefits.[23] The main problem from the point of view of the New Deal planners, however, was that veterans were granted types of benefits that other citizens were not. The GI bill included housing benefits that contradicted previous administration efforts in public housing, notably loan guarantees at below-market interest rates to help able-bodied veterans purchase homes.[24] Most of all, reformers lost the chance of channeling the enthusiasm to aid those who sacrificed in the war effort into New Deal programs for all citizens.

THE FAILURE TO REVIVE AND EXTEND NEW DEAL
SOCIAL POLICY, 1945-1950

There was to be no more rolling back of the New Deal, and the reformers remained hopeful. In 1944 Roosevelt put his name again before the nation, running again on domestic issues, and again the people reelected him. Although Roosevelt did not live to see the end of the war, his successor Harry S. Truman was a follower of the New Deal and was thought likely to revive it. Nevertheless, bids to change national social policy mainly sputtered. U.S. social policy muddled through during a time when other countries were enacting welfare states.

Relative to the wartime plans and the Depression-era achievements, gains in employment policies were minor in the immediate postwar era. The New Dealers found themselves in a much weaker position than before the war. The dismantled employment programs would have to be created anew merely to begin to address the planners' objectives. If massive unemployment had resurfaced, as experts expected and people feared, perhaps there would have been a drive to reinstate the WPA. But neither another depression nor a new WPA was in the cards.

Instead proponents of employment policy focused their attention on the so-called Full Employment bill of 1945. The bill granted a guarantee of jobs for citizens—something never achieved during the 1930s—and would have restored some of the presidential planning capacities that had resided in the NRPB. Some have argued that, had it passed, the employment bill would have forced the government to spend its way to full employment, according to the Keynesian principles of aggregate demand on which the bill was based. However, it seems unlikely that the bill or any bill could have forced Congress to spend *in general*. As the *New Republic* argued, at best the bill would have induced the president to submit a yearly budget with employment goals linked clearly to spending proposals. Less well noted at the time was the undue faith that the bill placed in the theories of Keynes. In any case, the legislation could not designate the government as the employer of the last resort—not without a public employment program. In the end, this bill was diluted, eliminating the full-employment budget and creating a Council of Economic Advisors, an advisory body to be staffed by economists, though not necessarily Keynesians.[25]

One means of augmenting national employment policy had a seemingly good chance to be realized after the war. When the USES was nationalized in order to handle wartime manpower problems, the bureaucratic machinery was in place to ease the nationalization of Unemployment Compensation. A nationalized USES might also make it simpler to reestablish public employment programs, and on a more secure footing, as the NRPB committee had envisioned them. However, at the end of the war congressional con-

Plate 6.2 "This Way to a Job" (photographer unknown). The offices of the United States Employment Service were nationalized during the Second World War. Many New Dealers thought national control should be retained, in order to facilitate a postwar national work program. Instead Congress returned the authority over employment offices to states and localities.

servatives agitated to return the offices back to the control of the states. Congress passed a bill reasserting the prewar status quo, and the Truman Administration did not fight it.[26]

More failures were in store for social spending advocates. Many of their hopes were bound up in the titles of the 1945 version of the Wagner-Murray-Dingell bill. Like its predecessor, the bill envisaged comprehensive social insurance, including national health insurance, and reforms of the social assistance system. Yet the bill received only minor consideration, as issues of war and reconversion predominated over issues of social reconstruction. Some of the programs included in the bill appeared later in piecemeal form and suffered various fates.

Reforming Unemployment Compensation was given a lower priority by the Truman Administration, perhaps in part because the dread postwar depression did not materialize. UC was not nationalized and remained controlled by the states with their many levels of benefits and taxation. In addition, in 1949 it was removed from the purview of the Social Security

Administration (renamed in 1946) and placed under that of the Department of Labor—by way of the presidential powers of reorganization won by Roosevelt in the late 1930s. That change may have made the processing of UC claims more efficient, but it cut forever the program's ties to the national OASI program.[27] States would always control UC, and so its marginalization was ensured.

Reversing its fortunes was OASI. The program received a final setback in 1947, when Congress passed legislation, over Truman's veto, to restrict its coverage. But in January 1950, a one-percentage-point increase in the payroll tax was finally allowed by Congress to go into effect. In August 1950, the program achieved expanded eligibility and benefits, as well as coverage by more than 8 million people to about three-fourths of the labor force. Benefits were increased by 80 percent. Another one-percentage-point increase in the tax was scheduled for 1953. The 1950 Social Security Act amendments mainly improved existing programs. Disability insurance was conspicuously rejected. But the achievement should not be discounted. Reformers had turned back bids to destroy or alter OASI, by thawing the frozen payroll tax and by preventing the program's transmutation into a flat benefit. No doubt it is for these reasons that Altmeyer, the head of the SSB, refers to this time as the "Crucial Years."[28]

Special assistance programs did not advance greatly in the immediate postwar period, but survived. Following the recommendation of the SSB, in 1946 Congress changed the reimbursement formula to one of "variable grants" that benefited states that paid low amounts per recipient. The federal government would now pay a higher proportion of the first increments paid out for special assistance grants and a lower percentage for additional increments; two years later the formula was made even more advantageous to states making small payments per child. In effect, these changes penalized the states with more generous special assistance programs in order to induce states with less generous programs to cover more people with minimal pensions. In addition, though, the maximum monthly payments subject to matching were increased slightly. For OAA, the maximum figure went from forty dollars to forty-five dollars per recipient. For ADC, the maximum increased from eighteen dollars to twenty-four dollars for the first child and from twelve dollars to fifteen dollars each for additional children. In 1947, new regulations from the Bureau of Public Assistance required states to process ADC applications promptly and provide benefits to all eligible applicants. The regulations were devised to end the practice of maintaining waiting lists—used by some states to limit the number of recipients or to discriminate against them. Still, the option to discriminate was provided by the "suitable home" provisions in many state ADC laws.[29]

Only in the 1950 amendments to the Social Security Act was ADC made more generous. For the first time the caregiver became eligible in the determination of benefits. This provision greatly increased the level of benefits

TABLE 6.1
U.S. National Taxation Sources as a Percentage of GNP, 1932–1949

| | | | | Income | | Estate | Capital |
	Customs	Excises	Social Insurance	Corporation	Individual	and Gift	Stock
1932	0.57	0.78	0.00	1.09	0.74	0.08	0.00
1939	0.35	1.95	0.82	1.28	1.14	0.40	0.14
1940	0.33	1.85	1.72	0.98	1.11	0.35	0.13
1949	0.14	2.93	1.49	4.36	6.06	0.30	0.00

Source: U.S. Bureau of the Census, *Historical Statistics*, series F 1-5, Y 343-351, Y 352-357, Y 358-373, pp. 224, 1105–7.

Note: For the years 1932 and 1939, the administrative budget is the source for taxation figures, and for 1940 and 1949, cash receipts are used.

subject to federal reimbursement by adding twenty-seven dollars to the existing maximums. At the same time, however, Congress passed an amendment requiring welfare agencies to notify law enforcement officials of cases in which a child had been abandoned or deserted, signaling the beginning of greater congressional interest in the characteristics of ADC beneficiaries. OAA did not receive any increase in its matching maximum, however, which remained at fifty dollars per recipient per month.[30]

Major public assistance achievements were lacking, however. The unification of the public assistance programs, a prime goal of the NRPB planners, was lost, as was the less ambitious bid to get the federal government to pay a share of state and local general assistance. In 1949, Truman proposed a grant-in-aid for general assistance programs, but gained instead a new special assistance for permanent disability, a risk that did not apply to very many people and which the NRPB committee and the Social Security Administration had thought should be covered by social insurance.[31]

A similar stop-and-go pattern appeared in taxation policy. Conservatives won the speedy end of taxes specifically designed for wartime and the cutting of income taxes soon after the war. More cuts in income taxes were made in 1948, after Congress was able to override Truman's third veto. But, even so, the income tax system remained largely intact. As Table 6.1 shows, in 1949 personal and corporate income taxes accounted for more than 10 percent of gross national product, much greater than the approximately 2 percent of 1939. All in all, the national American tax state had grown tremendously, mostly during the 1940s and mostly by way of income taxes. For the rest of the postwar period, the government relied on rises in incomes or in inflation to increase governmental revenues, rather than on changes in taxation policy.[32]

Attempts to pass national health insurance on its own failed completely, however. Truman paid lip service to the issue in 1945 and 1946, but placed it at the center of his "Fair Deal" in 1949. His proposal for a single, universal health insurance program was designed to make the government responsible for more than 4 percent of the GNP. Although it did not call for the reorganization of medical services, the proposal faced strong opposition from the American Medical Association and other health care interest groups, as well as the Republican Senator Robert Taft of Ohio. Despite considerable support in public opinion for various forms of government intervention, Truman failed. All the administration gained for its efforts were grants-in-aid for the building of hospitals, for state public health systems, and for medical research.[33]

EXPLAINING THE CHECKERED CAREER OF U.S. SOCIAL POLICY IN THE 1940s

The central question about New Deal social policy in the 1940s is what accounts for its ups and, mainly, downs. The answer is not the war—for war has much potential to build the domestic state. Given the circumstances, though, the war did not help the proponents of completing the New Deal. And just as the rise of New Deal social policy was not due to a strong labor movement, the decline of New Deal social policy was not due to a weak labor movement. As was the case in the previous decade, labor continued to support New Deal social policy and sometimes radical alternatives to it, and never had the labor movement been more powerful and active. If anything, labor's muscle-flexing by way of strikes harmed the prospects of New Deal social policy in the 1940s. Nor was the answer a lack of state capacities. The adoption of new social policy in the 1930s and the reorganization of the executive branch made it a much powerful instrument for analyzing, proposing, and implementing social policies. Most reform proposals reflected these new capacities. Centralized administration of social policy resulted in proposals that called for more national control and these dominated the political agenda. But greater control over reform proposals did not much matter—the main reason that there were no extensions of the New Deal was that partisan politics did not allow for them. To put it in the terms I have used before, in the 1940s the American political regime was far from reform-oriented.

What, then, accounted for that? Again, the war was important as it drew attention away from domestic policy, but it was not decisive. And the inauspicious political situation was not a matter mainly of lack of public support. After all, the American people continued to elect presidents backing the New Deal—and by considerable margins. The lack of a reform regime was not due mainly to the long-standing divisions in power and authority within the national government and across the state governments. It was true that separations of powers and federalism tended to disperse the forces for social policy and that states were now major players in social policy. The experience of the 1930s showed, however, that states would respond to national incentives if they were powerful enough. The problem lay mainly in the undemocratic nature of the American political process. Because of that the few were able to thwart the many. Then the moment passed.

The Impact of War on New Deal Social Policy

Like the Depression, the war had a significant impact on the possibilities of American social policy. Also like the Depression and its decade, however, the war does not provide an adequate explanation of U.S. social policy in the 1940s. To the contrary, social scientists generally argue that major wars do not typically provoke the decline of social policy—the results of the American 1940s—but have a stimulant effect on it. Wars tend to induce states to make commitments to citizens in return for citizens' efforts on behalf of the state. Wars also tend to increase the fiscal capacities of states, making greater social spending possible. In the next chapter, which compares American and British policy developments in the 1940s, I argue that neither of these processes is certain or likely to lead to greater social policy. Although I postpone a sustained discussion until then, a few words here are in order.

There is no doubt that how the war was run, who was running it, and what happened during wartime worked to the detriment of New Deal social policy. In the United States, the war took attention away from those most in favor of expanded domestic policy. Having spent the Depression concerned mainly with domestic issues, the Roosevelt Administration had to put them aside just before and during the war. The administration needed to marshal its political capital to gain control over the prosecution of the war. Moreover, some consequences of the Second World War tended to mitigate in the short run some of the domestic problems New Deal social policy was designed to solve. In America, the war temporarily ended unemployment, removing the urgency from the high-profile employment programs of the 1930s. The war was not always working against New Deal reformers, however. The buildup for war and the war itself gave taxation reform a boost up on the political agenda. Other social problems, notably health issues, also gained greater currency.

As the impact of the Depression on social policy was contingent on other political developments, so, too, was the impact of the war. For political reasons, neither taxation nor health policy went as far as they might have, despite being boosted by the war. The greatest gains were made in taxation, on which New Dealers were primed before the war—a time when the Left was still powerful in Congress. Policy for health had not advanced far during the Depression, and because of political conditions proponents of new policy were unable to capitalize on the issue after the war. Although the war mattered in all these ways, it did not itself decisively influence social policy. If the war had taken place under different political and policy circumstances, much of New Deal policy might have survived. The war period might have resulted in net gains for social policy, not its rollback and redefinition.

State Administrative Authority and Proposals for Social Policy

Sometimes lost in discussions of 1940s reform proposals is the fact that these differed in form from their counterparts of the early 1930s. The 1940s proposals typically called for centralization and nationalization and with them restrictions on the power of states and localities. These changes were due mainly to the changes in the nature of the administration of public policy. In 1934, the Roosevelt Administration had to construct a Committee on Economic Security from various governmental agencies and outside experts. In 1940, the administration had its own policymaking body in the National Resources Planning Board. Situated in the Executive Office of the President, the NRPB took a more centralized view of social policy and called not for incremental change or additional power-sharing programs like the CES, but for a complete reorganization and centralization of social policy, especially in employment. The NRPB committee also proposed the elimination of the special assistance programs and their incorporation into a larger, more nationally regulated program of assistance, as well as for the upgrading of social insurance.

During the war, the Social Security Board, with its oversight and administration of the special assistance and social insurance programs, was also devising improvements in social policy. The SSB wanted to rationalize and standardize social insurance and public assistance programs and proposed changes in them. As we have seen, the board wanted to use the war especially to upgrade America's commitment to social insurance. It hoped that an increase in payroll taxes could be converted into new commitments for health insurance as well as increased national control over unemployment compensation. It also wanted a new national commitment to general assistance as well as improved ADC programs.[34]

Some of these proposals made it onto the political agenda in bills sponsored by New York's Senator Robert Wagner. In the 1930s, Wagner, a sponsor of the Social Security Act, was mainly compiling proposals building on the best of state and local social policy developments. In the 1940s, the "American Plan" of the Wagner-Murray-Dingell bills was based almost wholly on the output of the NRPB and the SSB. Even the GI bill, cobbled together by the American Legion, consisted of remnants of proposals devised under the auspices of the NRPB—after the legion had sheared away the programs for all Americans. It fits, too, that the postwar employment bills placed more emphasis on economists and budgetary manipulations and than on public employment or supply-side interventions. These strictly fiscal concerns reflected the central role of the Bureau of the Budget in planning social policy after the demise of the NRPB and the WPA.[35]

In taxation, too, what appeared on the political agenda was determined mainly by the Treasury Department. Although Secretary Henry Morgenthau was a fiscal conservative, he wanted to ensure that wartime taxation upheld the social mission of the New Deal. For him that meant progressive taxation. Also, he was surrounded by disciples of Keynes, such as Assistant Secretary Harry Dexter White. Given the economic and fiscal problems posed by war—inflation and revenue generation—Morgenthau was not out of step with his advisors. The administration wanted to pay two-thirds of wartime expenses through taxation—a substantially higher percentage than raised for World War I—and the Treasury proposed to reform taxation in doing so. The Treasury battled the tax-writing committees of Congress and sometimes lost. That was the case concerning a new progressive spending tax, the nature of the excess profits tax, and the degree of personal income taxation. All the same, the Treasury's agenda set the tone for the reforms that occurred in 1940 through 1942. The Treasury notably was in favor of steep excess profits taxes to fund the war and the reform of the income tax as a matter of permanent policy, and it sought successfully to keep a national sales tax off the political agenda. Although it opposed the giveaways in the Ruml plan, the department had initially proposed the prior withholding of income taxes.[36] As with social policy, however, the degree to which its proposals would result in law depended on circumstances the Treasury could not control.

The End of Reform-Oriented Regimes

When Franklin Roosevelt decided to run for a third term, war was on his mind. He discussed military preparedness often and distortions of his position even more frequently. All the same, Roosevelt ran largely on his record of achievement and on the ineptness of the Republicans. He blamed the Republicans for the Depression and for doing nothing about it by way of social policy when they had the chance. He took credit for a record of recovery and reform—an economy much improved from 1932 and New Deal social policy that helped millions. Social policy, including the right to work, was an important theme in his campaign.[37]

Although Roosevelt's bid for a second reelection in 1940 did not receive the kind of overwhelming reception his first one did, in comparison with most American presidential elections Roosevelt's triumph in 1940 was impressive. He won with 54.8 percent of the popular vote and swamped his Republican opponent Wendell Willkie in the electoral college, 449 to 82. As went Maine and Vermont, so went a mere eight Midwestern states to the Republicans. As was the case in 1936, Roosevelt would have won reelection even if all the electoral votes of the states of the former Confederacy, 124 of

Plate 6.3 Roosevelt's Third Inauguration (Royden Dixon). Franklin D. Roosevelt won a second reelection in 1940 by yet another landslide and on the basis of his New Deals. Here he is seen at his unprecedented third inauguration. But soon war overwhelmed his political agenda, and conservative Congresses undercut his mandate. Although Roosevelt was elected a fourth time, he could not make good on his promise to complete New Deal social policy.

them, had gone to his opponent. To the extent that the president ran on the basis of his social policy, he had a clear mandate to continue to pursue it.[38]

But things had changed from the previous decade. The buildup to war did not dim so much Roosevelt's orientation toward reform as his ability to pursue it. A president has only so much attention to spare, and Roosevelt's was soon preempted by military matters. He admitted an already obvious change in 1943 when he claimed famously that he had transmogrified himself from Dr. New Deal to Dr. Win-the-War. Once his concerns had shifted, the domestic policies he pursued furthest were war-related ones such as the revamping of taxation. When he sought an extraordinary fourth term in 1944, the results were similar to those of 1940. He ran on his record in peace and war, against the Republicans, and on the basis of an economic bill of rights, winning handily over a Republican, Thomas Dewey. Roosevelt dropped only slightly in popularity, winning 53.6 percent of the vote, and captured nearly all the same states he won in 1940. Still, even in 1945 Roosevelt could not yet devote himself to domestic policy. If he was betting

TABLE 6.2
U.S. National Election Results, 1940–1950

	House			Senate			President
	Dem.	*Rep.*	*Dem. Margin*	*Dem.*	*Rep.*	*Dem. Margin*	
1940	268	162	106	66	28	38	Roosevelt, Democrat 54.8%, 449–82 electoral
1942	218	208	10	58	37	21	
1944	242	190	52	56	38	18	Roosevelt, Democrat 53.6%, 432–99 electoral
1946	188	245	−57	45	51	−6	
1948	263	171	92	54	42	12	Truman, Democrat 49.6%, 303–189–39 electoral[a]
1950	234	199	35	49	47	2	

Sources: Congressional Quarterly, *Guide to U.S Congress* (Washington, D.C.: Congressional Quarterly, 1985), p. 896. U.S. Bureau of the Census, *Historical Statistics of the United States From Colonial Times to 1970* (Washington, D.C.: U.S. Government Printing Office, 1975), series Y 79–83, p. 1073.

[a] All electoral votes were for the two major parties, save in 1948, when Strom Thurmond of the States' Rights Party won thirty-nine votes.

that he could set social policy right after the war, a plausible interpretation of his campaign, he lost. Upon taking office after Roosevelt's death in April 1945, Harry Truman also had to concern himself largely with the war and its aftermath.[39]

The problem was that except in taxation, Congress had to take the lead on social policy and was not positioned to advance it. After the election of 1940, the alignment in Congress was about as favorable to national social spending as it was in 1939 through 1940. The Democrats had a majority of 106 in the House, a net gain of nine seats from the previous Congress. Although the party could not hold all its seats in the Senate, it retained a large majority, of 38. The election did not, however, provide a congressional alignment such as that from 1935 through 1938. Still, the reform-oriented contingent in both houses of Congress was relatively large, making it possible for Roosevelt to win much of his agenda for taxation—though not nearly all of it. Then again, if Roosevelt merely had representatives of the democratized northern polity to work with, he very likely would have had his way completely on taxation. Some minor social policy gains in unrelated areas also might have been possible.

The real rise of conservative power came after the off-year congressional elections of 1942. The Democratic majority in the House fell to ten and the majority in the Senate dropped to twenty-one. Using the terminology I have

TABLE 6.3.

Pro– and Anti–Social Spending Contingents in the U.S. House of Representatives, 1939–1950

	Pro-Spending Members		Anti-Spending Members		
	Very Probable[a]	Probable[b]	Probable[c]	Very Probable[d]	Size of Pro-Spending Contingent[e]
1939–40	90	86	73	186	Medium
1941–42	72	107	73	183	Medium
1943–44	68	57	88	222	Small
1945–46	73	70	84	208	Medium/Small
1947–48	47	41	102	245	Small
1949–50	71	91	85	188	Medium

Source: Congressional Quarterly, *Guide to U.S. Elections* (Washington, D.C.: Congressional Quarterly, 1985), pp. 786–815.

[a] Includes radical third parties, Democrats elected in open polities, and Democrats or Republicans affiliated with radical third parties.

[b] Includes Democrats affiliated with the Republican Party and Democrats from states dominated by traditional patronage parties.

[c] Includes Republicans from open polities and Republicans affiliated with the Democratic Party.

[d] Includes Republicans from the South and from states dominated by traditional patronage-party organizations, Democrats or Republicans affiliated with conservative third parties, and southern Democrats.

[e] The size of the pro-spending contingent is a judgment based on the relative sizes of each grouping.

employed in previous chapters, the very probable supporters of national social spending—Democrats and third-party representatives from democratized and non-patronage-oriented polities—dropped to sixty-eight in the House. More important, the very probable anti-spenders—Republicans from patronage-oriented parties and Democrats from the underdemocratized South—were in a majority for the first time during the Roosevelt era. This off-year election was also notable for its very low level of voter participation.[40] The drop-off in support was compounded in its impact on social policy by the fact that Roosevelt was preoccupied by war issues and could no longer take charge in domestic policy. Still, had the New Dealers only Republican opposition with which to contend, they would have likely held the line in social policy.

Instead, however, congressional conservatives were numerous enough to roll back the New Deal. Hoping to ward off an embarrassing fight, Roosevelt called it quits for the WPA, and Congress eliminated the NRPB and the NYA. No new tax reforms were possible either, and instead Congress passed the offensive Revenue Act of 1944. The Social Security Board was scrambling in trying to save its OASI program in the face of taxation freezes. In 1943, moreover, Congress claimed the lead in questions of reconstruction, incorporating postwar planning into its committee system. The congressional planning committees were so weighed down by conservatives that "Mr. Republican," Senator Taft, was named to head one key Senate subcommittee.[41]

Despite another overwhelming victory, Roosevelt's final campaign did not return with him to Congress enough support to revive the New Deal. That would have been the case even if he or his successor had been able to focus on domestic policy. The Democratic majority in the House was increased to fifty-two seats, better than two years previous, but not nearly the margin provided by the 1938 or 1940 elections, not to mention the period before then. The very probable anti-spenders stood at 208. The Democratic majority in the Senate continued to drop as well, to eighteen seats, a far cry from the forty-six-seat majority after the 1938 elections. As a result of continuing war and the only moderately pro-spending orientation of Congress, made moderate by the structure of the American polity, only minor social spending reform was able to pass—the Employment Act of 1945 and some housing and health initiatives.

After the off-year elections of 1946, the Republicans gained control of Congress for the first time since the 1920s. They had a fifty-seven-seat majority in the House and a six-seat majority in the Senate. Given that and the consistently large representation of southern Democrats, it was no surprise that the New Deal was not revived. Just the opposite—Congress provided tax cuts rather than expanded social policy commitments. The only changes in social policy were to make it easier for states with stingy benefits in special assistance programs to continue their practices by way of a variable grant formula more favorable to them. Congress went beyond social policy, too, in reducing the rights of labor unions with the Taft-Hartley Act in 1947.

In 1948, Truman won election to the presidency in his own right. He faced opposition from as usual a Republican, again Thomas Dewey, but also from former Democrats to his left and right—the Progressive Henry Wallace, Roosevelt's previous vice president, and the States' Rights candidate Strom Thurmond, from South Carolina. All the same, Truman won in his campaign to continue what was left of the New Deal and to combat what he labeled, erroneously, a "do-nothing" Republican Congress. It was not the sort of mandate Roosevelt typically received, as Truman took only 49.6 percent of the popular vote and only 303 electoral votes, to Dewey's 189 and Thurmond's 39. But Truman brought with him a Democratic majority of ninety-two in the House and twelve in the Senate. In the House, the very probable anti-spenders fell back to 188.

And so for the third consecutive time in the decade a president endorsing New Deal social policy won an election with a clear mandate. But given the structure of American politics, the alignment in Congress was not one that could produce substantial reform. After his election Truman was able to pass significant improvements to the Social Security Act. OASI was saved, and ADC was upgraded. As was the case near the end of the 1930s, it was not possible, though, to make new social policy commitments. Truman's health insurance initiative went down to defeat. The lobbying of the American Medical Association and its business allies was magnified in its effect by a weakly reform-oriented Congress unwilling to enact a popular policy. Other New Deal initiatives had already been removed from the political agenda and would not be returning.

Social Movements and Social Policy in the 1940s

Many challengers declined in the 1940s, but the impact of movements also depended heavily on the political situation. When movements were doing well, as was the case for the Townsendites and labor in the early 1940s, unfavorable political conditions minimized their influence. The Townsend Movement followed up its gains in the late 1930s on OAA with further mobilization. In 1941, it seemed as though the Movement might transform Old-Age and Survivors' Insurance (OASI) into something akin to the Townsend Plan. The labor movement never had a better decade in terms of mobilization and was energetic in striking to secure gains in organization and wages. Both wings of the labor movement backed plans to expand social policy. If anything, however, labor's collective action campaign harmed its allies and induced demands to curb its power.

The Townsend Movement could not make a great impact during the war years. In the early 1940s the Movement sustained its membership and successfully endorsed members of Congress, as Table 6.4 shows. At perhaps the apex of its political power, the Movement was set to make its greatest influence on the issue of old-age security. Partly in reaction to the Movement, the head of the Federal Security Agency, Paul McNutt, was set to propose a flat-benefit old-age pension financed by an income tax in 1940. Altmeyer succeeded, though, in getting Roosevelt to stop him. Hearings led by the Townsend-backed Senator Sheridan Downey of California in 1941 drew further attention to the issue. Against its inclinations, the SSB was ready to compromise by converting OASI into a "double-decker" program. Each person sixty-five years or older would receive at least a minimum national pension—the basic Townsend idea. But some would receive higher benefits determined according to previous earnings—the essence of social insurance.[42] The hearings, however, were interrupted by the bad news from Pearl Harbor, and the issue was dropped.

Afterward a highly unfavorable election removed the issue of improving old-age benefits from the political agenda. The only proposals that made any headway at all were ones to freeze the OASI payroll tax. The absence of otherwise favorable political conditions thwarted the impact of the Townsend Movement, which focused instead on passing "baby" Townsend plans for individual states of the Union.[43] The war period demonstrated that a moderate level of challenger strength in membership and political

TABLE 6.4.
The Townsend Movement: Membership, Resources, and Political Activity, and Democratic
Majorities in the U.S. House of Representatives, 1940–1949

	Paid Members (thousands)	*Gross Receipts (thousands of dollars)*	*Membership as Percentage of U.S. Population 65 and Over*	*Townsend-Backed House Candidates (Percent Elected)*	*Democratic House Majority (Size)*
1940	646.9	689	7.16	132 (58.1)	106 (medium)
1941	468.7	636	5.05		
1942	297.6	486	3.11	172 (60.3)	10 (small)
1943	271.8	424	2.75		
1944	269.6	628	2.66	172 (75.1)	52 (medium)
1945	234.8	512	2.23		
1946	173.6	519	1.60	182 (66.2)	−57 (negative)
1947	134.3	418	1.20		
1948	92.7	353	0.80	135 (65.5)	92 (medium)
1949	52.8	328	0.44		

Source: Edwin Amenta, Bruce G. Carruthers, and Yvonne Zylan, "A Hero For the Aged? The Townsend Movement, The Political Mediation Model, and U.S. Old-Age Policy, 1934–1950." *American Journal of Sociology* 98 (1992): 308–39.

action was not enough in itself to cause changes in spending. When the political alignment is unfavorable, little is possible in the way of gaining spending innovations and improvements. The Townsend Movement declined after the war.

Organized labor remained committed to the Roosevelt Administration and largely backed its goals on social policy in the 1940s. Although John L. Lewis, the head of the Congress of Industrial Organizations (CIO) did not support Roosevelt in 1940, the vast majority of CIO workers did. When Lewis was deposed a year later, the CIO backed social insurance. The more conservative, but still growing American Federation of Labor (AFL), backed the proposals of the Social Security Board, including the Eliot bill of 1941 to increase payroll taxes. Labor's Non-Partisan League adopted ideas from the NRPB's *Security, Work, and Relief Policies*. Both CIO and AFL rallied behind the Wagner-Murray-Dingell bill in 1943, cementing a labor-state expert coalition behind it.[44]

All the same, increasing mobilization and collective action by a challenger favoring new social policy was not enough to make it happen. The labor movement remained concerned mainly with organizing workers in the 1940s, and gains in unionization were dramatic, as tight labor-market conditions worked hand in hand with governmental policy. After Pearl Harbor, Roosevelt obtained a no-strike pledge from leaders of the AFL and CIO. In return, "maintenance of membership" for unions became official policy, while workers' wages were expected to grow gradually. Falling away were bastions of anti-unionism in the industrial sector, notably "little steel,"

Plate 6.4 A Member of a Local Townsend Club (John Vachon). The Townsend Movement continued to flourish in the early 1940s and almost induced a major change in old-age policy. Here an Indiana man reads the *Townsend National Weekly* in 1941. But the issue was dropped during the war, and the Townsend Movement faded afterward.

which had repelled unionization in the 1930s. From 1939 to 1947 union membership grew from about 8.7 million to about 14.8 million, or 33.7 percent of the nonagricultural labor force. In addition, the wartime agreements and production helped unions to achieve collective bargaining rights, in practice resisted by employers. Despite the pledge, strike activity was higher during the war than during the New Deal 1930s, and strikes peaked after the war. Yet the war years brought the retrenchment of social policy, and the postwar years saw only marginal gains.[45]

Rather than aiding social spending legislation, the wartime and postwar strike waves probably harmed its chances, particularly those of the Wagner-Murray-Dingell bill. In the 1930s, the public viewed labor as struggling against unfair and often unlawful opponents. In the 1940s, strikes were viewed widely by the public as capitalizing on tight labor-market conditions at the expense of the war effort and the common sacrifice. Lewis, still head of the United Mine Workers, was vilified in particular for a series of strikes in 1943. Labor's opponents in Congress were encouraged to advance antilabor legislation. Two important bills passed, including the 1943

Plate 6.5 "Partners in Crime" (photographer unknown). Labor strikes were ubiquitous during the Second World War—more numerous than during the New Deal 1930s. The strikes were also unpopular as they slowed the production of munitions for war. In this photo, a sign accuses John L. Lewis of the United Mine Workers of being allied with the enemy.

Smith-Connally Act, which discouraged strikes and passed over Roosevelt's veto. At the end of war, the largest strike wave in American history was followed by the antilabor Taft-Hartley Act, which passed over Truman's veto in 1947 and limited the rights of labor under the National Labor Relations Act.[46]

Despite the attacks on organized labor or perhaps because of them, the alliance between labor and northern Democrats grew stronger, as friends and enemies were sorted out in the political battle. In the long-run, organizational gains made by labor in wartime probably improved the future prospects of new and expanded social policy. In the postwar period, moreover, about half of congressional districts had a strong labor presence in them.[47] That combined with both wings of labor agreeing to the agenda of the Social Security Administration augured well for social insurance. Yet labor was largely unsuccessful in organizing the South—no surprise, given the political weapons in the hands of those opposing labor. Little countervailing influence could be applied in anti-social spending, undemocratic districts.

The Democratic party diverged from social democratic parties also in that neither the party nor labor was bound by the policies of the other. The looseness of the connection made it possible for organized labor to win social welfare battles with business, while losing them in the political arena. In the 1940s labor's strength with respect to employers outran the strength of its allies in the national government. Public failure and private success eventually resulted in a greater selectivity in the provision of pensions and health benefits, as labor added a private tier of benefits for organized workers to existing public ones. This private welfare state, with its origins during and right after the war, now accounts for most consumer spending on health and about one-quarter of American social spending.[48]

WHY SOME PROGRAMS SURVIVED THE WAR, WHILE OTHERS DID NOT

The rollback and slowing of the New Deal was due to political conditions, but they do not explain why the New Deal was retrenched in the selective way that it was. Some programs were threatened, such as OASI. Others were left alone, such as the special assistance programs. Yet others, notably work programs, were decimated. Why did some programs survive, while others did not?

Why We Lost the WPA

The elimination of the WPA and allied work programs is an issue often ignored. It is typically assumed that the WPA was designed to be temporary and thus would naturally end as the Depression ended, also naturally. But the demise of the WPA was not inevitable. After all, the program was at the center of the first reform of welfare, and the commitment to the WPA was reaffirmed in the recession of 1938. In 1939, the WPA and other public employment programs employed more than 3 million people, accounting for about 2 percent of the gross national product and about 20 percent of national government expenditures, and put America in the lead in social spending efforts at the time. Although unemployment was subdued by the war, policymakers expected unemployment to return. The NRPB committee saw work programs as central to postwar social policy, as did left-wing Keynesians. What is more, the retrenchment of social spending programs is always difficult. Cutting and eliminating social programs provides direct and substantial harm to identifiable people, while providing only diffuse or theoretical benefits to many. Thus politicians have a difficult chore on their hands when they want to destroy a program and need to devise strategies to shift blame.[49] And there was no program bigger than the WPA.

General arguments about the retrenchment of social policies suggest that the WPA would be a likely target. Theodore Lowi argues that distributive programs engender interest-group support, while redistributive programs, like the WPA, do not. Theda Skocpol's arguments about "policy feed-backs" suggest that insufficient administrative capacities can doom a program to failure as well as make it unlikely that it will be chosen in the first place. Along these lines, the historian Michael Katz suggests that administrative problems limited the WPA. Paul Pierson argues that because of the temporary nature of unemployment, programs for the unemployed only rarely engender strong interest-group support in the manner of programs for the aged and thus are more vulnerable.[50]

All the same, none of these arguments fully explains the WPA's demise. Means testing may have been a disadvantage, but other means-tested programs, such as OAA and ADC, were not terminated. The WPA was built very quickly and ran into numerous administrative troubles, but other New Deal programs were built as quickly, and perhaps more so. The WPA was able to benefit from the examples of work relief through the Civil Works Administration and the Federal Emergency Relief Administration and was able to put a great many people to work quickly. By the end of the Depression decade few New Deal social spending programs had stronger administrative capabilities. At the end of 1939, the WPA included some eighteen hundred central or regional administrative employees, with divisions responsible for statistics, research, investigation, and information. Although unemployment plunged during the war, that did not mean the end of unemployment compensation programs, and most experts expected high unemployment after the war. In any case, an unemployed workers' organization developed around the WPA, which had also forged relationships with local governments around the country.[51]

What mattered more were other program characteristics—the WPA's far-reaching nature and the national executive authority embodied in it. These aspects of the WPA made its opponents more determined to stop it and its supporters more equivocal in favor of it. Because of institutional circumstances of American politics, notably the lack of democracy in the South and the patronage nature of many local party systems, the opponents of the WPA had greater means to fight it than they might otherwise have had. Despite the dominance of the Democratic party throughout the WPA era, pro-social spenders could never control the government and make the WPA more secure.[52]

The opponents of the WPA were more numerous and determined than those of other social spending programs because it was a work-relief program that aspired to pay higher than relief wages. Businessmen generally opposed any programs that might lead to higher taxes for them and accordingly were no fans of the WPA—the most expensive New Deal program. Also, although the WPA was supposed to avoid work projects that competed with private business, capitalists typically did not think this line was drawn tightly enough around the activities of the WPA. The WPA had the added disadvantage of potentially bidding up the wages of workers. In a 1939 poll asking business executives to name their least favorite New Deal program, the WPA placed third, behind only the Wagner Act and the undistributed profits tax. Republicans were typically united behind any attempt to lower the appropriations or wage rates for the WPA.[53]

The wage-inflating potential of the WPA made it especially threatening to southern political leaders, who also fought generous standards in OAA and ADC. A WPA that could deliver on its promise to employ all employable people without minimum-wage jobs would doubtless constitute a tempting alternative for the rural labor force. High wages for the WPA, consistent work, fair and routinized treatment of recipients, and moves to make the WPA permanent were all opposed by southern Democrats. They also wanted to prevent excessive sums from being spent on the rest of the country. These concerns were balanced only somewhat by the need of a poor region for federal money. Southern members of Congress led various efforts to investigate, water down, and slow the expenditures for the WPA, especially after 1938.[54]

The partisan nature of the Roosevelt regime and the national executive's control over the WPA also posed a more specific threat to political conservatives, including Democrats outside the South. In 1938, the WPA was perceived by many to be the means by which Roosevelt was attempting to "purge" his conservative enemies. Hopkins avoided using WPA funds to finance Democrats concerned chiefly with oiling their political machines at the expense of the program. He was, though, willing to deploy the WPA to aid the New Deal's allies and harm its opponents. Political organizations could pressure WPA workers to canvass or kick back a percentage of their wages. Even if that pressure did not often succeed it might still prove important as WPA workers usually greatly outnumbered municipal employees. Although Roosevelt's attempted purges were unsuccessful in the South and only marginally successful elsewhere, non-Democrats and conservative Democrats alike feared the WPA was being used or might be used against them and thus had more than ideological reasons to oppose the program.[55]

The great power the WPA vested in the executive branch and the administrators of the program made threats to deny grants all too plausible. The WPA typically relied on project proposals developed by sponsors, but did not automatically fund them and made state and local governments compete for grants. Denying federal grants was much easier for the WPA than for the SSB, which would have to cut off funds for all of the dependent children or aged in the state—a big and possibly self-defeating step. OASI provided benefits according to a formula that was subject to congressional decision, not administrative fiat. For members of Congress favorable to New Deal social policy but opposed bids for power by the executive branch, the WPA was a mixed blessing. Despite its specific social mission, the WPA resembled Roosevelt's plans to undermine the Supreme Court and radically to upgrade the executive branch. Sometimes attempts to remove the administration's discretion found unlikely allies. When South Carolina

Senator James Byrnes's Special Senate Unemployment Committee called for the earmarking of WPA funds to the states, Senator James Murray, Democrat of Montana and stalwart New Dealer, spoke out in favor of the plan.[56]

As Katz argues, the WPA's policy on wages was always a balancing act. Increases in wages would provoke increasing opposition by employers, but if wages were too low they would be opposed by workers. Much of the labor movement preferred no WPA at all to one that paid a "security" wage. In most of the South, however, a security wage was the highest wage possible, and in 1939 Congress established minimum monthly hours for WPA workers, in effect lowering WPA wage rates. The AFL and CIO lobbied unsuccessfully for repeal of the 130-hour provision, and authorized its construction locals to strike at WPA projects, with 50,000 to 100,000 workers doing so. After failing to repeal the wage provisions, labor turned its back on the WPA and focused on obtaining larger appropriations for the PWA and housing construction—for which workers could be employed under union conditions and without applying for relief.[57]

Although the Workers' Alliance of America consisted entirely of WPA workers and numbered some 200,000 at its peak, it was politically disadvantaged. In July 1939, the alliance organized a one-day strike against the new wage provisions, but its turnout of approximately 50,000 was low, coming as it did in the wake of threats to dismiss striking workers. Much of the congressional investigation of the WPA in 1939 and 1940 focused on alleged Communist influence in the Worker's Alliance. The institution of an eighteen-month time limit on WPA employment was devised partly to hinder the organizing tasks of the Worker's Alliance, which had enough on its hands with the inherent difficulties of mobilizing unemployed workers.[58]

Despite the efforts of Hopkins to reduce standard patronage politics in the WPA, such politics were endemic to it. State and local officials had various means to influence the process. One way that patronage politics seeped into the WPA was through the requirement that state-level heads of the WPA be confirmed by the Senate. By standard courtesy procedures, the choices were typically beholden to at least one of the state's senators. Another way was through the requirement that almost all WPA workers were to be taken from general assistance rolls. WPA employment was gained only by way of applying for relief, but not all relief applicants were guaranteed relief, and not all relief recipients were guaranteed WPA employment. Deciding who was to receive relief and nominating recipients for work relief gave local officials great influence. The lack of a national grant-in-aid for general assistance meant little federal leverage to ensure fairness in the relief-granting process. In the South, as we have seen, almost everyone accepted for general relief was transferred to the rolls of the WPA. Such problems led reformers to suggest federal grants-in-aid for general relief, in order to provide some federal leverage over the process, and for WPA employment to be connected to public employment offices.[59]

The WPA was bound to suffer the public-relations problems of any program with great political discretion in it. Designing a social program as a kind of pork barrel may make it easier to assemble an initial coalition behind it; politicians not interested in the social mission of the program may find other reasons to support it. But discretion can cloud the long-term prospects of a program, as it is likely to be portrayed as unfair or corrupt, or both, and lose the support of the general public who might be otherwise sympathetic to the program's mission. The WPA was neither subject to a standard formula nor administered under tight merit standards, as were other social programs after the Social Security Act amendments of 1939. The administration continued to allocate WPA jobs according to criteria it never fully disclosed, inviting suspicion in many state and local leaders who feared that they were not getting their fair share. And inequities of whatever sort provided ammunition for WPA's foes, who may have opposed it for other reasons.

Roosevelt had especially difficult decisions to make in the thirteen states characterized by David Mayhew as "regular organization" or "persistent factionalism" states, where patronage-oriented political parties predominated.[60] The president often found himself damned if he did and damned if he did not run the WPA through the regular Democratic organization. Supporting the regular organization might have been the only way to deliver the votes needed to continue the New Deal, but such organizations were usually indifferent or opposed to the ideology of the New Deal. Worse than that, they were often corrupt and in their administration of New Deal programs tended to discredit them by courting bad publicity. Running around the regular organization avoided such problems, but made the regulars sworn enemies of the program and often of the administration as well. Although Roosevelt and Hopkins tried nearly every possible configuration, only few worked to the long-term advantage of the program, as a few examples can show.

The choice to support a patronage-oriented machine was invariably an unhappy one with negative consequences for the prospects of the program. The administration made a devil's bargain with some corrupt political machines, especially, as Stephen P. Erie has argued, where they dominated states considered electorally crucial to Roosevelt. The most notorious examples were Frank Hague's machine in Jersey City and Thomas Pendergast's in Kansas City, where in each state the WPA was employed fraudulently. In New Jersey, Roosevelt bolstered with the WPA a regime that fought organized labor and other New Deal policies. In Missouri, the eventual fall of Pendergast, due to income tax evasion, caused the administration to take over the WPA. Where the administration had to choose between patronage-oriented organizations, it invariably incurred the wrath of the one left empty-handed. This was the case as we have seen in Illinois, where the administration tilted toward Mayor Kelly of Chicago and against

Governor Horner, a Democrat who never became friendly to the New Deal. Similar problems arose in West Virginia.[61]

Taking the high road was not without its problems, though. In New York City, Roosevelt ran the WPA around Tammany Hall and through Mayor Fiorello La Guardia, a New Deal supporter elected on the Fusion Reform ticket in 1933. La Guardia was granted a separate relief unit for New York City, with one-seventh of all the WPA expenditures, and helped select several successive nonpartisan WPA administrators. In return La Guardia campaigned for Roosevelt, lobbied for New Deal programs as head of the National Conference of Mayors, and founded the American Labor party in 1936 to provide a liberal alternative to the Democratic party in New York City.[62] All in all, the WPA was generous and efficient in the city, but no durable pro-New Deal faction of the Democratic party was built by way of it. Having a plausible alternative to patronage-oriented politicians was a luxury, however. In some states, notably Ohio, the administration did not have this option, nor would it ally with the existing patronage party organizations. Hopkins had encountered trouble with Democratic Governor Martin Davey in the administration of the Federal Emergency Relief Administration (FERA) and did not want to work with him on the WPA. By choosing the FERA head to run the WPA in Ohio Hopkins essentially cut out Davey—resulting in another Democratic regime that opposed the national New Deal.[63]

The WPA had attributes that made it less attractive to members of Congress than patronage usually is. Many of the negotiations central to the WPA, between the national administration and localities, ran somewhat outside the bounds of congressional deliberation. The WPA also favored some members of Congress over others. Although the confirmation of WPA officials provided many senators with significant control over WPA activities, it offered no such advantages to representatives. The WPA was investigated in both the Senate and the House, but the House investigation led by Clifton Woodrum of Virginia, the chair of an appropriations subcommittee, was far more mean-spirited. The House was also the site of the drastic restrictions enacted as part of the fiscal year 1940 appropriation bill.[64]

In short, the way the WPA was structured harmed its prospects for long-term survival. The WPA was a threatening program to influential groups and political conservatives. The centralized aspects of the program and its influence over wages and employment prospects gave them strong incentives to fight the program. The institutional limitations on pro-spending regimes ensured that the WPA would not be funded at an adequate level and provided a platform of strength from which political conservatives could contest the program and alter it in ways that made its supporters uneasy with it. The same aspects of the program made supporters at best ambivalent. Congressional support for the mission of the program did not translate into support for executive discretion. Wage rates might be made too low for the comfort of organized labor, and amendments to the program seemed to realize its worst fears. Although the WPA provided a kind of patronage, patronage-oriented politicians not aided by it were opposed to it, and the ones that were aided by it typically harmed the WPA's reputation. All conservatives needed were greater numbers in Congress and plausible economic reasons to end the WPA, and during the war they received both.

Why Special Assistance and Old-Age and Survivors' Insurance Survived

OASI, ADC, and OAA were constructed differently from the WPA in ways that enhanced their security and aided their survival. Although business organizations and southern economic and political elites fought the enactment of these programs, each had been amended from the start to make them less threatening. After the first few years of the programs had passed, moreover, there was little opportunity for patronage politics in them. Each program had some form of national fiscal backing. It helped, too, that each was managed by the SSB. But because the special assistance and social insurance programs were different in form they also lasted for reasons that differed.

The most beneficial circumstance shared by special assistance programs was the federal government's financial backing. Federal matching payments gave OAA and ADC a leg up on general assistance, which aided many more people at the end of the 1930s than OAA and ADC, but suffered a worse fate. Because the special assistance programs were grants-in-aid with few national standards, moreover, states and localities could greatly vary payments and eligibility standards. That flexibility made the programs less threatening, as it allowed discrimination and the denial of adequate benefits. In addition, after 1939 most opportunities for blatant patronage politics were eliminated from the programs—costing them some support from patronage-oriented parties, but making the programs more difficult to attack in the long run. Although the SSB was not as powerful as the WPA organization and was only an uneven ally of OAA, the board's support was far better than having no national administrative backing, and it ensured that the programs were run honestly.

The SSB was especially crucial in promoting ADC, which, unlike OAA, had little social movement or interest group support. Partly the board wanted to prevent the expansion of OAA programs for fear that they would undercut the nascent old-age insurance program, but doing that was consistent with seeking ways to bridge the disparity between OAA and ADC.[65] The board's proposed variable-grant formula, with its higher rate of reimbursement for the first portions of a state's grant and low overall matching ceilings, was a strategy designed to increase the extension of ADC as it ratified the minimal payments being made in some states for it. Providing national reimbursements that were much higher for the first portion of a monthly grant meant nearly to nationalize the funding for the stingiest states. Holding down the maximum benefit for matching reimbursement undercut the opposition of such states to the program. Without taxes being increased at the state level, benefits could be given out to more people. Also, there would be a limit on federal dollars going to more generous states. The plans of the NRPB and Senator Wagner to end the limits on matching payments would have had the opposite effect.

Why OASI survived is also rarely discussed, as if the answer to that, too, were obvious. As we have seen, however, the prospects of the OASI program in its formative years were doubtful at best. Not yet present were the conditions considered central to its current hold on the American people — its more numerous recipients and larger benefits than the means-tested programs, its supposed fiscal responsibility, organized interest-group backing, and the power of its program executives and their peculiarly influential social insurance imagery.[66] The SSB was overshadowed by other New Deal agencies until the postwar period. What is more, OASI had opponents who easily outweighed its supporters in terms of power and numbers. The program was attacked by business organizations and other conservatives, who did not like the payroll tax and feared that building a trust fund would facilitate open-ended commitments to further social benefits. Left-wing Keynesians within the Roosevelt and Truman administrations opposed the payroll tax for the program as both regressive and inimical to economic growth. Though mainly for the aged, OASI did not receive great support from old-age organizations like the Townsend Movement, which were far more sympathetic to and engaged with OAA. Even in 1949, the average old-age benefit for OAA was about forty-five dollars per month, dwarfing the twenty-five dollars received by the average OASI recipient. About 2.7 million individuals received retirement benefits under OAA, only 1.6 million under OASI. Under the circumstances, it is not surprising that the social insurance imagery had yet to capture the public imagination.[67]

Some reasons for OASI's survival have to be categorized under the heading of good fortune. President Roosevelt always favored the program, although he understood its political aspects far better than its technical ones. He was determined at the start that the program was to be "self-financing," by "contributions," which did not sound like the taxes they were. But Roosevelt was happy to undermine the program's finances when it suited his political purposes, as it did in 1939. And, relatively speaking, wartime events were good to OASI. The war took old-age policy off the political agenda just as the administration was knuckling under to the Townsend Movement and other groups to convert OASI into a double-decker program. Although the conservative Congress that gained power after 1942 froze OASI payroll taxes, it made a stronger advance on powerful New Deal agencies that conflicted with the SSB — the NRPB and the WPA. The economic prosperity also finished off the Townsend Movement, whose premises were based on the Depression.

Why OASI survived was also due to its program characteristics. It excluded agricultural and domestic workers, reducing some opposition to the program—not only from the South, but from farmers around the country. Its taxes were widespread enough, though, that Roosevelt could proclaim to good rhetorical effect in 1940 that millions were covered by a "system of social insurance" when almost no one was receiving benefits from it. Although OASI was run and funded by the national government, it did not grant the executive branch the kind of polarizing discretionary power it had with the WPA. Congress could legislate OASI benefit levels in minute detail, and the executive branch mainly administered these changes.

Most of all, OASI was well designed to take advantage of prosperity and provided a defensible way to give out great benefits without correspondingly great increases in taxes. It was a responsible-seeming way to spend irresponsibly. The OASI trust fund grew from about $2 billion in 1940 to about $12 billion in 1949, an increase that outstripped the growth in GNP by a factor of two. That happened despite the tax freeze and despite the rolls of aged recipients having grown more than tenfold, from about 113,000 to about 1.6 million. The way the program was structured—as a mainly pay-as-you-go program with a dedicated tax—made it possible, during economic growth, to give away much to many without great cost. And the economy was growing greatly during the 1940s and would continue to do so throughout the postwar period. Under the circumstances, political leaders could grant to recipients far more in benefits than what they could have expected given the "contributions" made by them or on their behalf. Although the first beneficiaries gained much more than later ones, all recipients for the rest of the century could be expected to receive much more on average than what they paid in taxes.[68]

CONCLUSION

The 1940s did not witness the consolidation of New Deal social policy, but its failure and redefinition. The comprehensive plans of the New Dealers to complete the work and relief policy of the 1930s went down to defeat. There was to be no guaranteed minimum income through work, relief, or social insurance. Employment programs, the cornerstone of New Deal social policy, were dismantled, and even attempts to make presidents propose symbolic "full-employment budgets" were deflected. Public assistance systems remained chaotic with few national standards, and federal grants-in-aid for general assistance were rejected. Social insurance did not advance very far either. National unemployment insurance was prevented, as was the creation of social insurance for sicknesses and disabilities. The battle of national health insurance was joined for the first time and lost.

The destruction of employment programs was perhaps the most surprising development, for they had the greatest administrative popular support among all New Deal programs, as well as great popular support. The WPA was ended, however, as were other employment programs. Going down with them was the NRPB—a White House organization designed to promote supply-side initiatives like the WPA.

By contrast, national taxation initiatives were largely successful. Because of the efforts of New Deal reformers, taxation policy was more transformed than consolidated. Early New Deal policies depended on regressive excise taxes and payroll taxes as well as some increased progressive taxes on corporations and incomes. In 1941 and 1942, the individual income tax was transformed from a tax on upper incomes to a steeply graduated tax on almost all incomes. It became simultaneously much more progressive and productive of revenue. Income taxes produced a steadily increasing stream of revenue as the economy grew in the postwar period. Impressive as they were, taxation innovations were not as dramatic as they might have been. There was little increase in payroll taxes for social insurance purposes. The new income taxes also underlined the political separation between social policy and taxation. It became possible to propose new spending increases without new taxes, leaving new social spending ungrounded in that way.

Other New Deal programs survived the war, but some were in better condition than others. OASI was threatened, but was in the clear by 1950. It had been expanded and amended to the point of being almost universal. From there it could constitute a foundation for increases in benefits and coverage and the extension of social insurance to other risks. However, the program was still not yet very generous and was never going to be united with UC. And the improvement in the fortunes of OASI came at the expense of OAA, a surviving relief program that had aided far more of the aged with greater sums than OASI. ADC also survived and was marginally improved, but became isolated.

What is more, America gained a program that confounded the plans of the New Dealers: a comprehensive system of veterans' benefits. These benefits included "readjustment allowances," educational benefits, free medical care, and incentives to purchase homes. This group of benefits came in addition to those for disabled veterans, who automatically gained from categorical legislation enacted after previous wars. Although many of these new benefits were planned by New Dealers, the planners did not expect that only veterans would gain such benefits and thus gain rights greater than those of other citizens.

By the end of the 1940s American public social provision was divided and confused. There was no longer a work program, and new initiatives to revamp relief policy and social insurance had failed. What was left ran along two tracks. On the one side, OASI, separated programmatically and fiscally, combined national fiscal decisions and bureaucratic administration with minimal surveillance of the recipient population. Veterans, too, were favored with separate programs. On the other side were the remnants of the New Deal relief policy, a policy of providing jobs for the unemployed and retirement from the labor force with a stipend for others. The WPA was finished, though, and the popular OAA program was in eclipse. In the assistance programs, benefits and eligibility were controlled by the states, which applied means tests and local surveillance. ADC and the less-favored general assistance programs became isolated. ADC's purpose would seem less and less clear as more and more women joined the labor force in the postwar period.

The New Deal failed during the war and was not resuscitated after it, but the failures were not due to the war itself. The war had the effect of removing social policy from the political agenda for the moment and highlighting some social problems rather than others—to some extent at the expense of employment policy. But the war provided positive opportunities, especially for changes in taxation policy, and might have resulted in the completion of the New Deal.

The reasons for the failures had more to do with institutional and political circumstances. As during the 1930s, when social policy initiatives had greater success, most of the planning for them was done by the administration. As in the 1930s, the plans followed from the structure of government agencies. Their greater centralization resulted in plans that reflected it. Political circumstances were much different from those in the 1930s, however, ensuring that most of these proposals would languish. President Roosevelt was consumed by the war effort and could pay attention to only those aspects of social policy, essentially taxation, that mattered for prosecuting the war. The same was true for his successor, Harry Truman. Compounding that were Congresses far from reform-oriented and actively hostile to the New Deal. These political conditions owed much in turn to the structure of American politics. One-fourth of Congress was held by legislators from relatively underdemocratized areas. For that reason these representatives were less likely to be in favor of social spending with national standards and enforcement—the direction in which the New Deal was heading. This combined with a resurgence of the Republican party and Democratic presidents unable to attend to social policy—much to its disadvantage.

Political circumstances explain why the New Deal was attacked and failed to be extended, but do not explain why some programs failed and others did not. Survival depended greatly on program characteristics. The characteristics that mattered most, though, were not whether the programs were means-tested or universal. The WPA was lost not because it was means-tested, but because it was structured in a way that was highly threatening. A national program with national standards, the WPA was greatly disliked by economic elites around the country and, because of its potential for low wages, was not greatly supported by organized labor either. Other means-tested programs, including ADC and OAA, did not share the WPA's qualities and largely survived. These programs did not gain the sort of national standards and controls proposed by the NRPB, however. OASI also lasted partly because of how it was constructed. It was not universal and did not benefit nearly as many people as ADC and OAA, and it was attacked during the war like much of the rest of the New Deal. But its payroll tax produced as the economy improved, leaving the trust fund in far better fiscal health than when the decade began. As a result, OASI was a strong candidate for minor expansion—much preferable to conservative forces than creating a new national health insurance program.

In the next chapter I contrast the decline and redefinition of the New Deal work and relief policy with wartime developments in Great Britain. There the war and postwar period brought success to the plans of reformers. At the end of the war the British government was legislating what people were now calling the "welfare state."

CHAPTER SEVEN

A Welfare State for Britain

> The USA is supplying us with munitions and with a large part of our food in time of war. I personally believe that when the war is over the USA will not be disposed to continue that operation and from my experience of America. . . . I hold the distinct view that the working classes of America will not be a party to supplying money to us in order to preserve social services which are higher than those provided for their own people.
>
> —*Sir John Forbes Watson, British Employers' Confederation, to William Beveridge, May 1942*

> The main feature of the Plan for Social Security is a scheme of social insurance against interruption and destruction of earning power and for special expenditure arising at birth, marriage or death.
>
> —*William Beveridge, November 1942*

SIR JOHN FORBES WATSON was one of many who testified in the spring of 1942 before William Beveridge, the academic and former civil servant who was charged the previous year with studying and making recommendations for British social policy.[1] Like his American business counterparts, Watson was attacking proposed augmentations in social policy—Beveridge's proposals for increased social insurance payments and his call for new health benefits for the British people after the war. Like their American counterparts, the members of the confederation counseled delay, urging Beveridge and the government to wait until after the war to ascertain whether Britain could afford new public spending commitments. And like the views of his American counterparts in 1935, Watson's "distinct" view was ignored. Beveridge went ahead with his proposals.

Although the United States was aiding its ally Britain, this did not end when the Beveridge Report was published at the end of 1942. Nor did aid cease when Britain provided protection for workers that went well beyond what was offered by America. By the end of the 1940s, America had enacted only a foundation for "social security" or Old-Age and Survivors' Insurance (OASI) and veterans' benefits through the GI Bill, while it had discarded most of its work and relief policy. By the end of the 1940s, Britain had enacted something so remarkable that a term was coined to describe it — the "welfare state," which provided for all the major risks of industrial capitalism. Comparing Britain and America begs one big question: Why did the 1940s produce a welfare state for Britain, while in America the completion of social policy was rejected?

This difference in policy outcomes is paradoxical because the United States aided Britain during the war, but refused to make similar policy commitments to Americans. Also, the wartime allies shared many circumstances that might influence social policy. First of all, each country was a major industrial power and therefore able to set its own course in public policymaking. In addition, both countries had long-standing democratic political institutions. Unlike some other large capitalist nations, notably Germany, the United States and Britain retained democratic political institutions throughout the Depression and the war. Each was a major participant on the winning side. Although British civilians felt the war's impact much more than their American counterparts, each country was comparatively unscathed by the war. Each managed to escape the social and political transformations that can follow from defeat or occupation. If anything, one might have expected greater wartime gains in U.S. social policy. After all, Roosevelt, the founder of the New Deal, remained in office, while in Britain basically the same Conservative-dominated parliament persisted from 1935 until the middle of 1945.

In other ways American students may find historical accounts of British public policy surprising. In histories of U.S. public policies, innovations are often attributed to the Great Depression. In histories of British policies, by contrast, innovations are often attributed to war, especially the Second World War. The standard answer to the big question is that despite the many similarities between the United States and Britain during the Second World War, there was something different about the British wartime experience. Scholars have argued that wartime conditions ranging from the British fiscal mobilization for war to the risk of civilian deaths from bombing account for the rise of the first welfare state.

Here, however, I argue that the influence of war cannot explain these differences in public policy outcomes and trajectories. Like economic depression, war has only indirect effects on the construction and the passage of public spending policies. I try to show instead that the institutional politics theory explains these outcomes better. In the United States during the Great Depression, social policy was planned mainly by way of state officials and changes in policy were based on previous innovations. The same was true for British social policy innovations in the 1940s. In the United States in the 1930s, innovations did not become law until a reform-oriented regime grasped firm control of political institutions. The same was true for Britain in the 1940s. To make this case, I start with the person most associated with the planning of the British welfare state, William Beveridge.

BRITISH SOCIAL POLITICS DURING THE SECOND WORLD WAR

Planning the Welfare State

An architect of British social policy from his former position in the Board of Trade, Beveridge had mainly pursued an academic career throughout the 1920s and 1930s. He received a commission in June 1941 from the Coalition government. That all-party grouping had been created to prosecute the war as it began to go badly for Britain early in 1940. The Coalition was led by the Conservative Prime Minister Winston Churchill, Beveridge's former chief at the Board of Trade. Churchill had moved right in the meantime and in 1940 completed his march from political obscurity at the expense of Neville Chamberlain.[2]

Beveridge was summoned from his ivory tower not by Churchill, but by Arthur Greenwood, the Labour minister without portfolio in charge of reconstruction and a member of the Cabinet. Beveridge's mission was to study and make recommendations for all of social policy, and he worked with a committee of civil servants from the ministries involved in the field. The outcome of this inquiry was *Social Insurance and Allied Services*, more commonly known as the Beveridge Report, which was released in December 1942. Though not immediately adopted by the government, the Beveridge Report set the tone for comprehensive social policy changes in Britain, in sharp contrast to the fate of the National Resources Planning Board (NRPB)'s proposals in the United States.

The Beveridge Report began with idealistic rhetoric, calling for "freedom from want." It also made three "assumptions." These included the introduction of family allowances, the creation of a national health service to buttress health insurance, and a commitment to maintain full employment. Beveridge's bold words and sweeping vision of the British social policy of the future captured the public imagination, but were not central to his report. The bulk of it dealt with social insurance in a nuts-and-bolts fashion more suitable for experts than for the general public on both sides of the Atlantic who purchased the report.

Beveridge's main recommendation was to reorganize, revamp, and augment social insurance programs. All programs would pay similar flat subsistence benefits—the "national minimum." All programs would be financed by equal flat taxes on employer and employee, with the final third provided by general state revenues, a scheme of financing that was along the lines envisioned in the original 1911 social insurance reforms. According to the report, social insurance benefits would be extended to include housewives, in addition to the mostly male workers long since included in British public social provision. Also, Beveridge proposed to add workmen's compensation to this scheme. Beveridge called for freedom from want, but little more than that. He did not call for a high standard of benefits, in the manner of the Townsend Movement. Moreover, he did not envisage that social insurance would replace earnings proportionately, in the manner of American OASI.

These changes in coverage and benefits required changes in administration. In Beveridge's social insurance vision, means-tested programs would be cut back and the scope of means-tested public assistance substantially reduced. To achieve this, he called for the end of the Assistance Board and proposed that all social insurance programs be combined in one ministry devoted exclusively to them.

Other British plans for social reconstruction did not crystalize until military victory was nearer. In November 1943, Prime Minister Churchill bowed to pressure and appointed a minister of reconstruction. Absorbed by the war effort, however, Churchill paid little attention to this area, and the one mandate he imposed regarding it was negative: a moratorium on passing measures costing the Treasury until after a postwar general election. Most of the planning for the postwar period was undertaken by the 1943 Reconstruction Committee, led by Lord Woolton, but with four Labour members, including Sir William Jowitt, formerly the head of the Reconstruction Problems Committee. In 1944, the Reconstruction Committee and its many subcommittees drafted a series of White Papers dealing with social insurance, health, and employment policy.[3] The first of these, *Social Insurance*, dealt mainly with the same issues Beveridge had grappled with. Perhaps because of the widespread public approval of the Beveridge Report, the government's White Paper mainly endorsed Beveridge's reorganization of social insurance and his guarantee of a "national minimum."[4]

A second White Paper concerned one of Beveridge's "assumptions" for postwar policy: the creation of a national health service. The White Paper, drafted under the direction of the Conservative Henry Willink, the minister of health, called for a free national health system financed mainly by the Treasury with general revenues, but with a small payroll tax. The system would be administered by central and local authorities. Voluntary hospitals would be coordinated with the system, but would remain private. Neither doctors nor patients would be required to join the system; doctors connected to health centers would be paid partly through salaries and partly through fees based on the number of persons treated.[5]

Following up Beveridge's assumption that the government would maintain full employment, the government produced a White Paper on this topic, *Employment Policy*. Like the report, the White Paper called for the state to accept the responsibility for high and stable employment. For the short run, the paper proposed to maintain munitions factories in depressed areas by way of licenses, government contracts, and financial assistance. This industrial policy was to be coordinated through the Board of Trade. For the long run, *Employment Policy* called for the use of Keynesian spending categories to analyze economic trends and for the use of public works to offset declines in private capital expenditure. The report also called for tax rates for social insurance to vary depending on economic conditions. In addition, local authorities were expected to submit five-year plans for public improvements.[6] But these public works plans provided more exhortation than enforcement. For the White Paper neither proposed to fund the local projects nor suggested inducements for the local authorities to create the five-year plans. Nor were there proposals for public employment programs on the model of the WPA.

Meantime, Labour backbenchers hoped to force the Coalition government to rescind Churchill's rule of no new social commitments until military victory. In February 1943, 121 Labour Members of Parliament supported an amendment to implement the Beveridge Report immediately. This uprising was quashed, though, and did not harm the Coalition as the Labour ministers of the government did not endorse it.[7] Reforms would have to await the next general election, if they were to come at all. And the campaign was delayed until the war in Europe reached its endgame as winter ended in 1945.

The Labour Government and the Enactment of Wartime Plans

In the June 1945 campaign, Labour won a landslide. It ousted a Conservative majority that had been seated since 1935 and took majority control of the Commons for the first time, installing Clement Attlee as prime minister. After the election the plans for social reform were largely realized. Attlee's Labour government made good on almost all of them before the end of the decade and, in some cases, went beyond them.

With respect to the recommendations for insurance, the Labour government acted quickly. James Griffiths, minister of national insurance, introduced the government bill in October 1945. Parliament adopted the bill, which ran mainly along the lines of the Beveridge Report and the Coalition White Paper based on it. Parliament revamped old-age insurance, unemployment insurance, disability insurance, and workmen's compensation. It also created the new program of family allowances. On the related question of relief, Beveridge had called for the end of the locally based poor law. This goal was accomplished, though by different means. Beveridge called for the end of means-tested assistance; the Labour government nationalized it instead. In 1948 the National Assistance Act was introduced by Aneurin Bevan, the minister of health and left-most member of the cabinet. With this act the Labour government created a National Assistance Board to take charge of all of those not covered by insurance programs, including the chronically disabled and the blind. This board, an administrative descendent of the 1935 Unemployment Assistance Board, had a less stringent means test and would reduce local differences in eligibility.[8]

The new National Health Service lived up to the controversial recommendations for universal and free medical care of the Coalition's 1944

White Paper. The Labour government even went beyond these recommendations in its 1946 bill. The program was financed mainly through general revenues, avoiding the high regressive payroll taxes of social insurance. The government also nationalized the hospitals. Led by Bevan the government induced the reluctant medical profession to enlist in 1948.[9]

In their own limited terms, the wartime plans for British employment policy also were achieved. These chiefly involved direct controls rather than Keynesian-inspired spending or public employment. The new British government manipulated industrial policy to direct development to depressed areas. Yet the use of Keynesian techniques, such as managing aggregate demand, was limited. This was due in part to Labour's preference for direct industrial controls.[10]

Policy Achievements in the United States and Britain: A Comparison

These developments highlight some similarities and differences in the social policy evolution of the Allies during and after the war. Both countries began planning for postwar social policies. Both countries devised comprehensive reforms. In America, the main set of plans was embodied in the NRPB's *Security, Work and Relief Policies* and other planning documents covering a range of social and economic issues. In Britain, social policy planning and political attention centered on Beveridge's *Social Insurance and Allied Services*, which was followed by related White Papers from the Coalition government. These plans were similar in their desire to fill programmatic gaps in policies, to mesh social insurance and relief, and to achieve full employment.

Yet the emphases in postwar planning differed considerably between Britain and the United States. The American plans dealt mainly with work and relief; new social insurance programs and the nationalization of Unemployment Compensation (UC) were secondary. By contrast, the British plans concentrated on the rationalization and extension of existing social insurance. The new British proposals for family allowances and the national health service had nothing to do with unemployment and Depression, and the reform of relief programs was an afterthought. Moreover, the British plans for preventing postwar unemployment were conspicuously underdeveloped as compared to the elaborate American proposals for public works and public employment.

The fates of the plans diverged more than their content. American reformers' dreams of a national system of economic security turned to nightmares before the Axis threat was stilled. They could only watch as Congress dismantled much of the work and relief policy of the Depression. By contrast, Britain was enjoined by Churchill against passing any costly legislation during the struggle. Difficult as this moratorium was for proponents of British public policy, it also meant that there would be no attempts at

destroying programs in existence. American reformers might have settled
for that.

After the war, Britain offered a relatively complete system of protection
designed to benefit all citizens, by adding several important national programs, including a public health service and family allowances. These reforms were tied to social insurance programs that were made more inclusive
and systematic. Programs were no longer backed by a stingy, locally administered poor law, but by a comprehensive and national means-tested safety
net. By comparison the United States ended the 1940s with only one universal national spending program—Old-Age and Survivors' Insurance (OASI).
The only American citizens who gained something like the protection of a
comprehensive welfare state were World War II veterans. But the veterans'
welfare state was expected to fade away with the passing of the generation
that went to war. Britain passed almost everything on its agenda and was
able to convert wartime controls into peacetime reforms. In the United
States, the reform achievements declined during the war and were rejuvenated only slightly afterward. How much did the war itself have to do with
these differences?

War as an Explanation for the Welfare State

In 1955 Richard Titmuss famously argued that war went far in explaining
them. Using British history as his model, Titmuss claimed that as states become more concerned with war, they must ensure that their subjects are fit
for battle and do so through public social provision. To remain battle-
ready, states eventually must safeguard the health of the entire population
and bolster civilian morale with equitable distributions of income and
wealth. To support his case, Titmuss claimed that the story of social policy
was one of unbroken expansion as war steadily became more total in the
twentieth century.[11] Since then, the Titmuss thesis—that war promotes social policy—has become part of the conventional wisdom in analyses of
British social policy.

However, the needs of the state in war-making do not automatically lead
to long-term social policies for large groups of people across risks, especially prior to the era of modern social policy, in nondemocracies, or when
the state loses the war. Any impulse for winning democratic states to compensate citizens after a war, moreover, might be confined to veterans. Titmuss's account also misses much of the history of social policy in Britain.
There the Liberal party inaugurated modern pension and social insurance
programs in 1906–1911—before World War I. In short, Titmuss's argument is too evolutionary, simplistic, and narrowly based to explain social
policy developments. But others have modified Titmuss's basic thesis, and
it is worth examining whether these arguments explain contrasts in policy
developments between the United States and Britain.

The Displacement Effect or Peace Dividend Thesis

A few years after Titmuss gave his famous lecture, Alan R. Peacock and Jack Wiseman also posited that war had an impact on social policy and developed their hypotheses from the British experience in World War II and afterward. They claimed, however, that crises like war lead indirectly to social policy innovations or increased social spending through what they called the "displacement effect": Taxes are more easily raised during large-scale social disturbances, such as depressions and wars. When the crisis ends, the taxation level remains high because people tolerate higher taxes once they have had experience with them. The higher taxes then lead to increased social spending because people also desire higher social spending than they are usually willing to tax themselves for.[12] Basically, they expect wars to provide a "peace dividend" that is easily diverted to social spending.

Some differences in social spending between the United States and Britain may be due to a kind of variable displacement effect, because the two countries had different geopolitical trajectories. There was no great displacement of public spending from military to civilian purposes in the United States because the war did not end—at least in the minds of American policymakers. After the Second World War the United States assumed a much greater role in world politics and engaged in a Cold War with the Soviet Union. Many of the revenues of the new income tax system were devoted to military rather than social purposes. In addition, the United States had to build executive institutions devoted to geopolitics. In his battles with Congress, the president used his influence to gain foreign policy objectives, focusing less on domestic public policies than was the case in the 1930s. The British geopolitical trajectory was in the opposite direction. The transition was marked in 1947, in a sort of changing of the international guard, as Britain renounced military commitments in Greece and Turkey which were then assumed by the United States. There was greater opportunity for the displacement of wartime taxes in Britain than in the United States.

Other facts do not fit as well. If the displacement argument were valid, the United States should have experienced a much greater expansion of social policy than Britain. After all, the United States benefited economically from the war while the British government was financially decimated. Lend Lease—U.S. wartime aid to Britain—had come to an end, and Britain was forced to turn to the United States, sending Keynes himself to ask for loans immediately after the war. Later the United States provided grants to Britain through the Marshall Plan. Matters turned out just the opposite of what Watson had expected: America did in fact help to pay for a series of nationalizing reforms of British social spending policy that it would not grant its own citizens.[13]

War, Uncertainty, and Moral Preferences

Like Peacock and Wiseman, John Dryzek and Robert E. Goodin have employed rational choice theory and British wartime experience to support their claims that war has a direct influence on public spending policies. They argue that the intention of the welfare state is social justice, and that justice is a matter of impartiality. From here, they argue that people will act on the basis of moral preferences when uncertain about their future positions in society. During war and other crises, uncertainty prevails and so people are more willing to act morally. War-induced preferences for morality are thus expected to result in postwar social spending increases, as, they claim, was the case in Britain. In short, they argue that the greater the uncertainty a country experienced, through wartime deaths and destruction, the greater the extensiveness of its wartime and postwar social insurance programs.[14]

The thesis that war makes you moral has analytical problems, too. Its portrayal of the types of risks and uncertainty produced by war is not fully convincing. In war, uncertainty centers not on one's potential economic status in the postwar world, but on whether one will live to see that world. If so, the thesis would have implications only for war-related programs, such as health and disability. The thesis also implies that public preferences are rapidly translated into social policy decisions. This assertion seems problematic, especially for Britain, which had no general election from 1935 until 1945 and a government that declared a moratorium on social policy during the war.

Empirically speaking, Dryzek and Goodin's arguments would expect similar developments in social policy in the United States and Britain during the war. From a cross-national perspective, the two had war experiences whose similarities outweighed their differences. Both countries were major allies on the winning side, both populations underwent substantial mobilizations for both military and economic activities, and both countries escaped occupation and large-scale domestic destruction. Moreover, in terms of casualties, the two countries did not differ much. The percentage of the British population killed during the war was 0.97; in America it was 0.23. To be sure, the British percentage was higher, but compare it to that of countries that endured the brunt of the war's destruction. Germany lost 6.4 percent of its population, Poland lost 9.7 percent, and Yugoslavia some 11.1 percent. British losses were even much less severe than those of other Western European countries, almost all of which suffered occupation. The Netherlands lost 2.4 percent of its population, for instance, and Finland 2.3 percent.[15]

Perhaps a weaker version of the argument helps to explain differences in wartime policies between the United States and Britain. Wars produce different kinds of social problems—and thus economic uncertainty—and these dislocations may then produce pressure for specific public programs. And there is no doubt that World War II affected British civilians, who had to contend with successive bombing campaigns in 1940 and 1944, more than their U.S. counterparts. British civilian deaths numbered sixty thousand.[16] This difference may help to explain war-related health programs for British civilians. Many civilians were covered along with servicemen in a sort of emergency national health service, and that fact probably inspired Beveridge's assumption that a national health service would emerge after the war.[17] Yet in other areas, differences in the degree of intensity of social problems engendered by the war does little to account for differences in public policies. The wartime boom in the U.S. domestic economy induced countless American workers to abandon rural homes for urban employment. To ease these dislocations, which were no doubt greater than those in Britain, America might have adopted national unemployment insurance and family support measures. But American proposals along these lines failed.

The Second World War had different effects on the two countries, but does not explain much of the differences in social policy proposals and achievements. The displacement of taxes from military to social purposes is never automatic. Tax cuts or new military objectives might also result. In the long run, military spending may preempt social spending, and military bureaucracies may grow at the expense of domestic bureaucracies. The British welfare state may have been possible only because Britain's geopolitical status was being greatly reduced.[18] I argue below the effects of war on social policy were mainly indirect, but not through the displacement effect. Some aspects about the British experience of war helped it toward its welfare state. But they would never have mattered if not for developments in the British state and politics.

The Institutional Politics Theory and Divergences in Policy

According to the institutional politics theory, war and other crises do not explain the main characteristics of policies and why they pass. The theory holds that major differences in political institutions will be key in explaining overall differences in public policies. Notably, American state political institutions made matters more difficult than British ones did for those pursuing innovations and augmentations in public social provision. First, the American polity was not fully democratized, and was much less democratic than the British one. In many parts of the United States the political voices of everyday people were stilled—especially those of impoverished African Americans in the South who would have likely favored increased social spending. What is more, America was pocked with patronage-oriented political parties. These parties were more likely to deflect national spending policies that provided rights automatically to large categories of citizens.

Moreover, American political institutions were more fragmented and unco-
ordinated, aiding those political forces hoping to prevent strong, national
public policies by making it easier to deflect national innovation in public
policy. Finally, the American executive bureaucracies were underdeveloped
as compared to British ones in the area of public social provision.[19]

All the same, structural conditions cannot entirely explain changes in
public policy. According to the institutional politics theory, innovations are
likely when a pro-social spending or reform-oriented regime overcomes the
structural obstacles provided by the political system and takes power—an
unlikely, but not impossible scenario in America. To understand policy proposals and the content of policy the theory points to the structure of domestic bureaucratic agencies and spending programs already in existence. The
structure and scope of these bureaucracies influence the type of proposals
generated. National planners will propose national plans; if state-level initiatives exist in the absence of such national planners, these initiatives will be
proposed. Administrators are likely to attempt to complete the missions of
their bureaus or agencies, if these missions are underfunded or incomplete.
Although crises can help to set the political agenda and can also sap the
power of regimes, the impact of crisis on public policy depends on who
happens to be in power when the crisis hits.

*Previous Policies, Domestic Bureaucracies, and Planning
for the Postwar World*

America and Britain converged at the end of 1942, both releasing blueprints
for postwar reform. In both countries the war encouraged such planning.
The Beveridge Report and the NRPB's *Security, Work, and Relief Policies*
were released within a few months of each another. Yet the two plans
differed considerably. The NRPB's planners had a radical redistributive approach to public policymaking. They wanted all Americans to be guaranteed a certain standard of living and planned to provide this through a
public job, if necessary, or through public relief or social insurance. The
NRPB committee was skeptical about the regressive payroll taxes that accompanied social insurance and instead called for the use of progressive
general revenues to finance these improvements. In Britain planning centered on rationalizing social insurance and creating two new programs
consistent with the national-minimum version of social insurance: family
allowances and a National Health Service.[20] Why did the plans diverge so
greatly in content?

These divergences reflected differences in the prior social policies of the
two countries. In the United States, most nationwide social policies were
initiated as responses to the Depression of the 1930s, while the basic British
social policies had been in existence since the 1910s and 1920s. Moreover,
the two nations had previously coped in contrasting ways with economic
crisis and mass unemployment. During both the 1920s and 1930s, the Brit-

ish avoided public works and jobs programs and provided relief to the unemployed through extensions of unemployment insurance. The United States, however, stressed work and wages to aid the unemployed as well as means-tested relief for others.

British and American reformers did not want to revolutionize their spending systems. Rather they wanted to build on what had already been constructed. If the Beveridge Report did not include public works or employment programs, it was because Britain had little experience with such programs. And so the Coalition White Paper on employment did little in this respect. The long-term British experience with nationally organized and publicly funded social insurance allowed Beveridge to assess the previous performance of various programs and suggest what appeared to be adjustments, extensions, and rationalizations.[21]

In the United States, the NRPB committee did something similar, but with different results. American planners hoped to use the wartime period to complete the New Deal by adding new programs and nationalizing old ones, mainly along the lines projected by the 1934–35 Committee on Economic Security. The NRPB committee presumed that work programs like the Works Progress Administration (WPA) were not merely emergency measures.[22] Public employment programs had been around for as long as most of the programs of the Social Security Act. There had been much greater experience with employment programs and public assistance programs of all types than with the program nowadays associated with the term social security, old-age insurance. From their vantage point of the end of the 1930s, providing adequate benefits to the needy and work to the unemployed seemed more important than preserving and extending strict contributory financing by taxes on employers and employees.

Because the Beveridge Report and the "American Beveridge Report," as its proponents called the NRPB report, differed considerably, the war had a different impact on their prospects. Because of their construction, the British plans secured a more favorable administrative reception. British plans could employ visionary rhetoric without veering far from existing administrative and fiscal arrangements, and thus they soothed officials in charge of these programs. Beveridge consulted with an interdepartmental committee of administrators familiar with the details of social policy. Beveridge and these officials shared the same outlook, and his report coincided sufficiently with their views to make it seem feasible to the British government.[23]

Although the NRPB committee included administrators of New Deal agencies, it was most closely associated with the president, leaving the U.S. planners with a less solid base within the national executive than Beveridge had. As we have seen, the NRPB committee had different emphases from the Social Security Board (SSB), which stood firm for social insurance based on payroll taxes and could not disagree more with the NRPB committee's desire to decouple social insurance benefits from payroll taxes. The differences in outlook between the NRPB and the SSB, however, were not so great as the differences between the both of them and the Veterans' Administration (VA). The NRPB received the VA's support for proposals that benefited veterans, but not for proposals that might conflict with the VA's programs for veterans. After the NRPB sponsored the Postwar Manpower Conference, it managed to shape many of the programs that were included in the GI Bill of Rights: veterans received readjustment allowances, improved unemployment benefits, and educational subsidies, rather than bonuses. But on matters such as health insurance and disability programs, the VA's control over national programs exclusively for veterans worked against the possibility of national programs for all citizens. Whenever the opportunity arose to win benefits for veterans that would be denied other citizens, the VA jumped at it.[24]

In Britain, the veteran population had a completely different system of public social provision to come home to. The health insurance policies of Britain were applied to the influx of World War II veterans. The new needs of the veterans in the context of an existing system of benefits increased the chances for a comprehensive National Health Service rather than diminishing it.

Mobilization for War and Implications for Permanent Social Policy

The two national polities managed the war quite differently, and these differences had an impact on the possibilities for postwar social reform in each country. The parts of the British state that ran the war promoted postwar reform, while the parts of American state that ran the war undercut the possibility of postwar reform. The British state had more powerful controls in wartime and thus greater opportunity to convert wartime mobilization efforts into postwar reforms.

In Britain wartime controls were crucial in establishing planning for industrial location and housing during the war. The continuation of controls into the postwar period allowed the Labour party to follow up the wartime reforms in planning and employment with vigorous public housing and industrial location policies. What was more important, the war brought to power policymaking departments eager to promote reforms. The trouble experienced by Britain early in the war provoked more than a Coalition government with a new prime minister. It also undermined the central role of the Treasury, which had been the main bureaucratic force behind fiscal conservatism, discouraging military as well as domestic expenditure. Wartime losses discredited both the Chamberlain government and the Treasury, and key powers over the economic mobilization were accrued by the Ministry of Labour, which was historically identified with social policy improvements. The Treasury, with its long history of thwarting social reforms, became marginal to the process.[25]

In the United States, too, economic mobilization for war meant centralization, but the United States managed the war through temporary civil agencies intended to coordinate the activities of industries and government. Roosevelt relied heavily on businessmen to staff these agencies, partly because the U.S. state lacked sufficient administrative capacities and partly because he wished to leave behind the political divisions of the late 1930s. At the apex of the U.S. system of war mobilization, several oversight agencies were created within the Office of Emergency Management, a temporary part of the Executive Office of the President. Notably, however, the NRPB was kept out of process. Had it been involved it would have at least outlived the war and might have been better positioned to transform wartime public controls into postwar social policy reforms. Instead, the final coordinating agency was the 1944 Office of Mobilization and Reconversion, which was subject to congressional oversight.[26] The wartime Roosevelt administration never achieved the degree of control over the economy that the British wartime Coalition did.

In Britain the war was run with comprehensive public controls administered through permanent ministries of the longstanding national civil service. At the inauguration of the Coalition government in May 1940, the Emergency Powers Act called for conscripting property and controlling labor as well as rationing food. Every year the controls were extended, and in 1944 the Conservatives and Labour agreed to keep them for two years after the war. These controls helped to prevent destructive wartime strikes. In the United States, the wartime economy was managed with weaker and more fragmented public controls; the key leadership roles went to business leaders and military officials, rather than civil administrators and leaders of labor. The upshot was that the U.S. approach to mobilization encouraged politically volatile labor disputes—and the weakening of forces in favor of expanded social policies.

Bipartisanship in Wartime and the Power of
Reform-Oriented Legislators

At first glance, it seems as though the makeup of the U.S. wartime leadership should have led to greater gains in social policy. A reform-minded Democrat held the presidency, and there was a Democratic majority in the Congress. The legislative following commanded by Roosevelt after the 1940 elections was large enough to continue and extend New Deal programs, even if too small to embark on major new reforms. Meanwhile, the British wartime Coalition government was led by Conservatives—who enjoyed more than a two-hundred-vote margin in the House of Commons.

Running a democratic nation during total modern war requires an unusual degree of bipartisan political compromise, however. Wartime political partnerships were formed in both Britain and the United States, and their dynamics had implications for social policy as well as war management. Bipartisanship, though, did more to harm reformers in America. In the United States, wartime cooperation meant reaching out to businessmen, conservatives, and Republicans—and often these characteristics inhered in the same person. President Roosevelt named the Hoover Administration official Henry Stimson to head the War Department. Roosevelt also appointed many Republican-leaning businessmen, or at least businessmen acceptable to Republicans, to the planning bureaus for wartime production. This bought the president some autonomy in plotting war strategy, but the agreement was strictly informal. Republicans remained free to attack the administration whenever there was an opportunity, as did southern Democrats.

Moreover, the immediate impact of war harmed the prospects, and the policies, of the ruling parties in each country. The Roosevelt Administration and the Democrats were blamed in the public mind for losses in the war as well as the domestic difficulties that wartime mobilization engendered. Likewise, British defeats in the early years of the war harmed the credibility of the Conservative party. With the formation of the Coalition, parties other than the Conservatives benefited from disasters having little to do with the government's domestic record. Public support for the Conservatives dropped, and they lost by-elections in the first half of 1942.[27]

What is more, although British electoral activity was confined to by-elections, in America partisan electoral politics proceeded on schedule. In both places the dominant party was taking a beating in public opinion, but in the United States, the electorate had a chance to act on its grievances—which it did when congressional elections took place on the regular schedule in November 1942. For the Democrats and for social spending advocates, it was unfortunate that this election followed immediately after the nation had suffered loss after loss in the Pacific theater and after it had become evident that makeshift domestic controls were unable to prevent inflation or labor unrest.[28] The result was about twice as harmful as the typical off-year election for the presidential party. The Democrats lost fifty seats in the House, weakening the reform element of the party at a crucial point.

In Britain, the formalization of a bipartisan Coalition government to run the war opened the Conservatives to reforming influences. Labour party leaders were brought into the War Cabinet and into other key positions. The trade union leader Ernest Bevin was given the Ministry of Labour, and Hugh Dalton led the Board of Trade. Arthur Greenwood was able to set in motion the creation of the Beveridge Report in his capacity as minister without portfolio, and reconstruction issues were kept in public view by Sir William Jowitt, the head of the 1942 Reconstruction Problems Committee. Bevin, Herbert Morrison, and Clement Attlee, each of them members of the War Cabinet, served on the important Reconstruction Committee of 1943. Throughout the war, these Labour leaders were able to use their positions to promote reform planning.[29]

In the United States, the existence of nonparliamentary parties and the separation of powers within the U.S. federal government aggravated the troubles of reformers during wartime. When Roosevelt put the New Deal on the back burner in exchange for a freer hand to run the war, struggles over social policy did not end. Instead, liberals in Congress, not the administration, took the initiative in reform and constructed their own postwar plans, with the help of strategically placed administrative agencies. For instance, the Wagner-Murray-Dingell bills drew on the NRPB and the SSB, and Senator James Murray relied on the Bureau of the Budget in formulating his 1945 full-employment bill. Similarly, congressional representatives working with the VA were key proponents of veterans' legislation. New U.S. social policies progressed only as far as congressional forces could move them—not very far, as it happened.

The difference in the political situations of the two countries is illuminated by a coincidence: Beveridge's voyage to America in the spring of 1943. With the publication of his report in December 1942, he became an international symbol of social policy. Later that month he was invited to America by the Rockefeller Foundation. Almost immediately he was warned by various U.S. officials, including Arthur Altmeyer of the SSB, to delay his trip because political conditions were not propitious. Despite a brief delay, matters did not improve. Arriving in New York May 11 on the *Queen Mary*, Beveridge was overshadowed by another passenger. Prime Minister Churchill was making his third wartime trip to the States, and for his fortnight in America Churchill stayed at the White House, as he had on previous visits. With constant access to the president and his close aides, the prime minister talked strategy, in this case promoting an invasion of Italy— and drank his way through late nights. Beveridge, in contrast, was conceded one brief, pre-lunch appointment with Roosevelt. During that interview the president ignored the Beveridge Report and its author and spoke mainly to Beveridge's wife Janet. Roosevelt turned to William Beveridge only to encourage him to visit the South and to assure him that he would aid the Beveridges' speedy return to England.[30]

During his stay the "man with the plan," as one journalist called Beveridge, bore witness to the introduction and removal from the political agenda of America's bold plans to augment social policy. Newspapers noted the similarities in scope between the Beveridge Report and the NRPB's "American Beveridge Report." And Beveridge was on hand for the introduction of the Wagner-Murray-Dingell bill, popularly called the "American Plan," on June 2. But the bill went nowhere. Congress was more concerned with passing the antistrike Smith-Connally bill over the president's veto, only the eighth time Roosevelt had suffered such a rebuke in his long tenure. Worse, the NRPB itself had its funds cut off later that month.[31]

If politics sometimes makes strange bedfellows, that is never more true than in wartime. Because of the war, a Democratic president rolled out the red carpet for a Conservative prime minister standing fast against both fascism and social reform. Roosevelt's views on social policy were so close to Beveridge's that the president was said to be displeased that Beveridge was associated with the term "cradle-to-grave" coverage, thinking that he should receive the credit.[32] But when Beveridge arrived in America, Roosevelt had nothing to say to the man who symbolized social insurance around the world.

Roosevelt's continuing concern with war and the small number of reform-oriented legislators returned with him made it unlikely that his victory in 1944 would reap new social benefits, except those targeted specifically on veterans. Where generosity toward veterans was concerned, anti-spenders opposing other strong federal measures beat a strategic retreat. Veterans' benefits were a bargain for conservatives who feared increasingly high taxation and the extension of New Deal national government agencies. Veterans' benefits would go to a small group without long-term implications for others, and the programs would be administered by the VA, diverting power from New Deal bureaucracies. Such benefits were likely to hamper New Dealers in their attempts to win a postwar battle over a permanent system of social policy for everyone.[33]

For social policies promoted by liberals, organized labor, and other pro-spending groups, it was a different story. When Harry Truman moved into the White House in April 1945 several questions important to the liberal reformers had already been decided against them in Congress. When he was elected in his own right in 1948, the regime that came to power was not functionally equivalent to having a Labour government like the one elected in Britain in 1945. In the United States, it was necessary to elect a left-wing Democratic president and a majority of northern and western Democrats to Congress. The Democratic victory in 1948 was only nominal, because in neither case was there sufficient congressional strength for general social reform. Truman could pass only part of what was left on the dwindling wartime social policy agenda, including funding for public housing—without national controls—and the upgrading of OASI to include more contributors and beneficiaries. A new national health insurance program was out of the question.[34] By contrast, the Labour party's great 1945 victory, producing a majority of 146, ensured that something resembling all the Coalition White Papers on social policy would pass.

CONCLUSION

In both Britain and the United States, social policy reformers made plans to complete systems of public social provision. The plans were in many ways different. But the results were even more so. In America, politicians began to dismantle its newly constructed public spending system during the war; in Britain, politicians adopted the welfare state in the wake of the Second World War.

Some account for this difference by invoking the war. The civilian consequences of the Second World War were more dramatic in Britain, perhaps providing greater inducements to public social provision, especially in health policy. What is more, Britain was better able to convert wartime increases in taxation to postwar social purposes, as it scaled back international aspirations and commitments. Yet in some basic ways the United States and Britain had similar experiences of war, as neither suffered conquest or the tremendous loss of life faced either by the war's losers such as Germany or its winners such as the Soviet Union.

What mattered more was differences in political institutions, previous domestic bureaucracies and programs, and domestic political conditions. The war had an impact mainly in how it interacted with and influenced these conditions. In both countries, the war was part of the reason that domestic planners produced postwar plans building on previous policies. In both countries, prosecuting the war meant bipartisanship. In both countries, losses and deprivations in war damaged the ruling party and its prewar administrative means. In both countries, the electorate turned to the reform-oriented party after the war was over. What was different was the institutional and political situation faced prior to the war and during it.

In Britain, the Conservatives had dominated Parliament since 1935 and so bipartisanship meant giving the Labour party a big role on issues facing the home front. Wartime losses and deprivations meant the discrediting of the Treasury and a loss of prestige, if not immediate power, for the Conservatives. There were greater possibilities for wartime controls, and questions of postwar reconstruction were decided in executive committees weighted to the advantage of the Labour party. Building on prior social programs, moreover, meant building on established social insurance and wartime health services. Because of the nature of the wartime Coalition, agreements were reached—on social insurance, employment policy, and the health service. In 1945, a strong Labour government inherited these plans and put them into effect, creating the British welfare state, and used the wartime controls to further its employment goals.

In the United States, the institutional and political conditions prior to the war led to a different result. Domestic planners devised more radical postwar plans, based on work and relief programs pioneered during the Depression. Yet the war put the New Deal planners on the defensive and marginalized them. Bipartisanship meant that the Administration would widen its support by relying less on its own planners and more on previously shunned conservatives and business leaders. That in turn resulted in a wartime planning apparatus that would be of little use for purposes of postwar reform. Bipartisanship in America also meant the president's ceding effective authority over domestic policy to Congress. Congress was taken over by anti-spenders, as wartime deprivations and losses were converted into electoral defeat in 1942 for the administration and the Democrats. Because the American coalition was only informal, the New Deal policy agenda, unlike the Beveridge Report, was not set aside, to be picked up after the war. Instead, liberal sponsors in Congress could pick and choose from available plans, and their proposals failed upon encountering a hostile, conservative

Congress. Except for policies benefiting veterans, Congress would not channel the dividends from a revolutionized income tax into a more national and comprehensive social policy for all Americans.

At the end of the war, the American people once again chose the Democrats and Roosevelt, whose campaign relied greatly on domestic promises. Yet given differences in structural circumstances, electoral victory in America did not mean control of the government by reform-oriented legislators. Roosevelt and Truman found that a Democratic victory ushered in a Congress that still included many Democratic representatives from undemocratic political systems and from patronage-oriented party organizations—who held the balance of power in any domestic legislative battles. Congressional liberal forces were strong enough only to improve domestic policies under the control of states, localities, and private enterprises and to improve OASI under the Social Security Act. As a result, America ended this period with a national OASI program and a kind of short-term welfare state for veterans.

As Sir John Forbes Watson noted, the two countries were becoming more and more linked through their wartime alliance. But he was wrong about their public policies: the United States was willing to aid a British state that was making social commitments at which America balked. The plans made by Beveridge were central to postwar British reform. As it happened, after the climax that was the publication of his report, Beveridge came to America and saw at first hand a low point in the history of American public policy.

CONCLUSION

IN THE TWO DECADES spanning the Great Depression, the Second World War, and its aftermath, modern American social policy traveled a great distance. In the 1930s alone, it had been transformed from a few locally based programs controlling only a minuscule proportion of the country's income to a national arrangement taking a share of income larger than that of other industrial countries. Reformers around the world demanded "New Deals" for their countries, too.

At the center of New Deal social policy begun in 1935 was work through the Works Progress Administration (WPA). The program employed many whom the market had failed, though not nearly everyone who needed work. It was supplemented by relief programs in which citizens were to be provided stipends for retiring or removing themselves from the labor force. These programs included Old-Age Assistance (OAA) and Aid to Dependent Children (ADC). Each program shared power between states and localities. Two social insurance programs were also added—Unemployment Compensation (UC) through incentives to the states and an experimental, national old-age insurance program.

This work and relief policy was consolidated in the late 1930s. The Fair Labor Standards Act introduced the minimum wage in 1938, and the WPA was reinforced by executive reorganization. The relief and social insurance programs were upgraded as well through amendments to the Social Security Act. By the end of the decade each state had adopted almost every key social program, and the United States was vying for world leadership in social spending. That happened despite the many things seeming to work against it—notably, a highly fragmented political system and a party system that lacked a social democratic contender.

In the 1940s, reformers attempted to complete the work and relief policy. They wanted to expand the work programs and connect the recipients more closely to a nationalized employment service. They also called for more national control over relief, while augmenting social insurance. In short, they wanted to ensure an American standard of living, preferably through private employment, but through public policy in situations where such employment was expected to fail.

But the plans came to nothing. Instead American social policy was retrenched, as the work programs were eliminated and redefined. What survived were programs constructed in ways that enabled them to withstand the inhospitable political climate of the period. These programs included the old-age insurance and special assistance programs—social security and welfare. The reformers failed despite a number of circumstances working in their favor—notably, a president who stood for social policy and kept getting reelected by landslides and state machinery that had been considerably strengthened.

What accounts for this two-sided paradox—America's unexpected emergence as a social spending leader and then the abandonment of its policy? More generally, what accounts for what happened in American social policy across the 1930s and 1940s, when a work and relief policy was created, consolidated, and abandoned, with a divided social security and welfare policy emerging in its place?

Here I return to these questions and reprise the central arguments of the book—that institutional and political conditions account for social policy outcomes. I want especially to explain why America was so slow in adopting modern social policy, why it was possible for America to become an innovator, and why it was likely that its innovations would falter. I do so by examining policy outcomes as they varied across time, across programs, across states, and across countries. My purpose is mainly to appraise my institutional politics argument. The last section discusses the legacy of the two decades for postwar social policy.

THE INSTITUTIONAL POLITICS THEORY: A RECAPITULATION

One standard institutional reason that the United States generally fails in social policy is that it was born with an excessively fragmented polity. The Constitution created divisions so great between and among the levels of government that determined minorities can always gain a foothold to block social spending innovations—even when majorities want them. Another institutional reason is that the American executive state has been so weak that it has inhibited social policy. According to this way of thinking, having little administrative capacity to run social policy can stunt the imaginations of American policymakers and doom the chances of far-reaching social policy, which would be difficult to run well.[1]

Each institutional argument is partly right, but each is at best incomplete. American federalism constitutes hindrances for reformers—especially those who want to create national social policy. They must negotiate the various levels of government asserting control over social policy. States and localities typically hope to retain control. Also important are the divisions of authority within the national government—notably the structure of the national legislature. Left to itself Congress tends to promote a kind of national policy by default, a sum of programs for individual districts, and congressional committees are battlegrounds in which social legislation can be laid waste. It takes state authority to administer and enforce social legislation, and state actors also are frequently resourceful proponents of the programs they administer. Reformers find it difficult to back social spending programs that they do not think will be run properly, and poorly run social programs are always vulnerable to political attacks. When strong domestic bureaucracies are lacking, proponents of social spending are missing key allies.

Although fragmented polities and weak state administrative institutions facilitate struggles against modern social spending, they do not constitute daunting obstacles to it. They do not provide compelling motivations for opponents of modern social policy, and having so many footholds in the polity makes it easier for opponents, but does not ensure their victory. I argue instead that the fragmented polity influences the process of social politics more than its ultimate outcome. And although a lack of state capacities makes the going rougher for proponents of social policy, such capacities can be created, and the openness of the state makes it possible even for radical projects to be housed there. Preexisting state capacities and state programs have great influence over the form of social policy, but previously weak domestic administration does not doom social policy to failure.

One institutional condition that matters more is the degree to which the polity is democratized. The more democratic rights are protected, I argue, the greater the influence of everyday people in politics and the greater the possibilities for far-reaching and generous social policy. When democratic rights are not protected, political leaders will tend to ignore the views and unarticulated desires of poorer people and take their lead from upper economic classes. In an underdemocratized polity politicians have little incentive to go the extra distance for the less well-off and every reason to aid the well heeled. Public money is often desired by the leaders of such polities, but it must be kept out of the hands of those who might threaten economic elites, who may also oppose the means to fund public policy.

There is little doubt that the American polity was poorly democratized for most of the twentieth century. In the North at the turn of the century there were numerous restrictions on the franchise, such as registration rules designed to keep less well-off immigrants from voting. These restrictions paled in comparison with those in the South, where great restrictions on voting were sustained by various means, from poll taxes to intimidation. Basic political rights such as speech and association were also restricted, especially for African Americans, and conservative Democratic parties held a monopoly on power. Undemocratic districts constituted about a quarter of Congress and the Electoral College—daunting obstacles for social reformers.[2]

A second key obstacle to modern social policy is a political party system devoted to using the government for the purposes of patronage. Patronage-party organizations are unfavorably disposed to modern social policy for reasons of their own. They oppose the creation of public bureaucracies, such as the efficient models required to run modern social policy, that cannot be easily used to reward the party faithful. Money earmarked for social policy cannot be diverted for spoils and often requires making difficult taxation decisions that could undermine the party's support from business. Re-

formers in turn would need to know that the programs would not be subject to the whims of these parties before pushing for them—a situation
likely to result in stalemate. In the Northeast and Midwest, patronage-party
organizations dominated the political life of many states and localities, and
their influence permeated the political system.[1]

Advocates for a national and generous social policy in America, in short,
faced severe obstacles. Significant parts of America's polity were not well
democratized, and other parts were not characterized by modern political
parties. For both reasons it was difficult to generate a political force ready
to back national social spending policy with national standards, retarding
modern social policy in America early in the twentieth century. The fragmentation of the polity and weakness in state policymaking capacities were
secondary hindrances, but facilitated those actors who opposed strong, national modern social policy.

Although the United States never had a social democratic party, I argue
that other political formations can break through these obstacles. A social
democratic party is one version of what I call a reform-oriented regime—
one that can create far-reaching modern social policy. And the possibility of
constructing a reform-oriented regime in America is connected to the nature
of American political institutions. Because only the president has impetus to
create national policies with national standards, such a regime requires first
that a president be favorably disposed to modern social policy. A president's orientation depends on several circumstances. It helps to be affiliated
with a party not opposed to social spending or historically in favor of it, to
be allied with pro-spending groups, to have a personal political history of
supporting social policy, and to serve when domestic policy is more salient
than foreign policy. The more of these conditions that hold good and the
more that they hold good, the more likely the president will favor national
social policy with high standards. For such a president to be effective, it
takes a mandate from the voters. A president will be in a stronger position
when winning landslides and thus not beholden to politicians from underdemocratized or patronage-oriented polities.

To get action on proposals a reform-oriented president also requires a
large contingent of the like-minded in Congress. That requirement is similarly connected to the main structural obstacles to reform. I argue that the
legislators with the greatest affinity to national and generous social policy
are likely to be Democratic and third-party legislators from democratic political systems and non-patronage-oriented party systems. What I call a reform-oriented regime consists of a president of the aforementioned type and
a contingent of such pro-spenders sizeable enough to overcome Republicans
and Democrats from undemocratic regimes. Such a regime is likely to
support a wide range of social spending proposals and will result in innovations in social policy. A reform-oriented president working with medium-
sized contingents of spenders is expected to produce an extension of exist-

ing programs, but no new innovations. Social policy will likely be rolled back when the president is not reform-oriented and when the presumed pro-spenders are greatly outnumbered by anti-spenders.

Other forces, however, impinge on policy. Once reform-oriented regimes come to power, the most highly developed domestic bureaucracies will likely influence what appears on the political agenda. Proposals with high-level bureaucratic sponsorship will be more likely to rise to the top. What is more, how domestic bureaucrats, policies, and abilities are spread throughout the polity influences the nature of proposals. If domestic planning capacities are centralized, coherent proposals are likely to result. If planning is dominated by competition among domestic bureaucracies, incoherent proposals shaped by varied modes of thinking about public policy are likely to result.

In addition, in federal polities like the American one, it is difficult for higher levels of government to wrest control of programs from lower levels. That is due not merely to the existence of federalism, but to the fact that political actors in much of the polity have reasons to retain as much local control as possible. When state and local programs already exist, those who oppose national policies can form coalitions with those who support existing lower-level policy arrangements, and most politicians and domestic bureaucrats at lower levels do so. For these reasons programs already enacted in some states and localities are likely to be boosted greatly by the national government, but not placed firmly under its control. In areas without state-level programs there are greater openings for immediate national experimentation and control.

Challengers hoping to change social policy can also influence outcomes in this area. The most influential challengers will be highly mobilized with an established political presence. Such challengers may put an issue on the political agenda or keep one from leaving it. They may also induce policymakers to increase benefits in proposals appealing to the groups represented by the challenger. Either way, their impact is typically contingent on other political conditions. The reform-oriented forces have to be in power or of moderate size and strength for challengers to have much impact.[2]

Although I discuss these different conditions and actors individually, I expect them to work interactively to produce policy outcomes. Different combinations of reform-oriented regimes, previous programs and domestic bureaucratic actors, and challengers will lead to different outcomes. My arguments also have implications for likely sequences of events in policymaking. Programs founded at the state level are likely candidates for national support, but unlikely ones for immediate nationalization. National programs are likely to result from episodes of experimentation and consolidation. And the initial makeup of programs will influence their chances for later growth. The more that programs are threatening to political and economic elites and the less they are run relatively automatically, the more likely they are to suffer retrenchment under anti–social spending political alignments. Creating state capacities in domestic policy takes the kind of political power needed to create new programs. And so in a polity like the American one, in which the structural hindrances to reform-oriented regimes are great, social policy is likely to be incoherent at first and subject to bids for rationalization later. Given these hindrances, moreover, the nature of early innovations is crucial, for it is far more likely that pro-spenders will be sizeable enough to extend existing programs than to create new ones.

These arguments address as well why some little New Deals—the state-level responses to national policy—were littler than others. I consider the states with democratic political systems and program-oriented party systems to be "open" to generous responses. In those polities, I expect generous social policy to be effected by specific sorts of political activity—a left or center party regime, powerful, long-standing domestic bureaucracies, and challengers demanding new or increased social spending. States with more of this activity are likely to be more generous. I expect the stingiest responses in the underdemocratized polities where the obstacles to social policy are most daunting.

A BRIEF DEMONSTRATION

But do these claims explain anything? In what follows I provide a brief summary and demonstration of my claims as they concern the overall trajectory of the policy, the form that policy took, the patterns of evolution of policy and programs, and the differences in policy across the states of the Union. In each case, outcomes largely lived up to expectations.

Across Time and Programs at the National Level

The historical trajectory of U.S. social policy in the 1930s and 1940s is the easiest place to start. (Needless to say, the first three decades of the twentieth century saw nothing resembling a reform-oriented regime at the national level.) Of the seven periods into which I divide it,[3] the single one, 1935–38, in which a reform-oriented regime was in power, saw the greatest innovations in American social policy. Among them were the WPA, the Social Security Act including the Social Security Board (SSB), and the Fair Labor Standards Act, which introduced the minimum wage. During the reform-oriented regime of 1935 through 1938, these programs avoided Supreme Court nullification and were partly consolidated as they got underway.

Significant gains in social policy also were made in the periods 1933–34, 1939–42, 1946–46, and 1949–50, when the reform-oriented forces were moderately powerful. In 1933, the United States established the Federal Emergency Relief Administration (FERA), setting the stage for the "welfare reform" of the Second New Deal. The end of the 1930s and the beginning of the 1940s witnessed important amendments to the Social Security

Act and to the income tax. The last period brought additional important Social Security Act amendments. In no case, however, were new major initiatives enacted, with the most notable failures being the rejection of the Wagner-Murray-Dingell bill in 1945 and Truman's health insurance initiative in 1949.

The times when the reform forces were weakest saw a lack of social spending or the rolling back of New Deal social policy. In the first part of the Depression, despite the crisis, Hoover did not make a concerted effort to provide relief until 1932, when its hand was forced by Congress, and even then had allocated little money by the time that he was ousted by the electorate. In any case, his relief program had no permanent implications for social policy. Reform forces were also weak in 1943–44 and 1947–48. In the middle of the war, which preoccupied the president and which saw the election of more conservatives to Congress than at any time since 1930, the New Deal was rolled back. Notably, the WPA, other employment programs, and the NRPB were terminated. In 1947, an income tax cut was passed over the administration's veto, a law that followed the antilabor Taft-Hartley Act.

My arguments also concern the development of policy and programs. Policy decided at one point in time will constrain what is possible and channel what happens later. Reform-oriented regimes, state domestic bureaucrats and programs, and challengers combine to affect the nature and extent of social policy. The programs and bureaucratic capacities that result in one wave of reform influence policy developments further down the line.

A reform-oriented regime took power during the Second New Deal of 1935, but the specific forms of programs depended on state actors, challengers, and previous programs. Figure 8.1 summarizes my expectations and what happened.[4] In 1935, support by state administrative political actors was important for work programs, the top priority of New Deal social policy and pressed by the powerful FERA. National bureaucratic support was also crucial for ADC, the pet program of the Children's Bureau. Movement support was key for old-age programs, which were backed by the Townsend Movement and to some extent for unemployment insurance, demanded by radicals in Congress and up to a point by unemployed workers. Other issues and programs did not have either sort of backing and did not appear on the political agenda. Such was the case for health policy, aside from the maternal programs previously overseen by the Children's Bureau. Nor was there national bureaucratic or movement support for workmen's compensation, run completely at the state level, or general relief, which the FERA had abandoned. In old-age insurance and work programs, moreover, there were no real state or local precedents. National programs resulted. By contrast, there were already programs to aid the aged and children, one state had adopted unemployment compensation, and many more were working on it. In each case, national legislation enhanced previous initiatives, while allowing substantial state and local control. Only for work pro-

FIGURE 8.1
Expected and Actual Program Outcomes under a Reform-Oriented Regime,
According to National Bureaucratic or Social Movement Influence and
State-Level Precedents

		Bureaucratic or Movement Influence	
		Present	Absent
Prior State-Level Program	**Absent**	National experiments: WPA Old-age insurance	No action: Health policy
	Present	Power-sharing programs: OAA UC ADC	Continued state or local programs: Workmen's compensation General relief

grams and old-age insurance was bureaucratic or movement support combined with a lack of preexisting programs at the state level (see the shaded
box in Figure 8.1).

The programs with greater administration and movement support resulted in programs with better funding and administrative procedures. On
that point, the comparison between OAA and ADC, both of them grants-in-
aid through the Social Security Act, is instructive. There was much greater
political pressure to do something for the aged, generated by the Townsend
Movement, than for dependent children. As a result, OAA had a higher
matching rate and greater benefits written into legislation than did ADC.
The Movement's political clout also ensured that ADC did not catch up to
OAA in 1939. All the same, neither program provided as generous and extensive benefits as the WPA, which was backed by the powerful FERA and
was Roosevelt's top priority in social policy.

The development of social policy generally depended on the fate of the
reform-oriented regime and the building of national-level policymaking capacities. Figure 8.2 reprises my expectations given different combinations of
the strength of pro-spending political contingents and state policymaking
abilities and precedents. This time the figure also arrays the political situations approximately as they existed between 1930 and 1950. The lower
right part of the figure—in which the reform forces were weak and the na-

FIGURE 8.2
Institutional Politics Theory: Short-Term Expectations and Policy Outcomes

National State Capacities
for Social Policy

	Strong	Weak
Strong	Adoption of national, collective social spending programs (Britian, 1945–50)	Adoption of power-sharing programs, some national experiments (1935–38)
Medium	Extension of national experiments in social spending (1939–42)	Extension of power-sharing programs in benefits, coverage (1933–34, 1939–42)
Weak	Failed national proposals; rollback of social spending programs (1943–45, 1947–48)	No national proposals; rollback of social spending programs (1930–31, 1947–48)

Reform Group's Power

tional state policymaking capacities were minimal—corresponds to the early 1930s under Hoover.[5] As expected, little happened in the way of social policy innovations at the national level. After that, pro-spenders became stronger in national politics, as shown higher up on the right side of the figure, culminating in the national experiments and power-sharing programs of 1935–38.

In the Second New Deal, new national policies and policymaking capacities were built, but they were only partial and fragmented in the WPA organization and the SSB. In some other areas, Unemployment Compensation and the power-sharing programs, state and local policymaking abilities grew relative to those at the national level. As a result of government reorganization in the late 1930s, planning capability for social policy was centralized in the National Resources Planning Board (NRPB), an upgrading of a bureau with origins in the Second New Deal. With a moderately sized pro-spending contingent behind Roosevelt, social policy advanced, mainly along the lines of previous action. There was also increased national control in the WPA. By contrast, the power-sharing programs of the Social Security Act produced struggles between the SSB and the states and localities.[6]

The time when policymaking capacities were most greatly centralized was also the time when the political power of reformers decisively weakened. The United States never found itself near the situation summarized at the shaded upper left of the figure—a reform-oriented regime coexisting with centralized policymaking abilities and nationalized domestic bureaucracies—the best case for national social policy. By contrast, Britain reached that point in 1945 and enacted its welfare state.[7] In the United States, a reform-oriented regime was not to appear again for decades, and even the moderately powerful pro-spending alignments of the late 1930s and early 1940s soon became a thing of the past.

What happened in the middle of the 1940s was unusual. It resembled as much as anything the familiar image of a cartoon figure running off a precipice and traveling some distance by sheer feet-churning before the inevitable fall. Made bold by the consolidation of the New Deal, with its newly reinforced and centralized policymaking agencies, reformers within the state spun out extensive national plans to reform the work and relief policy. Although health issues were downplayed, and family allowances did not appear, the WPA was to be revamped. General relief—the state and local program most closely connected to the WPA—and Unemployment Compensation were to be nationalized.

But the political ground had disappeared from beneath the vehement New Dealers. Roosevelt's support of social policy was temporarily neutralized by the war, and the makeup of Congress was the most anti-spending since Hoover was president. The plans were rejected and retrenchment ensued. Much of the centralized policymaking authority, including the NRPB and the WPA organization, were in for a fall. As a result, executive-based capabilities in social policy were reduced to less aggressive participants: the Bureau of the Budget and the SSB. Later proposals tended to follow their more cautious points of view. The Bureau of the Budget devised a wholly fiscal approach to unemployment through aggregate government spending and taxing, as embodied in the Full Employment bill of 1945. And the SSB called for the improvement of social insurance by way of the Old-Age and Survivors' Insurance (OASI) program.[8]

During the retrenchment, the WPA and employment programs were destroyed, while other programs such as OASI were merely reduced. What accounts for that? In standard treatments, the programs considered vulnerable to retrenchment are ones that are need-based and thus politically vulnerable or ones that are administratively weak. But although the WPA was need-based, other such programs, including OAA and ADC, were not eliminated. And although the WPA did not run without hitches, the WPA organization was perhaps the nation's most powerful domestic agency. Part of the reason that it was targeted for elimination was that it was more threatening to upper economic classes than most social spending programs. For it proposed to reinforce a prevailing wage in the North and establish a minimum wage in the South. Although the WPA had discretion built in it, the program raised the ire of powerful patronage-oriented Democrats cut out of the deal by the Roosevelt Administration. Where the administration worked with patronage-oriented Democrats, however, these allies often discredited the program by abusing it. But the WPA did not have strong support from groups typically in favor of public spending—in part because of the discretion built into the program. Congressional social policy advocates feared it because it granted tremendous authority to the executive branch. Unions also feared that the program might undercut wages. The OASI program was national, but highly limited in its benefits, recipients, and the discretion given to the SSB. It was not nearly as threatening.[9]

Points of Order

Other questions about developments at the national level concern issues of timing and sequence. To what degree did the timing of events, the order in which they took place, and initial decisions determine policy outcomes? Was the process of American policymaking "path-dependent"? That is to say, did initial choices make some outcomes much more likely, while precluding others? It is possible that initial choices ensured the success of some programs, precluded the nationalization of others, and doomed yet others to defeat. It is also possible that outcomes were basically decided at the outset by institutional conditions, such as hindrances to reform in the political system.

There are some conspicuous ways in which the timing of events mattered for policy outcomes. The fact that the reform-oriented regime took power when it did had an impact on the kind of policy that was adopted. The regime appeared in the middle of the Depression and at a time when American women had a relatively small presence in the paid labor force. Each had implications for the public policy that followed. Deciding a set of social policies in the middle of the Great Depression meant that some issues and types of programs were going to be emphasized at the expense of others. The issue of unemployment and programs based on need were both favored by the circumstances. If the regime had come to power just after the war undoubtedly other issues, such as health, might have been more prominent and need basing might not have been such an emphatic theme. Similarly, the fact that women were only a minor part of the paid labor force tended to influence the thinking inhering in some of the programs. If the regime had first come to power in the last generation, with women represented on such a large scale in the paid labor force, the assumptions behind programs would undoubtedly have been different.

Initial decisions and the order of events mattered concerning whether programs would become national in form, but here the issues are trickier. In constructing any program, policymakers have to make decisions about program type that might influence later program development. Among these decisions are whether to create national programs or power-sharing programs, whether to run programs on a merit basis with relatively automatic criteria to decide beneficiaries and benefits, whether to have high benefits, and whether to grant discretionary power to the executive. Taking the options that would reduce initial conflict was likely to produce programs relatively impervious to later nationalization.

I have argued that in issue areas in which previous lower-level programs were present, for instance, creating a power-sharing program at the national level was likely. Taking the power-sharing option was the path of least resistance and could create a lasting and nationwide, if uneven, commitment to a program. For legislatures around the country could decide exactly how they wanted to participate, and once they did they became committed to their decisions. That process, however, reduces the chances of later nationalization. For foes of nationalization have greater means to fight it, and the enthusiasm of pro-spending groups may be diminished. As it happened, moderately reform-oriented regimes that appeared after 1938 were able to improve power-sharing programs, by inducing merit standards in the administration of grant-in-aid programs and increasing payments for them. But the reformers could not nationalize them, as they proposed in the 1940s.

Creating a power-sharing program did not, however, completely preclude its later nationalization. Had a reform-oriented regime reappeared in the 1940s, power-sharing relief programs probably would have been nationalized, and so the initial decision was at least potentially retrievable. What is more, in areas where previous programs existed, an initial alternative to creating a power-sharing program would have been to delay, by creating policymaking capacities first or by expert study. That would mean to hold out for national policies by postponing the struggle until the terms of the debate could be transformed. A strategy like that, though, could easily be undone in the meantime by pro-spender losses in Congress. In a polity like the American one, in which reform-oriented regimes come only infrequently, a waiting game may provide the best chances for nationalization in the long run, but is highly risky.

Better prospects for a truly national policy appeared in policy areas with few or no lower-level programs. In relatively uncovered areas, I argue, it is easier to create national experiments, as there are not as many plausible alternatives. Politically and bureaucratically, the way is clearer. Such experiments can be augmented later, with something less than a completely pro-spending political alignment. That was the case for the WPA and old-age insurance, each created in 1935 and augmented later.

Initial decisions concerning the form of national programs can have tremendous consequences, too, however. For these programs there was a conspicuous trade-off between making an impact quickly and devising a program sustainable for the long run. Getting the WPA off to an impressive start required great executive discretion—to ensure that a relatively fair program would provide large amounts of reasonably remunerative work to many people quickly. Yet executive discretion can come at the long-term expense of a program, making it vulnerable later to antireform alignments, as happened with the WPA. Because anti-spending political alignments are endemic to the American polity, longevity for a national program may require initiating it in a modest way, but with the potential for later growth. That was the case for old-age insurance. Even so, it took a great deal of good fortune for that program to survive.

Initial decisions taken in policymaking, in short, had substantial impact on future developments. That social policy was adopted in the peculiar social conditions of the Depression had an impact on its form and outlook. Designing a program in a power-sharing fashion also made it difficult to nationalize later. And creating discretion in national programs made them vulnerable to later retrenchment, though it might have been possible to undo some of these decisions. Most of all, the structural obstacles to reform-oriented regimes ensured that the routes to the creation of national policy would be few and difficult.

Across the States of the Union

Perhaps more compelling evidence can come from the responses to the New Deal of the states of the Union. The states can afford a simultaneous appraisal of institutional and political claims. What I consider the best-case scenario for generous responses (type I) is for a state to be in favorable structural circumstances with a reform-oriented regime, powerful domestic bureaucracies, and significant challengers. The next most favorable scenarios are the state with a structurally open polity and with one or more powerful political forces for change (type II); and one with a structurally open polity and no powerful political forces for change was (type III). I consider an underdemocratized state the worst-case scenario (type VI). The next worst scenarios were states with patronage-oriented party systems (type V), and states with patronage-oriented parties, but with countervailing political forces for change (type IV).[10]

The four states I examined closely responded according to type. The biggest little New Deal was in Wisconsin, a state with an open polity and each of three political characteristics I expect to stimulate social policy. Wisconsin's New Deal was strong across all major social spending programs. All the same, Wisconsin was rarely in front of the Roosevelt Administration and its reform-oriented regime did not last long. A second-best case was California, which was similar to Wisconsin in most ways. But California lacked a reform-oriented regime, despite the 1938 election of Culbert Olson, a former adherent of End Poverty in California. There powerful challengers such as EPIC and the Townsend Movement pushed the OAA program to the limits of the acceptable for the Roosevelt Administration. In other policy areas, California's response to the New Deal was not negligible, but not as enthusiastic. Olson's far-reaching New Deal for California was largely blocked.

By contrast, states in what I consider unfavorable institutional circumstances responded far less eagerly to the New Deal. In Illinois, a patronage-oriented Democratic party gained control of government and took a highly selective stance toward the New Deal. The Democratic Chicago machine was especially favorable to the WPA. Although WPA wages were not particularly high there, the Democrats strongly supported the program and general assistance—the feeder program for the WPA. They dragged their heels, though, on enacting Social Security Act programs that required increased taxes and more standardized treatment across recipients. Illinois was the last state to adopt Unemployment Compensation and began the 1940s with an outmoded mothers' pension program.

In Virginia, a nondemocratic polity deflected as much of the New Deal as it could. It was the last state in the Union to adopt OAA and among the last to adopt Unemployment Compensation, and, like Illinois, it did not have an ADC program when the 1940s began. Most of its programs, moreover, were near the bottom in the efforts they made on behalf of their recipients. All of this happened, or did not happen, despite the fact that Virginia was among the South's most "organized" polities—the characteristic which V. O. Key argued was lacking from southern politics and accounted for its stunted social policy.[11]

It seems possible, though, that these cases do not embody the experiences of other states. Although my choices were made mainly to maximize the variability in institutional and political aspects of my theoretical claims, the four states do not cover each category of states and do not necessarily represent the categories they cover. For there were only four cases, and they were not chosen randomly. I might have picked ones, however inadvertently, that support my arguments, while missing many others that do not. More convincing would be to examine all of the states on important social policy results. If responses to the New Deal in all the states had turned out according to expectations, there could be no doubt. Unfortunately, such a book of case studies might have more sedative than instructional value, and those hoping for analyses employing inferential statistical methods or other quantitative techniques will have to look elsewhere.[12] Nonetheless, I can show that the reactions of the states with the strongest and weakest efforts in social spending largely conformed to my claims.

The list of states with the highest and lowest WPA wage efforts from chapter 5 reappears here, this time supplemented by the relevant institutional and political characteristics of each state. Five of the top ten states

TABLE 8.1
States with the Highest and Lowest WPA Wage Efforts, and Selected Institutional
and Political Indicators

Rank, State (Type)	Voting Rights[a]	Patronage Party[b]	Left/Center-Party Rule[c]	Administrative Powers[d]	Labor Movement[e]
1. Colorado (I)	Yes	No	Yes	Yes	Yes
2. Utah (I)	Yes	No	Yes	Yes	Yes
3. Arizona (I)	Yes	No	Yes	Yes	Yes
4. Oregon (II)	Yes	No	No	Yes	Yes
5. New Mexico (II)	Yes	No	Yes	No	No
6. New York (IV)	Yes	Yes	No	Yes	No
7. Minnesota (II)	Yes	No	Yes	No	Yes
8. Idaho (II)	Yes	No	Yes	Yes	No
9. Washington (I)	Yes	No	Yes	Yes	Yes
10. Montana (I)	Yes	No	Yes	Yes	Yes
39. Kentucky (V)	Yes	Yes	Yes	No	No
40. N. Carolina (VI)	No	No	Yes	No	No
41. Tennessee (VI)	No	No	Yes	Yes	No
42. Florida (VI)	No	No	Yes	No	No
43. Oklahoma (II)	Yes	No	Yes	No	No
44. Texas (VI)	No	No	Yes	No	No
45. Connecticut (V)	Yes	Yes	No	No	No
46. Virginia (VI)	No	No	Yes	No	No
47. Nevada (II)	Yes	No	Yes	No	Yes
48. Delaware (V)	Yes	Yes	No	No	No

[a] Refers to the right to vote, as manifested in relatively high voting participation.

[b] Refers to whether a state had centralized, patronage-oriented electioneering organizations.

[c] Refers to whether the Democratic party or a radical third party controlled the state government for four years or more during the 1930s.

[d] Refers to whether the state labor commissioner had rule-making authority in safety issues by the end of the 1920s and is used as a general indicator of power in domestic bureaucracies before 1930.

[e] Refers to whether the state had a powerful labor movement in the 1930s.

See chapter 5 for complete definitions and measurements.

approached the best-case scenario, as Table 8.1 shows. Another four states were in favorable institutional circumstances with at least one favorable political condition, and three of the four states had two such conditions. The only state that stands out is New York, which had relatively high WPA wages despite its patronage-oriented party system. That result, however, is mainly a quirk of the WPA's structure and New York politics. For administrative purposes New York City was treated as a state by the WPA. The city was led, moreover, by a "fusion" candidate of Republican and reform groups, Mayor Fiorello La Guardia, who eventually ran, as did Roosevelt in 1936, on the American Labor Party line. The city's previously dominant patronage-oriented Democratic party was dealt out of the WPA by Roose-

TABLE 8.2
States with the Highest and Lowest OAA Pension Efforts in 1940, and Selected
Institutional and Political Indicators

Rank, State (Type)	Voting Rights	Patronage Party	Left/Center- Party Rule	Administrative Powers	Townsend Movement[a]
1. Colorado (I)	Yes	No	Yes	Yes	Yes
2. California (II)	Yes	No	No	Yes	Yes
3. Arizona (I)	Yes	No	Yes	Yes	Yes
4. Idaho (I)	Yes	No	Yes	Yes	Yes
5. Utah (II)	Yes	No	Yes	Yes	No
6. Massachusetts (II)	Yes	No	Yes	Yes	No
7. South Dakota (II)	Yes	No	Yes	No	Yes
8. Kansas (II)	Yes	No	No	No	Yes
9. Wyoming (II)	Yes	No	Yes	No	Yes
10. Wisconsin (I)	Yes	No	Yes	Yes	Yes
39. Tennessee (VI)	No	No	Yes	Yes	No
40. Arkansas (VI)	No	No	Yes	No	No
41. Maryland (IV)	Yes	Yes	No	Yes	No
42. Kentucky (V)	Yes	Yes	Yes	No	No
43. Texas (VI)	No	No	Yes	No	No
44. Florida (VI)	No	No	Yes	No	No
45. S. Carolina (VI)	No	No	Yes	No	No
46. Georgia (VI)	No	No	Yes	No	No
47. Virginia (VI)	No	No	Yes	No	No
48. Delaware (V)	Yes	Yes	No	No	No

[a] Refers to whether the state's Townsend Movement was both large in clubs per capita and politically powerful in terms of successful endorsements of political candidates. For the other terms see Table 8.1.

velt.[13] Eight of the bottom ten, moreover, are types V and VI—undemocratic or patronage-oriented polities with no countervailing forces for change. The other two states—Oklahoma and Nevada—fall under type II. Oklahoma barely missed the cutoff point for being underdemocratized, however, and could easily be seen as type VI. As for Nevada, well, you can't win them all.[14] In almost every case, though, the results support the argument.

The argument holds up better for OAA perhaps because OAA pensions were more completely under the control of state governments than the WPA wages were. As Table 8.2 shows, each of the top ten states in OAA pension efforts was in favorable institutional circumstances, with a largely democratic political system and a program-oriented party system. Each also included a left- or center-party regime, strong domestic bureaucracies, or well mobilized Townsend Movements. Three of the top four states were type I, and most of the rest were type II. The bottom ten also correspond to expectations. Seven of the ten were former states of the Confederacy, lacking strong voting rights, and the other three are from patronage-oriented party systems. Each of the top ten OAA states were either type I or II, and each of the bottom ten were either type IV, V, or VI.

No matter how one looks at it—over time, across programs, across countries, or across states—the institutional and political arguments explain much about the development of American social policy. The times in which reform-oriented forces were powerful were the periods in which the greatest social policy gains were made. When these forces were weak, so were social policy responses. The nature of reform depended greatly on the character of previous programs and national bureaucratic actors. Unlike Britain just after the war, the United States never had a reform-oriented regime that coincided with centralized domestic policymaking actors. When and where they had established followings and a political presence, moreover, challengers pressed forward social policy. In the states, underdemocratized polities and patronage oriented polities ensured little New Deals that were very little, while open polities with powerful pro-spending forces of different kinds promoted more enthusiastic reactions.

The Legacy of the 1930s and 1940s for Postwar Social Policy

Though mostly unintended, the main results of the formative decades of U.S. social policy were to establish the OASI program and several power-sharing programs, notably ADC—social security and welfare. A modernized taxation system remained, too, and promised increased revenues, so long as the economy boomed and no one targeted taxation schedules for cuts. The employment programs were dropped, though, and replaced only by a weak form of Keynesian demand management. Other social policy was either highly selective or private. Veterans won a welfare state of their own, and a series of private social programs negotiated between employers and employees was begun in earnest.

Policy was transformed, but so was politics. American progressive liberalism centered on the New Deal. Roosevelt transformed the state and sought to redefine American politics, making it national and revolving about his initiatives. Democratic parties around the country began to realign themselves accordingly. As policy narrowed, though, so did the possibilities of politics. When New Deal social policy was centered on work and relatively direct governmental interventions to promote it, progressive liberalism had an interventionist aspect. By the end of the 1940s, that had receded, as New Deal social policy was thinned. Liberalism meant in part what remained from New Deal social policy and a weakened form of Keynesian economics.[15] Favorable action on even these less venturesome issues was difficult to secure in the postwar period.

Despite the war's end, the United States remained absorbed by geopolitical matters, sustaining a military presence far beyond anything existing in the first four decades of the century. This newfound military mission constituted a permanent diversion from social politics, commanding the attention of presidents, preempting executive authority, and delegating more control over social policy to Congress. When military matters were added to other structural obstacles in the American setting, the prospects for advocates of social policy became even less hopeful than they had been.

Partly as a result, the power of policy advocates in postwar America oscillated between moderate and weak. Most postwar developments in social policy accordingly have been augmentations along the lines set by OASI and ADC—the key "social security" and "welfare" programs. Insurance for permanent and total disability for workers was annexed to OASI in 1956. The social security and welfare programs reached their peaks in the early 1970s, after many years of Democratic presidents and congresses. Since then, social security has held its ground, backed as it has been by a powerful domestic bureaucracy and political constituency, its own taxation system, and a unique ideology of social insurance. Despite various declared "crises," the payroll taxes for the program were increased in 1977 and again after the elections of 1982. By contrast, the ADC program, (renamed Aid to Families with Dependent Children [AFDC] in 1962), suffered. Social security's eclipse of OAA removed a more politically favored group from the purview of state and local assistance systems, and neither welfare mothers nor children have proved especially politically powerful. What is more, AFDC was increasingly out of step with the increase in women in the paid labor force. It takes national and state-level legislation to upgrade AFDC benefits—neither of which was greatly forthcoming since 1970. As a result they deteriorated from inflation until the national grant-in-aid was replaced by a block grant in 1996.[16]

The one major exception came in the middle 1960s during the administration of the Democratic President Lyndon B. Johnson. At that time, Democrats completely dominated Congress, adopting reform of a scope reminiscent of the middle 1930s. Johnson's "war on poverty" brought innovations in public health care policy, establishing the social insurance program Medicare and grants-in-aid for the need-based Medicaid program—along the lines of the social security and welfare programs. Other initiatives, in housing and employment, were short-lived, however.[17]

Direct government employment on the order of the WPA has been mainly off the political agenda since the New Deal. Because any national social policy has been difficult to establish in the American setting, a "spending" Keynesian policy, as imagined by some New Dealers, has never been practicable either. Partly as a result American income taxation—a legacy of the New Deal and war—was pressed into service as both economic and employment policy in the postwar period. Various tax cuts were

adopted by presidents of both parties to stimulate the economy and employment. Often these general cuts were purchased by way of taxation "expenditures"—selective breaks from income taxes for small groups.[18] These
deals came at the ultimate expense of the fiscal health of the state.

The use of the income tax system as a means to nourish social policy in
the absence of new commitments was ended in the 1980s. Under the Ronald
Reagan Administration and the conservative Congresses elected with him,
income taxes were permanently curtailed. In 1981, Congress passed a three-
year, 25 percent reduction in personal income tax rates and even greater
reductions in the corporation income tax. Those changes were secured by
the Tax Reform Act of 1986, which increased corporation income taxes,
but drastically reduced the number of income tax brackets, lowered rates,
and indexed the brackets to inflation. The act ended the practice of increasing social spending on the basis of revenues produced by the interaction of
economic growth or inflation on the tax system. The "era of easy finance,"
the second one in American history, was over.[19]

The structural obstacles to constructing a reform-oriented regime have
loosened and tightened since the middle of the century. On the one hand, in
the wake of the civil rights movement, the Johnson Administration pushed
and the Democratic Congress passed the Voting Rights Act of 1965, marking the beginning of the end of underdemocratization in the South. Although the process took more than a decade to work, this barrier to reform
has been removed for good from the American scene. Still remaining,
though, are significant restrictions by way of voter registration throughout
the country. These restrictions still result in electoral participation that is
lower in America than in other rich countries.[20]

On the other hand, the prospects of social policy have been hampered by
the increased role of money in American politics. The requirements and results of fund-raising have tended to moderate the views of Democratic
candidates. As a result, the party as a whole has shifted to the right. Reforms in the process of nominating presidential candidates also have
worked against the Democratic candidate's incentive to form strong alliances with the increasingly shrinking labor movement or with other pro-
spending groups.[21]

The 1992 election of the Arkansas Democrat Bill Clinton to the presidency with small Democratic majorities in Congress provided hope for
social spending advocates that America would end its status as an outlaw
nation in national health insurance and reform welfare in part by replacing
it with work programs. Clinton's proposed health security program
reflected the fact that most non-poor and non-aged Americans who receive
health benefits get them at work. The employer "mandates" in the program
also reflected the fact that new commitments that required high taxation
would be difficult to gain. Although the earned income tax credit was
expanded in 1993, welfare reform was put on hold until the health security
issue was resolved. But the Clinton Administration gave up on it and

saw the electorate install a Republican Congress in 1994. Under its prodding Clinton signed a "reform" bill that gave few incentives for states to create employment, but every incentive to remove welfare mothers from the rolls.[22]

Although it is possible, It seems unlikely that reform-oriented regimes like those of the middle 1930s will ever appear again in the absence of a significant break in the connection between money and politics in America. That connection is far more powerful now than it was during the 1960s or the 1930s. Until then, the future of social policy is likely to remain on hold. A national commitment to health and a program to providing work for all those who need it in the manner of the WPA will have to wait.[23] In the meantime, we will endure with the divided system of social policy that was the legacy of the New Deal.

FRANKLIN ROOSEVELT in 1934 and Bill Clinton in 1993 faced parallel circumstances and made similar proposals in their bids to reform welfare. Each convened a study group, and each group proposed a work program, among other things. Here, though, the similarities end. Although Roosevelt was in a better political situation, with stronger Democratic majorities, the comparison is not flattering to President Clinton. It may, however, be instructive to those who hope to revitalize employment policy.

One thing that differed was how the two presidents talked and what they talked about. Roosevelt and his advisors talked more about ways to aid the unemployed and fight the consequences of poverty than about the unsatisfactory programs currently dealing with those problems. Although Roosevelt denounced the dole, he more often proclaimed the need for the government to employ people. Clinton and his advisors spoke mainly of ending welfare.

Another thing that differed was their timing. Roosevelt waited until the time was right. Facing a Congress in 1934 that was prepared only to deliver piecemeal reform, Roosevelt shunted aside its legislation. Only after the November elections fortifying the Democratic ranks in Congress did he introduce his proposals. By contrast, Clinton did not pursue his reforms in 1993 when he might have, and then, with his double-digit lead in the polls in the summer of 1996, he agreed to what Congress offered—an end to welfare, but with nothing to replace it.

What is more, Roosevelt and his advisors committed themselves to passing their proposals. In January 1935 Roosevelt pushed for a huge works appropriation. Once that was achieved he pressured Congress to pass his omnibus security bill, which provided federal support for aid to the aged, the blind, and dependent children, and unemployment compensation. Only Roosevelt's persistence kept Congress from gutting this legislation and removing from it the experimental old-age insurance program we now know as social security. Clinton let his welfare reform proposal die in Congress without pushing it, overshadowed as it was by the extensive debate over his health security plan, which also suffered from neglect.

Roosevelt knew that work was going to cost more than giving out checks and acted like it. To fund his "works program," Roosevelt sought an appropriation of almost $5 billion—far more than the Federal Emergency Relief Administration was receiving and an enormous sum for the time. As a result, less than a year later 3 million people were working for wages for the WPA. Clinton signed a bill that cut approximately $55 billion over six years from programs for poor people. Work programs will result only if fiscally strapped states in competition with one another to lower taxes decide to create them. If history is any indication, no national work policy will result.

The first episode of welfare reform provides lessons that seem to have been lost on Clinton and his band of would-be welfare reformers. One lesson has to do with how to talk about reform. If you want to provide work and wages for people on welfare, talk more about the need for a national commitment to a work program and less about the problems caused by welfare. People may get the mistaken impression that the welfare program itself is the main problem, rather than being a poor solution to a more fundamental problem—the lack of work opportunities.

Other lessons have to do with making the most of the political situation. If you have devised a workable program, use the powers of your office to sell it to the American people and Congress. Achieving reform takes more than merely convening experts and circulating their proposals in Congress—the Clinton Administration's failed approach. If Congress offers "welfare reform" that cuts aid to poor people without creating any program in return, deflect it. Accepting funding cuts will only make reform more difficult to achieve later. Solutions require money, and money has to come from somewhere. Any new work program in Bill Clinton's second term would require raising taxes—a much more difficult task, but one that needs facing.

Eliminating national standards and leaving decisions about aid to the states has already been tried and has failed. If the current policymakers need an example to follow, they might look back sixty years to Roosevelt and his social policy team. Their goal, to insure work for all those failed by the private market, is as relevant today as it was in the Great Depression. A similarly bold approach to the current welfare problem is in order.

Such an approach would have to encourage or provide work paying a living wage, provide or subsidize child care, and guarantee health benefits—solutions much like what the administration proposed, but did not pursue in 1994. Clinton's earned income-tax credit legislation of 1993 took one step down this path, as it effectively increased the minimum wage. But also needed is a national work program, perhaps beginning with a model program, and job training. Working women who head households also need affordable child care and cannot worry that taking a job will mean the end of their health benefits. To work, this program would have to be a commitment of the federal government. That approach may be impossible in the current political climate. But it is ultimately the only way to end welfare as we know it—a set of underfunded programs that do not address the lack of opportunities for work.

NOTES

INTRODUCTION
PARADOXES OF AMERICAN POLICY

1. "Annual Message to the Congress, January 4, 1935," in *The Public Papers and Addresses of Franklin D. Roosevelt* ed. Samuel I. Rosenman, 13 vols. (New York: Random House, 1938–50). See also "White House Statement Summarizing the Report for the President's Committee on Economic Security (Excerpts), January 17, 1935," ibid., p. 50. In its "summary of major recommendations," the Committee on Economic Security called first for "employment assurance." Project on the Federal Social Role, *The Report of the Committee on Economic Security of 1935 and Other Basic Documents Relating to the Development of the Social Security Act* (Washington, D.C.: National Conference on Social Welfare, 1985), p. 23.

2. The term "social security" sometimes includes as well the survivors', disability, and hospital insurance programs that were annexed to old-age insurance in the years after 1935. "Social security" also means the peculiar characteristics embedded in these programs—a payroll tax to fund them and benefits based in part on a person's taxation and earnings record. "Social security" also calls to mind the primary justification for these programs promoted by the Social Security Administration—that old-age insurance and associated programs resemble private insurance, and their beneficiaries are deemed deserving in that they supposedly have earned what they receive by paying an earmarked tax. However, the earliest recipients received far more in benefits than the amount they were taxed, and current retirees on average will still receive almost twice as much as they "contributed." Arthur Altmeyer, *The Formative Years of Social Security* (Madison, Wis.: University of Wisconsin Press, 1966), pp. 3–6. See also Margaret Weir, Ann Shola Orloff, and Theda Skocpol, "Understanding American Social Politics," *The Politics of Social Policy in the United States* (Princeton, N.J.: Princeton University Press, 1988), pp. 3–27.

3. Americans understand "welfare" as social policy for the poor. In recent times welfare has been centered on Aid to Families with Dependent Children—the need-based and means-tested program provided mainly to female heads of families that was the mainstay of the safety net until 1996. Also often considered welfare are other need-based programs, such as general assistance and Food Stamps. Although AFDC was and Food Stamps is an "entitlement," they have often been treated disparagingly—as if their recipients were undeserving. And the entitlement status of the various welfare programs varies greatly. The Food Stamp program, a national operation, corresponds to the more common understanding of entitlement: individuals fitting specific income and family status criteria are entitled to specified levels of support. The same is true for Supplemental Security Income, a national program for poor people who are aged, disabled, or blind. AFDC was an entitlement only in a more restricted sense: The federal government was required to "match" state-level spending at well-defined rates. States in turn were bound by federal standards for eligibility and equal treatment of recipients, but had the freedom to set eligibility and benefit standards within these limits. Its 1996 replacement, Temporary Aid to Needy Families, does not require the federal government to match state payments. General assistance programs are completely under the control of states and locali-

ties, with no matching from the federal government, and thus are entitlements in a local way. Medicaid, a grant-in-aid program like AFDC, is sometimes considered to be welfare, as eligibility for it is often determined in the same way as for AFDC and general assistance. See Weir et al., "Understanding American Social Politics"; David T. Ellwood, *Poor Support: Poverty in the American Family* (New York: Basic Books, 1988), chap. 1; Linda Gordon, *Pitied But Not Entitled* (New York: Basic Books, 1994), chap. 1; Herbert J. Gans, *The War Against the Poor: The Underclass and Anti-Poverty Policy* (New York: Basic Books, 1995).

4. Most contemporaneous studies of U.S. social policy in the 1930s employed the terminology of "relief." See, for instance, Josephine Chapin Brown, *Public Relief, 1929–1939* (New York: Holt, 1940); U.S. National Resources Planning Board Committee on Long-Range Work and Relief Policies, *Security, Work and Relief Policies* (Washington, D.C.: U.S. Government Printing Office, 1942); Donald S. Howard, *The WPA and Relief Policy* (New York: Sage, 1943).

5. Different programs at different times have been wrapped in the ideological embrace of social security. Notably, other programs of the Social Security Act, such as Aid to Dependent Children and Unemployment Compensation, were once included. When he discussed the Social Security Act, Roosevelt at first typically referred to "old-age pensions," "unemployment insurance," and "aid to dependent children"—not to "old-age insurance." See Rosenman, *Roosevelt Public Papers*, 4:326, 426. When people around the world today use the term "social security," they usually mean social insurance and assistance—following the initial American policy and usage. Altmeyer, *The Formative Years*, pp. 3–6.

6. Arthur M. Schlesinger, Jr., *The Age of Roosevelt: The Coming of the New Deal* (Boston: Houghton Mifflin, 1958), p. 12. The green ticket story appears in Altmeyer, *The Formative Years*, p. 12–13. As I argue below, when he was thinking about who would receive employment, Roosevelt was mainly thinking in terms of "he" and "him."

7. In his pioneering work, Harold Wilensky defined the welfare state as all government programs that tend to lead to equality of result. In practice these include the major social insurance and social assistance programs. From there Wilensky creates his index of "social security effort" to compare countries: *The Welfare State and Equality: Structural and Ideological Roots of Public Expenditures* (Berkeley: University of California Press, 1975), chap. 1. Peter Flora and Arnold J. Heidenheimer define the welfare state as all government programs contributing to equality and security. In practice, this leads them to examine the timing of adoption and the degree of inclusiveness of the major social insurance programs: "The Historical Core and Changing Boundaries of the Welfare State," in *The Development of Welfare States in Europe and America.* (New Brunswick, N.J.: Transaction, 1981), pp. 17–34. On the convergence in policy, see Arthur L. Stinchcombe, "The Functional Theory of Social Insurance," *Politics and Society* 15 (1986–87): 411–30.

8. Paul Pierson suggests that one strategy embraced by recent conservatives bidding to retrench social policies is to introduce means tests for programs that did not have them, and he is right about the last fifteen years: *Dismantling the Welfare State? Reagan, Thatcher, and the Politics of Retrenchment* (New York: Cambridge University Press, 1994), pp. 6, 14–15. But U.S. pro–social spending reformers fought to create modern, well-administered programs as a right for everyone who needed them. Need-based programs can be made relatively inclusive—by setting the level of eligibility at a high level of income and with liberal property provisions.

9. Gøsta Esping-Andersen, *The Three Worlds of Welfare Capitalism* (Princeton, N.J.: Princeton University Press, 1990), pp. 26–29, builds on the famous distinction between "institutional" and "residual" welfare states first proposed by Richard Titmuss: *Social Policy* (New York: Pantheon, 1974). For another tripartite scheme, see Norman Furniss and Timothy Tilton, *The Case for the Welfare State: From Social Security to Social Equality* (Bloomington: Indiana University Press, 1977). Esping-Andersen sees the conservative corporatist regime as standing somewhere between the social democratic and liberal regimes. For an analysis of his model, see Charles Ragin, "A Qualitative Comparative Analysis of Pension Systems," in *Methodological Advances in Comparative Political Economy*, ed. Thomas Janoski and Alexander Hicks (New York: Cambridge University Press, 1994), pp. 320–45. For feminist critiques, see Ann Shola Orloff, "Gender and the Social Rights of Citizenship: The Comparative Analysis of Gender Relations and Welfare States," *American Sociological Review* 58 (1993): 303–28; Julia O'Connor, "Gender, Class, and Citizenship in the Comparative Analysis of Welfare States: Theoretical and Methodological Issues," *British Journal of Sociology* 44 (1993): 501–18.

10. If they were to provide relatively automatic and generous benefits as a right to citizens, means-tested programs could be radically "decommodifying." Unlike universal old-age insurance, which one qualifies for by way of certifying one's lifetime connection to private employment, means-tested programs give benefits to people on the basis of their lack of a connection to the private market. Despite the efforts of reformers, the relief programs of the New Deal did not meet these standards. Neither have others since then.

11. The following discussion is based on Edwin Amenta and Theda Skocpol, "Taking Exception: Explaining the Distinctiveness of American Public Policies in the Last Century," in *The Comparative History of Public Policy*, Francis G. Castles, ed. (London: Polity Press, 1989), pp. 292–333.

CHAPTER ONE
AN INSTITUTIONAL POLITICS THEORY OF SOCIAL POLICY

1. In 1982, Sweden, the world's leader in public social provision, devoted approximately 32 percent of its gross domestic product to social spending. In contrast, the United States devoted only about 13 percent. Much research on public social spending over the last generation has been devoted to explaining postwar variation among capitalist democracies in social spending "efforts"—the share of its income that a country devotes to public social provision. See Harold Wilensky, *The Welfare State and Equality: Structural and Ideological Roots of Public Expenditures* (Berkeley: University of California Press, 1975); Alexander Hicks and Joya Misra, "Political Resources and the Growth of Welfare Effort: The Case of Affluent Capitalist Democracies, 1960–1982," *American Journal of Sociology* 99 (1993): 668–710; Evelyne Huber, Charles Ragin, and John D. Stephens, "Social Democracy, Christian Democracy, Constitutional Structure and the Welfare State: Towards a Resolution of Quantitative Studies," ibid., pp. 711–49.

2. Studies of the origins of public social provision have tended to take the form of case studies or close comparisons of a few carefully chosen nations. See, for instance, Gaston Rimlinger, *Welfare Policy and Industrialization in Europe, America, and Russia* (New York: Wiley, 1971); Hugh Heclo, *Modern Social Politics in Britain and Sweden* (New Haven, Conn.: Yale University Press, 1974); Ann Shola Or-

loff and Theda Skocpol, "Why Not Equal Protection? Explaining the Politics of
Public Social Welfare in Britain and the United States, 1880s–1920s," *American
Sociological Review* 49 (1984): 726–50; Peter Baldwin, *The Politics of Social Soli-
darity: Class Bases of the European Welfare State 1875–1975* (Cambridge: Cam-
bridge University Press, 1990); David Collier and Richard Messick, "Prerequisites
Versus Diffusion: Testing Alternative Explanations of Social Security Adoption,"
American Political Science Review 69 (1975): 1299–1315; Peter Flora and Jens
Alber, "Modernization, Democratization, and the Development of Welfare States in
Western Europe," in *The Development of Welfare States in Europe and America*,
ed. Peter Flora and Arnold Heidenheimer (New Brunswick, N.J.: Transaction
Books, 1981), pp. 37–80.

  3. Studies of American public policy across states of the Union were undertaken
at about the same time as the first wave of the cross-national studies. See, for instance, Thomas R. Dye, *Politics, Economics, and the Public: Policy Outcomes in the
American States* (Chicago: Rand McNally, 1966); Jack L. Walker, "The Diffusion
of Innovations Among the American States," *American Political Science Review* 63
(1969): 880–99. Recent studies taking the United States in comparative perspective
include the following: Edward D. Berkowitz, *America's Welfare State: From Roosevelt to Reagan* (Baltimore: Johns Hopkins University Press, 1991); Theda Skocpol,
*Protecting Soldiers and Mothers: The Political Origins of Social Policy in the United
States* (Cambridge, Mass.: Harvard University Press, 1992).

  4. For some notable social science analyses of the Social Security Act, see Frances
Fox Piven and Richard A. Cloward, *Regulating the Poor: The Functions of Public
Welfare*, 2d ed. (New York: Vintage Books, 1993); Theda Skocpol and G. John
Ikenberry, "The Political Formation of the American Welfare State in Historical and
Comparative Perspective," *Comparative Social Research* 6 (1983): 82–148; Jill S.
Quadagno, "Welfare Capitalism and the Social Security Act of 1935," *American
Sociological Review* 49 (1984): 632–47; Ann Shola Orloff, "The Political Origins of
America's Belated Welfare State," in *The Politics of Social Policy in the United
States*, ed. Margaret Weir, Ann Shola Orloff, and Theda Skocpol (Princeton, N.J.:
Princeton University Press, 1988), pp. 37–80; J. Craig Jenkins and Barbara G.
Brents, "Social Protest, Hegemonic Competition, and Social Reform: A Political
Struggle Interpretation of the Origins of the American Welfare State," *American
Sociological Review* 54 (1989): 891–909; Edwin Amenta and Sunita Parikh, "Capi-
talists Did Not Want the Social Security Act: A Critique of the 'Capitalist Domi-
nance' Thesis," ibid., 56 (1991): 124–29. G. William Domhoff, *The Power Elite
and the State: How Policy is Made in America* (New York: Aldine De Gruyter,
1990), chap. 3.

  5. For that reason I leave aside economic and modernization hypotheses that suggest that economic growth and related social changes account for developments in
public policy. These hypotheses have aided in indicating why richer countries spend
more and adopt policies sooner than poorer ones, but do not explain important
differences in spending and policy adoption among relatively rich countries. See, for
instance, Collier and Messick, "Prerequisites Versus Diffusion"; see also the review
of evidence in Theda Skocpol and Edwin Amenta, "States and Social Policies," *Annual Review of Sociology* 12 (1986): 131–57.

  6. Statist and institutional arguments about social policy hold that state structures and actions typically cannot be reduced to societal characteristics or events.
James G. March and Johan P. Olsen, "The New Institutionalism: Organizational

Factors in Political Life," *American Political Science Review* 78 (1984): 734–49; Theda Skocpol, "Bringing the State Back In: Strategies of Analysis in Current Research," in *Bringing the State Back In,* ed. Peter B. Evans, Dietrich Rueschemeyer, and Theda Skocpol (Cambridge: Cambridge University Press, 1985), pp. 3–37; Paul DiMaggio and Walter W. Powell, "Introduction," in *The New Institutionalism in Organizational Analysis* (Chicago: University of Chicago Press, 1991). Theorists taking this approach usually define the state as a set of organizations that extract resources and extend control and political authority over territory and people, but the state has two competing definitions as it has been applied to social policy. Following Tocqueville, some theorists argue that the structure of governmental institutions—the state in the wider sense—influences public social provision and political mobilization. Following Weber, others understand the state more narrowly and argue that executive bureaucracies propel social policy.

7. V. O. Key, *Southern Politics in State and Nation* (New York: Knopf, 1949), chap. 14. By contrast, the British sociologist T. H. Marshall posited an evolution of rights. He argued that the common man first achieved civil rights, then political rights, and finally the kind of social rights associated with modern social spending, with each set of rights building on the previous ones: *Class, Citizenship, and Social Development* (Chicago: University of Chicago Press, 1963), chap. 4. Recent research has found that democratic rights spur social policy adoption: Flora and Alber, "The Development of Welfare States in Western Europe"; Alexander Hicks, Joya Misra, and Tang Nah Ng, "The Programmatic Emergence of the Social Security State," *American Sociological Review* 60 (1995): 329–49. The early gain of the franchise by white men in America probably increased the chances of the provision of public benefits for lower economic classes in the nineteenth century, including Civil War pensions, education, and public employment through political hiring. Some U.S. public policies reflected the disfranchised status of African Americans in the South, and of women. Civil War pensions were less generous and had more restrictions for widows and women who had served in wartime roles. African Americans were treated unfairly in many New Deal social insurance programs. For Civil War veterans' pensions, see Skocpol, *Protecting Soldiers and Mothers,* chap. 2. On the New Deal, see Jill S. Quadagno, *The Transformation of Old-Age Security: Class and Politics in the American Welfare State* (Chicago: University of Chicago Press, 1988), and chap. 4 below. Yet early democratization did not bring *modern* public social spending to America. See, for instance, Ann Shola Orloff, *The Politics of Pensions: A Comparative Analysis of Britain, Canada, and the United States, 1880–1940* (Madison: University of Wisconsin Press, 1993), chap. 2.

8. Robert Dahl, *Polyarchy: Participation and Opposition* (New Haven, Conn.: Yale University Press, 1971).

9. See Frances Fox Piven and Richard A. Cloward, *Why Americans Don't Vote* (New York: Pantheon Books, 1989), especially chaps. 2 and 3 (the quote is from page 3); J. Morgan Kousser, *The Shaping of Southern Politics: Suffrage Restriction and the Establishment of the One-Party South, 1880–1910* (New Haven, Conn.: Yale University Press, 1974); Walter Dean Burnham, *Critical Elections and the Mainsprings of American Politics* (New York: Norton, 1970), chap. 4. For the impact of registration restrictions on U.S. voter turnout in comparative and historical perspective, see Ruy A. Teixeira, *The Disappearing American Voter* (Washington, D.C.: Brookings Institution, 1992), chap. 1.

10. On the means of disfranchisement of African Americans and poor whites in the South, see Kousser, *The Shaping of Southern Politics*, chaps. 2–7. Legal changes such as literacy tests also involved intimidation in their application. As Kousser argues (pp. 45–46), disfranchisers had to contend with the Fourteenth and Fifteenth Amendments. The former restricted the representation in the polity for districts disfranchising people for reasons other than crime and rebellion, while the latter prohibited discrimination on the basis of race, color, or previous condition of servitude. The early debates indicated that those attempting to restrict the electorate knew they would reduce white as well as black voting. Although he perceived a denial of voting rights as secondary to disorganized politics as a hindrance to social policy, Key did not ignore the former: "the scales in the have-have-not conflict have been tipped by the exclusion of a substantial sector of the have-not population—the Negroes—from effective participation in politics. Similarly substantial numbers of whites of the have-not group do not vote. . . . The have–have-not match is settled in part by the fact that substantial numbers of the have-nots never get into the ring" (*Southern Politics*, pp. 307–8). Key also discusses the use of force, chaps. 25–28.

11. See Jill S. Quadagno, "From Old-Age Assistance to Supplemental Security Income: The Political Economy of Relief in the South, 1935–1972," in Weir, Orloff, and Skocpol, *The Politics of Social Policy in the United States*, pp. 235–64. Because of the underdemocratized nature of the South, the views of its peculiar economic elites mattered greatly in politics. It seems likely, though, that if the southern elites had been similar to their counterparts in the North, political officials would still have likely opposed generous, national social spending, as the northern economic elites also opposed it.

12. Key, *Southern Politics*, chaps. 16–17. For an analysis of the records of southern Democrats on important votes, see Ira Katznelson, Kim Geiger, and Daniel Kryder, "Limiting Liberalism: The Southern Veto in Congress, 1933–1950." *Political Science Quarterly* 108 (1993): 283–306. They refer to southern representation in Congress as a "structural veto over Democratic party policy aims."

13. Max Weber, "Classes, Status Groups, and Parties" (1922), in *Weber: Selections in Translation*, ed. W. G. Runciman (Cambridge: Cambridge University Press, 1978), chap. 3. Mayhew refers to these as "traditional party organizations," and defines them as substantially autonomous, long-lasting, hierarchical, seeking to nominate candidates for a wide range of public offices, and relying substantially on material incentives. David Mayhew, *Placing Parties in American Politics* (Princeton, N.J.: Princeton University Press, 1986), pp. 19–20. For other notable arguments about "machine politics," see Harold Gosnell, *Machine Politics: Chicago Model*, 2d ed. (Chicago: University of Chicago Press, 1968); Edward C. Banfield and James Q. Wilson, *City Politics* (Cambridge, Mass.: Harvard University Press, 1963); Martin Shefter, "Party and Patronage: Germany, Italy, and England," *Politics and Society* 7 (1977): 404–51; Ira Katznelson, *City Trenches: Urban Politics and the Patterning of Class in the United States* (New York: Pantheon, 1981).

14. Mayhew claims specifically that the leaders of patronage-oriented party organizations are inclined to avoid programmatic benefits because the kind of person attracted to patronage parties is unlikely to be someone with an urge to build programs, pro-spending groups like the labor movement cannot easily exercise influence in them, and these parties promote issueless politics and discourage professional bureaucracies, while creating a political culture of pessimism about the utility of government: *Placing Parties*, pp. 292–94.

15. Martin Shefter, "Party and Patronage: Germany, Italy, and England," *Politics and Society* 7 (1977): 404–51; and "Regional Receptivity to Reform: the Legacy of the Progressive Era," *Political Science Quarterly* 98 (1983): 459–83. Mayhew, *Placing Parties*.

16. The twenty-four states in the upper left box are defined by their wide extension of voting rights and their lacking strong patronage-oriented or "traditional" party organizations: Arizona, California, Colorado, Idaho, Iowa, Kansas, Maine, Massachusetts, Michigan, Minnesota, Montana, Nebraska, Nevada, New Hampshire, New Mexico, North Dakota, Oklahoma, Oregon, South Dakota, Utah, Vermont, Washington, Wisconsin, and Wyoming. The thirteen states in the lower left box are Connecticut, Delaware, Illinois, Indiana, Kentucky, Maryland, Missouri, New Jersey, New York, Ohio, Pennsylvania, Rhode Island, and West Virginia. Each scores four or five on Mayhew's five-point ranking system: *Placing Parties*, p. 196. The eleven states in the upper right box include Alabama, Arkansas, Florida, Georgia, Louisiana, Mississippi, North Carolina, South Carolina, Tennessee, Texas, and Virginia, each of which exhibited greatly restricted voting rights throughout most of the twentieth century. No state fits the box at lower right.

17. Ellen Immergut, *The Political Construction of Interests: National Health Insurance Politics in Switzerland, France, and Sweden* (New York: Cambridge University Press, 1992). Sven Steinmo, *Taxation and Democracy: Swedish, British, and American Approaches to Financing the Modern State* (New Haven, Conn.: Yale University Press, 1993); Huber, Ragin, and Stephens, "Social Democracy, Christian Democracy." The classic statement is by Alexis de Tocqueville, *Democracy in America* (Garden City, N.Y.: Doubleday/Anchor Books, 1969), who argued that American political and administrative decentralization promoted liberty.

18. Paul Pierson, *Dismantling the Welfare State? Reagan, Thatcher, and the Politics of Retrenchment* (New York: Cambridge University Press, 1994), pp. 32–35.

19. See ibid., pp. 32–35. For the classic statement about the division of authority in the U.S. political system, see Samuel P. Huntington, *Political Order in Changing Societies* (New Haven, Conn.: Yale University Press, 1968), chap. 2.

20. Currently it takes 60 percent to close Senate debates, but at earlier times it took two-thirds.

21. On these points, see chapter 2.

22. Skowronek also argues that the presidency is order-affirming and order-creating. See *The Politics Presidents Make: Leadership from John Adams to George Bush* (Cambridge, Mass.: Harvard University Press, 1993), chap. 2. On the conflict between the president and the party organizations that typically control Congress, see Sidney Milkis, *The President and the Parties: The Transformation of the American Party System since the New Deal* (New York: Oxford, 1993).

23. Skocpol, "Bringing the State Back In"; Michael Mann, "The Autonomous Power of the State: Its Origins, Mechanisms, and Results," in *States in History*, ed. John A. Hall (Oxford and New York: Basil Blackwell, 1986), pp. 109–36; Bruce G. Carruthers, "When is the State Autonomous? Culture, Organization Theory, and the Political Sociology of the State," *Sociological Theory* 12 (1994): 19–44. On modern taxes, see Steinmo, *Taxation and Democracy*.

24. See the review of these arguments in Edwin Amenta and Bruce G. Carruthers, "The Formative Years of U.S. Social Spending Policies: Theories of the Welfare State and the American States During the Great Depression," *American Sociological Review* 53 (1988): 661–78.

25. From 1932 to 1939, civil service employment increased from 446,000 to 662,800, approximately 48.6 percent, a growth rate of about 5.9 percent per year. By contrast, for the Second World War period civil service employment jumped from 662,800 to 1,692,000—a 150.7 percent increase that translates into a rate of 12.1 percent per year. During the Progressive Era civil service employment grew at a rate of about 7.5 percent per year. U.S. Bureau of the Census, *Historical Statistics of the United States from Colonial Times to 1970* (Washington, D.C.: U.S. Government Printing Office, 1975), series Y 308–317, pp. 1102–3. Also, during the first years of the New Deal, Congress exempted most new agencies from merit system regulations: Paul P. Van Riper, *History of The United States Civil Service* (Westport, Conn.: Greenwood Press, 1958), chap. 13. For an argument about the importance of the type of state building, see Ira Katznelson and Bruce Pietrykowski, "Rebuilding the American State: Evidence from the 1940s," *Studies in American Political Development* 5 (1991): 301–99.

26. Margaret Weir, *Politics and Jobs: The Boundaries of Employment Policy in the United States* (Princeton, N.J.: Princeton University Press, 1992).

27. John D. Stephens, *The Transition From Capitalism to Socialism* (London: Macmillan, 1979). See also Walter Korpi, *The Democratic Class Struggle* (London: Routledge and Kegan Paul, 1983). John Myles, *Old Age in the Welfare State: The Political Economy of Public Pensions*, 2d ed. (Lawrence: University of Kansas Press, 1989). Gøsta Esping-Anderson, *Politics Against Markets: The Social Democratic Road to Power* (Princeton, N.J.: Princeton University Press, 1985). This argument, sometimes known as the power resources thesis, is usually measured with the parliamentary or cabinet representation of social democratic parties. See Michael Shalev, "The Social Democratic Model and Beyond: Two Generations of Comparative Research on the Welfare State," *Comparative Social Research* 6 (1983): 315–51; Skocpol and Amenta, "States and Social Policies," pp. 139–43; Gøsta Esping-Andersen and Kees van Kersbergen. "Contemporary Research on Social Democracy," *Annual Review of Sociology* 18 (1992): 187–208.

28. Francis G. Castles and Peter Mair, "Left-Right Political Scales: Some 'Expert' Judgments," *European Journal of Political Research* 12 (1984): 73–88. Alexander M. Hicks, "The Ascendance of Social Democracy: The Golden Age of Income Security Reform" (paper presented at the annual meeting of the American Sociological Association, Washington, 1995).

29. Esping-Andersen argues that a red-and-green coalition of workers and farmers was behind breakthrough Scandinavian social policies in the 1930s: *Three Worlds of Welfare Capitalism* (Princeton, N.J.: Princeton University Press, 1990), chap. 1. Orloff argues that a coalition of the organized working class and policy experts was necessary for the passage of old-age pensions in the United States, Canada, and Great Britain: *The Politics of Pensions*, chap. 2.

30. Morris Janowitz, *The Last Half Century* (Chicago: University of Chicago Press, 1980). Morris P. Fiorina, *Divided Government* (New York: Macmillan, 1992).

31. Organized labor rallied behind the programs of the Social Security Act and was mainly in alliance with reformers inside and outside the government to improve in the years after the initial enactment. See, for instance, Martha Derthick, *Policymaking for Social Security* (Washington, D.C.: Brookings Institution, 1979).

32. On the room for maneuver of presidents, see Skowronek, *The Politics Presidents Make,* chap. 2.

33. Heclo, *Modern Social Politics*, chap. 6. Skocpol, *Protecting Soldiers and Mothers*, introduction. According to Theodore J. Lowi, distributive programs engender greater interest group support than do redistributive programs, including most social spending, because the latter impose costs on specific people. "Four Systems of Policy, Politics, and Choice," *Public Administration Review* 32 (1972): 298–310. Theda Skocpol argues that limited state capacities can rule out certain lines of action. For instance, she argues that because of limited abilities to plan public works programs the United States could not rely on them to fight the Great Depression: "Political Response to Capitalist Crisis: Neo-Marxist Theories of the State and the Case of the New Deal," *Politics and Society* 10 (1980): 155–201. Ann Shola Orloff argues that the general public may refuse to support social spending programs if the agencies administering them are not staffed professionally: *The Politics of Pensions*, chap. 2. Sara A. Rosenberry also posits that if social policy systems hide redistributive goals through inclusiveness, they can avoid negative political reactions: "Social Insurance, Distributive Criteria, and the Welfare Backlash: A Comparative Analysis," *British Journal of Political Science* 12 (1982): 421–47. Paul Pierson argues further that mature programs have "lock-in" effects that counter bids to cut them: *Dismantling the Welfare State?* pp. 42–45. These contentions receive some support from American social policy experience. The abuses of Civil War pensions discouraged middle-class reformers from supporting new social spending programs during the Progressive Era. Since World War II, moreover, U.S. social insurance programs have been favored over means-tested public assistance programs. U.S. social security programs are backed by powerful interest groups, notably by the American Association for Retired Persons. Orloff and Skocpol, "Why Not Equal Protection?" Margaret Weir, Ann Shola Orloff, and Theda Skocpol, "Introduction: Understanding American Social Politics," in *The Politics of Social Policy in the United States*, pp. 3–29.

34. On the role of women's organizations in the fight for Aid to Dependent Children, see Nancy K. Cauthen and Edwin Amenta, "Not for Widows Only: Institutional Politics and the Formative Years of Aid to Dependent Children," *American Sociological Review* 61 (1996): 427–48. The early years of the Works Progress Administration and Old-Age Assistance are cases in point, as each were popular. Other means-tested programs, notably Aid to Dependent Children, grew consistently from their adoption through the 1960s. Nowadays long-term aid through Medicaid for nursing home patients is a means-tested benefit that state governments are reluctant to restrict.

35. I disagree with scholars who argue that enlightened businessmen constitute the major forces behind public spending innovations in order to strengthen capitalism in crises. Power elite theorists and hegemonic competition theorists, for instance, argue that individual capitalists in important firms and in organizations of capitalists representing these firms exerted great influence over reforms such as the New Deal. These theorists expect capitalists or capitalist-controlled experts to dominate the policy deliberation or "formulation" process. For a review of various arguments concerning the role of business in public policy and a statement of how the power elite thesis applies to the Social Security Act, see Domhoff, *The Power Elite and the State*. For the hegemonic competition thesis, see Jenkins and Brents, "Social Protest, Hegemonic Competition, and Social Reform." Yet capitalism has managed to flourish with the underdeveloped welfare state of Japan and the highly developed welfare state of Sweden. What is more, dividing capitalists interested in public pol-

icy into coherent class fractions is not easy. It is misleading, moreover, to treat experts as doing the bidding of capital. Should anyone working for a research institution taking money from capitalists or accepting a foundation grant be counted as advancing capital's interests? Probably not. Policy experts have professional interests and preoccupations that diverge from the interests and preoccupations of those who may at some point have employed them. These interests can be advanced by carving out permanent state employment for themselves and others with similar credentials. Experts may influence capitalists more than vice versa. For some of these criticisms, see Fred Block, "Rethinking the Political Economy of the Welfare State," in *The Mean Season: The Attack on the Welfare State*, ed. Fred Block, Richard A. Cloward, Barbara Ehrenreich, and Frances Fox Piven (New York: Pantheon Books), chap. 3; Skocpol, *Protecting Soldiers and Mothers*, chap. 3; David Vogel, "Why Businessmen Distrust Their State: The Political Consciousness of American Corporate Executives," *British Journal of Political Science* 8 (1978): 45–87.

36. Charles Tilly, *From Mobilization to Revolution* (New York: Addison Wesley, 1978). The classic statement about the role of protest in politics can be found in Frances Fox Piven and Richard A. Cloward, *Poor People's Movements: Why They Succeed, How They Fail* (New York: Random House, 1977), chap. 1. They claim that the protests of the poor during political crises have induced governments to pass unrestrictive spending programs and increase spending on existing ones. Sidney Tarrow argues also that protest groups usually bid to radically reorient state policy, but often leave behind them residues of reform: *Power in Movement* (New York: Cambridge University Press, 1994), chap. 10. More generally Theda Skocpol argues that "widespread federated interests"—challenging organizations or reform groups organized across congressional districts—have the best chance of influencing U.S. public social provision because their form of organization "fits" the American polity: *Protecting Soldiers and Mothers*, introduction. Ann Shola Orloff has argued that women's movements and advocacy groups have served to promote social policies that provide autonomy to women: "Gender and the Social Rights of Citizenship: The Comparative Analysis of Gender Relations and Welfare States," *American Sociological Review* 58 (1993): 303–28.

37. Doug McAdam, *Political Process and the Development of Black Insurgency, 1930–1970* (Chicago: University of Chicago Press, 1982). On the minor impact of the Townsend Movement, see W. Andrew Achenbaum, "The Formative Years of Social Security: a Test Case of the Piven and Cloward Thesis," in *Social Welfare or Social Control: Some Historical Reflections on Regulating the Poor*, ed. Walter I. Trattner (Knoxville: University of Tennessee Press, 1983), pp. 67–89. On the limited effect of labor strikes, see Skocpol, "Political Response to Capitalist Crisis." For analyses indicating moderate and meditated influences of New Deal social movements, see Edwin Amenta, Bruce G. Carruthers, and Yvonne Zylan, "A Hero For the Aged? The Townsend Movement, The Political Mediation Model, and U.S. Old-Age Policy, 1934–1950," *American Journal of Sociology* 98 (1992): 308–39; Edwin Amenta, Kathleen Dunleavy, and Mary Bernstein. "Stolen Thunder? Huey Long's Share Our Wealth, Political Mediation, and the Second New Deal," *American Sociological Review* 59 (1994): 678–702.

38. G. William Domhoff, for instance, argues that what he calls the ultraconservative segment of the power elite constitutes a strong opponent of public social spending: *The Power Elite and the State*, chap. 3. See also Quadagno, "Welfare Capitalism and the Social Security Act." A poll taken in 1939, four years *after* the

passage of the Social Security Act, indicates that only 24 percent of a sample of business executives supported it—much less than the 89 percent approval rating given a year earlier by the general public. Hadley Cantril, ed., *Public Opinion, 1935–1946* (Princeton, N.J.: Princeton University Press, 1951), p. 361; Michael E. Schiltz, *Public Attitudes toward Social Security, 1935–1965* (Washington, D.C.: U.S. Government Printing Office, 1970), chap. 2. On the business welfare programs, see Frank R. Dobbin, "The Privatization of American Social Insurance: Organizations, Fringe Benefits, and the State, 1920–1950," *American Journal of Sociology* 97 (1992): 1416–50. On the values of businessmen, see Vogel, "Why American Businessmen Distrust Their State"; Ann Shola Orloff and Eric Parker, "Business and Social Policy in Canada and the United States, 1920–1940," *Comparative Social Research* 12 (1990): 295–339. For attempts by organized business to stop or dilute the Social Security Act, see Amenta and Parikh, "Capitalists Did Not Want the Social Security Act."

39. The definition is from Anthony Orum, "Political Sociology," in *The Handbook of Sociology*, ed. Ronald Burt and Neil Smelser (Beverly Hills, Calif.: Sage, 1988). See also Steven Lukes, *Power: A Radical View* (London: Macmillan, 1974); Nelson W. Polsby, *Community Power and Political Theory: A Further Look at Problems of Evidence and Inference*, 2d ed. (New Haven, Conn.: Yale University Press, 1980), chaps. 11; Dennis Wrong, *Power: Its Forms, Bases and Uses* (Chicago: University of Chicago Press, 1988).

40. Skocpol, *Protecting Soldiers and Mothers*, introduction.

41. On retrenchment, see Pierson, *Dismantling the Welfare State?*, chap. 1. Because retrenchment imposes direct costs on the recipients of benefits, for politicians it becomes an exercise in blame-avoidance. Pierson argues persuasively that the 1980s and beyond constitute the main historical period of retrenchment, but social spending programs are subject to cutbacks at all times and thus the issues surrounding retrenchment are relevant at any time.

42. Peter Flora and Arnold J. Heidenheimer, "The Historical Core and Changing Boundaries of the Welfare State," in *The Development of Welfare States in Europe and America* (New Brunswick, N.J.: Transaction Books, 1981), pp. 17–34; Steinmo, *Taxation and Democracy*. Recent U.S. "welfare reform" proposals have increased the earned income tax credit, a refundable measure for poor people who work for wages. David Ellwood, "Welfare Reform As I Knew It: When Bad Things Happen to Good Policies," *American Prospect*, May–June, pp. 22–29.

43. Richard Rose, *Understanding Big Government: The Programme Approach* (London: Sage, 1984). Differences in social spending efforts are often greatly influenced by external economic events or demographic changes. Demographic or economic changes increase or decrease the size of the group eligible for benefits, and the amount of spending automatically follows, while policy remains the same. See John Myles, *Old Age in the Welfare State* (Lawrence: University of Kansas Press, 1989), chap. 3. Similarly when the economy grows, slumps, inflates, or deflates, taxation revenues rise or fall accordingly, without basic policy changing.

44. John Kingdon, *Agendas, Alternatives, and Public Policies* (Boston: Little, Brown, 1984). Paul Burstein, notably, has argued that the Civil Rights movement likely helped to set the political agenda for the Civil Rights Act of 1964, but may have had little to do with content of this legislation or its passage: "Explaining State Action and the Expansion of Civil Rights: The Civil Rights Act of 1964," *Research in Political Sociology* 6 (1993): 117–37. See also Deborah A. Stone, "Causal Stories

and the Formation of Policy Agendas," *Political Science Quarterly* 104 (1989): 281–300.

45. Charles C. Ragin, *The Comparative Method* (Berkeley: University of California Press, 1987). Gary King, Robert Keohane, and Sidney Verba, *Designing Social Inquiry: Scientific Inference in Qualitative Research* (Princeton, N.J.: Princeton University Press, 1994).

46. See also Edwin Amenta, "Making the Most of a Case Study: Theories of the Welfare State and the American Experience," *International Journal of Comparative Sociology* 32 (1991): 172–94.

47. On sequential arguments and appraisals, see Larry J. Griffin, "Temporality, Events, and Explanation in Historical Sociology: An Introduction," *Sociological Methods and Research* 20 (1992): 403–27; Andrew Abbott, "From Causes to Events: Notes on Narrative Positivism," ibid., 428–55.

48. James T. Patterson, *The New Deal and the States: Federalism in Transition* (Princeton, N.J.: Princeton University Press, 1969), p. vii.

49. These analyses take the form of "most different systems" comparisons. Adam Przeworski and Henry Teune, *Logic of Comparative Social Inquiry* (New York: Wiley, 1970).

50. Type I includes Arizona, Colorado, Idaho, Montana, Utah, Washington, Wisconsin. Type II, implying a positive score on at least one of the "political" conditions, but not all of them, includes California, Iowa, Kansas, Maine, Massachusetts, Minnesota, Nebraska, Nevada, New Hampshire, New Mexico, North Dakota, Oklahoma, Oregon, South Dakota, Wyoming. Type III includes Vermont and Michigan. Type IV, implying a positive score on one or more of the political conditions, includes Indiana, Illinois, Kentucky, Maryland, Missouri, New York, Ohio, Pennsylvania, West Virginia. Type V includes Delaware, New Jersey, Connecticut, Rhode Island. All eleven underdemocratized states were ruled by Democratic regimes: Alabama, Arkansas, Florida, Georgia, Louisiana, Mississippi, North Carolina, South Carolina, Tennessee, Texas, Virginia.

51. These analyses take the form of "most similar systems" comparisons. Przeworski and Teune, *Logic of Comparative Social Inquiry*.

52. For the best introduction to the basic, widely available primary sources for New Deal social policy, see the appendix in Berkowitz, *America's Welfare State*. As Berkowitz notes, students can go very far in studying New Deal social policy merely by examining such sources, including the *Report of the Committee on Economic Security* and congressional testimony.

CHAPTER TWO
AN INDIFFERENT COMMITMENT TO MODERN SOCIAL POLICY, 1880–1934

1. The sources of epigraph quotations are as follows: Blanche D. Coll, *Safety Net: Welfare and Social Security, 1929–1979* (New Brunswick, N.J.: Rutgers University Press, 1995), p. 3; Arthur M. Schlesinger, Jr., *The Age of Roosevelt: The Crisis of the Old Order, 1919–1933* (Boston: Houghton Mifflin, 1957), p. 232; "The Essentials of Unemployment Relief" (March 21, 1933), in *The Public Papers and Addresses of Franklin D. Roosevelt*, ed. Samuel I. Rosenman, 13 vols. (New York: Random House, 1938–50), 2:80. "A Call to War Veterans to Rally to the Colors in a Peacetime Sacrifice" (October 2, 1933), ibid., p. 376.

2. A number of excellent and trend-setting studies have pursued that narrative line, beginning with classics published in the 1940s. See, for instance, Grace Abbott,

From Relief to Social Security (Chicago: University of Chicago Press, 1966 [originally published in 1941]); Lewis Merriam, *Relief and Social Security* (Washington, D.C.: The Brookings Institution, 1946); Roy Lubove, *The Struggle For Social Security, 1900–1935* (Pittsburgh: University of Pittsburgh Press, 1968); Gaston Rimlinger, *Welfare Policy and Industrialization in Europe, America, and Russia* (New York: Wiley, 1971). For a recent evaluation of Progressive Era welfare and civil rights policy, see Eileen L. McDonagh, "The 'Welfare Rights State' and the 'Civil Rights State': Policy Paradox and State Building in the Progressive Era," *Studies in American Political Development* 7 (1993): 225–74.

3. Theda Skocpol, *Protecting Soldiers and Mothers: The Political Origins of Social Policy in the United States* (Cambridge, Mass.: Harvard University Press, 1992); Ann Shola Orloff, *The Politics of Pensions: A Comparative Analysis of Britain, Canada, and the United States, 1880–1940* (Madison: University of Wisconsin Press, 1993).

4. For one prominent exception, see Michael B. Katz, *In the Shadow of the Poorhouse: A Social History of Welfare in America* (New York: Basic Books, 1986), pp. 218–23.

5. Walter Dean Burnham, *Critical Elections and the Mainsprings of American Politics* (New York: Norton, 1970).

6. On Civil War pensions, see Skocpol, *Protecting Soldiers and Mothers*, chap. 2. See also J. W. Oliver, "History of Civil War Military Pensions, 1861–1885," *Bulletin of the University of Wisconsin,* no. 844 (1917), History Series, no. 1; W. H. Glasson, *Federal Military Pensions in the United States* (New York: Oxford University Press, 1918); Heywood Sanders, "'Paying for the 'Bloody Shirt': The Politics of Civil War Pensions," in *Political Benefits*, ed. Barry Rundquist (Lexington, Mass.: D. C. Heath, 1980), pp.137–60.

7. U.S. Bureau of the Census, *Historical Statistics of the United States from Colonial Times to 1970* (Washington, D.C.: U.S. Government Printing Office, 1975), series F 1–5, Y 352–57, Y 998–1009, pp. 224, 1106, 1149. Pensions peaked at 1.14 percent of GNP in 1893 and 1894.

8. See Skocpol, *Protecting Soldiers and Mothers*, p. 134.

9. Bureau of the Census, *Historical Statistics*, series Y 308–317, p. 1103; Amy Bridges, *A City in the Republic: Antebellum New York and the Origins of Machine Politics* (New York: Cambridge University Press, 1984); Morton Keller, *Affairs of State: Public Life in Late Nineteenth-Century America* (Cambridge, Mass.: Harvard University Press, 1977); Leonard White, *The Republican Era, 1869–1901: A Study in Administrative History* (New York: Macmillan, 1958); Alexander Keyssar, *Out of Work: The First Century of Unemployment in Massachusetts* (New York: Cambridge University Press, 1986).

10. Keller, *Affairs of State*, p. 307.

11. This was true even before the economic crisis of the late nineteenth century, when many other countries turned to protection. Peter Gourevitch, *Politics in Hard Times: Comparative Responses to International Economic Crises* (Ithaca, N.Y.: Cornell University Press, 1986).

12. American tariffs were not negotiated, however, by representatives of organized capital and labor, as they were in Australia. Francis G. Castles, *The Working Class and Welfare: Reflections on the Political Development of the Welfare State in Australia and New Zealand, 1890–1980* (Wellington: Allen & Unwin, 1985).

13. Bureau of the Census, *Historical Statistics*, series F1, Y338, pp. 224, 1104.

14. Robert Sharkey, *Money, Class, and Party: An Economic Study of Civil War and Reconstruction* (Baltimore: Johns Hopkins University Press, 1959); Irwin Unger, *The Greenback Era: A Social and Political History of American Finance, 1865–1879* (Princeton, N.J.: Princeton University Press, 1964).

15. For the Republicans' claim to protection, see their national party platforms of 1884, 1888, and 1892. In 1888 they explicitly denounced the tariff reductions of the Cleveland Administration and declared themselves "uncompromisingly in favor of the American system of protection." Kirk H. Porter and Donald Bruce Johnson, comps., *National Party Platforms, 1840–1968* (Urbana: University of Illinois Press, 1970), pp. 73, 80, 93.

16. For the political compromises and deals behind the customs tariffs and pensions, see Richard Franklin Bensel, *Sectionalism and American Political Development, 1880–1980* (Madison: University of Wisconsin Press, 1984). The following discussion is based on Festus P. Summers, *William J. Wilson and Tariff Reform* (New Brunswick, N.J.: Rutgers University Press, 1953); Sidney Ratner, *The Tariff in American History* (New York: Van Nostrand, 1973); Tom E. Terill, *The Tariff, Politics, and American Foreign Policy, 1874–1901* (Westport, Conn.: Greenwood Press, 1973); S. Walter Poulshock, "Pennsylvania and the Politics of the Tariff, 1880–1888," *Pennsylvania History* 29 (July 1962): 291–305; D. J. Rothman, *Politics and Power: The United States Senate, 1869–1901* (Cambridge, Mass.: Harvard University Press, 1966), chap. 3; Frank W. Taussig, *The Tariff History of the United States* (New York: Putnam, 1905).

17. On the income tax, see Sidney Ratner, *Taxation and Democracy in America* (New York: Norton, 1943); Roy G. Blakey and Gladys Blakey, *The Federal Income Tax* (New York: Longmans, Green, 1940).

18. Mary Dearing, *Veterans in Politics: The Story of the G.A.R.* (Baton Rouge: Louisiana State University Press, 1952).

19. Stephen Skowronek, *Building a New American State* (Cambridge: Cambridge University Press, 1982).

20. Martin Shefter, "Party and Patronage: Germany, Italy, and England," *Politics and Society* 7 (1977): 404–51.

21. On the American party systems, see Burnham, *Critical Elections*. On the settings of other party systems, see Seymour M. Lipset and Stein Rokkan, "Cleavage Structures, Party Systems, and Voter Alignments," in *Party Systems and Voter Alignments*, ed. Seymour M. Lipset and Stein Rokkan (New York: The Free Press, 1967), pp. 1–66.

22. On the fiscal differentiation of the parties, see Bensel, *Sectionalism and American Political Development*. On the divisions of parties along ethnic lines, see Paul Kleppner, *The Third Electoral System, 1853–1892* (Chapel Hill: University of North Carolina Press, 1979). Southern Democrats also tended to support temperance and later Prohibition.

23. Richard C. McCormick, *The Party Period and Public Policy: American Politics From the Age of Jackson to the Progressive Era* (New York: Oxford University Press, 1986). Paul Kleppner, *Continuity and Change in Electoral Politics, 1893–1928* (New York: Greenwood Press, 1987), p. 43.

24. Ira Katznelson, *City Trenches: Urban Politics and the Patterning of Class in the United States* (New York: Pantheon, 1981); Richard Oestreicher, "Urban Working-Class Political Behavior and Theories of American Electoral Politics, 1870–1940," *Journal of American History* 74 (1988): 1257–86. Vogel, "Why Business-

men Distrust Their State: The Political Consciousness of American Corporate Executives," *British Journal of Political Science* 8 (1978): 45–78; Paula Baker, "The Domestication of Politics: Women and American Political Society, 1780–1920," *American Historical Review* 89 (1984): 620–47; Martin Shefter, "Trade Unions and Political Machines: The Organization and Disorganization of the American Working Class in the Late Nineteenth Century," in *Working-Class Formation: Nineteenth-Century Patterns in Western Europe and the United States*, ed. Ira Katznelson and Aristide Zolberg (Princeton, N.J.: Princeton University Press, 1986), pp. 197–278.

25. Martin J. Schiesl, *The Politics of Efficiency: Municipal Administration and Reform in America, 1880–1920* (Berkeley: University of California Press, 1977); Martin Shefter, "Regional Receptivity to Reform: the Legacy of the Progressive Era," *Political Science Quarterly* 98 (1983): 459–83. Martin Sklar, *The Corporate Reconstruction of American Capitalism: The Market, the Law, and Politics* (New York: Cambridge University Press, 1988); Burnham, *The Mainsprings of Modern Politics*; Keller, *Affairs of State*; McDonagh, "State Building in the Progressive Era."

26. William P. Dillingham, *Federal Aid to Veterans, 1917–1941* (Gainesville: University of Florida Press, 1952), chap. 5; Davis R. B. Ross, *Preparing For Ulysses: Politics and Veterans During World War II* (New York: Columbia University Press, 1969), chap. 1; Orloff, *The Politics of Pensions*, chap. 7.

27. Bureau of the Census, *Historical Statistics*, series Y 308–11, p. 1102.

28. See Blakey and Blakey, *The Federal Income Tax*; John F. Witte, *The Politics and Development of the Federal Income Tax* (Madison: University of Wisconsin Press, 1984), chaps. 4, 5.

29. See Skocpol, *Protecting Soldiers and Mothers*; Jill S. Quadagno, *The Transformation of Old-Age Security: Class and Politics in the American Welfare State* (Chicago: University of Chicago Press, 1988); Philip Taft, *Labor Politics, American Style: The California State Federation of Labor* (Cambridge, Mass.: Harvard University Press, 1968); Morton Keller, *Regulating a New Society: Public Policy and Social Change in America, 1900–1933* (Cambridge, Mass.: Harvard University Press, 1994), chap. 6.

30. On Illinois, see Sophonisba P. Breckinridge, *The Illinois Poor Law and its Administration* (Chicago: University of Chicago Press, 1939), chap. 3; William R. Brock, *Welfare, Democracy and the New Deal* (Cambridge: Cambridge University Press, 1988), chap. 2.

31. These problems were somewhat mitigated by private charitable organizations, which aided those they deemed the most deserving. In larger cities, ethnic societies performed charitable functions. Joanna C. Colcord, *Cash Relief* (New York: Russell Sage, 1936), introduction, part I; Katz, *In the Shadow of the Poorhouse*, chaps. 1, 2, 4, quote from p. 293; Viviana A. Rotman Zelizer, *The Social Meaning of Money* (New York: Basic Books, 1994), chaps. 4–5. Brock, *Welfare, Democracy, and the New Deal*, chap. 2.

32. Abbott, *From Relief to Social Security*; Mark H. Leff, "Consensus for Reform: The Mothers' Pension Movement in the Progressive Era," *Social Service Review* 47 (1973): 397–417; Ann Shola Orloff, "Gender in Early U.S. Social Policy," *Journal of Policy History* 3 (1991): 249–81; Skocpol, *Protecting Soldiers and Mothers*, chap. 8; Christopher Howard, "Sowing the Seeds of 'Welfare': The Transformation of Mothers' Pensions, 1900–1940," *Journal of Policy History* 4 (1992): 188–227; Linda Gordon, *Pitied But Not Entitled: Single Mothers and the History of Welfare, 1890–1935* (New York: Free Press, 1994), chap. 3.

33. Elizabeth Brandeis, "Labor Legislation," in *History of Labor in the United States, 1896–1932*, ed. John R. Commons, vol. 3 (New York: Macmillan, 1935), pp. 399–700.

34. Brandeis, "Labor Legislation"; Walter F. Dodd, *Administration of Workmen's Compensation* (New York: The Commonwealth Fund, 1936); Robert Asher, "Workmen's Compensation in the United States, 1880–1935" (Ph.D. diss., University of Minnesota, 1971); Edward D. Berkowitz, *Disabled Policy: America's Programs for the Handicapped* (New York: Cambridge University Press, 1987), chap. 1.

35. Berkowitz, *Disabled Policy*, chap. 5.

36. Brandeis, "Labor Legislation"; James Leiby, *A History of Social Welfare and Social Work in the United States* (New York: Columbia University Press, 1978), chap. 11; Skocpol, *Protecting Solders and Mothers*, chap. 5. On health insurance, see Paul Starr, *The Social Transformation of American Medicine* (New York: Basic Books, 1982), pp. 235–66. On old-age pensions, see Orloff, *The Politics of Pensions*, chap. 7. On unemployment insurance, see Daniel Nelson, *Unemployment Insurance: The American Experience, 1915–1935* (Madison: University of Wisconsin Press, 1969), chap. 6. On Departments of Welfare, see Howard W. Odum, "Public Welfare Activities," in President's Committee on Social Trends, *Recent Social Trends in the United States* (New York: McGraw-Hill, 1933), chap. 24.

37. Derek Fraser, *The Evolution of the British Welfare State: A History of Social Policy Since the Industrial Revolution* (London: Macmillan, 1984), chap. 8; Bentley B. Gilbert, *British Social Policy, 1914–1939* (Ithaca, N.Y.: Cornell University Press, 1970); Hugh Heclo, *Modern Social Politics in Britain and Sweden* (New Haven, Conn.: Yale University Press, 1974); Orloff, *The Politics of Pensions*, chap. 6; Peter Flora, Jens Alber, Richard Eichenberg, Jurgen Kohl, Franz Kraus, Winfried Pfenning, and Kurt Seebohm, *State, Economy, and Society in Western Europe 1815–1975: The Growth of Mass Democracies and Welfare States* (Chicago: St. James, 1983), pp. 442, 446.

38. Bureau of the Census, *Historical Statistics*, series F 1–5, H 32–47, Y 998–1009, pp. 224, 341, 1149. Specifically, U.S. social spending constituted 0.47 percent of GNP in fiscal 1929 and veterans' benefits 0.42 percent. Social spending is taken from columns 33, 34, 39, 41, 42, 47 of the "H" series, including "social insurance," "public aid," and "other social welfare." See also Odum, "Public Welfare," p. 1258. The quote is from Keller, *Regulating a New Society*, p. 215.

39. Paul Kleppner, *Who Voted? The Dynamics of Electoral Turnout, 1870–1980* (New York: Praeger, 1982), chap. 4. See Burnham's explanatory note, Bureau of the Census, *Historical Statistics*, pp. 1067–69, series Y 27–78, pp. 1071–72. Among the potentially eligible he includes those allowed to vote under national or state law according to age group, race, sex, and citizenship status.

40. J. Morgan Kousser, *The Shaping of Southern Politics: Suffrage Restriction and the Establishment of the One-Party South, 1880–1910* (New Haven, Conn.: Yale University Press, 1974), especially pp. 45–46 on the role of amendments to the Constitution. Another key means of restriction was the white primary—important because the Democratic party dominated in most parts of the South to the point where the Republicans were powerless. As Kousser points out, Populists sometimes acquiesced in restrictions like the white primary, as they feared that Democrats in the Black Belt would steal votes. See also V. O. Key, *Southern Politics in State and Nation* (New York: Knopf, 1949), chaps. 25–28. Percentages calculated from Bu-

reau of the Census, *Historical Statistics*, series Y 27–78, pp. 1071–72. States had the right to make decisions about their electorates, so long as they did not contradict the Constitution as interpreted by the Supreme Court.

41. Kleppner, *Who Voted?*, chap. 4. Because women voted in approximately the same fashion that men did in the earliest elections, politicians also did not feel the need to appeal specifically to women.

42. See Skocpol, *Protecting Soldiers and Mothers*, especially chap. 5, on the divisions among Progressives. See also Orloff, *The Politics of Pensions*, pp. 233–39.

43. See Kleppner, *Continuity and Change*, chap. 5.

44. Bureau of the Census, *Historical Statistics*, series F 1–5,Y 352–357, pp. 224, 1106. Although it no longer brought in much revenue, tariff protection continued to be a central economic policy. Tariffs were reasserted in 1922 with the Fordney-McCumber Tariff Act. Ratner, *The Tariff in American History*, chap. 3. The last hurrah of tariff protection was the 1930 Hawley-Smoot Tariff Act, an agricultural relief measure that was amended to please the gamut of industrial interests. E. E. Schattschneider, *Politics, Pressures, Tariffs* (Hamden, Conn.: Archon Books, 1963).

45. Glasson, *Federal Military Pensions*. Orloff, *The Politics of Pensions*, pp. 275–80.

46. Bureau of the Census, *Historical Statistics*, series Y 352–357, 358–373, pp. 1106–7.

47. Kristi Andersen, *The Creation of a Democratic Majority, 1928–1936* (Chicago: University of Chicago Press, 1979).

48. On the economic policies of Hoover, see Albert U. Romasco, *The Poverty of Abundance: Hoover, the Nation, and the Depression* (New York: Oxford University Press, 1965), chaps. 2, 3.

49. For a discussion of the Hoover Administration's approach to relief, see Harry L. Hopkins, *Spending to Save: The Complete Story of Relief* (New York: Norton, 1936), chap. 2; Josephine Chapin Brown, *Public Relief, 1929–1939* (New York: Holt, 1940), chaps. 3–6; Merriam, *Relief and Social Security*, chap. 1; Irving Bernstein, *A History of the American Worker, 1920–1933: The Lean Years* (Boston: Houghton Mifflin, 1960), chaps. 7, 14; Romasco, *The Poverty of Abundance*, chap. 8. Jordan A. Schwarz, *The Interregnum of Despair: Hoover, Congress, and the Depression* (Urbana: University of Illinois Press, 1970), chap. 2; Bonnie Fox Schwartz, *The Civil Works Administration, 1933–34* (Princeton, N.J.: Princeton University Press, 1984), pp. 15–22; Brock, *Welfare, Democracy, and the New Deal*, chap. 3. See also Stephen Skowronek, *The Politics Presidents Make: Leadership from John Adams to George Bush* (Cambridge, Mass.: Harvard University Press, 1993), pp. 260–87.

50. Hopkins replaced Jesse I. Straus, president of R. H. Macy & Co. Brock, *Welfare, Democracy, and the New Deal*, pp. 84–104; Brown, *Public Relief*, pp. 89–95. On Hopkins, see Robert E. Sherwood, *Roosevelt and Hopkins: An Intimate History* (New York: Harper, 1942), chaps. 1, 2; George McJimsey, *Harry Hopkins: Ally of the Poor and Defender of Democracy* (Cambridge, Mass.: Harvard University Press, 1987), chaps. 2, 3. For a brief discussion of state and local finances, see Henry J. Bitterman, *State and Federal Grants-In-Aid* (New York: Mentzer, Bush, 1938), p. 149. U.S. Federal Works Agency, *Final Statistical Report of the Federal Emergency Relief Administration* (Washington, D.C.: U.S. Government Printing Office, 1942).

51. U.S. Children's Bureau, *Mothers' Aid, 1931*, Children's Bureau publication no. 220 (Washington, D.C.: U.S. Government Printing Office, 1933); U.S. Committee on Economic Security, *Social Security in America: The Factual Background of the Social Security Act as Summarized From Staff Reports to the Committee on Economic Security* (Washington, D.C.: U.S. Government Printing Office, 1937), p. 245.

52. Orloff, *The Politics of Pensions*, pp. 280–83. Quadagno, *The Transformation of Old-Age Security*.

53. Committee on Economic Security, *Social Security in America*, pp. 156–67.

54. Hopkins, *Spending to Save*, chap. 3; Schwartz, *The Interregnum of Despair*, chap. 2; Brock, *Welfare, Democracy, and the New Deal*, chap. 4; Udo Sautter, *Three Cheers for the Unemployed: Government and Unemployment Before the New Deal* (Cambridge: Cambridge University Press, 1991), pp. 305–13.

55. Schwarz, *Interregnum of Despair*, chap. 6; Brock, *Welfare, Democracy, and the New Deal*, chap. 4; Sautter, *Three Cheers for the Unemployed*, pp. 305–13. Almost all of the advances were canceled and the loans forgiven during legislation passed in 1934 and 1938, and thus they were converted into grants. Hoover also vetoed a bill sponsored by Wagner to revamp the United States Employment Service.

56. Roger Daniels, *The Bonus March: An Episode of the Great Depression* (Westport, Conn.: Greenwood Press, 1971), p. 40, chaps. 4–8; Bernstein, *The Lean Years*, chap. 13.

57. Herbert Stein, *The Fiscal Revolution in America* (Chicago: University of Chicago Press, 1969), chap. 1; Witte, *The Federal Income Tax*, chap. 5; Schwarz, *The Interregnum of Despair*, chap. 5.

58. For discussions of the NRA, see Ellis Hawley, *The New Deal and The Problem of Monopoly* (Princeton, N.J.: Princeton University Press, 1966); Albert U. Romasco, *The Politics of Recovery: Roosevelt's New Deal*, (New York: Oxford University Press, 1983). For a discussion of the politics of the NRA codes, see Theda Skocpol, "Political Response to Capitalist Crisis: Neo-Marxist Theories of the State and the Case of the New Deal," *Politics and Society* 10 (1980): 155–201; Kenneth Finegold and Theda Skocpol, *State and Party in America's New Deal* (Madison: University of Wisconsin Press, 1995), chap. 3; Skowronek, *The Politics Presidents Make*, pp. 288–313.

59. For the quote, see Arthur M. Schlesinger, Jr., *The Age of Roosevelt: The Coming of the New Deal* (Boston: Houghton Mifflin, 1958), p. 12. On the impact of the Economy Act, see Dillingham, *Federal Aid to Veterans*; Ross, *Preparing For Ulysses*, pp. 25–33; Daniels, *The Bonus March*, p. 227. The number of veterans receiving disability benefits dropped from about 1 million in 1933 to 580,000 in 1934. For statistics on veterans' pensions, see Bureau of the Census, *Historical Statistics*, series Y 984–97, 998–1009, pp. 1147–50.

60. Nelson, *Unemployment Insurance*, p. 198. See also J. Joseph Huthmacher, *Senator Robert F. Wagner and the Rise of Urban Liberalism* (New York: Atheneum, 1968), chap. 6; Bernstein, *The Lean Years*, pp. 267–86; Schwarz, *Interregnum of Despair*, chap. 2. For a discussion of the first incarnation of the USES, see Sautter, *Three Cheers for the Unemployed*, chap. 3, pp. 154–80. For a social-scientific treatment of U.S. employment services and benefits, see Desmond King, *Actively Seeking Work? The Politics of Unemployment and Welfare Policy in the United States and Great Britain* (Chicago: University of Chicago Press, 1995).

61. For the legislation funding the Federal Emergency Relief Administration, see Federal Works Agency, *Final Statistical Report of the FERA*, pp. 99–104. For the chronology of events, see Doris Carothers, *Chronology of the Federal Emergency Relief Administration: May 12, 1933 to December 31, 1935*, Research Monograph VI (Washington, D.C.: U.S. Government Printing Office, 1937). For other discussions, see Brown, *Public Relief*, chaps. 8–12; Edward Ainsworth Williams, *Federal Aid for Relief* (New York: Columbia University Press, 1939); Searle F. Charles, *Minister of Relief: Harry Hopkins and the Depression* (Syracuse, N.Y.: Syracuse University Press, 1963), chap. 2; McJimsey, *Harry Hopkins*, chap. 4; Brock, *Welfare, Democracy and the New Deal*, pp. 162–73. Many states, including most of the former Confederacy, provided little funding of their own for FERA aid. See discussion in Brown, *Public Relief*, p. 205.

62. John A. Salmond, *The Civilian Conservation Corps, 1933–1942: A New Deal Case Study* (Durham, N.C.: Duke University Press, 1967), chaps. 1, 2.

63. Carothers, *Chronology of the FERA*, chap. 2; Bonnie Fox Schwartz, *The Civil Works Administration, 1933–34: The Business of Emergency Employment in the New Deal* (Princeton, N.J.: Princeton University Press, 1984), chaps. 2–5. Veterans were given preference, and the jobs included health benefits. On the wage rates of the CWA, see "Statement of Corrington Gill, Assistant Federal Emergency Relief Administrator," U.S. House of Representatives, Committee on Appropriations, *Supplemental Hearings, Emergency Relief Appropriation* (Washington, D.C.: U.S. Government Printing Office, 1935), February 11, 1935, pp. 1–26.

64. Schwartz, *The Civil Works Administration*, chap. 2.

65. Ibid., chaps. 6–7. E. Wight Bakke, *The Unemployed Worker: A Study of the Task of Making a Living Without a Job* (New York: Archon Books, 1969 [originally published 1940]), chaps. 12–13.

66. For the changes in the types of aid and the number of cases, see Federal Works Agency, *Final Statistical Report of the FERA*, chap. 3. In May 1934, the modal urban person on relief was a white man, a head of household, thirty-eight years of age, who had ten years of experience in his usual occupation, but who had not worked in it regularly since the winter of 1931–32. Gladys L. Palmer and Katherine D. Wood, *Urban Workers on Relief*, WPA Research Monograph IV (New York: Da Capo, 1971 [originally published, 1936]), pp xxiii–xxiv.

67. The FERA also aided many of those, like destitute farmers, who needed help, but would not typically be looking for wage employment. On ADC, see committee on Economic Security, *Social Security in America*, chapter 13. See also Nancy K. Cauthen and Edwin Amenta, "Not for Widows Only: Institutional Politics and the Formative Years of Aid to Dependent Children," *American Sociological Review* 61 (1996): 431. In their study of relief in seventy-nine cities, Palmer and Wood found that more than 20 percent of relief families were headed by females and that 14 percent of those on relief were family heads without work experience: *Urban Workers on Relief*, Pt. 2, pp. 76, 84.

68. Stein, *The Fiscal Revolution*, chap. 4; Mark H. Leff, *The Limits of Symbolic Reform: The New Deal and Taxation, 1933–1939* (Cambridge: Cambridge University Press, 1984), p. 111. Similarly, New Deal agricultural policy combined payments with a processing tax.

69. On Hopkins's efforts to get state officials to pay their fair share of relief expenses, see Brock, *Welfare, Democracy, and the New Deal*, chap. 6. See also David J. Maurer, "Relief Problems and Politics in Ohio," in *The New Deal: The*

State and Local Levels, ed. John Braeman, Robert H. Bremner, and David Brody (Columbus: Ohio State University Press, 1975), pp. 77–102. For state-level taxation efforts, see Susan B. Hansen, *The Politics of Taxation: Revenue Without Representation* (New York: Praeger, 1983), chap. 5.

CHAPTER THREE
AMERICA'S FIRST WELFARE REFORM, 1935–1936

1. The sources of epigraph quotations are as follows: Robert E. Sherwood, *Roosevelt and Hopkins: An Intimate History* (New York: Harper and Brothers, 1948), p. 65 (supposedly Hopkins said this to Aubrey Williams); Franklin D. Roosevelt, "Annual Message to the Congress, January 4, 1935," in *The Public Papers and Addresses of Franklin D. Roosevelt*, ed. Samuel I. Rosenman, 13 vols. (New York: Random House, 1938–50), 4:19–20; U.S. Committee on Economic Security, *Report to the President* (Washington, D.C.: U.S. Government Printing Office, 1935), p. 9; Edith Abbott, "Don't Do It Mr. Hopkins!" *The Nation*, January, 9, 1935, pp. 41–42 (see also Lela B. Costin, *Two Sisters for Social Justice: A Biography of Grace and Edith Abbott* [Urbana: University of Illinois Press, 1983], pp. 219–21).

2. The classic accounts of this key period of reform have not been surpassed. See, for instance, James MacGregor Burns, *Roosevelt: The Lion and the Fox* (New York: Harcourt, Brace and World, 1956), chaps. 11–12; Arthur M. Schlesinger, Jr., *The Politics of Upheaval* (Boston: Houghton Mifflin, 1960), chaps. 21–22; William E. Leuchtenburg, *Franklin D. Roosevelt and the New Deal* (New York: Harper and Row, 1963), chap. 7. The U.S. old-age insurance program was initially called Federal Old-Age Benefits, but I use the former terminology for consistency's sake.

3. The accounts of contemporary participants most often relied upon are Edwin Witte, *The Development of the Social Security Act: A Memorandum on the History of the Committee on Economic Security and Drafting and Legislative History of the Social Security Act* (Madison: University of Wisconsin Press, 1962). Frances Perkins, *The Roosevelt I Knew* (New York: Harper and Row, 1946), chap. 23; Arthur Altmeyer, *The Formative Years of Social Security* (Madison: University of Wisconsin Press, 1966), chaps. 1–2; J. Douglas Brown, *An American Philosophy of Social Security: Evolution and Issues* (Princeton, N.J.: Princeton University Press, 1972), chap. 1. A study of the implementation of the act is Charles McKinley and Robert W. Frase, *Launching Social Security* (Madison: University of Wisconsin Press, 1970). A number of scholarly efforts examining social science arguments have been devoted to this issue, some of the more notable including Edward Berkowitz and Kim McQuaid, *Creating the Welfare State: The Political Economy of Twentieth Century Reform*, 2d ed. (New York: Praeger, 1989), chap. 6; Theda Skocpol and G. John Ikenberry, "The Political Formation of the American Welfare State in Historical and Comparative Perspective," *Comparative Social Research* 6 (1983): 87–148; Jill S. Quadagno, "Welfare Capitalism and the Social Security Act of 1935," *American Sociological Review* 49 (1984): 632–47; Ann Shola Orloff, "The Political Origins of America's Belated Welfare State," in *The Politics of Social Policy in the United States* ed. Margaret Weir, Ann Shola Orloff, and Theda Skocpol (Princeton, N.J.: Princeton University Press, 1988), pp. 37–80. Edward D. Berkowitz, *America's Welfare State: From Roosevelt to Reagan* (Baltimore: Johns Hopkins University Press, 1991), chap. 1; Blanche D. Coll, *Safety Net: Welfare and Social Security, 1929–1979* (New Brunswick, N.J.: Rutgers University Press, 1995), chap. 2.

4. "Message to Congress Reviewing the Broad Objectives and Accomplishments of the Administration" (June 8, 1934), Rosenman, *Roosevelt Public Papers*, 3: 287–93.

5. See Witte, *The Development of the Social Security Act*, pp. 9–10.

6. Committee on Economic Security, *Report to the President*, p. 9. The Holy Trinity of principal accounts—Witte, Perkins, and Altmeyer—do not discuss the work program very much, partly because the program was removed from the deliberations of the CES, much to the chagrin of Witte, and was never under the control of the Social Security Board. Also, all three were proponents of social insurance and do not discuss much the relief nature of New Deal social policy. Witte's account is the only one that is not retrospective and thus has the most credibility for the parts of the program he was overseeing. Perkins, though, the chair of the committee, vied for power over it with Hopkins, the federal emergency relief administrator and the de facto leader of U.S. social policy, with whom Perkins frequently disagreed. Hopkins's *Spending to Save: The Complete Story of Relief* (New York: Norton, 1936) is not his account of what happened, but a mass-market book hoping to turn public opinion in favor of a generous work program during the 1936 election year. In it he indicates that the work program was permanent to his way of thinking and the centerpiece of New Deal social policy. For a discussion of Hopkins's views, see George McJimsey, *Harry Hopkins: Ally of the Poor and Defender of Democracy* (Cambridge, Mass.: Harvard University Press, 1987), chap. 6, especially pp. 95–97. As late as December 24, 1934, Roosevelt wanted to combine the legislation for the work program and other economic security in one bill. Arthur W. Macmahon, John D. Millett, and Gladys Ogden, *The Administration of Federal Work Relief* (Chicago: Public Administration Service, 1941), pp. 26–27; Witte, *The Development of the Social Security Act*, p. 77. Altmeyer suggests that Roosevelt initially saw unemployment insurance and work relief as a combination, with those running out of insurance benefits to immediately gain work relief, *The Formative Years of Social Security*, pp. 12–13. Perhaps the most reliable general account of the entire decade of reform, focusing on relief aspects, is by the FERA's Josephine Chapin Brown, *Public Relief, 1929–1939* (New York: Holt, 1940).

7. The "dole" was a common term for the "uncovenanted" or transitional unemployment insurance benefits that aided the unemployed in Britain during the 1920s. In that country, unemployment insurance had been stretched beyond its original functions to aid those people who had already received the maximum amount of payments, but who were "genuinely seeking work." By 1931 these transitional benefits were cut back and a means test was applied to applicants for them. See, for instance, Derek Fraser, *The Evolution of the British Welfare State: A History of Social Policy since the Industrial Revolution*, 2d ed. (London: Macmillan, 1984), chap. 8; Corrington Gill, *Wasted Manpower: The Challenge of Unemployment* (New York: Norton, 1939), pp. 233–37.

8. That was the case even though the FERA was already administering work-relief projects and would continue to do so. Admitting that, though, would have made the president's works program seem not so new. Macmahon et al., *Federal Work Relief*, chap. 1.

9. Ickes's Advisory Committee on Allotments (ACA) included various people inside and outside the government and was to recommend projects to the president. Frank Walker was in charge of the Division of Applications and Information (DAI),

which was to gather suggested plans for work projects. In July, the WPA was granted the authority to fund projects of $25,000 or less, and the ACA and DAI were eliminated in September. See "Three White House Statements Outlining the Machinery for Handling the Four-Billion Dollar Works Relief Appropriation" (April 23, 25, 26, 1935), "The Creation of the Machinery for the Works Progress Administration: Executive Order No. 7034" (May 6, 1935), and "White House Release of Presidential Statement Fixing Respective Jurisdictions of PWA and WPA" (July 3, 1935); Rosenman, *Roosevelt Public Papers*, 4:126–29, 163–68, 291–94; Donald S. Howard, *The WPA and Relief Policy* (New York: Sage, 1943), chap. 1; Macmahon et al., *Federal Work Relief*, chaps. 2–3; Sherwood, *Roosevelt and Hopkins*, pp. 65–71; McJimsey, *Harry Hopkins*, chaps. 5–6; Searle F. Charles, *Minister of Relief: Harry Hopkins and the Depression* (Syracuse, N.Y.: Syracuse University Press, 1963), chaps. 6–7; Anthony Badger, *The New Deal: The Depression Years* (New York: Hill and Wang, 1989), pp. 200–215. See also Harold Ickes, *The Secret Diary of Harold Ickes: The First One Thousand Days 1933–1936* (New York: Simon and Schuster, 1953), pp. 429–46.

10. Federal Works Agency, *Final Report*, pp. 23–26. For Roosevelt's vision of the program, see "Informal Extemporaneous Remarks to State Works Progress Administrators" (June 17, 1935), Rosenman, *Roosevelt Public Papers*, 4:260–64.

11. The wages were to vary according to place and type of employee. There were slight variations across four regions of the country and across county size to take into account cost of living and greater variations across the five skill categories of wage employees and between wage employees and supervisory employees. Federal Works Agency, *Final Report*, pp. 23–26, 37–41. On wages of WPA workers, see also Howard, *The WPA*, chap. 6. For a case study of someone bidding to receive WPA work, but not already on relief, see Grace Adams, *Workers on Relief* (New Haven, Conn.: Yale University Press, 1939), chap. 2. For the influence of organized labor on the upgrading of WPA wages, see McJimsey, *Harry Hopkins*, pp. 81–83.

12. The National Youth Administration, led by Aubrey Williams, was created by executive order. See "Presidential Statement on the Establishment of the National Youth Administration" and "The National Youth Administration Is Established, Executive Order No. 7086" (June 26, 1936), Rosenman, *Roosevelt Public Papers*, 4:281–87. On the CCC, see John A. Salmond, *The Civilian Conservation Corps, 1933–1942: A New Deal Case Study* (Durham, N.C.: Duke University Press, 1967), chap. 3.

13. In its first two years, Roosevelt was susceptible to pressure by fiscal conservatives such as the secretary of the treasury, Henry Morgenthau, and his own desire to appear to be closing the budget deficit. As a result, Roosevelt cut expenditures for the WPA in late 1936, in order to claim that he was making progress on balancing the budget. But the New Deal planners had no intention of ending work relief through the WPA and were able to induce the president to back them. John Morton Blum, *Roosevelt and Morgenthau* (Boston: Houghton Mifflin, 1972); Dean L. May, *From New Deal to New Economics: The American Liberal Response to the Recession of 1937* (New York: Garland, 1981). See also McJimsey, *Harry Hopkins*, chap. 6.

14. Hopkins published *Spending To Save*, which advocated permanent works programs, before the election. The 1936 Democratic party platform, which was written by Roosevelt, was explicit about public employment: "Where business fails to supply such employment, we believe that work at prevailing wages should be

provided. . . ." The Republicans and their allies in the print media made a big issue of the WPA. The party rejected work relief in its 1936 platform. Kirk H. Porter and Donald Bruce Johnson, comps., *National Party Platforms, 1840–1968* (Urbana: University of Illinois Press, 1970), pp. 360–63, 366; Sherwood, *Roosevelt and Hopkins*, pp. 81–86.

15. A copy of the Roosevelt Administration's bill, the "Economic Security Act," is appended to the Committee on Economic Security, *Report to the President.*

16. Title I is on pp. 1–3 of the Social Security Act, which is reprinted in Project on the Federal Social Role, *The Report of the Committee on Economic Security of 1935 and Other Basic Documents Relating to the Development of the Social Security Act* (Washington, D.C.: National Conference on Social Welfare, 1985), chap. 3 (hereafter Social Security Act). Paul Douglas, *Social Security in the United States* (New York: Whittlesey House, 1936); Witte, *The Development of the Social Security Act*, pp. 5–7.

17. Abraham Holtzman, *The Townsend Movement: A Political Study* (New York: Bookman, 1963); Edwin Amenta, Bruce G. Carruthers, and Yvonne Zylan, "A Hero For the Aged? The Townsend Movement, The Political Mediation Model, and U.S. Old-Age Policy, 1934–1950," *American Journal of Sociology* 98 (1992): 308–39.

18. Witte, *The Development of the Social Security Act*, pp. 144–45; Altmeyer, *The Formative Years*, p. 35. Even if this language had not been removed, it seems likely that states would have interpreted "reasonable" in the ways that they wanted. The alternative would have been for the national government to deny matching funds and thus harm its objective to aid the needy.

19. Altmeyer, *The Formative Years*, pp. 35–36.

20. For the OAA program in California, see Jackson K. Putnam, *Old-Age Politics in California: From Richardson to Reagan* (Stanford, Calif.: Stanford University Press, 1970).

21. The quote is from U.S. House of Representatives, Committee on Ways and Means, *Hearings on the Economic Security Act* (Washington, D.C.: U.S. Government Printing Office, 1935), p. 211. For a discussion of the debate surrounding this program, see Nancy K. Cauthen and Edwin Amenta, "Not for Widows Only: Institutional Politics and the Formative Years of Aid to Dependent Children," *American Sociological Review* 61 (1996): 427–48.

22. Title IV is on pp. 9–11 of the Social Security Act. See also Witte, *The Development of the Social Security Act*, pp. 163–64. The assignment of the program to the Social Security Board was despite the recommendations of the CES to assign it to the FERA and the hopes of Katharine Lenroot, the recently appointed chief of the Children's Bureau, who wanted the bureau to administer the program. For Lenroot's testimony, see U.S. Congress, Senate Committee on Finance, *Hearings on the Economic Security Act* (Washington, D.C.: U.S. Government Printing Office, 1935), pp. 342–43. The new legislation also allowed for the provision of benefits to a number of relatives other than a child's mother. The House report on the bill specified that states were free to impose eligibility requirements on ADC families on the basis of "moral character." As with OAA, each qualifying state had to comply with federal requirements for one main administrative agency. See Cauthen and Amenta, "Not for Widows Only."

23. See Macmahon et al., *Federal Work Relief*, p. 37; Brown, *Public Relief*, chap. 13.

24. For a discussion of these differences, see below, pp. 173–74.

25. Witte, *The Development of the Social Security Act*, pp. 124–25.

26. Daniel Nelson, *Unemployment Insurance: The American Experience, 1915–1935* (Madison: University of Wisconsin Press, 1969), chap. 8.

27. Although the CES did not explicitly endorse merit rating, it was not ruled out and was included in an amendment by Senator Robert La Follette, Jr., of Wisconsin. Altmeyer, *The Formative Years*, pp. 12–13, 40.

28. Robert P. Ingalls, *Herbert H. Lehman and New York's Little New Deal* (New York: New York University Press, 1975), p. 18. The Supreme Court opinions in *Stewart Machine Co. v. Davis* and *Helvering v. Davis* appear in Project on the Federal Social Role, *The Report of the Committee on Economic Security*, chap. 4. Both majority opinions were written by Justice Benjamin Cardozo.

29. For a description of initial legislation, see Bryce Stewart, *Planning and Administration of Unemployment Compensation in the United States* (New York: Industrial Relations Counselors, 1938); Edwin Amenta, Elisabeth S. Clemens, Jefren Olsen, Sunita Parikh, and Theda Skocpol. "The Political Origins of Unemployment Insurance in Five American States," *Studies in American Political Development* 2 (1987): 137–82.

30. At least this is what is suggested by the principal accounts. See Witte, *The Development of the Social Security Act*, pp. 102–4, 146–62. Altmeyer, *The Formative Years*, pp. 34–35.

31. For a discussion of this imagery, see Jerry R. Cates, *Insuring Inequality* (Ann Arbor: University of Michigan Press, 1983).

32. Titles II and VIII are on pp. 3–7, 19–22 of the Social Security Act. For the amendments by Congress, see Witte, *The Development of the Social Security Act*, pp. 146–62.

33. Mark H. Leff, *The Limits of Symbolic Reform: The New Deal and Taxation, 1933–1939* (Cambridge: Cambridge University Press), chap. 1, especially pp. 45–47. Taxing the less well off was also characteristic of the first New Deal.

34. Title VIII of the Social Security Act appears on pp. 19–22.

35. "A Message to the Congress on Tax Revision," (June 19, 1935), Rosenman, *Roosevelt Public Papers*, 4:270–77. For a discussion of the origins of the proposal, see Schlesinger Jr., *The Politics of Upheaval*, chap. 18. For a discussion of the impact of these taxes, see Leff, *The New Deal and Taxation*, chaps. 2–3. For the reaction of Long, see Alan Brinkley, *Voices of Protest: Huey Long, Father Coughlin and the Great Depression* (New York: Random House, 1982), p. 80.

36. On the role of Patman, see Roger Daniels, *The Bonus March: An Episode of the Great Depression* (Westport, Conn.: Greenwood Press, 1971), chap. 3. See also William P. Dillingham, *Federal Aid to Veterans, 1917–1941* (Gainesville: University of Florida Press, 1952). For Roosevelt's message, see "The President Vetoes the Bonus Bill" (May 22, 1935), Rosenman, *Roosevelt Public Papers*, 4:182–93. To pay for the veterans' bonuses in 1936, the administration sought a tax on undistributed business profits and won one as well as more fiscally substantial increases in corporation income taxes. These provided more revenue, $800 million per year, than the previous "soak-the-rich" taxes. Schlesinger Jr., *The Politics of Upheaval*, pp. 509–12; Leff, *The New Deal and Taxation*, pp. 169–85.

37. See Christopher Leman, "Patterns of Policy Development: Social Security in the United States and Canada," *Public Policy* 25 (1977): 261–91; Fred Block, "The Ruling Class Does Not Rule," *Socialist Revolution* 33 (1977): 6–28.

38. For comparisons among industrial countries, see Peter Gourevitch, *Politics in Hard Times: Comparative Responses to International Economic Crises* (Ithaca, N.Y.: Cornell University Press, 1986). For a comparison of the United States and Britain in the adoption of Keynesian deficit spending techniques, see Margaret Weir, "Ideas and Politics: The Acceptance of Keynesianism in Britain and the United States," in *The Political Power of Economic Ideas: Keynesianism Across Nations*, ed. Peter A. Hall, (Princeton, N.J.: Princeton University Press, 1989), pp. 53–86. On British social policy, see Fraser, *The British Welfare State*, chap. 8. For a comprehensive analysis of the adoption of core social insurance programs in seventeen industrial countries in the 1930s, see Alexander Hicks, "The Ascendence of Social Democracy," (paper presented at the Annual Meeting of the American Sociological Association, Washington, D.C., 1995).

39. See Lester V. Chandler, *America's Greatest Depression, 1929–1941* (New York: Harper & Row, 1970), p. 21.

40. For more on those programs, see chapter two, p. 131.

41. Many large corporations had sought to ensure worker loyalty by way of "welfare capitalist" benefit programs, including stock ownership programs and old-age annuities. Although these programs covered only a small proportion of the labor force, companies could and did drop them. For the argument about private pensions constituting alternatives to public ones, see Ann Shola Orloff, *The Politics of Pensions: A Comparative Analysis of Britain, Canada, and the United States, 1880–1940.* (Madison: University of Wisconsin Press, 1993), chap. 9. On welfare capitalism in the 1920s, see Stuart Brandes, *American Welfare Capitalism, 1880–1940* (Chicago: University of Chicago Press, 1976). For an analysis of welfare capitalist programs in the 1920s through the 1940s, see Frank Dobbin, "The Privatization of American Social Insurance: Organizations, Fringe Benefits, and the State, 1920–1950," *American Journal of Sociology* 97 (1992): 1416–50.

42. Witte also commissioned a number of studies and reports outside the auspices of these committees. For a listing of these studies, see U.S. Committee on Economic Security, *Social Security in America: The Factual Background of the Social Security Act as Summarized From Staff Reports to the Committee on Economic Security* (Washington, D.C.: U.S. Government Printing Office, 1937), appendices 13–15.

43. See Witte, *The Development of the Social Security Act*, p. 25, for a discussion of the organization of the committee. Witte wrote the "Preliminary Outline of the Work of the Staff on the Committee on Economic Security" on August 10. A day later he wrote a memo concerning the shape of the program he thought should form the committee's agenda. He also wrote the staff's initial recommendations for the social security program on September 26. These appear in the "Preliminary Report of the Staff of the Committee on Economic Security." Witte appended to his recommendations the early conclusions of the staff subcommittees, some of which disagreed with him. See National Archives (NA), Reports of the Committee on Economic Security, Record Group (RG) 47, Box 6, Preliminary Reports File 3. The Technical Board developed its own preliminary recommendations on October 1, with its final "preliminary" report dated October 9. See NA, RG 47, Box 1, File 1.

44. Witte, *The Development of the Social Security Act*, pp. 9–12. For an analysis of the problems of mothers' pensions, see U.S. Children's Bureau, "Mothers' Aid, 1931," Children's Bureau Publication no. 220 (Washington, D.C.: U.S. Government Printing Office, 1933).

45. For the breaking away of the "public employment and relief" group from the CES, see Witte, *The Development of the Social Security Act*, pp. 11, 31. For the early deliberations on the work program and a discussion of the FERA memos, see Macmahon et al., *Federal Work Relief*, pp. 25–28, 57. Baker's memos are at the Franklin D. Roosevelt (FDR) Library, Hopkins Papers, Container 49, "Mr. Jacob Baker's Memoranda on 'A National Work Program.' " Some memos important to the story of the creation of the WPA can be found in the National Archives, "Records of the Work Projects Administration," RG 69, Box 140. On Aubrey Williams, see John A. Salmond, "Aubrey Williams: Atypical New Dealer?" in *The New Deal: The National Level*, ed. John Braeman, Robert H. Bremner, and David Brody (Columbus: Ohio State University Press, 1975), pp. 218–45.

46. See Witte's "Possible General Approaches to the Problem of Economic Security" (August 16, 1934), NA, RG 47, Box 1, File 8. For the reports of the Committee on Public Employment and Relief, see NA, RG 47, Box 1, File 2. Ross's initial report, "Relief, Employment, and Retraining in Relation to Economic Security," is dated August 13, 1934, NA, RG 47, Box 21. For details on the backgrounds of various FERA staff members, see Coll, *Safety Net*, pp. 13–20.

47. Witte, *The Development of the Social Security Act*, pp. 32, 162.

48. On the activities of the Children's Bureau during the New Deal, see Susan Ware, *Beyond Suffrage: Women in the New Deal* (Cambridge, Mass.: Harvard University Press, 1981), pp. 97–101; Michael B. Katz, *In the Shadow of the Poorhouse: A Social History of Welfare in America* (New York: Basic Books, 1986), chap. 8; Linda Gordon, *Pitied But Not Entitled: Single Mothers and the History of Welfare* (New York: The Free Press, 1994), chap. 7.

49. There is a great deal of literature on the differences between the Wisconsin and Ohio plans. For some early statements in favor of the Ohio type of reform, see Isaac M. Rubinow, "The Movement toward Unemployment Insurance in Ohio," *Social Service Review* 7 (1933): 186–224. See also Abraham Epstein, *Insecurity: A Challenge to America* (New York: Agathon Press, 1968), originally published in 1938. For discussions of the Wisconsin style of reform, see Nelson, *Unemployment Insurance*, chap. 6. For a discussion of Wisconsin's program and Witte's role in it, see Theron F. Schlabach, *Edwin Witte: Cautious Reformer* (Madison: State Historical Society of Wisconsin, 1969), chap. 6. For discussions of both approaches, see Roy Lubove, *The Struggle For Social Security, 1900–1935* (Pittsburgh: University of Pittsburgh Press, 1968), chap. 7; Skocpol and Ikenberry, "The Political Formation of the American Welfare State in Historical and Comparative Perspective"; Amenta et al., "The Political Origins of Unemployment Insurance in Five American States." Witte was running the Wisconsin unemployment compensation program when he was called to Washington in July 1934.

50. Witte, *The Development of the Social Security Act*, p. 29.

51. For Armstrong's views, see Barbara N. Armstrong, *Insuring the Essentials: Minimum Wage, Plus Social Insurance—A Living Wage Problem* (New York: Macmillan, 1932). For an account from another participant, see Brown, *An American Philosophy of Social Security*, chap. 1.

52. Witte, *The Development of the Social Security Act*, p. 30.

53. Committee on Economic Security, *Report to the President*, p. 3.

54. Witte himself notes the constraints placed on his proposals by prior legislation, *The Development of the Social Security Act*, pp. 3–4; Quadagno, "Welfare Capitalism and the Social Security Act of 1935," p. 636.

55. Stewart, *Unemployment Compensation in the United States*, p. 27; Nelson, *Unemployment Insurance*, chap. 8; Amenta et al., "The Political Origins of Unemployment Insurance."

56. For the view that the constitutionality of the bill was key, see Perkins, *The Roosevelt I Knew*, pp. 286–87. For the view that expert disagreement was important, see Paul Douglas, *Social Security in the United States* (New York: Whittlesey House, 1936); Schlabach, *Cautious Reformer*, chap. 6. For the view that the presence of Wisconsin reformers was crucial, see Skocpol and Ikenberry, "The Political Formation of the American Welfare State in Historical and Comparative Perspective."

57. For flaws in workmen's compensation, see Armstrong, *Insuring the Essentials*, pp. 171–283. Aid to Dependent Children was based on grants for veterans' dependents, but in an oversight omitted funds for the caretaker.

58. For the argument that OAI was nationalized because it was unencumbered by state-level initiatives, see Skocpol and Ikenberry, "The Political Formation of the American Welfare State." For the early development of the OAI program, see Brown, *An American Philosophy of Social Security*, chap. 1; Berkowitz and McQuaid, *Creating the Welfare State*, pp. 119–21; Carolyn Weaver, *The Crisis in Social Security* (Durham, N.C.: Duke Press Policy Studies, 1982), chaps. 4–5.

59. Schlabach, *Cautious Reformer*, p. 146.

60. Witte, *The Development of the Social Security Act*, p. 102–4, 146–62; Altmeyer, *The Formative Years*, pp. 34–35.

61. Leah Hannah Feder, *Unemployment Relief in Periods of Depression: A Study of Measures Adopted in Certain American Cities, 1857–1922* (New York: Sage, 1936); Amy Bridges, *A City in the Republic: Antebellum New York and the Origins of Machine Politics* (New York: Cambridge University Press, 1986).

62. On the state and local work relief programs, see Edward Ainsworth Williams, *Federal Aid for Relief* (New York: Columbia University Press, 1939), chap. 1; Macmahon et al., *Federal Work Relief*. On the fiscal crises of the states, see Irving Bernstein, *A History of the American Worker, 1920–1933: The Lean Years* (Boston: Houghton Mifflin, 1960).

63. For characterizations of the partisan nature of U.S. political parties and those of other rich capitalist democracies, see Alexander Hicks and Joya Misra, "Political Resources and the Growth of Welfare Effort: The Case of Affluent Capitalist Democracies, 1960–1982," *American Journal of Sociology* 99 (1993): 668–710.

64. Udo Sautter, *Three Cheers for the Unemployed: Government and Unemployment Before the New Deal* (Cambridge: Cambridge University Press, 1991); U. S. Bureau of the Census, *Historical Statistics of the United States From Colonial Times to 1970* (Washington, D.C.: U.S. Government Printing Office, 1976), series Y 84–134, p. 1075.

65. Smith was their choice. See, for instance, Arthur M. Schlesinger, Jr., *The Age of Roosevelt: The Crisis of the Old Order, 1919–1933* (Boston: Houghton Mifflin, 1957), pp. 390–95; Kenneth S. Davis, *FDR: The New York Years, 1928–1933* (New York: Random House, 1979), chaps. 3, 8; Jordan A. Schwarz, *The Interregnum of Despair: Hoover, Congress, and the Depression* (Urbana: University of Illinois Press, 1970), chap. 7; William R. Brock, *Welfare, Democracy, and the New Deal* (Cambridge: Cambridge University Press, 1988), chap. 4; Hopkins, *Spending to Save*, chap. 3; Sautter, *Three Cheers for the Unemployed*, pp. 305–13.

66. Bureau of the Census, *Historical Statistics*, series Y 84–134, Y 135–186, pp. 1075, 1077.

67. See, for instance, Witte, *The Development of the Social Security Act*, pp. 143–44; Altmeyer, *The Formative Years of Social Security*, pp. 35, 39. For more on Virginia, see chapter 5, pp. 174–76.

68. David R. Mayhew, *Party Loyalty Among Congressmen: The Difference Between Democrats and Republicans, 1947–1962* (Cambridge, Mass.: Harvard University Press, 1966).

69. Schlesinger Jr., *Politics of Upheaval*, pp. 142–46; Richard M. Valelly, *Radicalism in the States: The Minnesota Farmer-Labor Party and the American Political Economy* (Chicago: University of Chicago Press, 1989), pp. 168–69. See, especially, James J. Lorence, *Gerald J. Boileau and the Progressive–Farmer Labor Alliance: Politics of the New Deal* (Columbia: University of Missouri Press), chap. 3; Lorence lists the bloc (p. 110) and finds that it has a Rice index of cohesion on welfare/relief votes of .77 and on the work relief bill of .80.

70. Mack C. Shelley II, *The Permanent Majority: The Conservative Coalition in the United States Congress* (University: University of Alabama Press, 1983), p. 66.

71. See, for instance, Gary M. Fink, *Labor's Search for Political Order: The Political Behavior of the Missouri Labor Movement, 1890–1940* (Columbia: University of Missouri Press, 1973); Amenta et al., "The Political Origins of Unemployment Insurance in Five American States"; Jill S. Quadagno, *The Transformation of Old-Age Security: Class and Politics in the American Welfare State* (Chicago: University of Chicago Press, 1988), chap. 3; Theda Skocpol, *Protecting Soldiers and Mothers: The Political Origins of Social Policy in the United States* (Cambridge, Mass.: Harvard University Press, 1992), chap. 4; Nelson, *Unemployment Insurance*, chap. 7. On the growth of the labor movement see Milton Derber, "Growth and Expansion," in *Labor and The New Deal*, ed. Milton Derber and Edwin Young (Madison: University of Wisconsin Press, 1961), pp. 1–44; Milton Derber, "The New Deal and Labor," in Braeman et al., *The New Deal: The National Level*, pp. 110–32.

72. On the impact of labor on the New Deal and vice versa, see Michael Goldfield, "Worker Insurgency, Radical Organization, and New Deal Labor Legislation," *American Political Science Review* 83 (1989): 1257–82; Theda Skocpol and Kenneth Finegold, "Explaining New Deal Labor Policy," *American Political Science Review* 84 (1990): 1297–1304; Steve Fraser, "The 'Labor Question,'" chap. 3 in *The Rise and Fall of the New Deal Order, 1930–1980*, ed. Steve Fraser and Gary Gerstle (Princeton, N.J.: Princeton University Press, 1990); David Plotke, *Building a Democratic Political Order: Reshaping American Liberalism in the 1930s and 1940s* (New York: Cambridge University Press, 1996), chaps. 4 and 5.

73. See Derber, "Growth and Expansion"; Edwin Young, "The Split in Organized Labor," in Derber and Young, *Labor and the New Deal*, pp. 45–67. For the figures, see Bureau of the Census, *Historical Statistics*, series D 946–951, p. 178.

74. Witte, *The Development of the Social Security Act*, p. 252; Altmeyer, *The Formative Years*, pp. 32–33.

75. See "Statement of William Green," U.S. Senate, Committee on Appropriations, *Supplemental Hearings, Emergency Relief Appropriation*, February 12, 1935, pp. 27–46. Schwartz, *The Civil Works Administration*, chap. 4; Macmahon et al., *Federal Work Relief*, pp. 52–53.

76. J. David Greenstone, *Labor in American Politics* (New York: Knopf, 1969); Karen Orren, "Union Politics and Postwar Liberalism in the United States, 1946–1979," *Studies in American Political Development* 1 (1986): 215–52.

77. Steven Fraser, *Labor Will Rule: Sidney Hillman and the Rise of American Labor* (New York: Free Press, 1991), chap. 12.

78. James A. Farley, *Behind the Ballots: The Personal History of a Politician* (New York: Harcourt, Brace, 1938), p. 249; Raymond Moley, *After Seven Years* (New York: Harper, 1939), p. 308.

79. For an early version of the Long Plan, see Huey Long Scrapbooks, Hill Memorial Library Special Collections (HMLSC), Louisiana State University, no. 18. That number includes a Share Our Wealth Society circular, dated Feb. 19, 1934, with the usual six points: to limit poverty; to limit fortunes; old age pensions (thirty dollars per month, for people aged sixty and older); to limit the hours of work; to balance agricultural production with consumption; to care for the veterans of our wars. For more extended discussions of Share Our Wealth, see Brinkley, *Voices of Protest*, pp. 71–74; Donald R. McCoy, *Angry Voices: Left of Center Politics in the New Deal Era* (New York: Kennikat Press, 1967), pp. 122–23; T. Harry Williams, *Huey Long* (New York: Vintage, 1969), p. 693; William Ivy Hair, *The Kingfish and His Realm: The Life and Times of Huey P. Long* (Baton Rouge: Louisiana State University Press, 1991), chap. 15.

80. For a contemporaneous view of Long's plans, see Raymond G. Swing, *Forerunners of American Fascism* (New York: Julian Messner, 1935), chap. 3. On the Louisiana clubs, see Williams, *Huey Long*, p. 701. On the movement as a whole, see Brinkley, *Voices of Protest*, pp. 79–81. A number of useful articles concerning the ambitions of Long appear in the Long Scrapbooks, HMLSC, especially no. 19. See also U.S. Department of Justice, FBI files on Huey P. Long, HMLSC, Box 2, Folder 58.

81. The other states were Colorado, Illinois, New Jersey, and Ohio. For the polling documents, see the Emil Hurja Papers, FDR Library, "Materials Relating to the 'National Inquirer' Presidential Preference Polls," Box 72. For the state-by-state results of the poll and a detailed analysis of Hurja's interpretation of it and the impact of Share Our Wealth on the New Deal, see Edwin Amenta, Kathleen Dunleavy, and Mary Bernstein, "Stolen Thunder? Huey Long's Share Our Wealth, Political Mediation, and the Second New Deal," *American Sociological Review* 59 (1994): 678–702. Hurja almost certainly underestimated the support of Roosevelt, making the preferences of the voters seem more divided than they were. In January 1936 Roosevelt saw the election as fairly close, along the lines of the poll. Schlesinger Jr., *Politics of Upheaval*, pp. 571–72. Farley did not rely completely on polling, a still relatively untried technique, and gathered his own intelligence, sending letters inquiring about Roosevelt's chances locally, to congressmen, heads of local Democratic committees, newspaper editors, and lawyers. Covering each state by this method Farley guessed the results of each state correctly. See Farley, *Behind the Ballots*, pp. 321–28. For the correspondence between Farley and Democratic operatives, see the Papers of the Democratic National Committee, FDR Library, Boxes 1093–1103. Long appeared on the cover of the April 1, 1935, edition of *Time*. That story and several other magazine articles discussing the potential impact of Long appear in the T. Harry Williams Papers, HMLSC, Box 6, Folder 47.

82. See, for instance, Burns, *The Lion and the Fox*, pp. 210–15, 220–26, and Leuchtenburg, *Franklin D. Roosevelt and the New Deal*, p. 100.

83. See Williams, *Huey Long*, pp. 836–37. Schlesinger Jr., *The Politics of Upheaval*, chap. 18.

84. Leff, *The New Deal and Taxation*, chap. 3.

85. Among scholars, see Frances Fox Piven and Richard A. Cloward, *Regulating the Poor: The Functions of Public Welfare*, 2d ed. (New York: Vintage Books, 1993), chap. 3; Orloff, *The Politics of Pensions*, chap. 9. Among contemporaries, see Witte, *The Development of the Social Security Act*, pp. 83–84; Perkins, *The Roosevelt I Knew*, p. 294; Altmeyer, *The Formative Years*, pp. 13–14. The quote is from Francis E. Townsend, *New Horizons: An Autobiography* (Chicago: J. L. Stewart Publishing Co., 1943), p. 235.

86. Townsend's brother was a silent partner. Although some specifics changed over the years, the basic idea remained. For discussions of the Movement and the Plan, see Richard L. Neuberger and Kelley Loe, *An Army of the Aged: A History and Analysis of the Townsend Old Age Pension Plan* (Caldwell, Idaho: The Caxton Printers, Ltd., 1936); Hadley Cantril, *The Psychology of Social Movements* (New York: John Wiley and Sons, 1941), chaps. 7–8; Abraham Holtzman, *The Townsend Movement: A Political Study* (New York: Bookman, 1963); Edwin Amenta and Yvonne Zylan, "It Happened Here: Political Opportunity, the New Institutionalism, and the Townsend Movement," *American Sociological Review* 56 (1991): 250–65.

87. Two examples are Twentieth-Century Fund Committee on Old Age Security, *The Townsend Crusade: An Impartial Review of the Townsend Movement and the Probable Effects of the Townsend Plan* (New York: Twentieth Century Fund, 1936); National Industrial Conference Board, *The Townsend Scheme* (New York: National Industrial Conference Board, 1936).

88. Witte was also the author of a press release that attacked the plan and the credibility of the challenger. "Old Age Pension Organizations," September 6, 1934. NA, RG 47, Box 22, Witte—personal file.

89. In February 1935 Townsend estimated that there were approximately three thousand clubs with 150 members each—a total of 450,000 club members. Later he claimed that more than 20 million people supported the movement. In April, 1936, during the congressional investigation of the movement, Clements estimated membership at more than two million—approximately seven thousand clubs with 300 members each—but admitted that the figure might be as low as one million. The evidence provided by revenues, based on membership fees, suggests that the lower estimate is closer. OARP received only $85,000 in revenue in 1934, most of it in the last quarter of the year. OARP had gathered approximately $555,000 in the first three quarters of 1935, about $350,000 for the last quarter, and $180,000 for the first quarter of 1936. U.S. Congress, House of Representatives, *Hearings Before the Select Committee Investigating Old-Age Pension Organizations*, 74th Cong., 2d sess., vols. 1 and 2 (Washington, D.C.: U.S. Government Printing Office, 1936), pp. 65, 76, 82, 208. U.S. Congress, Senate Committee on Finances, *Hearings on the Economic Security Act* (Washington, D.C.: U.S. Government Printing Office, 1935), pp. 1047–48. The requirements for paid membership included both a "contribution" or fee to join and a "quota" or membership dues, and thus the number of paid members was probably much lower than Clements's high estimate. For a further discussion, see Amenta and Zylan, "It Happened Here." Holtzman estimates that the aged membership of the movement reached as high as 1.5 million or more than

10 percent of those sixty years old and over. For that and the political activity of the movement, see Holtzman, *The Townsend Movement*, pp. 47–49, chap. 6.

90. See Witte, *The Development of the Social Security Act*, pp. 41–47.

91. See the discussions in Amenta, Carruthers, and Zylan, "A Hero for the Aged?" Orloff, *The Politics of Pensions*, chap. 9; McKinley and Frase, *Launching Social Security*, pp. 148–49; Coll, *Safety Net*, chap. 3.

92. Particularly damning were Townsend's admission that two hundred dollars per month was more than the tax would bear, that seventy-five years was a more viable retirement age, and that the transactions tax was merely a sales tax by a different name. Senate Committee on Finances, *Hearings on the Economic Security Act*, pp. 1015–45.

93. House of Representatives, *Hearings Before the Select Committee Investigating Old-Age Pension Organizations*, especially p. 445; Brinkley, *Voices of Protest*, chaps. 10–11; David H. Bennett, *Demagogues in the Depression: American Radicals and the Union Party, 1932–1936* (New Brunswick, N.J.: Rutgers University Press, 1969).

94. Theda Skocpol, *Protecting Soldiers and Mothers*, chap. 6; Theda Skocpol, Marjorie Abend-Wein, Christopher Howard, and Susan G. Lehmann, "Women's Associations and the Enactment of Mothers' Pensions in the United States," *American Political Science Review* 87 (1993): 686–701. Elizabeth S. Clemens, "Organizational Repertoires and Institutional Change: Women's Groups and the Transformation of U.S. Politics," *American Journal of Sociology* 98 (1993): 755–98.

95. U.S. House of Representatives, *Hearings Before the House Committee on Ways and Means on the Economic Security Act*, p. 525. For a more detailed discussion of the demobilization of these groups and the origins of ADC, see Cauthen and Amenta, "Not for Widows Only."

96. Daniels, *The Bonus March*; Dillingham, *Federal Aid to Veterans*; Davis R. B. Ross, *Preparing For Ulysses: Politics and Veterans During World War II* (New York: Columbia University Press, 1969), chap. 1. For statistical details on the declines in veterans' pensions, see Bureau of the Census, *Historical Statistics*, series Y 984–97, Y998–1009, pp. 1147, 1149.

97. Accounts of the impact of capitalists and their organizations on the Social Security Act include the following: Quadagno, "Welfare Capitalism and the Social Security Act of 1935"; J. Craig Jenkins and Barbara G. Brents, "Social Protest, Hegemonic Competition, and Social Reform: A Political Struggle Interpretation of the Origins of the American Welfare State," *American Sociological Review* 54 (1989): 891–909; G. William Domhoff, *The Power Elite and the State: How Policy is Made in America* (New York: Aldine De Gruyter, 1990); Colin Gordon, *New Deals: Business, Labor, and Politics in America, 1920–1935* (New York: Cambridge University Press, 1994), chap. 7.

98. Kim McQuaid, "The Business Advisory Council of the Department of Commerce, 1933–1961: A Study in Corporate/Government Relations," *Research in Economic History* 1 (1976): 171–97.

99. Witte, *The Development of the Social Security Act*, p. 49; Theda Skocpol and Edwin Amenta, "Did Capitalists Shape Social Security?" *American Sociological Review* 50 (1985): 572–75.

100. Jenkins and Brents, for instance, note that William Leiserson took money from the Twentieth Century Fund, and William Domhoff argues that J. Douglas Brown and Murray Latimer—experts working on old-age security proposals—were

"part of the policy network that John D. Rockefeller, Jr., had put together. . . ." See Jenkins and Brents, "Social Protest, Hegemonic Competition, and Social Reform"; Domhoff, *The Power Elite and the State*, p. 51. Yet William Leiserson was an author of the Ohio plan for unemployment insurance, which opposed by almost all capitalist organizations. See Edwin Amenta and Sunita Parikh, "Capitalists Did Not Want the Social Security Act: A Critique of the 'Capitalist Dominance' Thesis," *American Sociological Review* 56 (1991): 124–29. Similarly, Mary Van Kleek, of the Russell Sage Foundation, helped to draft the radical Lundeen bill—whose provisions for open-ended unemployment payments under the control of workers were anathema to capitalist organizations and the more moderate CES. Altmeyer, *The Formative Years*, p. 31. Brown was a professor at Princeton and Latimer was employed by the government Railroad Retirement Board. Barbara Armstrong, a full-time academic, was a critic of private old-age pension efforts. See Armstrong, *Insuring the Essentials*, sec. 3.

101. For a summary of some of the programs the committee and its staff examined, see CES, *Social Security in America*.

102. Herman E. Krooss, *Executive Opinion: What Business Leaders Said and Thought on Economic Issues, 1920s–1960s* (Garden City, N.Y.: Doubleday, 1970), p. 20; Frederick Rudolph, "The American Liberty League, 1934–1940," *American Historical Review* 56 (1950): 19–33; George Wolfskill, *The Revolt of the Conservatives: A History of the American Liberty League, 1934–1940* (Boston: Houghton Mifflin, 1962); George Wolfskill and John A. Hudson, *All But the People: Franklin D. Roosevelt and His Critics, 1933–1939* (London: Macmillan, 1969), pp. 160–66, 304–8.

103. For capitalist opposition to the Social Security Act, see Krooss, *Executive Opinion*, p. 183; Ann Shola Orloff and Eric Parker, "Business and Social Policy in Canada and the United States, 1920–1940," *Comparative Social Research* 12 (1990): 295–339; Amenta and Parikh, "Capitalists Did Not Want the Social Security Act." The quote is from U.S. Senate Committee on Finance, *Hearings on the Economic Security Act*, p. 900.

104. Quadagno, "Welfare Capitalism and the Social Security Act."

105. Witte, *The Development of the Social Security Act*, pp. 105–6; Schlabach, *Cautious Reformer*, pp. 150–51.

CHAPTER FOUR
CONSOLIDATING THE WORK AND RELIEF POLICY, 1937–1939

1. The sources of epigraph quotations are "Second Inaugural Address" (January 20, 1937), in *The Public Papers and Addresses of Franklin D. Roosevelt*, ed. Samuel I. Rosenman, 13 vols. (New York: Random House, 1938–50), 11:5; "Annual Message to Congress" (January 5, 1938), ibid., 7:8.

2. James MacGregor Burns, *Roosevelt: The Lion and the Fox* (New York: Harcourt, Brace and World, 1956), chap. 17; William E. Leuchtenburg, *Franklin D. Roosevelt and the New Deal* (New York: Harper & Row, 1963), chap. 11. See also Richard Polenberg, "The Decline of the New Deal, 1937–1940," in *The New Deal: The National Level*, ed. John Braeman, Robert H. Bremner, and David Brody (Columbus: Ohio State University Press, 1975), pp. 246–66. The classic statement of the conservative bloc thesis is James T. Patterson, *Congressional Conservatism and the New Deal: The Growth of the Conservative Coalition in Congress, 1933–1939*

(Lexington: University of Kentucky Press, 1967). See also David L. Porter, *Congress and the Waning of the New Deal* (Port Washington, N.Y.: Kennikat Press, 1980).

3. Alan Brinkley, *The End of Reform: New Deal Liberalism in Recession and War* (New York: Knopf, 1995), chap. 4; Ellis Hawley, *The New Deal and the Problem of Monopoly* (Princeton, N.J.: Princeton University Press, 1967), chap. 24.

4. Barry Dean Karl, *The Uneasy State: The United States from 1915 to 1945* (Chicago: University of Chicago Press, 1983), chap. 8; Sidney Milkis, *The President and the Parties: The Transformation of the American Party System since the New Deal* (New York: Oxford University Press, 1993), chap. 5.

5. Leuchtenburg, *Franklin Roosevelt and the New Deal*, p. 231.

6. It is uncertain whether the "switch in time saved nine," as was once commonly held. Roberts had already changed his thinking on New Deal legislation, and Roosevelt might have lost the court packing battle even if Roberts had not done so. All the same, Leuchtenburg suggests that these decisions constituted a constitutional revolution. *The Supreme Court Reborn: The Constitutional Revolution in the Age of Roosevelt* (New York: Oxford University Press, 1995), pp. 168–79. See also Karl, *The Uneasy State*, chap. 7; Brinkley, *The End of Reform*, chap. 1.

7. Among other things, the law also provided for the forty–hour week and eliminated child labor in interstate commerce. For the story of the deliberations over this bill, see Frances Perkins, *The Roosevelt I Knew* (New York: Viking, 1946), chap. 21; Burns, *Roosevelt: The Lion and the Fox*, pp. 342–44; Leuchtenburg, *Franklin Roosevelt and The New Deal*, pp. 261–63.

8. "Depression" was thought by Hoover to be preferable to "crisis" or "panic"—the usual terms of the day for general economic trouble. Keynes published *The General Theory of Employment, Interest, and Money* in 1936, but among the New Deal spenders, Currie was notable for having read it. On administration spenders, see Brinkley, *The End of Reform*, chaps. 4–5; Hawley, *The Problem of Monopoly*, chaps. 20–21; Herbert Stein, *The Fiscal Revolution in America* (Chicago: University of Chicago Press, 1969), chap. 6; Dean L. May, *From New Deal to New Economics: The American Liberal Response to the Recession of 1937* (New York: Garland, 1981); Margaret Weir, *Politics and Jobs: The Boundaries of Employment Policy in the United States* (Princeton, N.J.: Princeton University Press, 1992), pp. 34–41. For an analysis of unemployment, see Lester V. Chandler, *America's Greatest Depression, 1929–1941* (New York: Harper & Row, 1970), chap. 3.

9. "Recommendations to Congress Designed to Stimulate Further Recovery," (April 14, 1938), in Rosenman, *Roosevelt Public Papers*, 7:227.

10. U.S. Congress, Senate Special Committee to Investigate Unemployment and Relief, *Unemployment and Relief: Report*, 76th Cong., 1st sess., January 14, 1939, pp. 3–6. On Hopkins and Byrnes, see Searle F. Charles, *Minister of Relief: Harry Hopkins and the Depression* (Syracuse, N.Y.: Syracuse University Press, 1963), p. 163.

11. May, *From New Deal to New Economics*; Arthur W. Macmahon, John D. Millett, and Gladys Ogden, *The Administration of Federal Work Relief* (Chicago: Public Administration Service, 1941), pp. 140–42; Porter, *Congress and the Waning of the New Deal*, chap. 4.

12. "The Annual Budget Message" (January 5, 1939), in Rosenman, *Roosevelt Public Papers*, 8:36–53; Stein, *The Fiscal Revolution*, p. 124; Macmahon et al., *Federal Work Relief*, chap. 6.

13. This paragraph and the next are based on the following: Arthur Altmeyer, *The Formative Years of Social Security* (Madison: University of Wisconsin Press, 1966), chap. 3; U.S. Social Security Administration, "History of Provisions," *Social Security Bulletin, Annual Statistical Supplement* (Washington, D.C.: Social Security Administration, 1991); Robert Ball, "The 1939 Amendments to the Social Security Act and What Followed," chap. 6 in Project on the Federal Social Role, *The Report of the Committee on Economic Security of 1935, and Other Basic Documents Relating to the Development of the Social Security Act* (Washington, D.C.: National Conference on Social Welfare, 1985) (the text of the amendments appears as chapter 8).

14. This new means-testing requirement served to rein in the generosity of some OAA programs, such as California's, which allowed the aged to keep up to fifteen dollars per month of income in addition to OAA benefits. See Jerry R. Cates, *Insuring Inequality* (Ann Arbor: University of Michigan Press, 1983), chap. 5; Blanche D. Coll, *Safety Net: Welfare and Social Security, 1929–1979* (New Brunswick, N.J.: Rutgers University Press, 1995), pp. 91–102, 110–11; Edwin Amenta, Robin Tamarelli, and Michael P. Young, "The Old Folks at Home: Political Mediation and the Impact of the Townsend Movement in California, 1934–1950," (paper presented at the meeting of the American Sociological Association, Los Angeles, 1994, revised 1997).

15. Monte M. Poen, *Harry S. Truman Versus the Medical Lobby: The Genesis of Medicare* (Columbia: University of Missouri Press, 1979), pp. 19–24; Paul Starr, *The Social Transformation of American Medicine* (New York: Basic Books, 1982), pp. 275–80; J. Joseph Huthmacher, *Senator Robert F. Wagner and the Rise of Urban Liberalism* (New York: Atheneum, 1968), pp. 263–67.

16. The following account is drawn from Barry Dean Karl, *Executive Reorganization and Reform in the New Deal: The Genesis of Administrative Management, 1900–1939* (Cambridge, Mass.: Harvard University Press, 1963); Richard Polenberg, *Reorganizing Roosevelt's Government, 1936–1939* (Cambridge, Mass.: Harvard University Press, 1966) chap. 9; Porter, *Congress and the Waning of the New Deal*, chap. 5; Brinkley, *The End of Reform*, chap. 1.

17. Marion Clawson, *New Deal Planning: The National Resources Planning Board* (Baltimore: Johns Hopkins University Press, 1981).

18. Macmahon et al., *Federal Work Relief*, chap. 6; Brown, *Public Relief*, pp. 344–48; Coll, *Safety Net*, pp. 124–27.

19. The WPA was handling the certification process itself in eleven states and the District of Columbia. U.S. National Resources Planning Board Committee on Long-Range Work and Relief Policies, *Security, Work and Relief Policies* (Washington, D.C.: U.S. Government Printing Office, 1942), p. 407; U.S. Federal Works Agency, *Final Report on the WPA Program, 1935–1943* (Washington, D.C.: U.S. Government Printing Office, 1946), pp. 8, 19; Donald S. Howard, *The WPA and Relief Policy* (New York: Sage, 1943), pp. 361–68.

20. Stein, *The Fiscal Revolution*, pp. 120–23.

21. Compare the evidence in Hadley Cantril, *Public Opinion, 1935–1946* (Princeton, N.J.: Princeton University Press, 1951), pp. 920–21, with the evidence in Stein, *The Fiscal Revolution*, p. 121. In May 1939, a question by the American Institute for Public Opinion asked if the government should "do away with work relief (such as the WPA)?" 73 percent said no. In August that year the same organi-

NOTES TO CHAPTER FOUR

zation found that about 68 percent of the public thought "that Congress was right in defeating the three-billion dollar Lending Bill." In November of that year, 70 percent of the public favored a food-stamp plan.

22. Mark H. Leff, *The Limits of Symbolic Reform: The New Deal and Taxation, 1933–1939* (Cambridge: Cambridge University Press, 1984), chap. 7.

23. Mark H. Leff, "Speculating in Social Security Futures," in *Social Security, The First Half-Century*, ed. Gerald D. Nash, Joel H. Pugach, and Richard F. Tomasson (Albuquerque: University of New Mexico Press, 1987), pp. 243–78.

24. Walter Dean Burnham, *Critical Elections and the Mainsprings of American Politics* (New York: Norton, 1970); Kristi Andersen, *The Creation of a Democratic Majority, 1928–1936* (Chicago: University of Chicago Press, 1979); Nancy J. Weiss, *Farewell to the Party of Lincoln: Black Politics in the Age of FDR* (Princeton, N.J.: Princeton University Press, 1981), p. 181.

25. Leuchtenburg, *Franklin Roosevelt and the New Deal*, p. 252.

26. Patterson, *Congressional Conservatism*, p. 50. In an appendix Patterson shows that most conservative Democrats from 1933 to 1939 were southerners. See also Richard Polenberg, "The Decline of the New Deal, 1937–1940," in Braeman et al., *The New Deal: The National Level*, pp. 246–66. Needless to say, not all southern members of Congress were conservative, just as all western Democrats were not all friendly to the New Deal. A number of liberal southerners found their way into Congress in the 1930s, including Maury Maverick and Lyndon Johnson of Texas and Claude Pepper of Florida, not to mention radicals such as Huey Long of Louisiana. Yet as Alan Brinkley points out, the list of southern progressives was short, their power bases weak: "The New Deal in Southern Politics," in *The New Deal and the South*, ed. James C. Cobb and Michael L. Namorato (Jackson: University of Mississippi Press, 1984), pp. 97–115.

27. Macmahon et al., *Federal Work Relief*, pp. 270–74; David J. Maurer, "Relief Problems and Politics in Ohio," in Braeman et al., *The New Deal: The State and Local Levels*, pp. 77–102.

28. Charles McKinley and Robert W. Frase, *Launching Social Security* (Madison: University of Wisconsin Press, 1970), pp. 155–63; Coll, *Safety Net*, chap. 3; Robert T. Lansdale, Elizabeth Long, Agnes Leisy, and Byron T. Hipple, *The Administration of Old-Age Assistance* (Chicago: Public Administration Service, 1939); Altmeyer, *The Formative Years*, chap. 2. Questions of personnel were so touchy that during one discussion Altmeyer was shoved by Congressmen Fred Vinson, who later served on the Supreme Court: ibid., p. 49.

29. Federal Works Agency, *Final Report*, pp. 10–14.

30. *The Final Report of the Advisory Council on Social Security* is reprinted in Project on the Federal Social Role, *The Report of the Committee on Economic Security*, chap. 7. See also "Social Security Act Amendments, 1939," in Altmeyer, *The Formative Years*, pp. 96–98; Martha Derthick, *Policymaking for Social Security* (Washington, D.C.: The Brookings Institution, 1979), pp. 90–92; Coll, *Safety Net*, pp. 91–94; Nancy K. Cauthen and Edwin Amenta, "Not for Widows Only: Institutional Politics and the Formative Years of Aid to Dependent Children," *American Sociological Review* 60 (1996):427–48; Jerry Cates, *Insuring Inequality*, chap. 1. Because of differences in staff makeup and organizational preference, the Bureau of Public Assistance was convinced that family budgeting by way of detailed assessment of need was the best way to ensure fairness and adequacy in granting aid. In

contrast, the WPA felt that such practices involved more work than they were worth, and therefore provided wages without regard even to family circumstances, in the manner of private employers.

31. In October 1936, a poll by Fortune magazine asked, "Do you believe that the WPA has been doing useful work in this locality?" and found that the "yes" answers outnumbered the "no" answers by a margin of four to one. Cantril, *Public Opinion*, p. 696. The 1936 Democratic party platform was explicit about public employment: "Where business fails to supply such employment, we believe that work at prevailing wages should be provided. . . ." The Republican platform criticized New Deal relief policies. Kirk H. Porter and Donald Bruce Johnson, *National Party Platforms, 1840–1968* (Urbana: University of Illinois Press, 1970), pp. 360–63, 366 (quote on p. 362). The Republicans and their allies in the print media tried to make a big issue of corruption and politics in the WPA and rejected work relief in their platform. They also employed a last-ditch, dirty-trick campaign against the payroll taxes of the Social Security Act, inducing employers to include in pay envelopes statements of how much workers would lose from the tax. Robert E. Sherwood, *Roosevelt and Hopkins: An Intimate History* (New York: Harper, 1948), pp. 81–86; Arthur M. Schlesinger, Jr., *The Politics of Upheaval* (Boston: Houghton Mifflin, 1960), chap. 33; Burns, *Roosevelt*, chap. 14.

32. For the secret polling, see the discussion in chapter 3, above, p. 220. Harvard Sitkoff, *A New Deal for Blacks: The Emergence of Civil Rights as a National Issue, vol. 1: The Depression Decade* (New York: Oxford, 1978), chap. 4; Weiss, *Farewell to the Party of Lincoln*, chaps. 9–10. She argues that "to black Americans, the single most important event" of the second New Deal was the creation of the WPA (p. 168). Only about one-third of African Americans of voting age lived in the North and about two-thirds of that group lived in large urban areas. See also Andersen, *The Creation of a Democratic Majority*.

33. Schlesinger, *The Politics of Upheaval*, chap. 32; Burns, *Roosevelt*, chap. 14; Milkis, *The President and the Parties*, pp. 62–74; Susan Ware, *Beyond Suffrage: Women in the New Deal* (Cambridge, Mass.: Harvard University Press, 1981), chap. 4; Weiss, *Farewell to the Party of Lincoln*, chaps. 7, 9. Like the Republican Party, the DNC had a "Colored Division."

34. U. S. Bureau of the Census, *Historical Statistics of the United States From Colonial Times to 1970* (Washington, D.C.: U.S. Government Printing Office, 1976), series Y 84–134, Y 135–86, pp. 1075, 1077.

35. U.S. Congress, Senate Special Committee to Investigate Unemployment and Relief, *Unemployment and Relief: Report*, 76th Cong., 1st sess., January 14, 1939, pp. 3–6; Sherwood, *Hopkins and Roosevelt*, pp. 91–99.

36. Bureau of the Census, *Historical Statistics*, series Y204–10, p. 1083; James J. Lorence, *Gerald J. Boileau and the Progressive Farmer-Labor Alliance: Politics of the New Deal* (Columbia: University of Missouri Press), chap. 5, esp. pp. 206–7.

37. Burns, *The Lion and the Fox*, pp. 342–44; Perkins, *The Roosevelt I Knew*, chap. 21. Votes concerning this bill also saw southern Democrats merge with Republicans against the rest of the Democratic party; Key, *Southern Politics*, p. 356. The liberal bloc was solidly in favor; Lorence, *The Progressive Farmer-Labor Alliance*, pp. 218–19.

38. Patterson, *Congressional Conservatism*.

39. Bureau of the Census, *Historical Statistics*, series Y 204–10, p. 1083; Lorence, *The Progressive Farmer-Labor Alliance*, pp. 241–42.

40. U.S. Senate Special Committee to Investigate Campaign Expenditures, *Investigation of Campaign Expenditures in 1936* (Washington, D.C.: U.S. Government Printing Office, 1937), pp. 127–33; Louise Overacker, "Campaign Funds in the Presidential Election of 1936," *American Political Science Review* 31 (1937): 473–98.

41. Milton Derber, "Growth and Expansion," in *Labor and The New Deal*, ed. Milton Derber and Edwin Young (Madison: University of Wisconsin Press, 1961), pp. 1–44; Edwin Young, "The Split in Organized Laborm" ibid., pp. 45–67. For figures, see Bureau of the Census, *Historical Statistics*, series D 927–34, D 946–51, pp. 177–78.

42. Derthick, *Policymaking for Social Security*, chap. 5; Ball, "The 1939 Amendments to the Social Security Act"; Macmahon et al., *Federal Work Relief*, pp. 52–53; Howard, *The WPA*, pp. 215–16; Richard Valelly shows that the effective sit-down strikes beginning in 1937 harmed organized labor in public opinion. *Radicalism in the States: The Minnesota Farmer-Labor Party and the American Political Economy* (Chicago: University of Chicago Press, 1989), pp. 134–35.

43. Edwin Amenta, Bruce G. Carruthers, and Yvonne Zylan, "A Hero For the Aged? The Townsend Movement, The Political Mediation Model, and U.S. Old-Age Policy, 1934–1950," *American Journal of Sociology* 98 (1992): 308–39; Abraham Holtzman, *The Townsend Movement: A Political Study* (New York: Bookman, 1963), chap. 6.

44. U.S. Congress, House of Representatives, *Hearings Relative to the Social Security Act Amendments of 1939*, vols. 1–3, 76th cong., 1st sess., 1939, pp. 3–43; U.S. Congress, Senate, *Hearings Before the Committee on Finance on H.R. 6635*, 76th Cong., 1st sess., 1939, pp. 95, 180, 188.

45. Lorence, *Progressive Farmer-Labor Alliance*, pp. 217–18; Steve Valocchi, "The Unemployed Workers Movement of the 1930s: A Reexamination of the Piven and Cloward Thesis," *Social Problems* 37 (1990): 191–205, esp. p. 201; Selden Rodman, "Lasser and the Workers' Alliance," *The Nation*, September 10, 1938, pp. 242–44.

46. Herman E. Krooss, *Executive Opinion: What Business Leaders Said and Thought on Economic Issues, 1920s–1960s* (Garden City, N.Y.: Doubleday, 1970), pp. 184–85.

47. Taking a sample of 589 major capitalists, Michael Patrick Allen found that more than one third gave at least one hundred dollars to the 1936 campaign, compared with about 1 percent of the public at large. Of the 207 capitalist contributors, 82 percent contributed to the Republican side. "Capitalist Response to State Intervention: Theories of the State and Political Finance in the New Deal," *American Sociological Review* 56 (1991): 679–89; See also Overacker, "Campaign Funds in the Presidential Election of 1936."

48. Edwin Amenta and Sunita Parikh, "Capitalists Did Not Want the Social Security Act: A Critique of the 'Capitalist Dominance' Thesis," *American Sociological Review* 56 (1991): 124–29. A poll taken by *Fortune* magazine in October 1939 asked a sample of businessmen which of many New Deal measures was "the worst of these acts." The WPA came in third (with 17.1 percent), behind the easily victorious Wagner Act (43.9 percent) and the undistributed profits tax (22.5 percent). Social security came in fifth (3.4 percent). Cantril, *Public Opinion*, p. 405.

49. Henry Roseveare, *The Treasury: The Evolution of a British Institution* (New York: Columbia University Press, 1969); Robert Skidelsky, "Keynes and the Trea-

sury View: The Case For and Against an Active Employment Policy," in *The Emergence of the Welfare State in Great Britain and Germany*, ed. W. J. Mommsen (London: Croom Helm, 1981), pp. 167–87. Derek Fraser, *The Evolution of the British Welfare State: A History of Social Policy since the Industrial Revolution, 2d ed.* (London: Macmillan, 1984), chap. 8.

50. Peter Flora, Jens Alber, Richard Eichenberg, Jurgen Kohl, Franz Kraus, Winfried Pfenning, and Kurt Seebohm, *State, Economy, and Society in Western Europe 1815–1975: The Growth of Mass Democracies and Welfare States* (Chicago: St. James, 1983).

51. NRPB Committee, *Security, Work and Relief*, pp. 558, 561. Social spending for the calendar year is taken by the NRPB Committee's definition of public aid, excluding earnings of persons employed on federal construction projects. The GNP is taken from Bureau of the Census, *Historical Statistics*, series F1, p. 224. The GNP was $90.5 billion in 1939. These definitions and figures are used in the following paragraphs. See also Howard, *The WPA*, pp. 854–57; Chandler, *America's Greatest Depression*, chap. 3.

52. NRPB Committee, *Security, Work and Relief*, pp. 557.

53. Cauthen and Amenta, "Not for Widows Only"; Josephine Chapin Brown, *Public Relief, 1929–1939* (New York: Holt, 1940), chaps. 13, 14, 17.

54. NRPB Committee, *Security, Work and Relief*, pp. 558, 561; Brown, *Public Relief*, chap. 14.

55. The program accounted for approximately $0.43 billion. See also Altmeyer, *The Formative Years*, chap. 3; Daniel Nelson, *Unemployment Insurance: The American Experience, 1915–1935* (Madison: University of Wisconsin Press), chap. 9.

56. Irving Bernstein, *A History of the American Worker, 1920–1933: The Lean Years* (Boston: Houghton Mifflin, 1960), chap. 13; William P. Dillingham, *Federal Aid to Veterans, 1917–1941* (Gainesville: University of Florida Press, 1952); Davis R. B. Ross, *Preparing For Ulysses: Politics and Veterans During World War II* (New York: Columbia University Press, 1969), chap. 1; Bureau of the Census, *Historical Statistics*, series Y 984–97, Y998–1009, pp. 1147, 1149; Polenberg, *Reorganizing Roosevelt's Government, 1936–1939*; William E. Pemberton, *Bureaucratic Politics: Executive Reorganization during the Truman Administration* (Columbia: University of Missouri Press, 1979), p. 33.

57. Bureau of the Census, *Historical Statistics*, series F 1–5, Y 352–57, Y 358–73, pp. 224, 1106–7. On tax incidence, see Joseph A. Pechman, *Federal Tax Policy* (Washington, D.C.: The Brookings Institution, 1977). Leff, "Speculating in Social Security Futures."

58. In the liberal type, public social policy has a small presence and a large need-based component, and is augmented by private social policy. Gøsta Esping-Andersen, *The Three Worlds of Welfare Capitalism* (Princeton, N.J.: Princeton University Press, 1990), especially chap. 2 on decommodification.

59. Universal programs, moreover, often follow a political process in which great numbers of recipients push for higher benefits and greater scope. By contrast, need-based programs trace a vicious circle: because of their few recipients they are reduced in benefits and scope, leading to fewer recipients and lower benefits, and so on. For some dissent from this prevailing view, see Jill Quadagno, *The Color of Welfare: How Racism Undermined the War on Poverty* (New York: Oxford University Press, 1994), chap. 8.

60. In the table scope and generosity are conflated, though of course these characteristics can vary in practice.

61. Ann Shola Orloff, "Gender and the Social Rights of Citizenship: The Comparative Analysis of Gender Relations and Welfare States," *American Sociological Review* 58 (1993): 303–28. Her critique also implies a more negative evaluation of the conservative corporatist regime, which discourages the participation of women in the paid labor force.

62. Almost all spouse and widow/widower benefits go to women. Spouse beneficiaries receive one-half of the benefit of the "contributor." The receipt and continuation of that benefit and the eventual receipt of the "widow" benefit, equal to the contributor benefit, depend on sustaining the marriage. Divorcees have a longer waiting period than first-married spouses. Madonna Harrington Meyer, "Making Claims as Workers or Wives: The Distribution of Social Security Benefits." *American Sociological Review* 61 (1996): 449–65.

63. Workers began to feel as though the provision of work was a right. See Lizabeth Cohen, *Making a New Deal: Industrial Workers in Chicago, 1919–1939* (New York: Cambridge University Press, 1990), chap. 6.

64. This act reinstated the initial 1936 federal regulations, which had been diluted somewhat by the Emergency Relief Act of 1937. This access to a job was also mitigated by the 1939 act's stricture that those working more than eighteen months continuously were to be automatically dismissed and not reinstated for thirty days. See Howard, *The WPA*, pp. 491, 517–20. For the wage rates and employment by wage classes, see Federal Works Agency, *Final Report*, pp. 23–25, 37–41.

65. See, for instance, Mirra Komarovsky, *The Unemployed Man and His Family: The Effect of Unemployment upon the Status of the Man in Fifty-Nine Families* (New York: Dryden Press, 1940). E. Wight Bakke, *The Unemployed Worker: A Study of the Task of Making a Living without a Job* (New Haven, Conn.: Yale University Press, 1940).

66. Federal Works Agency, *Final Report of the WPA*, pp. 42–43; Howard, *The WPA*, pp. 429–34. The median age of men on the WPA rose as war-related employment hired away younger men.

67. For more on this, see the next chapter, below, pp. 288–92.

68. John A. Salmond, *The Civilian Conservation Corps, 1933–1942: A New Deal Case Study* (Durham, N.C.: Duke University Press, 1967). Lewis L. Lorwin, *Youth Work Programs: Problems and Policies* (Washington, D.C.: American Council on Education, 1941); NRPB Committee, *Security, Work, and Relief*, pp. 260–80.

69. The WPA did not keep separate statistics concerning women with children and without husbands in the home, but admitted its policy openly. Initially this division was called "Women's and Professionals' Projects." Federal Works Agency, *Final Report*, pp. 44–45, 67–71; Howard, *The WPA*, pp. 429–34.

70. U.S. Social Security Board, "Changes in the Types of Families Accepted for Aid to Dependent Children," *Social Security Bulletin* 6 (June 1943): 30–32; Cauthen and Amenta, "Not for Widows Only."

71. "Social Security Act Amendments of 1939," pp. 4–7.

72. Howard, *The WPA*, pp. 285–86, 303–6, 325–31.

73. Federal Works Agency, *Final Report*, p. 45; Richard Sterner, *The Negro's Share: A Study of Income, Consumption, Housing, and Public Assistance* (New York: Harper, 1943), chap. 13.

74. Sterner, *The Negro's Share*, chap. 13; NRPB Committee, *Security, Work, and Relief*, pp. 116–18.

75. Sterner, *The Negro's Share*, chap. 15; NRPB Committee, *Security, Work, and Relief*, pp. 116–18; Cauthen and Amenta, "Not for Widows Only."

76. Sterner, *The Negro's Share*, chap. 11.

CHAPTER FIVE
SOME LITTLE NEW DEALS ARE LITTLER THAN OTHERS

1. The sources of epigraph quotations are as follows: Ronald L. Heinemann, *Depression and New Deal in Virginia* (Charlottesville: University Press of Virginia, 1983), p. 159; Roger Biles, *Big City Boss in Depression and War: Mayor Edward J. Kelly of Chicago* (DeKalb: Northern Illinois University Press, 1984), p. 157; Robert E. Burke, *Olson's New Deal for California* (Berkeley: University of California Press, 1953), p. 42; John E. Miller, *Governor Philip F. La Follette, The Wisconsin Progressives and the New Deal* (Columbia: University of Missouri Press, 1982), pp. 67, 121.

2. Robert P. Ingalls, *Herbert H. Lehman and New York's Little New Deal* (New York: New York University Press, 1975); Jackson K. Putnam, *Old-Age Politics in California: From Richardson to Reagan* (Stanford, Calif.: Stanford University Press, 1970). Richard M. Valelly, *Radicalism in the States: The Minnesota Farmer-Labor Party and the American Political Economy* (Chicago: University of Chicago Press, 1989); Alan P. Sindler, *Huey Long's Louisiana: State Politics, 1920–1952* (Baltimore: Johns Hopkins University Press, 1956), chaps. 4, 5; Edith Abbott, "Cruelties of the Illinois Three-Year Settlement Provisions," *Social Service Review* 14 (1940): 33–34. For more on Virginia, Illinois, California, and Wisconsin, see pp. 302–29.

3. U.S. Federal Works Agency, *Final Report on the WPA Program, 1935–1943* (Washington, D.C.: U.S. Government Printing Office, 1946), "Table 4," p. 116.

4. U.S. Social Security Administration, "Old-Age Assistance," *Social Security Bulletin* 13 (November 1950): 12.

5. The average benefits per child are taken from the *Social Security Bulletin* 3,4 (December 1940, December 1941). The share of female-headed families with children is taken from U.S. Bureau of the Census, *U.S. Census of Population* (Washington, D.C.: U.S. Government Printing Office, 1940). For a discussion about the potential recipient base for ADC, see Nancy K. Cauthen and Edwin Amenta, "Not for Widows Only: Institutional Politics and the Formative Years of Aid to Dependent Children," *American Sociological Review* 60 (1996): 427–48, esp. p. 439.

6. For WPA wages and OAA pensions I examine the results of a simple regression model of average benefits on per capita income, using the benefit figures above. The "residuals" of this model present the differences between the actual average payment and the payment that would be predicted by the state's income. A large positive residual score would indicate that the state had a higher average benefit than one would expect given its income. These scores are employed for the rankings. The measure of per capita income is derived from U.S. Bureau of the Census, *Historical Statistics of the United States from Colonial Times to 1970* (Washington, D.C.: U.S. Government Printing Office, 1975), series F 297–348, pp. 243–45. The ADC quality index is a simple product of two measures of generosity and coverage: the average payment per child recipient as a share of per capita income in 1940 multiplied by the number of recipient families as a share of female-headed households

with children. (Because of data limitations for the eight states without ADC programs in 1940, I employ an average of their indices for 1939 and 1941). For more details on the ADC index, see Cauthen and Amenta, "Not for Widows Only," p. 439.

7. For a discussion of little WPAs, see Donald S. Howard, *The WPA and Relief Policy* (New York: Sage, 1943), pp. 633–40. The number of WPA workers is for December 1939 and is taken from Federal Works Agency, *Final Report*, Table 2, p. 111. The general relief information is from January 1940 and is taken from U.S. Federal Security Agency, *Social Security Yearbook, 1940* (Washington, D.C.: U.S. Government Printing Office, 1941), pp. 283–84.

8. See Bureau of the Census, *Historical Statistics*, series F1–5, Y 710–35, pp. 224, 1129. U.S. GNP was about $94.9 billion in 1927, $103.1 billion in 1929, and $99.7 billion in 1940. For per capita tax increases, see U.S. Bureau of the Census, *Statistical Abstract of the United States* (Washington, D.C.: U.S. Government Printing Office, 1930, 1941). For the states' adoption of different sources of taxation, see Susan B. Hansen, *The Politics of Taxation: Revenue Without Representation* (New York: Praeger, 1983), chap. 5.

9. See chapter 1, pp. 44–46, and David R. Mayhew, *Placing Parties in American Politics* (Princeton, N.J.: Princeton University Press, 1986), chap. 10.

10. Edwin Amenta and Yvonne Zylan, "It Happened Here: Political Opportunity, the New Institutionalism, and the Townsend Movement," *American Sociological Review* 56 (1991): 250–65.

11. See Walter Dean Burnham's explanatory note and the data, Bureau of the Census, *Historical Statistics*, pp. 1067–69, series Y 27–78, pp. 1071–72. I relied on the presidential elections for 1932 and 1936. V. O. Key, *Southern Politics in State and Nation* (New York: Alfred A. Knopf, 1949).

12. Mayhew calls them traditional party organizations. On his scale of one to five, I count those states scoring four or five as patronage-oriented. Every state except Louisiana scores either at or near the extremes. Mayhew, *Placing Parties in American Politics*, p. 196.

13. For a quick summary of state regimes in the 1930s, see Hansen, *Politics of Taxation*, p. 158. For Wisconsin, see Miller, *Governor Philip F. La Follette*, chaps. 4–6. For Minnesota, see Richard M. Valelly, *Radicalism in the States: The Minnesota Farmer-Labor Party and the American Political Economy* (Chicago: University of Chicago Press, 1989).

14. Elizabeth Brandeis, "Labor Legislation," in *History of Labor in the United States, 1896–1932*, ed. John R. Commons vol. 3 (New York: Macmillan, 1935), pp. 399–700; Howard W. Odum, "Public Welfare Activities," chap. 24 in President's Committee on Social Trends, *Recent Social Trends in the United States* (New York: McGraw-Hill, 1933); Edwin Amenta, Elisabeth S. Clemens, Jefren Olsen, Sunita Parikh, and Theda Skocpol, "The Political Origins of Unemployment Insurance in Five American States," *Studies in American Political Development* 2 (1987): 137–82.

15. The size of labor's following is typically captured by unionization, which is measured by the percentage of the nonagricultural labor force in unions at the end of the 1930s. Leo Troy and Neil Sheflin, *U.S. Union Sourcebook* (West Orange, N.J.: Industrial Relations Data and Information Services, 1985), p. 7–3; U.S. Bureau of the Census, *Statistical Abstract of the United States, 1948* (Washington, D.C.: U.S. Government Printing Office, 1948), pp. 194, 196. Political presence is ascer-

tained by examining the resource mobilization of state federations of labor—the central lobbying organizations of labor in state-level politics. This is measured by the amount of income of the federation of labor between 1938 and 1940 as a percentage of the nonagricultural labor force, in a way similar to the unionization figure. Although it was impossible to gain information for state federations of labor in each state of the Union, such information was available for each state scoring high on unionization. For the details, see Edwin Amenta and Jane D. Poulsen, "Social Politics in Context: The Institutional Politics Theory and State-Level U.S. Social Spending Policies at the End of the New Deal," *Social Forces* 75 (1996): 33–60.

16. Membership strength can be ascertained by examining the per capita number of Townsend clubs, circa 1940, the only surviving systematic evidence across states. For information on Townsend clubs, see Abraham Holtzman, *The Townsend Movement: A Political Study* (New York: Bookman, 1963), pp. 48–49. For the per capita measure, see Amenta and Zylan, "Political Opportunity, the New Institutionalism, and the Townsend Movement," p 257. The measure of political presence is the percentage of a state's delegation won by Townsend candidates in the elections of 1938 and 1940. This gauges indirectly the influence of the movement on state-level officials, who were often politically connected to members of Congress and aware of the Townsend influence on their fates. The information is from Holtzman, *The Townsend Movement*, pp. 145–47, and the *Townsend National Weekly*. See Edwin Amenta, Bruce G. Carruthers, and Yvonne Zylan, "A Hero For the Aged? The Townsend Movement, The Political Mediation Model, and U.S. Old-Age Policy, 1934–1950," *American Journal of Sociology* 98 (1992): 308–39. States with more than ten clubs per 100,000 persons in 1940 and with one-half or more of their congressional delegations endorsed by the Townsend Movement are considered ones where the movement was powerful. These states include Arizona, California, Colorado, Florida, Idaho, Indiana, Kansas, Minnesota, Montana, Nevada, New Hampshire, Ohio, Oregon, South Dakota, Washington, Wisconsin, and Wyoming.

17. I discuss states from only four of the six categories listed in Table 1.5. The omitted categories are "patronage, no countervailing forces," states which I expect to have a negative reaction to New Deal social policy, and the "open, but no forces for change," which I expect to have an indifferent reaction to New Deal social policy. The first category includes four states and the second two states.

18. Earl Black and Merle Black, *Politics and Society in the South* (Cambridge, Mass.: Harvard University Press, 1987), chap. 1; Key, *Southern Politics*.

19. Amenta et al., "The Political Origins of Unemployment Insurance in Five American States." Illinois also had a Democratic regime in power for much of the 1930s.

20. The following discussion is based on Key, *Southern Politics*, chap. 2; Robert F. Hunter, "Virginia and the New Deal," in *The New Deal: The State and Local Levels*, ed. John Braeman, Robert H. Bremner, and David Brody (Columbus: Ohio State University Press, 1975), pp. 103–36; Heinemann, *Depression and New Deal in Virginia*; J. Harvie Wilkinson III, *Harry Byrd and the Changing Face of Virginia Politics, 1945–1966* (Charlottesville: University Press of Virginia, 1968).

21. See Key, *Southern Politics*, chap. 2; Wilkinson, *Harry Byrd*, pp. 37–39.

22. Wilkinson, *Harry Byrd*, introduction. Mayhew described the Byrd organization's policy aims as "a program of keeping the government honest, budgets balanced, the public sector small, unions weak, and blacks segregated." *Placing Parties in American Politics*, pp. 127–32, quote from p. 132.

23. U.S. Children's Bureau, *Mothers' Aid, 1931,* Children's Bureau Publication no. 220 (Washington, D.C.: U.S. Government Printing Office, 1933), pp. 17, 19.

24. See Heinemann, *Depression and the New Deal in Virginia,* chap. 5.

25. See Hunter, "Virginia and the New Deal," Tables 5.1 and 5.2, pp. 122ff; Heinemann, *The Depression and the New Deal in Virginia,* chap. 8.

26. For union figures, see note 15. For the Townsend Movement, see Amenta and Zylan, "It Happened Here," p. 257; Holtzman, *Townsend Movement,* chapter 3.

27. Heinemann, *Depression and New Deal in Virginia,* p. 171.

28. At the dawn of the Depression, Illinois ranked fourth in manufacturing, fifth in urbanization, and third in total population. It also had very high state federation of labor revenues as compared to wage earners. Amenta et al., "The Political Origins of Unemployment Insurance," pp. 142, 162. See also Eugene Staley, *The History of the Illinois State Federation of Labor* (Chicago: University of Chicago Press, 1930).

29. See Harold Gosnell, *Machine Politics: Chicago Model* (Chicago: University of Chicago Press, 1937); Alex Gottfried, *Boss Cermak of Chicago: A Study of Political Leadership* (Seattle: University of Washington Press, 1962); John H. Fenton, *Midwest Politics* (New York: Holt, Rinehart, and Winston, 1966), chap. 7; Lyle M. Dorsett, *Franklin D. Roosevelt and the Big City Bosses* (Port Washington, N.Y.: Kennikat Press, 1977), chap. 6; Biles, *Big City Boss*; Mayhew, *Placing Parties in American Politics,* pp. 73–77.

30. Factory inspectors did not have access to accident reports filed with the commission and thus had a difficult time enforcing laws. Earl Beckner, *A History of Illinois Labor Legislation* (Chicago: University of Chicago Press, 1929), pp. 425–26, 500–504. See also Amenta et al, "The Political Origins of Unemployment Insurance," pp. 150–51.

31. See Sophonisba P. Breckinridge, *The Illinois Poor Law and its Administration* (Chicago: University of Chicago Press, 1939), chap. 3.

32. Staley, *The Illinois State Federation of Labor*; Irving Bernstein, *The Lean Years: A History of the American Worker, 1920–1933* (New York: Houghton Mifflin, 1960), p. 467; Gosnell, *Machine Politics Chicago Model,* pp. 149–55; Gottfried, *Boss Cermak of Chicago,* pp. 210–18.

33. Searle F. Charles, *Minister of Relief: Harry Hopkins and the Depression* (Syracuse, N.Y.: Syracuse University Press, 1963), pp. 41–42.

34. Biles, *Big City Boss,* pp. 51–52. For a discussion of Kelly's claims about how he would aid Roosevelt, see David Plotke, *Building A Democratic Political Order: Reshaping American Liberalism in the 1930s and 1940s* (New York: Cambridge University Press, 1996), p. 138.

35. Stephen P. Erie, *Rainbow's End: Irish Americans and the Dilemmas of Urban Machine Politics, 1840–1945* (Berkeley: University of California Press, 1988), pp. 131, 134; Dorsett, *Roosevelt and the Big City Bosses,* chap. 6; Biles, *Big City Boss,* pp. 74–81.

36. Howard, *The WPA,* p. 637. Kelly's support came in handy for Roosevelt when he decided to run for a third term in 1940. Kelly publicly demanded that Roosevelt run again, hosted the convention, permitted Hopkins to run the floor, and packed the hall with regulars to shout down Roosevelt's opponents, such as Carter Glass of Virginia. Dorsett, *Roosevelt and the Big City Bosses,* chap. 6; Biles, *Big City Boss,* pp. 74–84; Doris Kearns Goodwin, *No Ordinary Time: Franklin and*

Eleanor Roosevelt: The Home Front in World War II (New York: Simon and Schuster, 1994), pp. 126–31.

37. See Tables 5.1 and 5.2 above; U.S. Committee on Economic Security, *Social Security in America: The Factual Background of the Social Security Act as Summarized From Staff Reports to the Committee on Economic Security* (Washington, D.C.: U.S. Government Printing Office, 1937), pp. 159–63; Charles McKinley and Robert W. Frase, *Launching Social Security* (Madison: University of Wisconsin Press, 1970), pp. 183–88; Blanche D. Coll, *Safety Net: Welfare and Social Security, 1935–1979* (New Brunswick, N.J.: Rutgers University Press, 1994), pp. 76–77; Alfred H. Kelly, "A History of the Illinois Manufacturers' Association" (Ph.D. thesis, University of Chicago, 1938), chap. 29; Amenta et al., "The Political Origins of Unemployment Insurance."

38. James T. Patterson, *The New Deal and the States: Federalism in Transition* (Princeton, N.J.: Princeton University Press, 1969), p. 159.

39. Royce D. Delmatier, Clarence F. McIntosh, and Earl G. Waters, *The Rumble of California Politics, 1848–1970* (New York: Wiley, 1970), chap. 6; Michael Paul Rogin and John L. Shover, *Political Change in California: Critical Elections and Social Movements, 1890–1966* (Westport, Conn.: Greenwood Press, 1970), chaps. 2, 3.

40. Delmatier et al., *California Politics*, chap. 7; Putnam, *Old-Age Politics*, chap. 2; Odom, "Public Welfare Activities"; Children's Bureau, *Mothers' Aid, 1931*; Committee on Economic Security, *Social Security in America*, p. 245.

41. Upton Sinclair, *I, Governor of California, and How I Ended Poverty: A True Story of the Future* (Los Angeles: Upton Sinclair, 1933), pp. 21–24; Delmatier et al., *California Politics*, chap. 8; Putnam, *Old-Age Politics*, chap. 3; Arthur M. Schlesinger, Jr., *The Age of Roosevelt: The Politics of Upheaval* (Boston: Houghton Mifflin, 1960), chap. 7.

42. Delmatier et al., *California Politics*, chap. 8; Putnam, *Old-Age Politics*, chaps. 3–4; Greg Mitchell, *The Campaign of the Century: Upton Sinclair's Race for Governor of California and the Birth of Media Politics* (New York: Random House, 1992). In April 1936, the Townsend state organizer for southern California, Edward E. Gordon, estimated that he had three hundred clubs with average membership of five hundred—probably twice the actual total, but still a high percentage of the approximately one million Townsend club members across the nation. Southern California Townsend revenues peaked in December 1935; U.S. Congress House of Representatives, *Hearings Before the Select Committee Investigating Old-Age Pension Organizations*, 74th Cong., 2d sess., 1:65, 82, 2:489, 495–96. During the campaign Sinclair stated that he would "put off the problem of pensions to see what the president does." Upton Sinclair, *Immediate EPIC* (Los Angeles: Upton Sinclair, 1934), p. 26; Upton Sinclair, *I, Candidate for Governor, and How I Got Licked* (Los Angeles: University of California Press, 1994 [originally 1934, 1935]). See also the introduction by James N. Gregory. Sinclair lost with 879,537 votes to 1,138,620 for Merriam and 302,519 for Raymond Haight, a moderate candidate running on the Progressive ballot line.

43. California's old-age pension program was officially known as Old Age Security, but I am calling it an OAA program, which it also was, for consistency's sake. In 1937, only 18 percent of those sixty-five and older received pensions, ranking California twenty-third. That year the Los Angeles County Board of Supervisors refused to release liens already taken out on pensioners, and the State Supreme

Court ruled in favor of the board, overturning the law and allowing counties to continue the practice. California Department of Social Welfare, *Public Assistance in California*, vol. 7 (Sacramento, Calif.: State Printing Office, 1940), pp. 3, 6; California Department of Social Welfare, *Public Assistance in California*, vol. 10 (Sacramento, Calif.: State Printing Office, 1940), pp. 2–5; Putnam, *Old-Age Politics*, pp. 76, 79, 84–85, 88; Jerry Cates, *Insuring Inequality: Administrative Leadership in Social Security, 1935–1954* (Ann Arbor: University of Michigan Press, 1983), pp. 113–14; Coll, *Safety Net*, pp. 84–91.

44. Burke, *Olson's New Deal for California*, chap. 7. The ADC figure is from the ADC pension index discussed above. Howard, *The WPA*, p. 638.

45. Burke, *Olson's New Deal*, chaps. 2–4. The American Federation of Labor Political League of California failed to endorse Olson, though most labor leaders worked in his behalf in the general election. Philip Taft, *Labor Politics American Style: The California State Federation of Labor* (Cambridge, Mass.: Harvard University Press, 1968), pp. 103–8. On Ham and Eggs, see Putnam, *Old-Age Politics*, pp. 94–100; Frank A. Pinner, Paul Jacobs, and Philip Selznick, *Old Age and Political Behavior: A Case Study* (Berkeley: University of California Press, 1959), pp. 4–5.

46. In California the maximum benefit was raised automatically to forty dollars per month because of a 1935 provision that California OAA grants would rise with federal matching. The amendments to the Social Security Act also restricted the resources that could be discounted, harming the position of many California pensioners. In 1939, another Ham and Eggs initiative was defeated by more than two to one. Two lien-repeal propositions passed by a more than half a million votes. Putnam, *Old-Age Politics*, pp. 111, 115–19, 123–24; Cates, *Insuring Inequality*, pp. 116–17.

47. Robert S. Maxwell, *La Follette and The Rise of the Progressives In Wisconsin* (Madison: State Historical Society of Wisconsin, 1956), pp. 153–73; Herbert F. Marguiles, *The Decline of the Progressive Movement in Wisconsin, 1890–1920* (Madison: State Historical Society of Wisconsin, 1968), chap. 4; Robert C. Nesbit, *Wisconsin: A History* (Madison: State Historical Society of Wisconsin, University of Wisconsin Press, 1973), chap. 26; Amenta et al., "The Political Origins of Unemployment Insurance," pp. 148–50.

48. Miller, *Governor Philip F. La Follette*, chaps. 1–2; Nesbit, *Wisconsin*, pp. 484–89; Amenta et al., "Political Origins of Unemployment Compensation"; Daniel Nelson, *Unemployment Insurance: The American Experience, 1915–1935* (Madison: University of Wisconsin Press, 1969), chapter 6. Although Wisconsin was at the top of states in the number of families aided per population, it was just below the median, $21.68 per family, in terms of average grant. Children's Bureau, *Mothers' Aid, 1931*, Odum, "Public Welfare." Its county-optional old-age pension program was adopted in 1925 and still operative in the Depression. Its benefits were among the highest at approximately twenty dollars per month, but with only about 5 percent of those seventy years and older receiving pensions. Committee on Economic Security, *Social Security in America*, pp. 156–67.

49. The FLPF was initially known as the League for Independent Political Action. Philip La Follette did not win as much presidential support in his gubernatorial race as did his counterpart in Minnesota, Governor Floyd Olson, but Wisconsin Democrats were highly displeased by Roosevelt's visit. Schlesinger Jr., *Politics of Upheaval*, chap. 6; Donald R. McCoy, *Angry Voices: Left-of-Center Politics in the New Deal Era* (Port Washington, N.Y.: Kennikat Press, 1958), chap. 2; Miller,

Governor Philip F. La Follette, chaps. 3–4; Patrick J. Maney, *"Young Bob" La Follette: A Biography of Robert M. La Follette, Jr., 1895–1953* (Columbia: University of Missouri Press, 1978), chap. 8; Valelly, *The Minnesota Farmer-Labor Party*, pp. 165–67; Nesbit, *Wisconsin*, chap. 29.

50. Miller, *Governor Philip F. La Follette*, chap. 4; Nesbit, *Wisconsin*, pp. 490–91; Howard, *The WPA*, pp. 637–38.

51. Miller, *Governor Philip F. La Follette*, chap. 6; Amenta et al, "Political Origins of Unemployment Insurance." Wisconsin had some trouble getting its unemployment compensation program certified by the SSB. McKinley and Frase, *Launching Social Security*, pp. 218–21.

52. James MacGregor Burns, *Roosevelt: The Lion and the Fox* (New York: Harcourt, Brace, and World, 1956), pp. 358–60; Maney, *"Young Bob"*, chap. 8; Miller, *Governor Philip F. La Follette*, chap. 8.

53. Roger T. Johnson, *Robert M. La Follette, Jr. and the Decline of the Progressive Party in Wisconsin* (Madison: State Historical Society of Wisconsin, 1964), chaps. 5–6; Miller, *Governor La Follette*, chaps. 7–8; Maney, *"Young Bob"*, chaps. 16–17.

CHAPTER SIX
REDEFINING THE NEW DEAL, 1940–1950

1. Sources of epigraph quotations are as follows: "The Opening of the 1940 Presidential Campaign" (October 23, 1940), in *The Public Papers and Addresses of Franklin D. Roosevelt*, ed. Samuel I. Rosenman, 13 vols. (New York: Macmillan, 1938–50), 9:494; U.S. National Resources Planning Board Committee on Long-Range Work and Relief Policies, *Security, Work and Relief Policies* (Washington, D.C.: U.S. Government Printing Office, 1942), p. 2; U.S. Federal Works Agency, *Final Report on the WPA Program, 1935–1943* (Washington, D.C.: U.S. Government Printing Office, 1946), p. v.

2. An influential case is made by David Brody, "The New Deal and World War II," in *The New Deal: The National Level*, ed. John Braeman, Robert H. Bremner, and David Brody (Columbus: Ohio State University Press, 1975), pp. 267–309. For the views that the war and postwar period consolidated and sustained the New Deal, see also Richard E. Neustadt, "Congress and the Fair Deal: A Legislative Balance Sheet," in *Public Policy* 5 (1953): 351–81; Richard O. Davies, "Social Welfare Policies," in *The Truman Period as a Research Field*, ed. Richard S. Kirkendall (Columbia: University of Missouri Press, 1967), pp. 149–86; David Plotke, *Building a Democratic Political Order: Reshaping American Liberalism in the 1930s and 1940s* (New York: Cambridge University Press, 1995), chap. 7. Whereas gains made by the labor movement in the 1930s were consolidated during the 1940s, as Brody persuasively argues, New Deal social policy was not consolidated, as I document below.

3. Harold G. Vatter, *The U.S. Economy in World War II* (New York: Columbia University Press 1985), chap. 1.

4. For a discussion of the NRPB and its committee, see Marion Clawson, *New Deal Planning: The National Resources Planning Board* (Baltimore: Johns Hopkins University Press, 1981); Philip W. Warken, *A History of the National Resources Planning Board* (New York: Garland, 1979). For the significance of the planning board for postwar American liberalism, see Alan Brinkley, *The End of Reform: New*

Deal Liberalism in Recession and War (New York: Knopf, 1995), pp. 245–53. See also Edwin Amenta and Theda Skocpol, "Redefining the New Deal: World War II and the Development of Social Provision in the United States," in *The Politics of Social Policy in the United States*, ed. Margaret Weir, Ann Shola Orloff, and Theda Skocpol (Princeton, N.J.: Princeton University Press, 1988), pp. 81–122. The following details on the recommendations of the committee are based on NRPB Committee, *Security, Work and Relief*, pp. 502–549.

5. NRPB Committee, *Security, Work and Relief*, pp. 514–15.

6. Ibid., pp. 523–24.

7. Ibid., pp. 522–28.

8. These recommendations are detailed in U.S. National Resources Planning Board, *Demobilization and Readjustment: Report of the Conference on Postwar Readjustment of Civilian and Military Personnel* (Washington, D.C.: U.S. Government Printing Office, 1943).

9. For the views and proposals generated by the SSB, see Wilbur Cohen, ed., *War and Post-War Social Security: The Outlines of an Expanded Program* (Washington, D.C.: American Council on Public Affairs, 1942). The following relies on essays in that volume by Arthur Altmeyer, the chairman of the SSB, Cohen, I. S. Falk, and William Haber. For the wartime activities of Cohen, who was central to the SSB's planning, see Edward D. Berkowitz, *Mr. Social Security: The Life of Wilbur J. Cohen* (Lawrence: University of Kansas Press, 1995), pp. 49–55. See also Jerry R. Cates, *Insuring Inequality* (Ann Arbor: University of Michigan Press, 1983); Bartholomew H. Sparrow, *From the Outside In: World War II and the American State* (Princeton, N.J.: Princeton University Press, 1996), chap. 2; Blanche D. Coll, *Safety Net: Welfare and Social Security, 1929–1979* (New Brunswick, N.J.: Rutgers University Press, 1995), esp. chaps. 6, 7.

10. Arthur Altmeyer, "War and Post-War Problems," in Cohen *War and Post-War Social Security*, pp. 20–30. See also Edward D. Berkowitz, "Social Security and the Financing of the American State," chap. 4 in *Funding the Modern American State, 1941–1995: The Rise and Fall of the Era of Easy Finance*, ed. W. Elliot Brownlee (New York: Cambridge University Press, 1995).

11. Leonard P. Adams, *The Public Employment Service in Transition, 1933–1968: Evolution of a Placement Service into a Manpower Agency* (Ithaca, N.Y.: The New York State School of Industrial and Labor Relations, 1969). For a discussion of how the USES fit into U.S. employment policy as a whole, see Margaret Weir, *Politics and Jobs: The Boundaries of U.S. Employment Policy* (Princeton, N.J.: Princeton University Press, 1992), chap. 2.

12. John Morton Blum, ed., *From the Morgenthau Diaries: Years of Urgency, 1938–1941* (Boston: Houghton Mifflin, 1964), pp. 304–18, and *From the Morgenthau Diaries: The War Years, 1941–1945* (Boston: Houghton Mifflin, 1967), chap. 2; Sidney Ratner, *Taxation and Democracy in America* (New York: Norton, 1943), pp. 501–8; Randolph E. Paul, *Taxation in the United States* (Boston: Little Brown, 1954); John F. Witte, *The Politics and Development of the Federal Income Tax* (Madison: University of Wisconsin Press, 1985), pp. 111–15.

13. Mark H. Leff, "Speculating in Social Security Futures," in *Social Security: The First Half-Century*, ed. Gerald D. Nash, Joel H. Pugach, and Richard F. Tomasson (Albuquerque: University of New Mexico Press, 1987), pp. 243–78.

14. John A. Salmond, *The Civilian Conservation Corps, 1933–1942: A New Deal Case Study* (Durham, N.C.: Duke University Press, 1967), chap. 12.

15. John Morton Blum, *V Was For Victory* (San Diego, Calif.: Harcourt Brace Jovanovich, 1976), pp. 234–37; Richard Polenberg, *War and Society: The United States, 1941–1945* (Philadelphia: Lippincott, 1972), pp. 80–82. On the conflicts in New Deal public employment policy, see Michael B. Katz, *In the Shadow of the Poor House: A Social History of Welfare in America* (New York: Basic Books, 1986), pp. 224–34.

16. Witte, *The Politics and Development of the Federal Income Tax*, pp. 119–20; Blum, *V was for Victory*, pp. 241–42.

17. Blum, *Morgenthau Diaries, 1941–1945*, pp. 73–78; Witte, *The Politics and Development of the Federal Income Tax*, pp. 119–20; Blum, *V was for Victory*, pp. 241–42; "The President Vetoes a Revenue Bill" (February 22, 1944), Rosenman, *Roosevelt Public Papers*, 13:80–84.

18. Leff, "Speculating in Social Security Futures."

19. This bill is reprinted in the *Congressional Record*. 78th Cong., 1st sess., June 3, 1943, pp. 5260–62

20. See, e.g., Edwin E. Witte, "What to Expect of Social Security," *American Economic Review* 34 (1943), (supp.), pp. 212–21; Edwin E. Witte, "American Post-War Social Security Proposals," *American Economic Review* 33 (1943): 825–38.

21. Barry Dean Karl, *Charles Merriam and the Study of Politics* (Chicago: University of Chicago Press, 1974), chap. 12; Clawson, *New Deal Planning*, chaps. 15–19; Warken, *A History of the National Resources Planning Board*, pp. 237–45; Brinkley, *The End of Reform*, pp. 254–57; Ira Katznelson and Bruce Pietrykowski, "Rebuilding the American State: Evidence from the 1940s," *Studies in American Political Development* 5 (1991): 301–99.

22. Davis R. B. Ross, *Preparing For Ulysses: Politics and Veterans During World War II* (New York: Columbia University Press, 1969), chap. 4.

23. Keith W. Olson, *The G.I. Bill, the Veterans, and the Colleges* (Lexington: University Press of Kentucky, 1974).

24. Ross, *Preparing for Ulysses*, chap. 4.

25. Stephen Kemp Bailey, *Congress Makes a Law: The Story of the Employment Act of 1946* (New York: Columbia University Press, 1950); Heinz Eulau, Alvin H. Hansen, Mordecai Ezekiel, James Loeb Jr., and George Soule, "What the [Full Employment] Bill Proposes," in "The Road to Freedom: Full Employment, A Special Section," *The New Republic*, September 24, 1945, pp. 396–97. See also Weir, *Politics and Jobs*, chap. 2; Brinkley, *The End of Reform*, pp. 259–64.

26. Mary Hedge Hinchey, "The Frustration of the New Deal Revival, 1944–1946" (Ph.D. diss., University of Missouri, 1965), chap. 6; Adams, *The Public Employment Service in Transition*, chap. 3.

27. Truman reunited the Bureau of Employment Services with the USES. Arthur Altmeyer, *The Formative Years of Social Security* (Madison: University of Wisconsin Press, 1966), chap. 7; Hinchey, "The Failure of the New Deal Revival," pp. 109–10.

28. Susan M. Hartmann, *Truman and the 80th Congress* (Columbia: University of Missouri Press, 1971), chap. 6; Altmeyer, *The Formative Years of Social Security*, chaps. 6–7; Wilbur J. Cohen and Robert J. Myers, "Social Security Act Amendments of 1950: A Summary and Legislative History," *Social Security Bulletin* 13 (October 1950): 3–14; Leff, "Speculating in Social Security Futures"; Berkowitz, *Mr. Social Security*, pp. 56–70; Cates, *Insuring Inequality*, chap. 3; Coll, *Safety Net*, pp. 155–64. The 1950 amendments added some 8 million uncovered workers to the pro-

gram, including "regularly employed" agricultural workers and domestics. Cates suggests that a flat benefit for OASI would have aided the poorer among the aged in the 1940s. This may probably be true, but as Cates notes, flat benefits became in the 1950s the goal of the program's conservative critics, who feared its expansion. The amendments helped to strengthen "social security" to face these attacks and allowed for the persistent, incremental growth of this program throughout the post-World War II period.

29. Gordon W. Blackwell and Raymond F. Gould, *Future Citizens All* (Chicago: American Public Welfare Association, 1952); Ellen J. Perkins, "Old-Age Assistance and Aid to Dependent Children, 1940–50," *Social Security Bulletin* 14 (November 1951): 11–29. Winifred Bell, *Aid to Dependent Children* (New York: Columbia University Press, 1965), chap. 3.

30. U.S. Social Security Administration, "History of Provisions," *Social Security Bulletin Annual Statistical Supplement* (Washington, D.C.: Social Security Administration, 1991); Gilbert Y. Steiner, *Social Insecurity: The Politics of Welfare* (Chicago: Rand McNally, 1966).

31. Altmeyer, *The Formative Years*, chap. 7; Cohen and Myers, "Social Security Act Amendments"; Coll, *Safety Net*, pp. 155–64.

32. Hartmann, *The 80th Congress*, pp. 74–79, 95–96, 132–37; Witte, *The Federal Income Tax*, pp. 131–44; W. Elliot Brownlee, *Federal Taxation in America: A Short History* (New York: Cambridge University Press, 1996), chap. 3. The 1948 income tax cuts were reinstated at the beginning of the Korean War in 1950. Brownlee calls the period from 1941 to 1986 the "era of easy finance"—which ended with the indexation of tax brackets.

33. Paul Starr, *The Social Transformation of American Medicine: The Rise of a Sovereign Profession and the Making of a Vast Industry* (New York: Basic Books, 1982), pp. 280–89; Donald E. Spritzer, *Senator James E. Murray and the Limits of Post-War Liberalism* (New York: Garland, 1985), pp. 133–35; Monte M. Poen, *Harry S. Truman Versus the Medical Lobby: The Genesis of Medicare* (Columbia: University of Missouri Press, 1979), chap. 6; J. Joseph Huthmacher, *Senator Robert F. Wagner and the Rise of Urban Liberalism* (New York: Atheneum, 1968); Hinchey, "The Failure of New Deal Revival," pp. 103–6.

34. See Altmeyer, *The Formative Years*, pp. 96–98; Martha Derthick, *Policymaking for Social Security* (Washington, D.C.: The Brookings Institution, 1979), pp. 90–92; Coll, *Safety Net*, chap. 7.

35. The origins of the Wagner-Murray-Dingell bill are contested. Martha Derthick, a scholar of old-age insurance, claims that the bill was written almost entirely by I. S. Falk and Wilbur Cohen of the Social Security Board. J. Joseph Huthmacher, Senator Wagner's biographer, claims that the senator had developed the bill with his own staff, as Wagner had with other major pieces of social spending legislation, and that he was influenced by the planners in the NRPB. Derthick, *Social Security*, pp. 111, 114; Huthmacher, *Senator Robert F. Wagner*, pp. 292–94.

36. Blum, *Morgenthau Diaries, 1938–1941*, pp. 304–18, and *Morgenthau Diaries, 1941–1945*, chap. 2; John Morton Blum, *Roosevelt and Morgenthau* (Boston: Houghton Mifflin, 1972), chap. 17; Brownlee, *Federal Taxation*, pp. 89–99.

37. See, for instance, Rosenman, *Roosevelt Public Papers*, 9, Items 119, 120, 123, 125, and 128.

38. Congressional Quarterly, *Guide to U.S. Elections* (Washington, D.C.: Congressional Quarterly, 1985), p. 34.

39. Roosevelt regained Michigan and Wyoming and lost Ohio with all other states staying the same, and accordingly the electoral college provided another overwhelming margin, 432 to 99. *Guide to U.S. Elections*, p. 35. For the economic bill of rights, see "Unless There Is Security Here at Home, There Cannot Be Lasting Peace in the World—Message to Congress on the State of the Union" (January 11, 1944), Rosenman, *Roosevelt Public Papers*, 13:32–44, especially p. 41. See also "Campaign Address at Soldiers' Field, Chicago" (October 28, 1944), ibid., pp. 369–77. On Truman, see Hinchey, "The Failure of the New Deal Revival," pp. 94–97.

40. Hadley Cantril and John Harding, "The 1942 Elections: A Case Study in Political Psychology," *Public Opinion Quarterly* 7 (1943):222–41. They chalk up the defeat to a low Democratic turnout.

41. Roland Young, *Congressional Politics in the Second World War* (New York: Da Capo Press, 1972), chap. 8.

42. Coll, *Safety Net*, pp. 125–26; Cates, *Insuring Inequality*, chap. 3.

43. Abraham Holtzman, *The Townsend Movement: A Political Study* (New York: Bookman, 1963), chap. 8; Edwin Amenta, Bruce G. Carruthers, and Yvonne Zylan, "A Hero For the Aged? The Townsend Movement, The Political Mediation Model, and U.S. Old-Age Policy, 1934–1950," *American Journal of Sociology* 98 (1992): 308–39.

44. Steven Fraser, *Labor Will Rule: Sidney Hillman and the Rise of American Labor* (New York: The Free Press, 1991), pp. 441–52, 506–10; Derthick, *Social Security*, pp. 111–15.

45. The similarity in strike activity is underscored by an examination of its frequency and "volume," which takes into account the frequency, the duration, and the number of workers involved in strikes. Volume is measured as the "man-days" lost due to strikes as a percentage of private, nonagricultural working time. Strike activity was similar for the period from 1933 through 1939, the New Deal years, when social spending gains were made, and the period from 1942 through 1945, the war years, when social spending was curtailed. The New Deal period averaged about 2,552 strikes per year and the strike volume averaged 0.30 percent. The war years averaged 4,107 strikes, and the strike volume was 0.19 percent. Moreover, the immediate postwar years from 1946 through 1949, an uneven period for social reform, witnessed the greatest strike activity: 3,926 strikes per year, with a strike volume of 0.70 percent. In every year from 1934 through 1940, moreover, more strikes concerned the right to organize than wages and hours. After 1940, more strikes concerned issues of wages and hours than organizational issues. On unionization and strike figures, see U.S. Bureau of the Census, *Historical Statistics of the United States from Colonial Times to 1970* (Washington, D.C.: U.S. Government Printing Office, 1975), series D 946–51, 970–85, pp. 177–79; P. K. Edwards, *Strikes in the United States, 1881–1974* (New York: St. Martin's Press, 1981), pp. 163, 260. See also David Brody, "The New Deal and World War II"; Fraser, *Labor Will Rule*, chaps. 16–17.

46. Under emergency wartime powers, the Smith-Connally Act called for a thirty-day cooling-off period and gave authority to the president to seize struck plants. The bill also called for a strike vote before one could be undertaken and gave a legal basis to the War Labor Board. Contributions to political campaigns from labor organizations were outlawed. The Taft-Hartley Act restricted the rights of labor organizations in several ways. Unions could be sued for breach of contract. The closed shop was outlawed. The automatic check-off for union dues required

written permission by the worker. Workers could ask for elections to withdraw the certification of the union. Secondary boycotts and strikes were prohibited. Strikes and lockouts were to be delayed with a sixty-day cooling off period. Strikes against the federal government were prohibited. The president was given powers to intervene in work stoppages under "national emergency strike" procedure. Featherbedding was outlawed. Unions were required also to present various paperwork to the Secretary of Labor, and union officers had to sign oaths that they were not Communists. Unions could not spend their funds on federal elections. The act also transformed the structure of the National Labor Relations Board, creating a general counsel to share functions with the five-member board. R. Alton Lee, *Truman and Taft-Hartley: A Question of Mandate* (Lexington: University of Kentucky Press, 1966); Arthur F. McClure, *The Truman Administration and the Problems of Postwar Labor, 1945–1948* (Cranbury, N.J.: Associated University Presses, 1969). See also Plotke, *Building a Democratic Political Order*, chaps. 7–8.

47. Plotke, *Building a Democratic Order*, chaps. 7–8; Karen Orren, "Union Politics and Postwar Liberalism in the United States, 1946–1979," *Studies in American Political Development* 1 (1986): 215–52; David R. Mayhew, *Party Loyalty Among Congressmen: The Difference Between Democrats and Republicans, 1947–1962* (Cambridge, Mass.: Harvard University Press, 1966), chap. 1.

48. Beth Stevens, "Blurring the Boundaries: How Federal Social Policy Has Shaped Private Sector Welfare Benefits," chap. 4 in Weir et al., *Social Policy in the United States*; Frank Dobbin, "The Privatization of American Social Insurance: Organizations, Fringe Benefits, and the State, 1920–1950," *American Journal of Sociology* 97 (1992): 1416–50.

49. Paul Pierson, *Dismantling the Welfare State? Reagan, Thatcher, and the Politics of Retrenchment* (New York: Cambridge University Press, 1994), chap. 1. For these reasons, cutting spending programs in isolation seems akin to increasing taxation without concomitant spending increases.

50. Lowi, "Four Systems of Policy, Politics, and Choice"; Theda Skocpol, *Protecting Soldiers and Mothers: The Political Origins of Social Policy in the United States* (Cambridge, Mass.: Harvard University Press, 1992), introduction; Katz, *In the Shadow of the Poorhouse*, pp. 224–34; Pierson, *Dismantling the Welfare State?* pp. 102–3. Katz also argues that the political dependence of the WPA, with its funding subject to congressional whim, undercut the program. In addition, the criteria for selection to the WPA, such as restriction of benefits to one family member, were discriminatory. Moreover, work relief programs have conflicting goals. Projects are supposed to provide high-quality output, yet employ the greatest number; to give relief, yet provide useful job training. Setting wages too high provides a disincentive to take private employment. Setting them too low undermines unions. Allowing variations means that equal work does not result in equal pay.

51. Federal Works Agency, *Final Report*, pp. 10–13.

52. For a more detailed argument, on which the following paragraphs are based, see Edwin Amenta, Ellen Benoit, Chris Bonastia, Nancy K. Cauthen, and Drew T. Halfmann, "Bring Back the WPA: The Origins of Modern American Social Policy in Welfare Reform," forthcoming in *Studies in American Political Development* 13 (1998).

53. On the poll of businessmen, see chapter 4, note 48. The negative view of the WPA was backed by business organizations. For instance, George F. Houston, chairman of the Committee on Industrial Financing of the National Association of

Manufacturers, called for an end to the WPA and the reverting of relief to the localities. U.S. Senate Special Committee to Investigate Unemployment and Relief, *Hearings*, vol. 2 (February 28–April 8, 1938) (Washington, D.C.: U.S. Government Printing Office, 1938), pp. 903–17. For evidence on the voting records of Republicans, see Amenta et al., "Bring Back the WPA."

54. Voting evidence supports the interpretation that southern Democrats were always uneasy with the WPA and merely waited until political conditions were more favorable to make a stand against it, or became opposed to the WPA after the administration took steps to make it permanent. For details, see Amenta et al., "Bring Back the WPA." On OAA and ADC, see Jill S. Quadagno, *The Transformation of Old-Age Security: Class and Politics in the American Welfare State* (Chicago: University of Chicago Press, 1988).

55. The WPA was investigated by congressional committees in 1938, 1939, and 1940. See Howard, *The WPA*, pp. 587–95; Charles, *The Minister of Relief*, p. 202.

56. See Amenta et al., "Bring Back the WPA."

57. The president of the Building and Trades Council, Thomas A. Murray, called for the abolition of the WPA activities in the building and construction field and their transfer to the PWA, "where our men would be employed full time without question under union conditions." See Amenta et al., "Bring Back the WPA."

58. Valocchi, "The Unemployed Workers Movement of the 1930s," p. 201; Selden Rodman, "Lasser and the Workers' Alliance," *The Nation*, September 10, 1938, pp. 242–44; Arthur W. Macmahon, John D. Millett, and Gladys Ogden, *The Administration of Federal Work Relief* (Chicago: Public Administration Service, 1941), p. 291.

59. Hopkins sought to find WPA heads who were sympathetic to the program—not necessarily Democrats or loyalists of either senator. To dodge senatorial prerogatives Hopkins chose to head the WPA in fourteen states the same person who headed the state emergency relief administration, but that was only a stopgap. The states included a number of southern ones: Alabama, Arkansas, Georgia, Indiana, Kentucky, Louisiana, Massachusetts, New Mexico, Ohio, South Dakota, Utah, Vermont, Virginia, and Wyoming. One analysis of WPA appointments revealed that of twenty-two studied, twelve were made for political reasons, and only four of the twelve were competent administrators. Macmahon, Millett, and Ogden, *The Administration of Federal Work Relief*, p. 270, 271, 274. On the unfairness in the program, see Katz, *In the Shadow of the Poorhouse*, pp. 224–34.

60. David Mayhew, *Placing Parties in American Politics*, (Princeton, N.J.: Princeton University Press, 1986).

61. Stephen P. Erie, *Rainbow's End: Irish Americans and the Dilemmas of Urban Machine Politics, 1840–1945* (Berkeley: University of California Press, 1988), p. 132.

62. Lyle M. Dorsett, *Franklin D. Roosevelt and the Big City Bosses* (Port Washington, N.Y.: Kennikat Press, 1977), pp. 49–55, 58, 60–62; Erie, *Rainbow's End*, p. 133.

63. Patterson, *The New Deal and the States*, p. 168; David J. Maurer, "Relief Problems and Politics in Ohio," in *The New Deal—The State and Local Levels*, ed. John Braeman, Robert H. Bremner, and David Brody (Columbus: Ohio State University Press, 1975), pp. 77–102.

64. For details, see Amenta et al., "Bring Back the WPA."

65. Cates, *Insuring Inequality*. Coll, *Safety Net*, chaps. 4–5.

66. See Pierson, *Dismantling the Welfare State?* chap. 3; Derthick, *Social Security*, chap. 3.

67. See above and Bureau of the Census, *Historical Statistics*, series H125–71, H346–67, pp. 346, 356; Leff, "Speculating in Social Security Futures"; Holtzman, *The Townsend Movement*, chap. 8.

68. Bureau of the Census, *Historical Statistics*, series F1–5, H125–71, H238–44, pp. 224, 346, 350.

CHAPTER SEVEN
A WELFARE STATE FOR BRITAIN

1. The sources of epigraph quotations are as follows: U.K., Public Record Office (PRO), Cabinet Papers, 87/77, May 20, 1942; William Beveridge, *Social Insurance and Allied Services* (New York: Macmillan, 1942), p. 9.

2. Beveridge exchanged memos with civil servants and then held hearings throughout 1942. The general outlines of his proposals were apparent in a three-page outline prepared in July 1941, "Social Insurance—General Considerations," British Library of Political Science, William Henry Beveridge Papers, VIII, 46. The following few paragraphs are based primarily on Beveridge, *Social Insurance*; Paul Addison, *The Road to 1945* (London: Jonathan Cape, 1975), chap. 8; Jose Harris, *William Beveridge: A Biography* (Oxford: Clarendon Press, 1977), chap. 16.

3. J. M. Lee, *The Churchill Coalition, 1940–1945* (Hamden, Conn.: Archon Books, 1980), pp. 127–38. Addison, *The Road to 1945*, pp. 221–22.

4. U.K. Ministry of Reconstruction, *Social Insurance* (New York: Macmillan, 1944).

5. Almont Lindsey, *Socialized Medicine in England and Wales: The National Health Service, 1948–1961* (Chapel Hill: University of North Carolina Press, 1962), pp. 32–39; Derek Fraser, *The Evolution of the British Welfare State* (London: Macmillan, 1973), p. 214; Henry Pelling, *The Labour Governments, 1945–51* (New York: St. Martin's Press, 1984), pp. 151–64.

6. U.K. Ministry of Reconstruction, *Employment Policy* (New York: Macmillan, 1945), pp. 10–15, 20–24; Kenneth O. Morgan, *Labour in Power, 1945–51* (Oxford: Clarendon Press, 1984), pp. 182–83.

7. Henry Pelling, *Britain and the Second World War* (Glasgow: Collins, 1970), pp. 168–73.

8. John Macnicol, *The Movement For Family Allowances, 1918–1945: A Study in Social Policy Development* (London: Heinemann, 1980), chap. 7; Fraser, *The Evolution of the British Welfare State*, p. 220; Pelling, *The Labour Governments*, p. 98; Morgan, *Labour in Power*, p. 143.

9. Fraser, *The Evolution of the British Welfare State*, p. 220; Pelling, *The Labour Governments*, pp. 101–18; Morgan, *Labour in Power*, pp. 151–74; Lindsey, *Socialized Medicine in England and Wales*, pp. 43–46.

10. The dismissal of Keynesianism was also due to the postwar economic situation; although Britain was suffering through austerity, its economy was characterized by inflation and high employment. According to Keynesian theory this situation called for restrictions on spending and increased taxation to slow the economy—neither of which materialized. Margaret Gowing, "The Organization of Manpower in Britain During the Second World War," *Journal of Contemporary History* 7 (1972): 147–67; Alan Booth, "The 'Keynesian Revolution' in Economic Policy-

making," *Economic History Review* 36 (1983): 103–23; Ben Pimlott, *Hugh Dalton* (London: Jonathan Cape, 1985), chap. 16; Margaret Weir, "Ideas and Politics: The Acceptance of Keynesianism in Britain and the United States," in *The Political Power of Economic Ideas: Keynesianism Across Nations*, ed. Peter A. Hall (Princeton, N.J.: Princeton University Press, 1989), pp. 53–86.

11. Richard M. Titmuss, "War and Social Policy," in *Essays on the "Welfare State"* (Boston: Beacon Press, 1969), chap. 4.

12. Alan R. Peacock and Jack Wiseman, *The Growth of Public Expenditure in the United Kingdom* (Princeton, N.J.: Princeton University Press, 1961), chap. 1.

13. Morgan, *Labour in Power*, pp. 144–50, 269–72. The peace dividend thesis has other explanatory problems. It is silent about the form that social policy might take and does not even distinguish between short-term veterans' benefits and permanent benefits for larger categories of people. Also, wartime taxes might not be nearly sufficient to pay for war, eliminating a potential peace dividend, or wartime taxes might be cut. The peace dividend may be returned to taxpayers—which is in part what happened in the United States.

14. "Risk-Sharing and Social Justice: The Motivational Foundations of the Post-War Welfare State," *British Journal of Political Science* 16 (1986): 1–34. Dryzek and Goodin appraise their argument by analyzing many participating nations of World War II. To measure uncertainty they construct a scale including two measures: the proportion of the population killed in the war and the length of time between 1933 and 1949 during which a state was active in the war or was a site of fighting. To measure increase in social expenditure they use the proportionate change from 1933 to 1949 in social security as a proportion of income. Under a number of specifications, the uncertainty index is significantly related to increases in social spending.

15. Ibid.

16. Arthur Marwick, *War and Social Change in the Twentieth Century: A Comparative Study of Britain, France, Germany, Russia, and the United States* (London: Macmillan, 1974).

17. Richard Titmuss, *Problems of Social Policy* (London: His Majesty's Stationery Office, 1950).

18. For an argument about the negative impact of small wars on social policy, see Harold Wilensky, *The Welfare State and Equality: Structural and Ideological Roots of Public Expenditures* (Berkeley: University of California Press, 1975), chap. 4. On the positive impact of the decline of Britian's geopolitical role on its welfare state, see Patrick Dunleavy, "The United Kingdom: Paradoxes of an Ungrounded Statism," in *The Comparative History of Public Policy*, ed. Francis G. Castles (London: Polity Press, 1989), pp. 242–91. The American geopolitical trajectory was greatly different from the British one and doubtless could not have been planned more poorly to promote modern public social provision. America's largest war came early enough to promote veterans' benefits. Then, as the rest of the capitalist world turned inward to complete welfare states, the United States became the world's foremost military power, ensuring that public social provision would have a large and long-term competitor in the military establishment. This trajectory is illuminated by examining wartime casualties. The Civil War claimed about 1.71 percent of the American population; this figure compares to the 0.13 percent and 0.31 percent killed in the First and Second World Wars, respectively. J. David Singer

and Melvin Small, *The Wages of War, 1816–1965: A Statistical Handbook* (New York: Wiley, 1972), p. 260. The smaller American wars, in Korea and Vietnam, which were analogous to the Boer War, came in the second half of the twentieth century.

19. For a discussion of these differences, see above, chapter 1, pp. 39–56.

20. The architects of the respective programs saw the differences between them. In an interview with the Rockefeller Foundation on May 16, 1943, Beveridge declared that the NRPB report was an "able document," but nothing like an American Beveridge Report, as many in the United States were calling it. He saw the NRPB report as mainly a fact-finding document and not nearly as detailed in its recommendations as his own report. Beveridge Papers, XI, 38. Eveline Burns, of the NRPB committee, compared the programs directly. She argued that the NRPB report was more radical than the Beveridge Report in providing employment assurance. "Comparison of the NRPB Report with the Beveridge Report," December 26, 1942. PRO, PIN 8/167. See also the discussion by Alan Brinkley, "The New Deal and the Idea of the State." Chapter 4 in Steve Fraser and Gary Gerstle, eds. *The Rise and Fall of the New Deal Order, 1930–1980* (Princeton, N.J.: Princeton University Press, 1989), p. 120.

21. Beveridge's committee, the War Cabinet Interdepartmental Committee on Social Insurance and Allied Services, met extensively and exchanged memoranda with officials from with all government agencies involved in social policy from July through December 1941. See the memoranda in the British PRO, Cabinet Papers, 87/76. Only afterwards did he stage hearings with such groups as the Trade Union Congress and the Townsend-like National Federation of Old Age Pensioners Associations. PRO, Cabinet Papers, 87/77. Beveridge rejected the claims of the latter for a high flat old-age pension, without a means test for all those sixty and older who would agree to retire. See also Bentley B. Gilbert, *British Social Policy, 1914–1939* (Ithaca, N.Y.: Cornell University Press, 1970), pp. 180–92; Fraser, *The Evolution of the British Welfare State*, pp. 185–97.

22. Philip W. Warken, *A History of the National Resources Planning Board* (New York: Garland, 1979), p. 229.

23. Jose Harris, "Some Aspects of Social Policy in Britain During the Second World War," in *The Emergence of the Welfare State in Great Britain and Germany*, ed. W. J. Mommsen (London: Croom Helm, 1981), pp. 247–62.

24. Sar A. Levitan and Karen A. Cleary, *Old Wars Remain Unfinished: The Veteran Benefits System* (Baltimore: Johns Hopkins University Press, 1973).

25. W. K. Hancock and M. M. Gowing, *British War Economy* (London: His Majesty's Stationery Office, 1949); Henry Roseveare, *The Treasury: The Evolution of a British Institution* (New York: Columbia University Press, 1969); Robert Skidelsky, "Keynes and the Treasury View: The Case For and Against an Active Employment Policy," in Mommsen, *The Emergence of the Welfare State*, pp. 167–87; James C. Cronin, *The Politics of State Expansion: War, State, and Society in Twentieth Century Britain* (London: Routledge, 1991).

26. Herman Miles Somers, *Presidential Agency: OWMR, The Office of War Mobilization and Reconversion* (New York: Greenwood Press, 1950); David Brody, "The New Deal and World War II," in *The New Deal: The National Level*, ed. John Braeman, Robert H. Bremner, and David Brody (Columbus: Ohio State University Press, 1975), pp. 267–309.

27. Paul Addison, "By-Elections of the Second World War," in *By-Elections in British Politics*, ed. Chris Cook and John Ramsden (London: Macmillan, 1973), pp. 165–90. In June 1943, after the war had started to go in the Allies' favor, a Gallup poll found that if British elections were to be held, 38 percent would vote Labor as opposed to 31 percent for the Conservatives, foreshadowing the election of 1945. George H. Gallup, ed., *The Gallup International Public Opinion Polls: Great Britain, 1937–1975* (New York: Random House, 1976), p. 73.

28. According to Doris Kearns Goodwin, Roosevelt was hoping that the military command would give the go-ahead to invade North Africa before the November elections, boosting the morale of the nation and his party's fortunes. But he did not attempt to influence the timing of this decision, which happened a few days after Election Day. Doris Kearns Goodwin, *No Ordinary Time: Franklin and Eleanor Roosevelt in the Second World War* (New York: Simon and Schuster, 1994), chap. 15.

29. Lee, *The Churchill Coalition*, pp. 32–35; Addison, *The Road to 1945*, pp. 235–37.

30. For Beveridge's invitation to visit America and warnings by American officials, including Arthur Altmeyer, for the Beveridges to delay their trip, see Beveridge Papers, XI, 31. The schedule of the trip appears in Beveridge Papers, XI, 36. For Churchill's stay in America, see Goodwin, *No Ordinary Time*, pp. 435–39.

31. American newspaper stories mentioning Beveridge were clipped and filed in Beveridge Papers, XI, 38. These include stories about the Wagner bill, of which Beveridge had a copy, and the NRPB. Dorothy Kilgallen called Beveridge "the man with the plan" in her syndicated column of June 5, in the New York *Journal American*. The only time Beveridge was widely cited in American papers was when he made an off-hand comment about why strikes were more common in the United States than Britain.

32. See the retrospective memoir by Frances Perkins, *The Roosevelt I Knew* (New York: Harper & Row, 1946), p. 283.

33. Davis R. B. Ross, *Preparing For Ulysses: Politics and Veterans During World War II* (New York: Columbia University Press, 1969).

34. Wilbur J. Cohen and Robert J. Myers, "Social Security Act Amendments of 1950: A Summary and Legislative History." *Social Security Bulletin* 13 (October 1950): 3–14.

CONCLUSION

1. See chapter 1, pp. 20–29.
2. See chapter 1, pp. 29–39.
3. See Table 1.1.
4. See chapter 3, pp. 80–93.
5. See chapter 2, pp. 69–72.
6. See chapter 4, pp. 126–30.
7. See chapter 7, pp. 235–36.
8. See chapter 6, pp. 203–7.
9. See chapter 6, pp. 219–27.
10. See chapter 1, pp. 47–50.
11. See chapter 5, pp. 172–88.

12. For multiple regression and qualitative comparative analyses of WPA wages and OAA pensions across states at the end of the New Deal, see Edwin Amenta and Jane D. Poulsen, "Social Politics in Context: The Institutional Politics Theory and State-Level U.S. Social Spending Policies at the End of the New Deal," *Social Forces* 75 (1996): 33–60. For multiple regression analyses of ADC, see Nancy K. Cauthen and Edwin Amenta, "Not for Widows Only: Institutional Politics and the Formative Years of Aid to Dependent Children," *American Sociological Review* 61 (1996): 427–48.

13. Lyle M. Dorsett, *Franklin D. Roosevelt and the Big City Bosses* (Port Washington, N.Y.: Kennikat Press, 1977), pp. 49–63. The evidence suggests, though, that La Guardia and Roosevelt had a mutually reinforcing relationship based on ideological agreement, not one in which the president used the mayor in a cynical way, as Dorsett implies.

14. Because of a significant number of high-income residents, Nevada's per capita income was about twice as high as that of its neighbors such as Arizona and Utah and was about the same as New York and Connecticut.

15. For the argument that liberalism narrowed even more significantly during the final Roosevelt years, see Alan Brinkley, *The End of Reform: New Deal Liberalism in Recession and War* (New York: Knopf, 1995).

16. On social security, see Martha Derthick, *Policymaking for Social Security* (Washington, D.C.: The Brookings Institution, 1979); Paul Pierson, *Dismantling the Welfare State? Reagan, Thatcher, and the Politics of Retrenchment* (New York: Cambridge University Press, 1994), chap. 3; Edward D. Berkowitz, "Social Security and the Financing of the American State," chap. 4 in *Funding the Modern American State, 1941–1995: The Rise and Fall of the Era of Easy Finance*, ed. W. Elliot Brownlee (New York: Cambridge University Press, 1995). On AFDC, see Blanche D. Coll, *Safety Net: Welfare and Social Security, 1929–1979* (New Brunswick, N.J.: Rutgers University Press, 1995), chaps. 8–12.

17. For a recent account of Johnson's program, see Jill Quadagno, *The Color of Welfare: How Racism Undermined the War on Poverty* (New York: Oxford University Press, 1994).

18. On "commercial" or tax-cut Keynesianism, see Robert Lekachman, *Age of Keynes* (New York: McGraw-Hill, 1966). From 1970 through 1981, there have been 105 modifications increasing "tax expenditures" and only 43 modifications decreasing them. These expenditures are deviations from the revenues that would have been generated under the structural provisions of tax laws—for instance, the deductions for mortgage interest to home owners and the individual income tax. Tax expenditures grew from 4.4 percent of GNP in 1967 to 8.4 percent in 1982. John F. Witte, *The Politics and Development of the Federal Income Tax* (Madison: University of Wisconsin Press, 1985), chap. 12.

19. See Witte, *The Federal Income Tax*, chap. 11; W. Elliot Brownlee, *Federal Taxation in America: A Short History* (New York: Cambridge University Press, 1996), pp. 115–50.

20. Frances Fox Piven and Richard A. Cloward, *Why Americans Don't Vote* (New York: Pantheon Books, 1989); Ruy A. Teixeira, *The Disappearing American Voter* (Washington, D.C.: The Brookings Institution, 1992).

21. See, for instance, Thomas Byrne Edsall, *The New Politics of Inequality* (New York: Norton, 1984). For an analysis of the role of political action committees, see

Dan Clawson, Alan Neustadtl, and Denise Scott, *Money Talks: Corporate PACs and Political Influence* (New York: Basic Books, 1992).

22. See Theda Skocpol, *Boomerang: Clinton's Health Security Effort and the Anti-Government Turn in U.S. Politics* (New York: Norton, 1996); David T. Ellwood, "Welfare Reform as I Knew It: When Bad Things Happen to Good Policies," *American Prospect*, May–June 1996, pp. 22–29.

23. For a call to create a modern WPA, see William Julius Wilson, *When Work Disappears: The World of the New Urban Poor* (New York: Knopf, 1996), chap. 8.

INITIALS OF ORGANIZATIONS AND PROGRAMS

ACA	Advisory Committee on Allotments
ADC	Aid to Dependent Children
AFDC	Aid to Families with Dependent Children
AFL	American Federation of Labor
ALL	American Liberty League
BAC	Business Advisory Council
BPA	Bureau of Public Assistance
CCC	Civilian Conservation Corps
CWA	Civil Works Administration
CES	Committee on Economic Security
CIO	Congress of Industrial Organizations
DAI	Division of Applications and Information
DNC	Democratic National Committee
EPIC	End Poverty in California
FERA	Federal Emergency Relief Administration
FLPF	Farmer-Labor Political Federation
FOE	Fraternal Order of Eagles
GFWC	General Federation of Women's Clubs
LNPL	Labor's Non-Partisan League
NA	National Archives
NCM	National Congress of Mothers
NCPT	National Congress of Parents and Teachers
NPA	National Progressives of America
NIRA	National Industrial Recovery Act
NRA	National Recovery Administration
NRPB	National Resources Planning Board
NYA	National Youth Administration
OAA	Old-Age Assistance
OAI	Old-age Insurance
OARP	Old-Age Revolving Pensions
OASI	Old-Age and Survivors' Insurance
PECE	President's Emergency Committee for Employment
POUR	President's Organization on Unemployment Relief
PWA	Public Works Administration
RFC	Reconstruction Finance Corporation
SRA	State Relief Agency
SSB	Social Security Board
TERA	Temporary Emergency Relief Administration

UC   Unemployment Compensation
USES   United States Employment Service
VA   Veterans Administration
WAA   Workers' Alliance of America
WPA   Works Progress Administration, Work Projects Administration

ALL THE PHOTOGRAPHS in this book are from the Library of Congress, Farm Security Administration, Office of War Information Collection (FSA-OWI). The Historical Section of the FSA, which was begun in 1935 as the Resettlement Administration, was led by Roy E. Stryker. The section was transferred to the OWI in 1942 as part of the Domestic Operations Branch, which was terminated by Congress in 1943. The section employed more than twenty photographers, including Walker Evans and Dorothea Lange, and generated more than seventy-seven hundred images. Stryker consulted with the famous sociologist Robert S. Lynd among others in devising his shooting assignments, which he allowed to range far beyond their ostensible rural subject matter. His approach led Ansel Adams to complain that the section employed not photographers, but "sociologists with cameras." All of the photographs in the collection are in the public domain, are available on microfiche, and can be ordered from the Library of Congress by way of the negative numbers, which are given below for each of the photographs reproduced here.

For discussion of the Historical Section and its collection of photographs, see F. Jack Hingley, *Portrait of a Decade: Roy Stryker and the Development of Documentary Photography in the 1930s* (Baton Rouge: University of Louisiana Press, 1972); Pete Daniel, Merry A. Forresta, Maren Stange, and Sally Stein, *Official Images: New Deal Photography* (Washington, D.C.: Smithsonian Institution, 1987), especially the essay by Stange; Carl Fleischhauer and Beverly W. Brannan, ed. *Documenting America, 1935–1943* (Berkeley: University of California Press, 1988); Nicholas Natanson, *The Black Image in the New Deal: The Politics of FSA Photography* (Knoxville: University of Tennessee Press, 1992). For some of the more prominent photographers, see Penelope Dixon, *Photographers of the Farm Security Administration: An Annotated Bibliography, 1930–1980* (New York: Garland, 1983). For the file itself, see *America 1935–1946* (Cambridge: Chadwick-Healey, 1981).

The photographs reproduced in each plate, with names of photographers, original captions, dates, and Library of Congress negative numbers, are as follows.

2.1. Russell Lee, "Sign, Mineola" [Texas] (January 1939). LC-USF 33–11961 M2.

2.2. Ben Shahn, "Colored inhabitant of Scotts Run, W.Va., who has just received a relief check" (October 1935). LC-USF 33-RA6128 M3.

2.3. Ben Shahn, "Applicants for jobs waiting in front of FERA offices, New Orleans, La." (October 1935). LC-USF 33–6160 M3.

3.1. Russell Lee, "The mail must go thru—line up of WPA workers during the flood at Cairo, Illinois" (February 1937). LC-USF 34–10252 E.

3.2. Russell Lee, "Sign, saw pit, Colorado" (September 1940). LC-USF 33–12910 M4.

3.3. Dorothea Lange, "New York City, Post Office, lower east side" (June 1936). LC-USF 34–9153 E.

3.4. Marion Post Wolcott, "Highway Signboards, southern Alabama" (March 1939). LC-USF 34–51789 D.

4.1. Russell Lee, "Mass meeting, San Augustine [*sic*], Texas. Notice that balcony is reserved for negroes [*sic*]" (April 1939). LC-USF 34–46614.

4.2. Jack Delano, "Pickets outside a textile mill in Greensboro, Greene County, Ga." (May 1941). LC-USF 33–20923-M3.

4.3. Dorothea Lange, "In front of city hall, San Francisco, Calif. The Worker's [*sic*] Alliance WPA organize simultaneous demonstrations in the large cities of the nation cut [*sic*] in the relief appropriation by the US Congress" (February 1939). LC-USF 34–18927 E.

4.4. Jack Delano, "Manati, Puerto Rico. Waiting for work projects [*sic*] Administration pay checks at the post office" (December 1941). LC-USF 34–46614 D.

4.5. Dorothea Lange, "Unemployment benefits aid begins, line of men inside a division office of the state employment service office [*sic*] at San Francisco, Calif. They will receive from 6 to 15 dollars per week for up to 16 weeks. Coincidental with the announcement that the Federal Unemployment Census showed close to 10 million persons out of work, 22 states begin paying unemployment compensation" (January 1938). LC-USF 34–18311 C.

5.1. Russell Lee, "Negroes working for a WPA project. Chicago" (April 1941). LC-USF 34–18927 E.

5.2. Dorothea Lange, "After 44 years of Republican administration, California gets a Democratic administration. The California 'New Deal' faces the same opposition as the national 'New Deal'" (January 1939). LC-USF 34–18791 E.

6.1. Gordon Parks, "Daytona Beach, Fla. Bethune-Cookman College. National youth administration [*sic*] students learning forging" (January 1943). LC-USW 3–14859 C.

6.2. Photographer unknown, no caption available. U.S. Office of War Information. LC-USW 3–23880 D.

6.3. Royden Dixon, "Inauguration Day—1941" (January 1941). LC-USF 34–14192.

6.4. John Vachon, "John W. Dillard, real estate and insurance man, and a member of the local Townsend club in his office. Washington, Indiana" (June 1941). LC-USF 34–62997 D.

6.5. Photographer unknown, no caption available. LC-USF 34–18927 E.

Abbott, Edith, 80, 81, 87, 177
Abbott, Grace, 87, 96
Advisory Council on Economic Security, 109, 117
African Americans, 132, 134–35; and civil rights, 21, 60, 66, 252; and social policy, 70, 89, 157–59, 277n. 7, 308n. 32
After the War, Full Employment, 201
Agricultural Adjustment Administration, 124
Aid to Dependent Children (ADC) (also Aid to Families with Dependent Children [AFDC]), 145–46, 149–51, 256–60; creation of, 81, 100, 115–16, 295n. 22; described, 86–88, 250, 273n. 3; during 1940s, 192, 215, 225; and inequality, 152–53, 157, 159; 1939 changes to, 127, 134; in postwar period, xi, 205, 266–67; and social policy planning, 195, 197, 209; and state-level policies, 11, 163, 166–69, 179, 183, 187
Altmeyer, Arthur, 11, 94, 100, 134, 196–98, 205, 215, 246
American Association for Labor Legislation, 62, 180
American Association for Social Security (also American Association for Old-Age Security), 62, 97
American Federation of Labor (AFL), 74, 138, 177, 180, 197, 216, 222
American Labor party, 107, 138, 224, 264
American Legion, 202, 209,
American Liberty League (ALL), 6, 117–18
American Medical Association (AMA), 207, 215
American party system, 60
American Progress, 111
Amlie, Thomas, 186
Andrews, John, 96
antidiscrimination policies, 152
Arrears Act (1879), 56, 59
Attlee, Clement, 235, 245

Bailey, Josiah, 132
Baker, Jacob, 96
Beck, James M., 118
benefits, distributive and collective, 43
Berger, Victor, 185
Berkowitz, Edward, 64

Bethune, Mary McLeod, 135
Bevan, Aneurin, 235–36
Beveridge Report (*Social Insurance and Allied Services*), 231, 233, 235, 236, 241–42, 245, 327n. 20
Beveridge, William, 231–33, 242, 246
Bevin, Ernest, 245
Black, Earl, 173
Black, Merle, 173
Board of Trade, Britain, 233–34, 245
Boileau, Gerald, 107
Bonus Army, 47, 71–73, 115–17, 296n. 36
Brandeis, Elizabeth, 96
Brandeis, Louis, 111
Brinkley, Alan, 123
Britain: social policy of, 50–51, 57, 64, 93, 142–44, 231–249; social spending "effort" of, 5, 143–44
Brown, J. Douglas, 97
Bureau of the Budget, U.S., 128, 202, 210, 246, 259
Bureau of Public Assistance, U.S., 205
Burnham, Walter Dean, 56, 65
Burns, Eveline, 193
Burns, James MacGregor, 122
Burstein, Paul, 283n. 44
Business Advisory Council (BAC), 117
business organizations, 117–19, 142, 220, 222, 281n. 35. *See also* Business Advisory Council, Chamber of Commerce, National Association of Manufacturers
Byrd, Harry F., 104, 174
Byrnes, James F., 126, 222

California, 169; and Old-Age Assistance, 87, 156, 165; and old-age pensions, 64, 70, 71; and social policy, 173–74, 180–84, 262
California Life Retirement Payments Association, 180, 183
California State Federation of Labor, 180, 183
campaign finance, 268, 309n. 47
Capone, Al, 177
Castles, Francis G., 31
Cates, Jerry, 134
Catt, Carrie Chapman, 135
Cermak, Anton, 176
challengers. *See* social movements

Chamber of Commerce, 40, 119, 142
Chamberlain, Neville, 233, 243
child labor laws, 63, 180
Children's Bureau, U.S., 68, 70, 95–96, 100, 115, 193
Churchill, Winston, 233–34, 236, 246
civil rights movement, 268
civil service, 280n. 25
Civil War pensions, 9–10, 35, 55–57, 61
Civil Works Administration (CWA), U.S., 74–76, 84
Civilian Conservation Corps (CCC), U.S., 10–11, 73–74, 84, 126, 144, 156, 199
Clements, Robert, 112, 139
Cleveland, Grover, 58
Clinton, Bill, xi, 268, 270–71
Cloward, Richard A., 21, 282n. 36
Coalition Government, Britain, 233, 235, 243
coalitions, 280n. 29
Cold War, 238
Committee on Economic Security (CES), U.S., xi, 3, 80, 114, 124, 209, 297n. 43; drafting of the Social Security Act by, 82–83, 94–101
Common Sense, 186
Commons, John R., 96, 185
comparable worth policy, 152
Congress of Industrial Organizations (CIO), 135, 138–39, 173, 180, 183, 216, 222
Congress, U.S., xi, 26, 86, 114, 137, 200, 210; composition of, 104–8, 135–38; conservative coalition in, 122, 142; and social policy, 27, 33, 199, 203–6, 212–13, 224, 245–46. *See also* "reform-oriented regimes"
Conservative party, Britain, 244
corporatism, 72, 148
Costigan, Edward, 71
Coughlin, Father Charles E., 115
Coughlin, John J., 176
Council of Economic Advisors (CEA), 203
courts, 25, 26, 59
Creel, George, 181
Cummings, Homer, 82
Currie, Lauchlin, 126, 128

Dalton, Hugh, 245
Davey, Martin, 224
Davis, John W., 118
"decommodification," 148, 153–54, 275n. 10
deficit spending, 125–26

democracy, 49, 65, 98, 103–4, 132, 208, 277n. 7, 268, 279n. 16, 278n. 10; and institutional politics theory, 13, 19–22, 24, 32, 171, 173, 252
Democratic National Committee (DNC), 110, 135
Democratic party, 56, 62, 68, 103, 134, 219. *See also* "reform-oriented regimes"
Department of Labor, 205
Dependent Pensions Act (1890), 57
Development of the Social Security Act, The, 82
Dewey, John, 186
Dewey, Thomas, 211, 214
Dewson, Mary, 135
Dill-Connery bill, 82, 100, 114
Dingley Tariff Act (1897), 59
disability insurance, 235
Disability Pensions Act (1890), 58
"displacement effect," 238
"dole, the," 80, 81, 83, 293n. 7
Domhoff, G. William, 282n. 38
Douglas, Paul, 97, 186
Downey, Sheridan, 182, 215
Dryzek, John, 239, 326n. 14
Dunham, Robert, 177
Du Pont, Pierre, 118

earned income tax credit, 268
Eccles, Marriner, 126
economic and modernization theories, 276n. 5
economic security bill (also Economic Security Act), development of, 81, 83; impact of previous programs on, 100; influence of business organizations on, 118; influence of social movements on, 110, 111, 114; proposals in, 86–90. *See also* Social Security Act
elections, 59, 62, 103, 241, 245; of 1936, 135, 301n. 81, 308n. 31; of 1938, 122, 221; of 1940, 160, 210–11; of 1944, 203, 211, 247, 322n. 39
Eliot bill, 197
Eliot, Martha, 96
Ellwood, David T., xi
Ely, Richard, 185
Emergency Powers Act (1944), 244
Emergency Relief and Construction Act (1932), 71
employables, 154
Employment Act (1945), 214
employment policy, 73–77, 198, 202, 203
Employment Policy, 234

End Poverty in California (EPIC), 180
Epstein, Abraham, 97, 100, 140
Erie, Stephen P., 223
Esping-Andersen, Gøsta, 31, 148
Executive Office of the President, 128, 244
Executive Reorganization Act (1939), 128

Fair Labor Standards Act (1938), 125, 159, 250
Falk, I. S., 97
family allowances, 11, 235
Farley, James, 110, 135, 177
Farm Security Administration, U.S., 126, 193, 333
Farmer-Labor party (Minnesota), 135, 137, 165, 171
Farmer-Labor Political Federation (FLPF), 186
Fechner, Robert, 74
Federal Emergency Relief Act (1933), 83
Federal Emergency Relief Administration (FERA), U.S., xi, 73, 74, 76, 175, 291nn. 66–67; and institutional politics theory, 256–60; relationship of to other programs, 55, 75, 84, 163; and social policy planning, 94–95, 99
Federal Reserve Board, U.S., 126
Federal Security Agency, U.S., 191, 193, 215
Federal Works Agency, U.S., 128
federalism, 13, 16, 25–26, 67, 251, 254
First New Deal, 16, 45, 46, 55; social policy in, 72–79
Flora, Peter, 143, 274n. 7
Folsom, Marion, 117
Food Stamps, 43, 63, 273n. 3
form of programs, 262
Forster, H. Walter, 118
fragmented political institutions, 24–27, 61, 251–52
Fraternal Order of Eagles (FOE), 62, 180
full employment bill, 203, 259

Garner, John Nance, 132
gender inequality: and social policy, 8–9, 151–53; and New Deal social policy, 9, 155–57. *See also* women
general assistance (general relief), 146, 151, 273n. 3; and institutional politics theory, 256–60; and social policy proposals, 201, 209; and state policies, 165, 182, 187
General Federation of Women's Clubs (GFWC), 62, 115

geopolitics and social policy. *See* war and social policy
George, Walter, 132
Germany, 23, 59, 239; and social policy, 5, 28, 57, 150
GI Bill of Rights (1944), 192, 202, 209, 243, 247
Gifford, Walter, 69
Gill, Corrington, 96
Glass, Carter, 175
Goodin, Robert E., 239, 326n. 14
Grand Army of the Republic, 59
Great Britain. *See* Britain
Great Depression, 6, 93–94, 260
Green, William, 74, 109
Greenwood, Arthur, 233, 245
Griffiths, James, 235
Guffey Coal Conservation Act (1935), 124

Haber, William, 193
Hague, Frank, 223
Ham and Eggs, 180, 183
Hansen, Alvin, 97, 201, 194
Harrison, Benjamin, 58
health and safety laws, 64
health policy, 208, 256–60; in Britain, 234, 240; and the Committee on Economic Security, 97, 138, 127; reform proposals concerning, 11, 195, 201, 204, 206, 215, 267–68
Hearst, William Randolph, 181
Heclo, Hugh, 35
Heidenheimer, Arnold J., 274n. 7
Heil, Julius, 187
Hickok, Lorena, 177
Hicks, Alexander, 31
historical sequence, 45
Hoey, Jane, 134
Hoover, Herbert, 54–55, 69, 71–72, 93, 102, 256
Hopkins, Harry L., 70, 73, 74, 128; 1940 presidential contention of, 135, 160–61; and patronage, 133, 221–22; and social policy planning, xi, 7, 80, 81, 82, 86, 95; and state-level social policy, 175, 177, 224; and the WPA, 3, 84, 86, 126
Hornblower, William B., 181–82
Horner, Henry, 177, 179, 223
House of Representatives, U.S., 22, 224; Appropriations Committee of, 26; Rules Committee of, 26; Ways and Means Committee of, 26, 140
Hurja, Emil, 111

Ickes, Harold, 84
Illinois, 85, 223; social policy in, 89, 165, 169, 173–74, 176–79, 263
Illinois Manufacturers' Association, 177
in-kind aid, 63
institutional and statist theories, 18, 276–77n. 6
institutional politics theory: appraised across time and program, 255–62; and Britain, 240–47; defined, 12–15, 18–53, 251–55; and New Deal social policy, 94–119, 130–42; and state-level social policy, 163, 170–72, 189, 262–66, 284n. 50
interest groups. See business organizations.
Italy, 5, 23, 59

Johnson, Hiram, 180
Johnson, Lyndon B., 267–68
Jowitt, Sir William, 234, 245

Karl, Barry Dean, 123
Katz, Michael, 63, 220, 222, 323n. 50
Katznelson, Ira, 61
Keller, Morton, 65
Kelly, Edward J., 162, 176–79, 223
Kenna, Michael, 176
Key, V. O., 20, 173–74, 263
Keynes, John Maynard, 12, 125–26
Keynesianism, 194, 203, 210, 226, 219, 266; in Britain, 234, 236, 325n. 10
King, William, 101
Kingdon, John, 42
Kleppner, Paul, 65
Kousser, J. Morgan, 278n. 10

labor, 207, 215–19, 268; and the New Deal, 74, 109–10, 134–35, 138–39, 222, 322n. 45; in state politics, 175, 176–77, 180, 184. See also American Federation of Labor, Congress of Industrial Organizations, Workers' Alliance of America
labor markets and social policy. See market forces: and social policy
Labor's Non-Partisan League, 183
Labour party, Britain, 93, 142, 234–36, 244–45, 247
La Follette, Philip, 162, 171, 185–86, 188
La Follette, Robert M. 171,
La Follette, Robert M., Jr., 71, 73, 171, 185, 186, 188
La Guardia, Fiorello, 138, 224, 264
Lasser, David, 141, 222
Latimer, Murray, 97
Leeds, Morris E., 117

left-center parties, 49. See also "reform-oriented regimes"
Leiserson, William, 97
Lemke, William, 115
Lenroot, Katharine, 96
Leuchtenburg, William, 122–23
Lewis, John L., 138, 216
Liberal party, Britain, 93, 237
liberalism, 266
logrolling, 27
Long, Huey P., 6, 91, 108. See also Share Our Wealth
Los Angeles Times, 180, 181
Louisiana, 70, 111, 165
Lowi, Theodore, 219, 281n. 33
Lundeen bill, 110

MacArthur, Douglas, 72, 116
Madison (Wisc.) Capital Times, 186
Marcantonio, Vito, 107
market forces: and social policy, 8, 148–53; and New Deal social policy, 9, 153–54
Marshall, T. H., 277n. 7
Marx, Karl, 12, 18
Massachusetts, 71, 169
maternal programs. See Aid to Dependent Children, mothers' pensions, Sheppard-Towner Act
Maverick, Maury, 107
Mayhew, David, 22, 171, 173, 223, 278nn. 13–14
McAdam, Doug, 38
McAdoo, William Gibbs, 181
McGovern, Francis E., 185
McKinley Tariff Act (1890), 58
McKinley, William, 59
McNutt, Paul, 215
McPherson, Aimee Semple, 181
means-tested programs, 220, 234–35, 281n. 34. See also Aid to Dependent Children, Food Stamps, general assistance, Medicaid, Old-Age Assistance, Works Progress Administration
Medicaid, 267, 273n. 3
Medicare, 267
Mellon, Andrew, 72
Merriam, Charles, 177
Merriam, Frank, 182
Meyers, Howard B., 96
Michigan, 111, 169
Midwest, U.S., 23–24, 166–67
Ministry of Labour, Britain, 243, 245
Minnesota, 107, 111, 165
Mississippi, 70, 168

Missouri, 133, 223
Moley, Raymond, 110
Morgenthau, Henry, 82, 90, 95, 210
Morrison, Herbert, 245
Morrow, L. C., 118
Mothers' Aid, 1931, 70, 96
mothers' pensions, 10, 63, 70, 76, 152–53; and ADC, 87, 96; in states, 166–69, 174, 175, 180, 181, 185–86
Murray, James, 222, 246
Murray, Merrill G., 97

Nash, Patrick A., 176
National Assistance Act, Britain, 235
National Association for the Advancement of Colored People (NAACP), 135
National Association of Manufacturers (NAM), 40, 118–19, 198
National Civic Federation, 67
National Conference of Mayors, 224
National Conference of Social Work, 62
National Congress of Mothers (NCM) (also National Congress of Parent's and Teachers [NCPT]), 62, 115
National Economy Act (1933), 117
National Health Service, Britain, 235, 243
National Industrial Recovery Act (1933) (NIRA), 72, 83, 109
National Labor Relations Act (1935) (also Wagner Act), 109–10, 138, 218
National Labor Relations Board, U.S., 109
National Progressives of America (NPA), 187
National Recovery Administration (NRA), U.S., 72, 124
National Resources Planning Board (NRPB), U.S., 128, 244, 226; and social policy planning, 5, 191–97, 209, 242, 258–59; social policy reports of, 201, 241, 246, 327n. 20; termination of, 201–2, 246; and work and relief policy, 193–96, 219
National Youth Administration (NYA), U.S., 11, 84, 126, 144, 156, 195, 199
nationalization of social policy, 209, 261
need-based programs, 35, 145, 148–50, 310n. 59. *See also* Aid to Dependent Children, Food Stamps, general assistance, means-tested programs, Medicaid, Old-Age Assistance, Works Progress Administration
needs assessment, 307–8n. 30
Netherlands, 5, 239
New York (city), 224, 264
New York (state), 111, 124; and social policy, 64, 70, 71, 73, 89, 157

New York *Times,* 118
Non-Partisan League, 216
nonparliamentary parties, 245
Norris, George, 135
Norris-La Guardia Act (1932), 186
North, U.S., 66
Northeast, U.S., 23–24

Office of Education, U.S., 202
Office of Emergency Management, U.S., 244
Office of Mobilization and Reconversion, U.S., 244
Office of War Information, U.S., 333
Ohio, 88, 97, 133, 169, 224
Ohio Chamber of Commerce, 118
Ohl, Henry, 109
Old-Age Assistance (OAA), 149–51, 250, 256–60; creation of, 81, 86, 97; during 1940s, 11, 205, 225; funding of, 145, 192; and inequality, 155, 159; in postwar period, 205, 267; and reform proposals, 195, 201; in states, 11, 100, 163, 165, 166–69, 175, 179, 183, 187, 265–66, 317n. 46; and Townsend Movement, 114, 140
old-age insurance, 235. *See also* Old-Age and Survivors' Insurance, "social security"
old-age pensions, 70–71, 180–81, 186
Old Age Revolving Pensions, Ltd. (OARP). *See* Townsend Movement
Old-Age and Survivors' Insurance (OASI), 101, 150, 221, 250, 256–60; creation of, 11, 81, 97; during 1940s and 1950s, 11, 205, 214, 225; and inequality, 152–53, 157, 159, 320–21n. 28; 1939 changes to, 127, 134; and payroll tax, 197, 201, 215; political support for, 118, 125, 140; in postwar period, 192, 266, 267; and reform proposals, 196, 215; WPA compared to, 221. *See also* old-age insurance, "social security"
Olson, Culbert L., 162, 182–84, 187
Olson, Floyd, 171
organized labor. *See* labor
Orloff, Ann Shola, 31, 54, 151, 281n. 33
outdoor relief, 63

path dependence, 260
Patman, Wright, 91
patronage, 57, 62, 63, 132–33, 225
patronage-oriented parties, 59, 67; and institutional politics theory, 13, 15, 19, 22–25, 32, 49, 252, 278nn. 13–14; and the New Deal, 103, 106; and state-level social policy, 171, 173, 176–79, 279n. 16

Patterson, James T., 47, 137, 179
peace dividend, 238, 326n. 14
Peacock, Alan R., 238–39
Pelletier, John B., 182
Pendergast, Thomas J., 133, 223
Perkins, Frances, 82
Pierson, Paul, 220, 274n. 8, 281n. 33, 283n. 41
Piven, Francis Fox, 21, 282n. 36
policy experts, 303–4n. 100
"policy feedbacks," 35, 98–101
political learning, 35
poor law, 62–63
Postwar Manpower Committee, U.S., 196, 202, 243
"power elite," 282n. 38
power resources thesis, 280n. 27. *See also* social democratic thesis
presidency, the, 24–27, 32
President's Emergency Committee for Employment (PECE), 69
President's Organization on Unemployment Relief (POUR), 69
previous programs, 98–101, 241–42, 254, 256–57, 261. *See also* "policy feedbacks"
Progressive party (Wisconsin), 135, 137, 185–88
progressivism, 10, 61–64, 67, 180
public employment, 81, 95, 101, 199, 208, 266–68. *See also* Civil Works Administration, Civilian Conservation Corps, Federal Emergency Relief Administration, National Youth Administration, Works Progress Administration
public works, 234. *See also* Public Works Administration
Public Works Administration (PWA), 72–73, 75, 128, 222

Quadagno, Jill, 21

race: and disfranchisement, 65–66; and New Deal social policy, 157–59, 277n. 7, 308n. 32. *See also* African Americans
Raskob, John J., 103
Rauschenbush, Paul, 96
Reagan, Ronald, 12, 268
recession, 122, 131
Reconstruction Committee, Britain, 234, 245
Reconstruction Finance Corporation (RFC), 71, 73, 94, 130
"reform-oriented regimes," 259, 260; and institutional politics theory, 14, 19, 29, 32,

253, 255; and New Deal social policy, 101–8, 134–38; in 1940s, 207, 244, 247; and state-level social policy, 171, 173
"relief," 4, 274n. 4. *See also* Aid to Dependent Children, Federal Emergency Relief Administration, in-kind benefits, general assistance, Old-Age Assistance, outdoor relief, work and relief policy, work and relief state, work relief, Works Progress Administration
Report of the Committee on Economic Security, 193
Republican party, 56–58, 68, 102, 142, 221. *See also* "reform-oriented regimes"
retrenchment of social policy: analytical discussions of, 41–42, 219–20, 274n. 8, 281n. 33, 283n. 41, 323n. 49; during World War II, 191–93; and institutional politics theory, 33; and the Work Projects Administration, 219–25
Richardson, Friend, 180
Richmond (Va.) *Times-Dispatch*, 162, 175
Roberts, Owen, 124–25
Rockefeller Foundation, 246
Roosevelt, Eleanor, 72–73, 135
Roosevelt, Franklin D.: and deficits, 76, 125–26, 294n. 13; and elections, 103, 135, 160, 203, 210–11, 221, 247, 301n. 81, 322n. 39; and general relief, 80, 81, 83; and the Great Depression, 69–72; and labor, 109–10, 134–35, 138, 216, 218; and New Deal social policy planning, 3–4, 7, 54, 81–2, 102–3, 122, 191, 193, 201, 209, 211; and old-age insurance, 89, 90, 101, 226–27; political support for, 6, 117, 134–35, 162; and public employment, 95, 122, 191, 223, 293n. 6; and state and local politics, 163, 176–79, 181, 183, 186, 224, 316n. 36; and the Supreme Court, 122, 124–25; and taxation, 111, 200; and veterans, 54, 72–73, 91, 192; welfare reform of, xi, 270–71; and World War II, 7, 193, 208, 244–46, 328n. 28
Ross, Emerson, 96
Rubinow, Isaac, 97
Ruml, Beardsley, 199

San Francisco *Examiner*, 181
Schlesinger, Arthur M., Jr., 111
Schmedeman, Albert B., 186
Second New Deal, 16, 45, 46, 55; social policy in, 80–121
Security, Work and Relief Policies, 192–93, 201, 236

Senate, U.S., 222, 224; Appropriations Committee of, 26; Finance Committee of, 26

Share Our Wealth, 110–12, 301n. 79. *See also* Long, Huey P.

Shefter, Martin, 23

Sheppard-Towner Act, 10, 55, 63, 68

Shouse, Jouett, 103, 118

Sinclair, Upton, 180, 181–83

Skocpol, Theda, 27, 41, 54, 220, 282n. 36, 281n. 33

Skowronek, Stephen, 27, 59

Sloan, Alfred, 118

Smith, Al, 103, 118

Smith, Ed, 132

Smith, Gerald L. K., 111, 115

Smith-Connally Act (1943), 218, 322n. 46

social democratic thesis, 31

social democracy, 18, 31, 148

Social Insurance, 234

Social Insurance and Allied Services. See Beveridge Report

social insurance programs, 149–50. *See also* health policy, Old-Age and Survivors' Insurance, unemployment compensation, unemployment insurance, workmen's compensation

social movements, 215–17; and institutional politics theory, 15, 21, 29–31, 37–40, 254, 256–57; and New Deal social policy, 49, 108–17, 139–41, 172–73. *See also* labor, Share Our Wealth, Townsend Movement, Workers' Alliance of America

social policy, 40–42. *See also* First New Deal, Second New Deal, "Third New Deal," "welfare state," work and relief policy

social policy "effort." *See* social spending "effort"

social policy planning, 191, 236, 241–42, 266–69. *See also* Children's Bureau, Committee on Economic Security, Federal Emergency Relief Administration, National Resources Planning Board, Social Security Board, Works Progress Administration

"social security," 149, 151, 273n. 2, 274n. 5

Social Security Act (1935), 11, 18, 43–44, 54, 214; creation of, xi, 3, 81, 86–90; 1939 amendments to, 127, 134; 1950 amendments to, 205–6; in states, 175, 176, 179. *See also* Committee on Economic Security, economic security bill

Social Security Board (SSB) (also Social Security Administration), U.S., 87, 89, 127,

128, 133, 205–6; and management of Social Security Act programs, 221, 225; and old-age assistance, 114, 140; and old-age insurance, 201, 215; and social policy planning, 133–34, 193, 196–98, 209, 221, 242, 246, 258–59

social spending "effort," 5, 46, 65, 76–77, 143–44, 275n. 1, 283n. 43, 288n. 38

Socialist party (Milwaukee, Wisc.), 185, 187

South, U.S., 125; deficiency of democracy in, 15, 21, 24, 65–66; and power in U.S. politics, 22, 107; and social policy, 20, 104, 132, 140, 165–67, 176, 221, 307n. 26, 324n. 54. *See also* "reform-oriented regimes"

Southern Pacific Railroad, 180

special assistance programs, 205–6. *See also* Aid to Dependent Children, Old-Age Assistance

Special Senate Committee to Investigate Unemployment and Relief, U.S., 126

spend-lend bill, 129–30, 138

Spingarn, Joel E., 135

state bureaucracies, 59, 207, 241–42; and institutional politics theory, 13, 27–31, 34–37, 39, 49, 252, 254, 281n. 33; and New Deal social policy, 6, 94–101, 128, 171, 256–57

state (-level) social policies, 48–50, 86–89, 146, 162–90, 258–59; before Second New Deal, 62, 76, 98–101

statist and institutional theories, 18, 276–77n. 6

Stayton, Will, 118

Stein, Herbert, 130

Stephens, John D., 31

Stewart, Bryce, 97

Stimson, Henry, 245

strikes, 322n. 45

Supplemental Security Income, 273n. 3

Supreme Court, U.S., 59, 90, 124–25, 305n. 6; and Roosevelt, 122, 124, 136

Sweden, 5, 275n. 1

Swope, Gerard, 117

Sydenstricker, Edgar L., 97

Taft, Robert, 207, 214

Taft-Hartley Act (1947), 214, 218, 322n. 46

Tammany Hall, 138, 224

Tarrow, Sidney, 282n. 36

Tax Reform Act (1986), 268

taxation, 27, 42, 46, 90, 147–48, 234, 238, 267–68; of corporation incomes, 91, 130,

taxation *(cont.)*
142, 148, 198, 206; customs tariffs, 10,
57–58, 286n. 15, 289n. 44; excises, 76,
147; "expenditures" in, 329n. 18; of incomes, in 1940s, 198, 206; of inheritances
and gifts, 91, 148; in 1940s, 192, 195,
198–200, 206, 208, 210, 228; of payrolls,
7, 90, 118, 130, 142, 147, 195, 198, 201,
215, 226, 234; of personal incomes, 7, 11,
58, 62, 72, 81, 91, 112, 130, 185, 195; reform proposals of, 197, 201, 209; of sales,
76, 177, 198; state policies concerning,
163, 165, 169, 187
Teagle, Walter, 117
Teamsters, 135
Temporary Aid to Needy Families, formation
of, xi, 273n. 3
Temporary Emergency Relief Admininstra-
tion (TERA) (New York), 70
Thalberg, Irving, 181
"Third New Deal," 16, 45, 46; social policy
in, 122–61
Thomas, Norman, 181
Thurmond, Strom, 214
Tilly, Charles, 37
Titmuss, Richard, 237
Tobin, Daniel, 135
Tocqueville, Alexis de, 12, 18, 24
Townsend bill, 110
Townsend, Dr. Francis E., 6, 86, 108, 112–
15, 139–40, 182, 301n. 92. *See also*
Townsend Movement, Townsend Plan
Townsend Movement, 15, 47, 112–15, 139–
40, 216–16, 226; in states, 172, 175, 180,
187; membership of, 301n. 89, 316n. 42.
See also Townsend Plan
Townsend National Weekly, 114, 217
Townsend Plan, 152–53
Treasury, Britain, 142–43, 243
Treasury Department, U.S., 210
Truman, Harry S., 203–4, 206–7, 212, 214,
218, 247
Tydings, Millard, 132

unemployables, 86, 154
unemployment compensation (UC), 118,
125, 134, 146, 159, 250, 256–60; creation
of, 88–89, 96–97; and labor markets, 150,
154; and reform proposals, 195, 197, 201–
4; and state policies, 100, 163–64, 165,
179, 185, 187
unemployment insurance, 235. *See also* unemployment compensation

United Mine Workers, 138, 217
United States Employment Service (USES),
73–77, 198, 202, 203
universal programs, 310n. 59

Vandenburg, Arthur, 201
veterans' benefits, 11, 146, 158, 196, 266;
and Bonus Army, 47, 71–73, 115–17,
296n. 36; Civil War pensions, 9–10, 35,
55–57, 61; GI Bill of Rights, 192, 202,
209, 243, 247; Roosevelt's opposition to,
54, 91, 192
Veterans Administration (VA), 202, 243, 246
Viner, Jacob, 97
Virginia, 162, 263; social policy in 173–76,
Virginia Manufacturers Association, 175
voting rights. *See* African Americans,
democracy
Voting Rights Act (1965), 268

wages and hours legislation. *See* Fair Labor
Standards Act
Wagner Act, 125, 138
Wagner, Senator Robert, 71, 73, 82, 103,
110, 192, 201, 209, 226
Wagner-Lewis bill, 82, 88, 97
Wagner-Murray-Dingell bill, 201, 204, 209,
246, 321n. 35
Wagner-Peyser Act (1933), 73
Wallace, Henry, 82, 214
war and social policy, 267, 326n. 18. *See also*
World War II
War Department, 245
war on poverty, 267
Watson, Sir John Forbes, 231, 238, 249
Weber, Max, 12, 18
Weir, Ernest, 118
"welfare," 4, 149, 273n. 3. *See also* Aid to
Dependent Children, Food Stamps, Medi-
caid, Old-Age Assistance, "relief," Supple-
mental Security Income
"welfare capitalists," 297n. 41
welfare reform, xi, 86, 269
"welfare state," 29, 55, 203; in Britain, 12,
17, 50, 230, 232, 233–36; as employed
by social scientists, 7–9, 40, 44; and
"regimes," 8, 148, 275n. 9. *See also*
social policy
West, U.S., 166–67
White, Harry Dexter, 210
Wilensky, Harold, 274n. 7
Williams, Aubrey, 84, 96, 128
Williams, T. Harry, 111

Willink, Henry, 234
Willkie, Wendell, 210
Wilson, William Julius, 330n. 23
Wilson, Woodrow, 62
Wilson-Gorman Act (1893), 58–59
Wisconsin, 169; social policy in, 173–74,
    184–88, 262; and unemployment
compensation, 64, 88–89, 100, 165
Wisconsin Finance Authority, 186
Wisconsin Idea, 185
Wisconsin Industrial Commission, 185
Wisconsin Supreme Court, 187
Wisconsin-Minnesota Progressive Group,
    107
Wiseman, Jack, 238–39
Witte, Edwin, 82–83, 94–95, 100–101, 104,
    113, 144, 148, 187
women, 8–9, 63, 260, 267, 277n. 7; and
    New Deal social policy, 74, 75, 87, 151–
    57, 311n. 62; and politics, 67, 135; and
    state-level social policy, 180, 185. *See also*
    Aid to Dependent Children, Children's
    Bureau, gender inequality, mothers'
    pensions, Sheppard-Towner Act
Woodrum, Clifton, 224
Woolton, Lord, 234
work and relief policy, xi, 3, 35, 42; com-
    pared to British social policy, 17, 236–37,
    242; consolidation of, 16, 123, 124–30;
    described, 8–10; enactment of, 12, 16,
    83–88, 101–8; at the end of the 1930s, 16,
    144–46; gender implications of, 75, 155–
    57; and institutional politics theory,
    92–93; market implications of, 153–54;
    planning of, 16, 82–83, 94–97; proposed

completion of, 191, 193–96; racial impli-
    cations of, 157–59; rejection of, 7, 17, 92,
    199–202; in states, 163, 164–68. *See also*
    Second New Deal, "Third New Deal,"
    welfare reform, work and relief state
work and relief state, 7, 8–10, 17, 144. *See
    also* work and relief policy
work relief, 182, 186. *See also* Federal Emer-
    gency Relief Administration, work and re-
    lief policy, Works Progress Administration
Workers' Alliance of America (WAA), 141,
    180, 183, 222
workmen's compensation, 10, 64, 256–60,
    235; in states, 177, 180, 185
Works Progress Administration (WPA)
    (also Work Projects Administration), 194–
    95, 203, 225, 250, 256–60, 293–94n. 9,
    306n. 21; creation of, xi, 3, 83–86; fund-
    ing of, 126–27, 138, 144; and inequality,
    152–53, 155–56, 158; and labor, 139,
    141, 222; and labor markets, 150–51,
    154; and 1936 elections, 294–95n. 14,
    308n. 31; opposition to, 142, 220–22,
    260, 323n. 50, 324n. 54; organization
    of, 128, 262; and patronage, 132–33,
    222–23; and social policy planning, 133–
    34, 191, 193, 258–59; and state policies,
    163–65, 166–69, 177–79, 183, 324n. 59;
    termination of, 7, 192, 199, 219–25;
    wages in, 84, 109, 166–69, 263–64,
    294n. 11, 312n. 6, *See also* work and relief
    policy, work relief
World War II: political impact of, 244–45;
    social policy impact of, 6, 7, 17, 31, 207–
    9, 226, 232, 237–40

About the Author

Edwin Amenta is Associate Professor of Sociology
at New York University.

PRINCETON STUDIES IN AMERICAN POLITICS:
HISTORICAL, INTERNATIONAL, AND COMPARATIVE PERSPECTIVES

*Labor Visions and State Power: The Origins of Business
Unionism in the United States* by Victoria C. Hattam

The Lincoln Persuasion: Remaking American Liberalism
by J. David Greenstone

*Politics and Industrialization: Early Railroads in the
United States and Prussia* by Colleen A. Dunlavy

Political Parties and the State: The American Historical Experience
by Martin Shefter

*Prisoners of Myth: The Leadership of the Tennessee
Valley Authority, 1933–1990* by Erwin C. Hargrove

*Bound by Our Constitution: Women, Workers, and the
Minimum Wage* by Vivien Hart

*Experts and Politicians: Reform Challenges to Machine Politics in
New York, Cleveland, and Chicago* by Kenneth Finegold

*Social Policy in the United States: Future Possibilities in
Historical Perspective* by Theda Skocpol

Political Organizations by James Q. Wilson

*Facing Up to the American Dream: Race, Class, and the Soul
of the Nation* by Jennifer L. Hochschild

Classifying by Race edited by Paul E. Peterson

From the Outside In: World War II and the American State
by Bartholomew H. Sparrow

*Kindred Strangers: The Uneasy Relationship between Politics
and Business in America* by David Vogel

*Why Movements Succeed or Fail: Opportunity, Culture, and
the Struggle for Woman Suffrage* by Lee Ann Banaszak

*The Power of Separation: American Constitutionalism and The Myth
of the Legislative Veto* by Jessica Korn

Losing Control: Party Decline in the Fiscal State
by John J. Coleman

*The Origins of the Urban Crisis: Race and Inequality
in Postwar Detroit* by Thomas J. Sugrue

*The Road to Nowhere: The Genesis of President Clinton's Plan
for Health Security* by Jacob Hacker

Imperiled Innocents: Anthony Comstock and Family Reproductioon in Victorian American by Nicola Beisel

Morning Glories: Municipal Reform in the Southwest by Amy Bridges

The Hidden Welfare State: Tax Expenditures and Social Policy in the United States by Christopher Howard

Bold Relief: Institutional Politics and the Origins of Modern American Social Policy by Edwin Amenta